The Eurovision Song Contest

Lugano 1956 - Copenhagen 2014

The Complete and Independent Guide

7th Year of Publication

Silverthorn Publishing

Simon Barclay
General Editor

ISBN 978-1-291-83175-7

Contents

Introduction to the 2014 Edition

Denmark hosted Eurovision this year with the organisers staging the 59th Contest in the B&W Hallerne, in Copenhagen. Broadcaster DR chose three presenters to host the semi-finals and final, Lise Rønne, Nikolaj Koppel and Pilou Asbæk . This was Denmark's and Copenhagen's third hosting of the Contest, following Contests in 1964 and 2001.

The Contest saw 37 countries taking part, two fewer than in 2013. Poland and Portugal returned but Cyprus, Serbia, Croatia and Bulgaria all dropped out, mostly due to funding reasons although Croatia also blamed a poor run of results in recent years. The Cypriot broadcaster stated that their absence in 2014 may continue indefinitely.

Valentina Monetta was San Marino's representative for the third successive year, becoming the fourth performer to do so in the history of Eurovision. Romania's Paula Seling and Ovi returned after their relative success in 2010. The winners of Junior Eurovision in 2006, Russia's Tolmachevy Sisters made history by participating in the main Contest this year.

Of the 37 entries, 32 were sung wholly or predominantly in English, a complete turnaround following 2013 which had seen a resurgence in the use of native languages.

Congratulations to Conchita Wurst and to Austria who won Eurovision for the first time since 1966. Netherlands were runners-up but have the honour of being awarded the highest number of 12 points in a semi-final without going on to win the final.

And a special mention for both Montenegro and San Marino who both made it through to the Grand Final for the first time. Every currently regularly participating country has now reached the final at least once.

It was another abject performance this year for most of the the Big 5, with Spain excepted. The UK, France, Germany and Italy averaged 28 points each this year, higher than last year but meaning they all finished in the bottom ten, with France ending with a woeful two points.

After nine consecutive years that the winner has come from the second half of the running order, Conchita won after performing 11th. There was a change this year compared to recent contests, with five of the top eight entries performing in the first half.

The 2014 Edition of the Complete & Independent Guide is the 7th edition of the book. It contains every detail of every Contest since 1956. We have expanded the Guide this year to include extra facts, statistics and records, including a section on the winning margins since 1975 and also a complete round-by-round scoreboard analysis so the movements of your favourites can be followed as the votes were announced.

So, now we can look forward to Austria in 2015, and the 60th Eurovision Song Contest.

Simon Barclay
Editor

silverthorn-publishing@outlook.com   http://eurovisionguide.blogspot.com

Eurovision Winners

Year	Host City	Winner	Artist	Song
1956	Lugano, Switzerland	Switzerland	Lys Assia	Refrain
1957	Frankfurt, Germany	Netherlands	Corry Brokken	Net Als Toen
1958	Hilversum, Netherlands	France	André Claveau	Dors Mon Amour
1959	Cannes, France	Netherlands	Teddy Scholten	Een Beetje
1960	London, United Kingdom	France	Jacqueline Boyer	Tom Pillibi
1961	Cannes, France	Luxembourg	Jean-Claude Pascal	Nous Les Amoureux
1962	Luxembourg City, Luxembourg	France	Isabelle Aubret	Un Premier Amour
1963	London, United Kingdom	Denmark	Grethe & Jørgen Ingmann	Dansevise
1964	Copenhagen, Denmark	Italy	Gigliola Cinquetti	Non Ho L'étà
1965	Naples, Italy	Luxembourg	France Gall	Poupée De Cire, Poupée De Son
1966	Luxembourg City, Luxembourg	Austria	Udo Jürgens	Merci Chérie
1967	Vienna, Austria	United Kingdom	Sandie Shaw	Puppet On A String
1968	London, United Kingdom	Spain	Massiel	La, La, La
1969	Madrid, Spain	= France	Frida Boccara	Un Jour, Un Enfant
		= United Kingdom	Lulu	Boom Bang-a-bang
		= Netherlands	Lenny Kuhr	De Troubadour
		= Spain	Salomé	Vivo Cantando
1970	Amsterdam, Netherlands	Ireland	Dana	All Kinds Of Everything
1971	Dublin, Ireland	Monaco	Séverine	Un Banc, Un Arbre, Une Rue
1972	Edinburgh, United Kingdom	Luxembourg	Vicky Leandros	Après Toi
1973	Luxembourg City, Luxembourg	Luxembourg	Anne-Marie David	Tu Te Reconnaîtras
1974	Brighton, United Kingdom	Sweden	ABBA	Waterloo
1975	Stockholm, Sweden	Netherlands	Teach-In	Teach-In
1976	The Hague, Netherlands	United Kingdom	Brotherhood of Man	Save Your Kisses For Me
1977	London, United Kingdom	France	Marie Myriam	L'oiseau Et L'enfant
1978	Paris, France	Israel	Izhar Cohen & the Alphabeta	Abanibi
1979	Jerusalem, Israel	Israel	Milk and Honey	Hallelujah
1980	The Hague, Netherlands	Ireland	Johnny Logan	What's Another Year
1981	Dublin, Ireland	United Kingdom	Bucks Fizz	Making Your Mind Up
1982	Harrogate, United Kingdom	Germany	Nicole	Ein bißchen Frieden
1983	Munich, Germany	Luxembourg	Corinne Hermès	Si La Vie Est Cadeau
1984	Luxembourg City, Luxembourg	Sweden	Herrey's	Diggi-loo diggy-ley
1985	Gothenburg, Sweden	Norway	Bobbysocks	La Det Swinge
1986	Bergen, Norway	Belgium	Sandra Kim	J'aime La Vie
1987	Brussels, Belgium	Ireland	Johnny Logan	Hold Me Now
1988	Dublin, Ireland	Switzerland	Céline Dion	Ne Partez Pas Sans Moi
1989	Lausanne, Switzerland	Yugoslavia	Riva	Rock Me
1990	Zagreb, Yugoslavia	Italy	Toto Cutugno	Insieme: 1992
1991	Rome, Italy	Sweden	Carola	Fångad Av En Stormvind
1992	Malmö, Sweden	Ireland	Linda Martin	Why Me
1993	Millstreet, Ireland	Ireland	Niamh Kavanagh	In Your Eyes
1994	Dublin, Ireland	Ireland	P Harrington & C McGettigan	Rock 'n' Roll Kids
1995	Dublin, Ireland	Norway	Secret Garden	Nocturne
1996	Oslo, Norway	Ireland	Eimear Quinn	The Voice
1997	Dublin, Ireland	United Kingdom	Katrina and The Waves	Love shine a light
1998	Birmingham, United Kingdom	Israel	Dana International	Diva
1999	Jerusalem, Israel	Sweden	Charlotte Nilsson	Take me to your heaven
2000	Stockholm, Sweden	Denmark	Olsen Brothers	Fly on the wings of love
2001	Copenhagen, Denmark	Estonia	Tanel Padar, Dave Benton & 2XL	Everybody
2002	Tallinn, Estonia	Latvia	Marie N	I Wanna
2003	Riga, Latvia	Turkey	Sertab Erener	Everyway That I Can
2004	Istanbul, Turkey	Ukraine	Ruslana	Wild Dances
2005	Kiev, Ukraine	Greece	Helena Paparizou	My Number One

Eurovision Winners (continued)

Year	Host City	Winner	Artist	Song
2006	Athens, Greece	Finland	Lordi	Hard Rock Hallelujah
2007	Helsinki, Finland	Serbia	Marija Šerifovic	Molitva
2008	Belgrade, Serbia	Russia	Dima Bilan	Believe
2009	Moscow, Russia	Norway	Alexander Rybak	Fairytale
2010	Oslo, Norway	Germany	Lena Meyer-Landrut	Satellite
2011	Düsseldorf, Germany	Azerbaijan	Ell/Nikki	Running Scared
2012	Baku, Azerbaijan	Sweden	Loreen	Euphoria
2013	Malmö, Sweden	Denmark	Emmelie de Forest	Only Teardrops
2014	Copenhagen, Denmark	Austria	Conchita Wurst	Rise Like a Phoenix

SECTION 1

Qualification for the 2014 Contest

Notes on each country's national competitions

Eurovision 2014: Qualification

Albania

Representative:	Hersi (real name Herciana Matmuja)
Born:	1990 in Kukës, Albania (age 24 during ESC2014)
Previous appearances:	none

This year's Albanian entry was selected from the 52nd edition of *Festivali I Këngës*, the national selection competition. There were two semi-finals, each with eight artists and their songs, but no voting took place and all 16 entries went on to perform in the national final on 28 December 2013. A jury panel awarded votes to their favourite 10 songs.

Top 3 Performers:

Artist	Song	Jury	Position
Hersi	Zemërimi i një nate	69	1
Klodian Kaçani	Me ty	45	2
Sajmir Braho	Grua	40	3

Armenia

Representative:	Aram MP3 (real name Aram Sargsyan)
Born:	1984 in Yerevan, Armenia (then Soviet Union) (age 30 during ESC2014)
Previous appearances:	none

Armenian broadcaster AMPTV selected their Eurovision candidate by internal selection on 31 December 2013 as part of the New Year's Eve *Big Night Gala Show*.

Austria

Representative:	Conchita Wurst (real name Thomas Neuwirth)
Born:	1988 in Gmunden, Austria (aged 25 during ESC2014)
Previous appearances:	none

Austrian broadcaster ORF selected their country's Eurovision candidate by internal selection on 10 September 2013. Eurovision wouldn't be Eurovision without some controversy and this year Wurst was subject of criticism both by Facebook members who objected to the lack of a proper selection competition and by the Belarus Ministry of Information who claimed that the Song Contest had become a "hotbed of sodomy" and that European liberal values were being imposed on Belarus and Russia.

Azerbaijan

Representative:	Dilara Kazimova
Born:	1984 in Baku, Azerbaijan (then Soviet Union) (age 29 during ESC2014)
Previous appearances:	none

Broadcaster İTV adopted a new format for this year, *Böyük Səhnə* (Big Stage). Five supercasting shows judged by juries reduced the number of artists to 14 who progessed to the next round. In Heat 1 of the next round of shows, the 14 artists performed cover versions of songs and again a jury voted for their favourites. Ten performers were successful and went on to Heat 2 where the process was repeated to find the 6 artists to compete in the final on 2 March 2014. Eventually, Dilara Kazimova was chosen by another jury.

Top 3 Performers:

Artist	Song	Jury	Position
Dilara Kazimova	Alone	50	1
Khana Hasanova	Run	46	2
Erkin Osmanli	Love Me Again	44	3

Eurovision 2014: Qualification

Belarus

Representative:	Teo (real name Yuriy Vaschuk)
Born:	1983 in Hidry, Belarus (then Soviet Union) (age 31 during ESC2014)
Previous appearances:	none

BTRC organised their national selection competition, 'Eurofest', again this year. A professional jury selected 15 performers to take part in the final on 10 January 2014. One performer withdrew after it was discovered that his song had been previously entered in Malta's selection competition. A combination of televoting and jury voting then selected Teo to represent Belarus, but not before a tie-breaker had to be introduced to split the two joint winners.

Top 3 Performers:

Artist	Song	Televoting	Jury	Position
Teo	Cheesecake	8	12	1
Max Lorens & DiDyuLya	Now You're Gone	12	8	2
Janette	You Will be Here	3	10	3

Belgium

Representative:	Axel Hirsoux
Born:	1982 in Manage, Belgium (age 31 during ESC2014)
Previous appearances:	none

The Flemish-speaking broadcaster VRT (who alternate sending ESC entries with the Flemish-speaking broadcaster RTBF) organised Eurosong 2014 this year. Two casting shows in front of a jury followed by a call-back round for initially unsuccessful acts produced 12 semi-finalists, four of whom took part in each of three shows. Again, jury voting saw the best two artists progressing to the national final on 16 March 2014. Here, seven international jury panels and a national televote with a quite convoluted percentage-based points method, chose Belgium's candidate.

Top 3 Performers:

Artist	Song	Televoting	Jury	Total
Axel Hirsoux	Mother	57.31% (160 pts)	74	234
Bandits	One	17.29% (48 pts)	42	90
Eva Jacobs	Nothing Is Impossible	13.12% (37 pts)	52	89

Denmark

Representative:	Basim (real name Anis Basim Moujahid)
Born:	1992 in Morocco (age 21 during ESC2014)
Previous appearances:	none

Host broadcaster DR held the national contest, Dansk Melodi Grand Prix 2014 on 8 March 2014. Ten acts competed in the first round, with the top three in the televote and jury voting progressing to the super-final. The winner was then chosen by viewers and a jury.

Super-final:

Artist	Song	Televote	Jury	Total
Basim	Cliché Love Song	15	15	30
Rebekkah Thornbech	Your Lies	7	8	15
Michael Rune feat Natasha Bessez	Wanna Be Loved	8	7	15

Eurovision 2014: Qualification

Estonia

Representative:	Tanja Mihhailova
Born:	1983 in Kaliningrad, Russia (then Soviet Union) (age 30 during ESC2014)
Previous appearances:	none

Broadcaster ERR held two semi-finals with 10 acts in each. The top five performers in each semi-final decided by a combination of jury votes and televoting advanced to the final, *Eesti Laul*, on 1 March 2014. Then, further jury and public voting selected the top two from these ten finalists, who progressed to a super-final and the eventual winner was chosen by viewer voting alone.

Super-final:

Artist	Song	Televote	Position
Tanja	Amazing	53%	1
Super Hot Cosmos Blues	Maybe-Maybe	47%	2

Finland

Representative:	Softengine
Group Members:	Topi Latukka, Ossi Mäkelä, Eero Keskinen, Henri Oskár, Tuomo Alarinta
Previous appearances:	none

Broadcaster YLE again organised the national selection competition, *Uuden Musiikin Kilpailu*. Two initial heats were held, each with 6 entrants. Jury and televoting chose the winner of each heat who progressed direct to the final, plus 4 runners-up who went on to take part in a semi-final. Two performers were eliminated and the remaining six joined the two direct finalists in the final show on 1 February 2014.

Top 3 Performers:

Artist	Song	Jury	Televote	Position
Softengine	Something Better	18.3%	28.3%	1
Mikko Pohjola	Sängyn reunalla	16.8%	19.5%	2
MIAU	God/Drug	15.4%	13.9%	3

France

Representative:	Twin Twin
Born:	Lorent Idir, François Djemel, Patrick Biyik
Previous appearances:	none

Broadcaster France 3 reverted to a national selection competition for the first time since 2007. A 14 member panel chose three artists to compete in the national final on 26 January 2014. The public then had around month to vote for their favourite and these votes were combined with those of a jury to select the winner.

National Finalists:

Artist	Song	Position
Twin Tin	Moustache	1
Destan	Sans toi	
Joanna	Ma liberté	

Eurovision 2014: Qualification

FYR Macedonia

Representative: Tijana Dapčević
Born: 1976 in Skopje, FYR Macedonia (then Yugoslavia) (age 38 during ESC2014)
Previous appearances: none

Broadcaster MRT chose Tijana Dapčević by internal selection on 28 August 2013.

Georgia

Representative: The Shin (Zaza Miminoshvili, Zurab Gagnidze, Mamuka Gaganidze)
                         Mariko Ebralidze
Born: (Mariko) 1984 in Tbilisi, Georgia (then Soviet Union) (age 29 during ESC2014)
Previous appearances: none

Broadcaster GPB chose The Shin & Mariko as Georgia's Eurovision representatives by internal selection on 4 February 2014. The Shin is a Georgian fusion jazz band.

Germany

Representative: Elaiza (Elżbieta "Ela" Steinmetz, Yvonne Grünwald, Natalie Plöger)
Previous appearances: none

Broadcaster NDR organised the selection competition *Unser Song für Dänemark* this year. Eight acts took part in the national final on 13 March 2014. There were three rounds of public televoting with the final round deciding Germany's representative from two remaining performers.

Top 2 Performers:

Artist	Song	Televoting	Position
Elaiza	Is it Right	55%	1
Unheilig	Wir sind alle wie eins	45%	2

Greece

Representative: Freaky Fortune (Nick Raptakis, Theofilos Pouzbouris)
                         Riskykidd (real name Shane Schuller)
Born: (Shane) 1994 in London, UK (age 19 during ESC2014)
Previous appearances: none

Broadcaster ERT had been closed down by the Greek government since the 2013 Contest and the new broadcaster NERIT was set up. Interim channel DT and private music channel MAD TV held a national final on 11 March 2014. Four acts took part and the winner was selected by a combination of jury and public televoting.

Final:

Artist	Song	Televoting	Jury	Position
Freaky Fortune feat Riskykidd	Rise Up	22%	15%	1
Kostas Martakis	Kanemas de me stamata	14%	14%	2
Crystallia	Petalouda stin Athina	10%	12%	3
Mark Angelo feat Josephine	Dancing Night	4%	9%	4

Eurovision 2014: Qualification

Hungary

Representative:	András Kállay-Saunders
Born:	1985 in New York, USA (age 29 during ESC2014)
Previous appearances:	none

Broadcaster MTV again organised a national selection competition for this year, called *A Dal*. Three heats, each with 10 performers, produced 18 semi-finalists. Three acts in each heat were chosen by a jury and three by a televote. In the semi-finals, two acts were chosen by the jury and two by the public. The final on 22 February 2014 comprised two rounds of voting, a jury reduced the number of performers to four, then a public televote decided the winner.

Top 4:

Artist	Song	Position
András Kállay-Saunders	Running	1
Bogi	We All	2
Fool Moon	It Can't Be Over	2
Viktor Király	Running Out of Time	4

Iceland

Representative:	Pollapönk (Heiðar Örn Kristjánsson, Haraldur Freyr Gíslason, Guðni Finnsson, & Arnar Þór Gíslason)
Previous appearances:	none

Broadcaster RÚV held their *Söngvakeppnin 2014* with two semi-finals each with five acts. From each semi-final, the top two artists decided by a public televote qualified for the final on 15 February 2014. A further two wildcards were chosen by the jury alone.
In the final, the top two acts with the highest combined scores from jury and televoting went through to a superfinal and then it was up to public televoting to decide the winner.

Superfinal

Artist	Song	Position
Pollapönk	Enga fordóma	1
Sigríður Eyrún Friðriksdóttir	Up and Away	2

Ireland

Representative:	Can-Linn feat. Kasey Smith
Born:	(Kasey) 1990 in Dublin, Ireland (age 23 during ESC2014)
Previous appearances:	none

RTE organised Ireland's national final, *Eurosong 2014*, which took place on 28 February 2014 with five acts. A combination of five juries based in Cork, Limerick, Galway, Sligo and Dublin plus a viewers' televote selected chose Ireland's Eurovision representative.

Top 3 Performers:

Artist	Song	Juries	Televote	Total	Position
Can-Linn feat. Kasey Smith	Heartbeat	54	60	114	1
Eoghan Quigg	The Movie Song	52	50	102	2
Laura O'Neill	You Don't Remember Me	44	40	84	3

Israel

Representative:	Mei Finegold
Born:	1982 in Rishon LeZion, Israel (age 31 during ESC2014)
Previous appearances:	none

Broadcaster IBA continued with their national selection competition this year, *Kdam Eurovision 2014*, but with a change of format. The IBA first chose Mei Finegold by internal selection to be the artist at Eurovision, and then a three song national final was held with the winning song chosen by a public televote.

Eurovision 2014: Qualification

Italy

Representative:	Emma (real name Emmanuela Marrone)
Born:	1984 in Florence, Italy (age 29 during ESC2014)
Previous appearances:	None

Unlike in the previous two years, broadcaster RAI this year decided not to select an artist from performers at the Festival di San Remo and instead chose Emma by internal selection.

Latvia

Representative:	Aarzemniecki (Jöran Steinhauer, Guntis Veilands, Katrīna Dinanta, Raitis Vilumovs)
Previous appearances:	none

For Latvia's *Dziesma 2014,* a panel created by broadcaster LTV selected 24 acts to compete in two semi-finals. In each semi-final, the top six performers chosen by a combination of viewers votes and a jury progressed to the final on 22 February 2014. The same voting procedure selected three acts to then go through to a Super Final where internet voting also took place.

Super-Final:

Artist	Song	Jury	Televoting	Position
Aarzemniecki	Cake to Bake	2	1	1
Dons	Pēdējā vēstule	1	2	2
Samanta Tina	Stay	3	3	3

Lithuania

Representative:	Vilija Matačiūnaitė
Born:	1986 in Vilnius, Lithuania (age 27 during ESC2014)
Previous appearances:	none

Eurovision selection competitions can be simple or very, very complicated and it's good to see Lithuania opting for the latter this year. Twelve weeks of selection shows, a Jubilee Concert, two semi-finals and final later and their representative was announced, probably with a big sigh of relief. Twenty artists were initially chosen to take part and they could be potentially paired with any of the songs the composers had written for them. Each week's show had a different theme, and gradually one artist left the competition each week. The winning song was selected in week 11. A jury and public televote on 1 March 2014 decided the winning artist.

Top 3 Performers:

Artist	Jury	Televote	Position
Vilija Matačiūnaitė	13	9596	1
Mia	12	7506	2
Vaidas Baumila	5	962	3

Malta

Representative:	Firelight (Michelle Mifsud, Richard Edward Micallef, Tony Polidano, Daniel Micallef, & Leslie Decesare)
Previous appearances:	none

Broadcaster PBS held a single semi-final this year, from which a jury selected 14 acts to perform in the Final on 2 February 2013. The winner was chosen by a 5 member jury and televoting but the jury votes were 5/6ths of the total points, with the public vote only 1/6th.

Top 3 Performers:

Artist	Song	Televote	Jury	Total	Position
Firelight	Coming Home	7	56	63	1
De Bee	Pin the Middle	8	38	46	2
Daniel Testa	One Last Ride	10	31	41	3

Eurovision 2014: Qualification

Moldova

Representative:	Cristina Scarlat
Born:	1981 in Chișinău, Moldova (then Soviet Union) (age 33 during ESC2014)
Previous appearances:	none

Broadcaster TRM held their national competition, *O Melodie Pentru Europa 2014*, with 24 acts taking part in two semi-finals. The usual combination of jury and televoting selected the 16 performers who would progress to the final on 15 March 2014. Further jury and televoting decided the winner.

Top 3 Performers:

Artist	Song	Televote	Jury	Total	Position
Cristina Scarlat	Wild Soul	10	12	22	1
Boris Covali	Perfect Day	12	8	20	2
Lucia S	Frozen	7	10	17	3

Montenegro

Representative:	Sergej Ćetković
Born:	1976 in Podgorica, Montenegro (then Titograd, Yugoslavia) (age 38 during ESC2014)
Previous appearances:	none

Broadcaster RTCG chose Montenegro's entry by internal selection.

Netherlands

Representative:	The Common Linnets (Ilse DeLange & Waylon)
Born:	(Ilse) 1977 in Almelo, Netherlands (age 36 during ESC2014)
	(Waylon, real name Willem Bijkerk) 1980 in Apeldoorn, Netherlands (age 34 during ESC2014)
Previous appearances:	none

Following their relatively successful performance last year, broadcaster AVROTROS continued with an internal selection process this year.

Norway

Representative:	Carl Espen
Born:	1982 in Bergen, Norway (age 31 during ESC2014)
Previous appearances:	none

Broadcaster NRK organised a simplified competition this year. From three semi-finals with five acts performing in each show, three artists were chosen by viewers to progress to the Melodi Grand Prix final. There, two rounds of public voting took place, firstly to reduce the finalists to a top 4 and then to decide the winner.

Gold Final:

Artist	Song	Televote	Position
Carl Espen	Silent Storm	53712	1
Linnea Dale	High Hopes	39086	2
Mo	Heal	37405	3
Knut Kippersund Nesdal	Taste of You	27757	4

Eurovision 2014: Qualification

Poland

Representative:	Donatan & Cleo
Born:	(Donatan , real name Witold Czamara) 1984 in Krakow, Poland (age 29 during ESC2014)
	(Cleo, real name Joanna Klepko) 1983 in Warsaw, Poland (age 30 during ESC2014)
Previous appearances:	none

Returning to Eurovision after two years in the wilderness, Poland's entry was decided by broadcaster TVP who chose Donatan & Cleo by internal selection.

Portugal

Representative:	Suzy (real name Susana Guerra)
Born:	Figueira da Foz, Portugal (age 34 during ESC2014)
Previous appearances:	none

Another country making a welcome return to Eurovision this year, Portugal's entry was selected through the national final *Festival da Canção 2014*, organised by the Portuguese broadcaster Rádio e Televisão de Portugal (RTP). A single semi-final was held with 10 performers, with public voting deciding which five should go on to the national final on 15 March 2014. Suzy was selected solely on the basis of a public vote.

Top 3 performers:

Artist	Song	Televote	Position
Suzy	Quero ser tua	41.56%	1
Catarina Pereira	Mea Culpa	23.58%	2
Rui Andrade	Ao teu encontro	14.56%	3

Romania

Representative:	Paula Seling & Ovi
Born:	(Paula) 1978 in Baia Mare, Romania (age 35 during ESC2014)
	(Ovi, real name Ovidiu Cernăuţeanu) 1974 in Botoşani, Romania (age 39 during ESC2014)
Previous appearances:	3rd in the final of Eurovision 2010

Broadcaster TVR held a selection contest with 12 artists taking part in a single show, Selecţia Naţională 2014, held on 1 March 2014. Jury and a public televote chose 2010 ESC entrants Paula Seling & Ovi as Romania's representatives for a second time.

Top 3 Performers:

Artist	Song	Televote	Jury	Total	Position
Paula Seling & Ovi	Miracle	10	12	22	1
Vaida	One More Time	12	4	16	2
Vizi Imre	Kind of Girl	6	10	16	2

Russia

Representative:	Tolmachevy Sisters (Anastasia Tolmacheva, Maria Tolmacheva)
Born:	1997 in Kursk, Russia (age 17 during ESC2014)
Previous appearances:	none

Continuing with the decision taken in 2012, broadcaster RTR did not hold a national competition and instead chose their entry by internal selection. Twins, the Tolmachevy Sisters, won Junior Eurovision in 2006.

Eurovision 2014: Qualification

San Marino

Representative:	Valentina Monetta
Born:	1975 in San Marino City, San Marino (age 39 during ESC2014)
Previous appearances:	2012 (finished 14th in semi-final), 2013 (finished 11th in semi-final)

Hoping it is third time lucky, or perhaps there is only one singer in San Marino, SMTV again chose Valentina Monetta as San Marino's representative by internal selection using a jury of music professionals. This will be the third consecutive appearance for Valentina, she failed to qualify for the final on the previous two occasions.

Slovenia

Representative:	Tinkara Kovač
Born:	1978 in Koper, Slovenia (then Yugoslavia) (age 35 during ESC2014)
Previous appearances:	none

Broadcaster RTVSLO reverted to the national selection competition this year, Evrovizijska Melodija 2014. The final, on 8 March 2014,

Superfinal:

Artist	Song	Televote	Position
Tinkara Kovač	Spet (Round & Round)	7932	1
Muff	Let Me Be	3450	2

Spain

Representative:	Ruth Lorenzo
Born:	1982 in Murcia, Spain (age 31 during ESC2014)
Previous appearances:	none

TVE held a national selection competition to find Spain's entry for the first time since 2011. Five invited artists performed in a final called Mira

Top 3 finalists:

Artist	Song	Televote	Jury	Total	Position
Ruth Lorenzo	Dancing in the Rain	36	30	66	1
Brequette	Más (Run)	30	36	66	2
Jorge González	Aunque se acabe el mundo	24	24	48	3

Sweden

Representative:	Sanna Nielsen
Born:	1984 in Edenryd, Sweden (age 29 during ESC2014)
Previous appearances:	none

Broadcaster SVT held its annual *Melodifestivalen* to select its representative. In each of the four semi-finals the two acts with the most televotes went through to the final, the third and fourth placed act went into a Second Chance round. This second chance round was eventually a head to head elimination, with the two acts remaining after the quarter and semi finals going on to the main final, held on 8 March 2014. Here, the ten finalists were judged by a combination of jury votes and televoting, with the jury votes being made up of the scores from 11 international panels, from Denmark, Estonia, France, Israel, Italy, Malta, Netherlands, Russia, Spain, the United Kingdom and Germany.

Top 3 Performers:

Artist	Song	Televote	Jury	Total	Position
Sanna Nielsen	Undo	122	90	212	1
Ace Wilder	Busy Doin' Nothin'	113	97	210	2
Alcazar	Blame it on the Disco	48	62	110	3

Eurovision 2014: Qualification

Switzerland

Representative:	Sebalter (real name Sebastiano Paù-Lessi)
Born:	1985 in Ticino, Switzerland (age 28 during ESC2014)
Previous appearances:	none

Broadcaster SRG SSR once again held the competion this year to choose the Swiss representative. Broadcasters from the German, French and Italian speaking media each put forward artists from which six were chosen to go forward to the national final, *Die grosse Entscheidungs Show*, on 1 February 2014. The winner was selected by 50/50 jury and televoting.

Top 3 Performers:

Artist	Song	Position
Sebalter	Hunter of Stars	1
Yasmina Hunzinger	I Still Believe	2
3 for All	Together Forever	3

Ukraine

Representative:	Mariya Yaremchuk
Born:	1993 in Chernivtsi, Ukraine (then Soviet Union) (age 21 during ESC2014)
Previous appearances:	none

Broadcaster NTU organised Ukraine's national final, *Evrobachennya 2014*, held on 21 December 2013. Twenty acts were selected by a professional jury to take part in the final. There, the usual combination of jury and public televoting decided Ukraine's representative.

Top 3 Performers:

Artist	Song	Televote	Jury	Total	Position
Mariya Yaremchuk	Tick-Tock	12	12	24	1
Viktoria Petryk	Love is Lord	7	10	17	2
Volodimir Tkachenko	Byti tam de ti	5	11	16	3

United Kingdom

Representative:	Molly (real name Molly Smitten-Downes)
Born:	1987 in Anstey, England (age 27 during ESC2014)
Previous appearances:	none

The BBC again decided not to hold a selection competition and on 3 March 2014 announced that Molly would represent the UK.

SECTION 2

Contest Details and Voting Tables

All the performers, song titles, writers & composers

Plus a full breakdown of all the votes awarded in every contest
including semi-finals

1956 Eurovision 1: Lugano, Switzerland

24 May 1956

Rank	Start	Country	Artist	Song	Writer	Composer
1	9	Switzerland	Lys Assia	Refrain	Emile Gardaz	Géo Voumard
2	10	Belgium	Mony Marc	Le Plus Beau Jour De Ma Vie	David Bée	Claude Alix
3	11	Germany	Freddy Quinn	So Geht Das Jede Nacht	Peter Mösser	Lothar Olias
4	12	France	Dany Dauberson	Il Est Là	Simone Vallauris	Simone Vallauris
5	14	Italy	Tonina Torielli	Amami Se Vuoi	Mario Panzeri	Vittorio Mascheroni
6	13	Luxembourg	Michèle Arnaud	Les Amants De Minuit	Pierre Lambry	Simone Laurencin
7	8	Netherlands	Corry Brokken	Voorgoed Voorbij	Jelle de Vries	Jelle de Vries
8	7	Italy	Franca Raimondi	Aprite Le Finestre	Pinchi	Virgilio Panzito
9	3	Belgium	Fud Leclerc	Messieurs Les Noyés De La Seine	Robert Montal	Jean Miret, Jacques Say
10	2	Switzerland	Lys Assia	Das Alte Karussell	Fernando Paggi	George Betz-Stahl
11	4	Germany	Walter Andreas Schwarz	Im Wartesaal Zum Großen Glück	Walter Andreas Schwarz	Walter Andreas Schwarz
12	5	France	Mathé Altéry	Le Temps Perdu	Rachèle Thoreau	André Lodge
13	6	Luxembourg	Michèle Arnaud	Ne Crois Pas	Jacques Lassry	Christian Guittreau
14	1	Netherlands	Jetty Paerl	De Vogels Van Holland	Annie Schmidt	Cor Lemaire

Note: Two songs were performed per country. Each country had 10 jurors who could award 1 point each to their favourite act, including those entries from their own country. The votes awarded have never been disclosed.

1957 Eurovision 2: Frankfurt, Germany

3 March 1957

Rank	Start	Country	Artist	Song	Writer	Composer	POINTS
1	6	Netherlands	Corry Brokken	Net Als Toen	Willy van Hemert	Guus Jansen	31
2	8	France	Paule Desjardins	La Belle Amour	Francis Carco	Guy Lefarge	17
3	9	Denmark	Birthe Wilke & Gustav Winckler	Skibet Skal Sejle I Nat	Paul Sörensen	Erik Fiehn	10
4	7	Germany	Margot Hielscher	Telefon, Telefon	Ralph Maria Siegel	Friedrich Meyer	8
5	2	Luxembourg	Danièle Dupré	Tant De Peine	Jacques Taber	Jean-Pierre Kemmer	8
6	4	Italy	Nunzio Gallo	Corde Della Mia Chitarra	Giuseppi Cavaliere	Mario Ruccione	7
7	3	United Kingdom	Patricia Bredin	All	Alan Stranks	Reynell Wreford	6
8	1	Belgium	Bobbejaan Schoepen	Straatdeuntje	Eric Franssen	Harry Frekin	5
9	10	Switzerland	Lys Assia	L'enfant Que J'étais	Emile Gardaz	Géo Voumard	5
10	5	Austria	Bob Martin	Wohin, Kleines Pony	Hans Werner, Kurt Svab	Kurt Svab	3

1957 Eurovision 2: Frankfurt, Germany

	Austria	Belgium	Denmark	France	Germany	Italy	Monaco	Netherlands	Switzerland	United Kingdom	TOTAL
Belgium			2		2				1		5
Luxembourg	3					4				1	8
United Kingdom	1	1					1	1	2		6
Italy		1	1				2	1		2	7
Austria						1	1			1	3
Netherlands	6	5	3	4	1	1		3	7	1	31
Germany		1		6						1	8
France		2	2		6		1	4		2	17
Denmark						3	5			2	10
Switzerland			2		1	1		1			5

Note: each country had 10 jurors who could award 1 point each to their favourite act.

1958 Eurovision 3: Hilversum, Netherlands

12 March 1958

Rank	Start	Country	Artist	Song	Writer	Composer	POINTS
1	3	France	André Claveau	Dors Mon Amour	Hubert Giraud	Pierre Delanoë	27
2	10	Switzerland	Lys Assia	Giorgio	Fridolin Tschudi	Paul Burkhard	24
3	1	Italy	Domenico Modugno	Nel Blu Dipinto Di Blu	Franco Migliacci, Domenico Modugno	Domenico Modugno	13
4	5	Sweden	Alice Babs	Lilla Stjärna	Åke Gerhard	Åke Gerhard	10
5	9	Austria	Liane Augustin	Die Ganze Welt Braucht Liebe	Günther Léopold, Kurt Werner	Günther Léopold, Kurt Werner	8
6	7	Belgium	Fud Leclerc	Ma Petite Chatte	André Dohet	André Dohet	8
7	8	Germany	Margot Hielscher	Für Zwei Groschen Musik	Fred Rauch, Walter Brandin	Friedrich Meyer	5
8	6	Denmark	Raquel Rastenni	Jeg Rev Et Blad Ud Af Min Dagbog	Harry Jensen	Harry Jensen	3
9	2	Netherlands	Corry Brokken	Heel De Wereld	Benny Vreden	Benny Vreden	1
10	4	Luxembourg	Solange Berry	Un Grand Amour	Monique Laniece, Raymond Roche	Michel Eric	1

1958 Eurovision 3: Hilversum, Netherlands

12 March 1958

	Austria	Belgium	Denmark	France	Germany	Italy	Monaco	Netherlands	Sweden	Switzerland	TOTAL
Italy	1	4		1	4		1		1	1	**13**
Netherlands										1	**1**
France	7	1	9		1	6	1	1		1	**27**
Luxembourg										1	**1**
Sweden	1	1						3	2	3	**10**
Denmark				1			1		1		**3**
Belgium			1		5		1			1	**8**
Germany		2		2			1				**5**
Austria		1		3			1	1		2	**8**
Switzerland	2	2		3		4	4	5	6		**24**

Note: each country had 10 jurors who could award 1 point each to their favourite act.

25

Rank	Start	Country	Artist	Song	Writer	Composer	POINTS
1	5	Netherlands	Teddy Scholten	Een Beetje	Willy van Hemert	Dick Schallies	21
2	10	United Kingdom	Pearl Carr & Teddy Johnson	Sing Little Birdie	Syd Cordell	Stan Butcher	16
3	1	France	Jean Philippe	Oui, Oui, Oui, Oui	Pierre Cour	Hubert Giraud	15
4	8	Switzerland	Christa Williams	Irgendwoher	Lothar Löffler	Lothar Löffler	14
5	2	Denmark	Birthe Wilke	Uh-jeg Ville Ønske Jeg Var Dig	Carl Andersen	Otto Lington	12
6	11	Belgium	Bob Benny	Hou Toch Van Mij	Ke Riema	Hans Flower	9
7	3	Italy	Domenico Modugno	Piove	Dino Verde	Domenico Modugno	9
8	6	Germany	Alice & Ellen Kessler	Heut' Woll'n Wir Tanzen Geh'n	Astrid Voltmann	Helmut Zander	5
9	9	Austria	Ferry Graf	Der K Und K Kalypso Aus Wien	Günther Léopold	Norbert Pawlicki	4
10	7	Sweden	Brita Borg	Augustin	Åke Gerhard	Harry Sandin	4
11	4	Monaco	Jacques Pills	Mon Ami Pierrot	Raymond Bravard	Florence Veran	1

1959 Eurovision 4: Cannes, France

	Austria	Belgium	Denmark	France	Germany	Italy	Monaco	Netherlands	Sweden	Switzerland	United Kingdom	TOTAL
France	1	2	4		4	1	2	1		1		15
Denmark	2	1		3		1	1	1	4	1	2	12
Italy		1		3			1		1	3		9
Monaco	1						1					1
Netherlands	3	3		4	2	7	1				1	21
Germany		1		2	1	1				1		5
Sweden			1		1			3				4
Switzerland	1	1	2	1			1		3		5	14
Austria							1	5	2	1		4
United Kingdom	2	2	1	1			2			3		16
Belgium			2		3		1	1			2	9

Note: each country had 10 jurors who could award 1 point each to their favourite act.

Rank	Start	Country	Artist	Song	Writer	Composer	POINTS
1	13	France	Jacqueline Boyer	Tom Pillibi	Pierre Cour	André Popp	32
2	1	United Kingdom	Bryan Johnson	Looking High, High, High	John Watson	John Watson	25
3	8	Monaco	François Deguelt	Ce Soir-là	Pierre Dorsey	Hubert Giraud	15
4	6	Norway	Nora Brockstedt	Voi-voi	George Elgaaen	George Elgaaen	11
5	11	Germany	Wyn Hoop	Bonne Nuit, Ma Chérie!	Kurt Schwabach	Franz-Josef Breuer	11
6	5	Belgium	Fud Leclerc	Mon Amour Pour Toi	Robert Montal	Jack Say	9
7	7	Austria	Harry Winter	Du Hast Mich So Fasziniert	Robert Gilbert	Robert Stolz	6
8	12	Italy	Renato Rascel	Romantica	Dino Verde	Renato Rascel	5
9	9	Switzerland	Anita Traversi	Cielo E Terra	Mario Robbiani	Mario Robbiani	5
10	2	Sweden	Siw Malmkvist	Alla Andra Får Varann	Åke Gerhard	Ulf Kjellqvist	4
11	4	Denmark	Katy Bødtger	Det Var En Yndig Tid	Sven Buemann	Vilfred Kjær	4
12	10	Netherlands	Rudi Carrell	Wat Een Geluk	Willy van Hemert	Dick Schallies	2
13	3	Luxembourg	Camillo Felgen	So Laang We's Du Do Bast	Henri Mootz	Henri Mootz, Jean Roderes	1

1960 Eurovision 5: London, United Kingdom

	Austria	Belgium	Denmark	France	Germany	Italy	Luxembourg	Monaco	Netherlands	Norway	Sweden	Switzerland	United Kingdom	TOTAL
United Kingdom	3	1			1	2	5	1	5	2	1	4		25
Sweden				2		1			1					4
Luxembourg						1								1
Denmark		1					1			2				4
Belgium					1	3			1		4			9
Norway	1		2	1					1			4	2	11
Austria		1	2			1							2	6
Monaco			2	3	7		1					1	1	15
Switzerland	1				1	1	1			1				5
Netherlands		1				1								2
Germany	2	2		4				2			1			11
Italy	1	1					1		2					5
France	2	3	4				1	7		5	4	1	5	32

Note: each country had 10 jurors who could award 1 point each to their favourite act.

1961 Eurovision 6: Cannes, France

Rank	Start	Country	Artist	Song	Writer	Composer	POINTS
1	14	Luxembourg	Jean-Claude Pascal	Nous Les Amoureux	Maurice Vidalin	Jacques Datin	31
2	15	United Kingdom	The Allisons	Are You Sure?	John Alford, Bob Day	John Alford, Bob Day	24
3	10	Switzerland	Franca di Rienzo	Nous Aurons Demain	Emile Gardaz	Géo Voumard	16
4	9	France	Jean-Paul Mauric	Printemps (avril Carillonne)	Guy Favereau	Francis Baxter	13
5	16	Italy	Betty Curtis	Al Di Là	Giulio Rapetti	Carlo Donida	12
6	13	Denmark	Dario Campeotto	Angelique	Aksel Rasmussen	Aksel Rasmussen	12
7	12	Norway	Nora Brockstedt	Sommer I Palma	Egil Hagen	Jan Wolner	10
8	5	Yugoslavia	Ljiljana Petrovic	Neke Davne Zvezde	Miroslav Antic	Jože Privšek	9
9	1	Spain	Conchita Bautista	Estando Contigo	Antonio Guijarro	Augusto Algueró	8
10	6	Netherlands	Greetje Kauffeld	Wat Een Dag	Pieter Goemans	Dick Schallies	6
11	2	Monaco	Colette Deréal	Allons, Allons Les Enfants	Pierre Delanoë	Hubert Giraud	6
12	4	Finland	Laila Kinnunen	Valoa Ikkunassa	Sauvo Puhtila	Eino Hurme	6
13	8	Germany	Lale Andersen	Einmal Sehen Wir Uns Wieder	Ernst Bader	Rudolf Maluck	3
14	7	Sweden	Lill-Babs	April, April	Bo Eneby	Bobby Ericsson	2
15	3	Austria	Jimmy Makulis	Sehnsucht	Leopold Andrejewirsch	Leopold Andrejewirsch	1
16	11	Belgium	Bob Benny	September, Gouden Roos	Wim Brabants	Hans Flower	1

1961 Eurovision 6: Cannes, France

	Yugoslavia	United Kingdom	Switzerland	Sweden	Spain	Norway	Netherlands	Monaco	Luxembourg	Italy	Germany	France	Finland	Denmark	Belgium	Austria	TOTAL
Spain		1		1		2	1	1				2					**8**
Monaco		1	1		1								3				**6**
Austria		1															**1**
Finland		2								2		1		1			**6**
Yugoslavia		1	1				1					2		1		3	**9**
Netherlands	2									2	1	1					**6**
Sweden												2					**2**
Germany				1										1		1	**3**
France		2		1	2			2	1		4		1				**13**
Switzerland		2		4	1		2	2		2			1			2	**16**
Belgium									1								**1**
Norway	1				1		1						1	1	5		**10**
Denmark				2		8	1					1					**12**
Luxembourg	5		1	1	2		3	4		3	5	1	1	1		4	**31**
United Kingdom	1		7		3				8	1			2	1	1		**24**
Italy	1						1	1					1	4	4		**12**

Note: each country had 10 jurors who could award 1 point each to their favourite act.

1962 Eurovision 7: Luxembourg

Rank	Start	Country	Artist	Song	Writer	Composer	POINTS
1	9	France	Isabelle Aubret	Un Premier Amour	Roland Valade	Claude Henri Vic	26
2	16	Monaco	François Deguelt	Dis Rien	René Rouzaud	Henri Salvador	13
3	14	Luxembourg	Camillo Felgen	Petit Bonhomme	Maurice Vidalin	Jacques Datin	11
4	13	United Kingdom	Ronnie Carroll	Ring-a-ding Girl	Stan Butcher	Syd Cordell	10
5	12	Yugoslavia	Lola Novakovic	Ne Pali Svetlo U Sumrak	Dragutin Britvic	Jozé Privšek	10
6	7	Germany	Conny Froboess	Zwei Kleine Italiener	Georg Buschor	Christian Bruhn	9
7	1	Finland	Marion Rung	Tipi-tii	Kari Tuomisaari	Kari Tuomisaari	4
8	6	Sweden	Inger Berggren	Sol Och Vår	Ulf Kjellqvist, Åke Gerhard	Ulf Kjellqvist, Åke Gerhard	4
9	15	Italy	Claudio Villa	Addio, Addio	Franco Migliacci	Domenico Modugno	3
10	11	Switzerland	Jean Philippe	Le Retour	Emile Gardaz	Géo Voumard	2
11	10	Norway	Inger Jacobsen	Kom Sol, Kom Regn	Ivar Andersen	Kjell Karlsen	2
12	5	Denmark	Ellen Winther	Vuggevise	Sejr Volmer-Sørensen	Kjeld Bonfils	2
13	8	Netherlands	De Spelbrekers	Katinka	Henry Hamhuis	Joop Stokkermans	0
14	2	Belgium	Fud Leclerc	Ton Nom	Tony Golan	Eric Channe	0
15	3	Spain	Victor Balaguer	Llámame	Miguel Portoles	Mario Selles	0
16	4	Austria	Eleonore Schwarz	Nur In Der Wiener Luft	Bruno Uher	Bruno Uher	0

1962 Eurovision 7: Luxembourg

Receiving \ Voting	Austria	Belgium	Denmark	Finland	France	Germany	Italy	Luxembourg	Monaco	Netherlands	Norway	Spain	Sweden	Switzerland	United Kingdom	Yugoslavia	TOTAL
Finland											1				3		4
Belgium																	0
Spain																	0
Austria																	0
Denmark							1						1				2
Sweden			3							1							4
Germany			1	2					2	2					2		9
Netherlands																	0
France	2	2				3	2	1	1	3	3	2	3	3	1	3	26
Norway					2												2
Switzerland						2											2
Yugoslavia		1	2	1			3						2	2			10
United Kingdom	1	1			1			2	1		1	1		1		1	10
Luxembourg		3		3					3							2	11
Italy					3												3
Monaco	3				1	1		3			2	3					13

Note: Each country awarded from 3 points to 1 point in descending order for their 3 favourite acts.

1963 Eurovision 8: London, United Kingdom

Rank	Start	Country	Artist	Song	Writer	Composer	POINTS
1	8	Denmark	Grethe & Jørgen Ingmann	Dansevise	Sejr Volmer-Sørensen	Otto Francker	42
2	10	Switzerland	Esther Ofarim	Ten Va Pas	Emile Gardaz	Géo Voumard	40
3	6	Italy	Emilio Pericoli	Uno Per Tutte	Alberto Testa, Giulio Rapetti	Tony Renis	37
4	1	United Kingdom	Ronnie Carroll	Say Wonderful Things	Norman Newell	Philip Green	28
5	11	France	Alain Barrière	Elle était Si Jolie	Alain Barrière	Alain Barrière	25
6	15	Monaco	Françoise Hardy	L'amour S'en Va	Françoise Hardy	Françoise Hardy	25
7	4	Austria	Carmela Corren	Vielleicht Geschieht Ein Wunder	Peter Wehle	Erwin Halletz	16
8	16	Luxembourg	Nana Mouskouri	A Force De Prier	Pierre Delanoë	Raymond Bernard	13
9	3	Germany	Heidi Brühl	Marcel	Charly Niessen	Charly Niessen	5
10	14	Belgium	Jacques Raymond	Waarom	Wim Brabants	Hans Flower	4
11	9	Yugoslavia	Vice Vukov	Brodovi	Mario Nardelli	Mario Nardelli	3
12	12	Spain	José Guardiola	Algo Prodigioso	Camillo Murillo Janero	Fernando Garcia Morcillo	2
13	5	Norway	Anita Thallaug	Solhverv	Dag Kristoffersen	Dag Kristoffersen	0
14	7	Finland	Laila Halme	Muistojeni Laulu	Börje Sundgren	Börje Sundgren	0
15	2	Netherlands	Annie Palmen	Een Speeldoos	Pieter Goemans	Pieter Goemans	0
16	13	Sweden	Monica Zetterlund	En Gång i Stockholm	Beppe Wolgers	Bobbie Ericsson	0

1963 Eurovision 8: London, United Kingdom

Receiving \ Voting	Austria	Belgium	Denmark	Finland	France	Germany	Italy	Luxembourg	Monaco	Netherlands	Norway	Spain	Sweden	Switzerland	United Kingdom	Yugoslavia	TOTAL
United Kingdom			3	3	3				1	3	5	5	2			3	28
Netherlands																	0
Germany									3		2						5
Austria			3	4	2								3		4		16
Norway																	0
Italy				2		3		4	5	1	3	3	5	5	2	4	37
Finland																	0
Denmark	3	5		5	4	2	2	5		5	4		1	3	3		42
Yugoslavia					1							2					3
Switzerland	5	4	4		5	4	5	3			1	4			5		40
France	2	1				1	4	1	2	4		1		4			25
Spain																2	2
Sweden																	0
Belgium	4																4
Monaco		3		1	4	5	3	2		2			4		1		25
Luxembourg			5			3	1		2					2			13

Note: Each country awarded from 5 points to 1 point in descending order for their 5 favourite acts.

1964 Eurovision 9: Copenhagen, Denmark

Rank	Start	Country	Artist	Song	Writer	Composer	POINTS
1	12	Italy	Gigliola Cinquetti	Non Ho L'età	Mario Panzeri	Nicola Salerno	49
2	8	United Kingdom	Matt Monro	I Love The Little Things	Tony Hatch	Tony Hatch	17
3	10	Monaco	Romuald	Où Sont-elles Passées?	Pierre Barouh	Francis Lai	15
4	7	France	Rachel	Le Chant De Mallory	Pierre Cour	André Popp	14
5	1	Luxembourg	Hugues Aufray	Dès Que Le Printemps Revient	Jacques Plante	Hugues Aufray	14
6	6	Austria	Udo Jürgens	Warum Nur, Warum?	Udo Jürgen Bockelmann	Udo Jürgen Bockelmann	11
7	5	Finland	Lasse Mårtenson	Laiskotellen	Sauvo Puhtila	Lasse Mårtenson	9
8	3	Norway	Arne Bendiksen	Spiral	Egil Hagen	Sigurd Jansen	6
9	4	Denmark	Bjørn Tidmand	Sangen Om Dig	Morgens Dam	Aksel Rasmussen	4
10	15	Belgium	Robert Cogoi	Près De Ma Rivière	Robert Cogoi	Robert Cogoi	2
11	2	Netherlands	Anneke Grönloh	Jij Bent Mijn Leven	René de Vos	Ted Powder	2
12	16	Spain	Tim, Nelly & Tony	Caracola	Fina de Calderón	Fina de Calderón	1
13	14	Switzerland	Anita Traversi	I Miei Pensieri	Sanzio Chiesa	Giovanni Pelli	0
14	9	Germany	Nora Nova	Man Gewöhnt Sich So Schnell An Das Schöne	Niels Nobach	Rudi von der Dovenmühle	0
15	11	Portugal	António Calvário	Oração	Francisco Nicholson, Rogério Braçinha	João Nobre	0
16	13	Yugoslavia	Sabahudin Kurt	Zivot Je Sklopio Krug	Stevan Raickovic	Srcan Matijevic	0

1964 Eurovision 9: Copenhagen, Denmark

	Austria	Belgium	Denmark	Finland	France	Germany	Italy	Luxembourg	Monaco	Netherlands	Norway	Portugal	Spain	Switzerland	United Kingdom	Yugoslavia	TOTAL
Luxembourg	3					5			3	3							14
Netherlands				1											1		2
Norway			5		1												6
Denmark							3				1						4
Finland											3		3		3		9
Austria		3			3								5				11
France		1					1	1	5	1		3	1			1	14
United Kingdom	1	5				1	5							5			17
Germany																	0
Monaco			3	5				3						1		3	15
Portugal																	0
Italy	5			3	5	3		5		5	5	5		3	5	5	49
Yugoslavia																	0
Switzerland																	0
Belgium									1			1					2
Spain			1														1

Note: Each country awarded their three favourite acts either 5 points, 3 points or 1 point.

1965 Eurovision 10: Naples, Italy

Rank	Start	Country	Artist	Song	Writer	Composer	POINTS
1	15	Luxembourg	France Gall	Poupée De Cire, Poupée De Son	Serge Gainsbourg	Serge Gainsbourg	32
2	2	United Kingdom	Kathy Kirby	I Belong	Phil Peters	Peter Lee-Sterling	26
3	11	France	Guy Mardel	N'avoue Jamais	Françoise Dorin	Guy Mardel	22
4	6	Austria	Udo Jürgens	Sag Ihr, Ich Lass' Sie Grüßen	Frank Bohlen	Udo Jürgen Bockelmann	16
5	13	Italy	Bobby Solo	Se Piangi, Se Ridi	Giulio Rapetti	Roberto Satti, Gianni Marchetti	15
6	4	Ireland	Butch Moore	I'm Walking The Streets In The Rain	Teresa Conlon	Joe Harrigan, George Prendergast	11
7	14	Denmark	Birgit Brüel	For Din Skyld	Poul Henningsen	Jørgen Jersild	10
8	18	Switzerland	Yovanna	Non à Jamais Sans Toi	Jean Charles	Bob Calfati	8
9	9	Monaco	Marjorie Noël	Va Dire à L'amour	Jacques Mareuil	Raymond Bernard	7
10	10	Sweden	Ingvar Wixell	Absent Friend	Alf Henriksson	Dag Wiren	6
11	1	Netherlands	Conny Van den Bos	Het Is Genoeg	Karel Prior	Johnny Holshuyzen	5
12	17	Yugoslavia	Vice Vukov	Ceznja	Zarko Roje	Julijo Maric	2
13	7	Norway	Kirsti Sparboe	Karusell	Jolly Kramer-Johansen	Jolly Kramer-Johansen	1
14	12	Portugal	Simone de Oliviera	Sol De Inverno	Jeronimo Bragança	Carlos Nobrega e Sousa	1
15	3	Spain	Conchita Bautista	Qué Bueno, Qué Bueno	Antonio Figueroa Egea	Antonio Figueroa Egea	0
16	16	Finland	Viktor Klimenko	Aurinko Laskee Länteen	Reino Helismaa	Toivo Kärki	0
17	5	Germany	Ulla Wiesner	Paradies, Wo Bist Du?	Barbara Kist, Hans Blüm	Barbara Kist, Hans Blüm	0
18	8	Belgium	Lize Marke	Als Het Weer Lente Is	Jaak Dreesen	Jef van den Berg	0

1965 Eurovision 10: Naples, Italy

Receiving ↓ / Voting →	Austria	Belgium	Denmark	Finland	France	Germany	Ireland	Italy	Luxembourg	Monaco	Netherlands	Norway	Portugal	Spain	Sweden	Switzerland	United Kingdom	Yugoslavia	TOTAL
Netherlands												5							5
United Kingdom		6	5					1				1		5	3	5			26
Spain																			0
Ireland								5					3					3	11
Germany																			0
Austria							5	3					5				3		16
Norway																		1	1
Belgium																			0
Monaco											1					1	5		7
Sweden				3		3													6
France	3								3	5	3			3				5	22
Portugal										1									1
Italy		3		1	1				1	3					5		1		15
Denmark	5								5										10
Luxembourg			3	5	5	5	1				5	3		1	1	3			32
Finland																			0
Yugoslavia						1							1						2
Switzerland	1		1		3		3												8

Note: Each country awarded their three favourite acts either 5 points, 3 points or 1 point, apart from Belgium which chose only two favourites and awarded 6 and 3 points.

1966 Eurovision 11: Luxembourg

Rank	Start	Country	Artist	Song	Writer	Composer	POINTS
1	9	Austria	Udo Jürgens	Merci Chérie	Udo Jürgen Bockelmann, Thomas Hörbiger	Udo Jürgen Bockelmann	31
2	10	Sweden	Lill Lindfors & Svante Thuresson	Nygammal Vals Eller Hip Man Svinaherde	Björn Lindroth	Bengt-Arne Wallin	16
3	6	Norway	Åse Kleveland	Intet Er Nytt Under Solen	Arne Bendiksen	Arne Bendiksen	15
4	17	Ireland	Dickie Rock	Come Back To Stay	Rowland Soper	Rowland Soper	14
5	3	Belgium	Tonia	Un Peu De Poivre, Un Peu De Sel	Phil van Cauwenbergh	Paul Quintens	14
6	12	Switzerland	Madeleine Pascal	Ne Vois-tu Pas?	Roland Schweizer	Pierre Brenner	12
7	5	Yugoslavia	Berta Ambroz	Brez Besed	Elza Budav	Mojmir Sepe	9
8	11	Spain	Raphael	Yo Soy Aquél	Manuel Alejandro	Manuel Alejandro	9
9	18	United Kingdom	Kenneth McKellar	A Man Without Love	Peter Callander	Cyril Ornadel	8
10	7	Finland	Ann-Christine Nyström	Play-boy	Ossi Runne	Ossi Runne	7
11	4	Luxembourg	Michèle Torr	Ce Soir Je T'attendais	Jacques Chaumelle	Bernard Kesslair	7
12	1	Germany	Margot Eskens	Die Zeiger Der Uhr	Hans Bradtke	Walter Dobschinski	7
13	8	Portugal	Madalena Iglesias	Ele E Ela	Carlos Canelhas	Carlos Canelhas	6
14	2	Denmark	Ulla Pia	Stop, Ja Stop - Ja Stop, Mens Legen Er Go	Erik Kåre	Erik Kåre	4
15	16	Netherlands	Milly Scott	Fernando En Philippo	Gerrit den Braber	Kees de Bruyn	2
16	15	France	Dominique Walter	Chez Nous	Jacques Plante	Claude Carrère	1
17	13	Monaco	Tereza	Bien Plus Fort	Jean-Max Rivière	Gérard Bourgeois	0
18	14	Italy	Domenico Modugno	Dio Come Ti Amo	Domenico Modugno	Domenico Modugno	0

1966 Eurovision 11: Luxembourg

	Yugoslavia	United Kingdom	Switzerland	Sweden	Spain	Portugal	Norway	Netherlands	Monaco	Luxembourg	Italy	Ireland	Germany	France	Finland	Denmark	Belgium	Austria	TOTAL
Germany			5								1						1		7
Denmark							1								3				4
Belgium				1		3		5					5						14
Luxembourg				5										1				1	7
Yugoslavia		5											3		1				9
Norway		3			3						5		1						12
Finland							3	1								3			7
Portugal					5											1			6
Austria	5		3		1	1			5	5	3			3			5		31
Sweden			1				5								5	5			16
Spain	1			3		5													9
Switzerland									3	1		3						5	12
Monaco																			0
Italy																			0
France									1										1
Netherlands		1										1							2
Ireland	3							3						5			3		14
United Kingdom										3		5							8

Note: Each country awarded their three favourite acts either 5 points, 3 points or 1 point.

Rank	Start	Country	Artist	Song	Writer	Composer	POINTS
1	11	United Kingdom	Sandie Shaw	Puppet On A String	Bill Martin, Phil Coulter	Bill Martin, Phil Coulter	47
2	17	Ireland	Sean Dunphy	If I Could Choose	Wesley Burrows	Michael Coffey	22
3	4	France	Noëlle Cordier	Il Doit Faire Beau Là-bas	Pierre Delanoë	Hubert Giraud	20
4	2	Luxembourg	Vicky	L'amour Est Bleu	Pierre Cour	André Popp	17
5	14	Monaco	Minouche Barelli	Boum-badaboum	Serge Gainsbourg	Serge Gainsbourg, Michel Colombier	10
6	12	Spain	Raphael	Hablemos Del Amor	Manuel Alejandro	Manuel Alejandro	9
7	10	Belgium	Louis Neefs	Ik Heb Zorgen	Phil van Cauwenbergh	Paul Quintens	8
8	15	Yugoslavia	Lado Leskovar	Vse Roze Sveta	Milan Lindic	Urban Koder	7
9	9	Germany	Inge Brück	Anouschka	Hans Blüm	Hans Blüm	7
10	7	Sweden	Östen Warnebring	Som En Dröm	Curt Peterson, Marcus Österdahl, Patrice Hellberg	Curt Peterson, Marcus Österdahl, Patrice Hellberg	7
11	16	Italy	Claudio Villa	Non Andare Più Lontano	Vito Pallavicini	Gianni Mescoli	4
12	5	Portugal	Eduardo Nascimento	O Vento Mudou	João Magalhães Pereira	Nuño Nazareth Fernandes	3
13	8	Finland	Fredi	Varjoon-suojaan	Alvi Vuorinen	Lasse Mårtenson	3
14	3	Austria	Peter Horten	Warum Es Hunderttausend Sterne Gibt	Karin Bognar	Kurt Peche	2
15	13	Norway	Kirsti Sparboe	Dukkemann	Ola Johannessen	Tor Hultin	2
16	1	Netherlands	Thérèse Steinmetz	Ring-dinge	Gerrit den Braber	Johnny Holshuysen	2
17	6	Switzerland	Géraldine	Quel Coeur Vas-tu Briser?	Gérard Gray	Daniël Faure	0

1967 Eurovision 12: Vienna, Austria

	TOTAL	Yugoslavia	United Kingdom	Switzerland	Sweden	Spain	Portugal	Norway	Netherlands	Monaco	Luxembourg	Italy	Ireland	Germany	France	Finland	Belgium	Austria
Netherlands	2		1															1
Luxembourg	17	1	2			1			4	1		3	2			2	1	
Austria	2	1					1											
France	20	4	2	1	4					2				2		2	3	
Portugal	3			1					1						1			
Switzerland	0																	
Sweden	7	1					1	2					2			1		
Finland	3						1		1			1						
Germany	7	1	1		1		1	1				1	1					
Belgium	8		1				1						1	1		3		
United Kingdom	47			7	1		1	7	2	3	5	2	1	3	7	2	3	3
Spain	9						2		1	2	1							1
Norway	2				1				1									
Monaco	10				1	5						1			1			2
Yugoslavia	7		1			2	1				1	1			1			
Italy	4			1		1												
Ireland	22	1	2		2		1			2	1	1		4			3	3

Note: Ten jurors from each country each awarded 1 point to their favourite act.

43

Rank	Start	Country	Artist	Song	Writer	Composer	POINTS
1	15	Spain	Massiel	La, La, La	Ramón Arcusa, Manuel de la Calva	Ramón Arcusa, Manuel de la Calva	29
2	12	United Kingdom	Cliff Richard	Congratulations	Bill Martin, Phil Coulter	Bill Martin, Phil Coulter	28
3	10	France	Isabelle Aubret	La Source	Guy Bonnet, Henri Dijan	Daniël Faure	20
4	14	Ireland	Pat McGeegan	Chance Of A Lifetime	John Kennedy	John Kennedy	18
5	8	Sweden	Claes-Göran Hederström	Det Börjar Verka Kärlek, Banne Mej	Peter Himmelstrand	Peter Himmelstrand	15
6	16	Germany	Wencke Myhre	Ein Hoch Der Liebe	Carl Schäuble	Horst Jankowski	11
7	17	Yugoslavia	Luci Kapurso & Hamo Hajdarhodzic	Jedan Dan	Stijepo Strazicic	Djelo Jusic, Stipica Kalogjera	8
8	7	Monaco	Line & Willy	A Chacun Sa Chanson	Roland Valade	Jean-Claude Olivier	8
9	3	Belgium	Claude Lombard	Quand Tu Reviendras	Roland Dero	Jo van Wetter	8
10	11	Italy	Sergio Endrigo	Marianne	Sergio Endrigo	Sergio Endrigo	7
11	5	Luxembourg	Chris Baldo & Sophie Garel	Nous Vivrons D'amour	Jacques Demarny	Carlos Leresche	5
12	1	Portugal	Carlos Mendes	Verão	José Alberto Diogo	Pedro Osório	5
13	6	Switzerland	Gianni Mascolo	Guardando Il Sole	Sanzio Chiesa	Aldo d'Addario	2
14	13	Norway	Odd Børre	Stress	Ola Johannessen	Tor Hultin	2
15	4	Austria	Karel Gott	Tausend Fenster	Walter Brandin	Udo Jürgen Bockelmann	2
16	9	Finland	Kristina Hautala	Kun Kello Käy	Juha Vainio	Esko Linnavalli	1
17	2	Netherlands	Ronnie Tober	Morgen	Theo Strengers	Joop Stokkermans	1

1968 Eurovision 13: London, United Kingdom

6 April 1968

Country	TOTAL	Yugoslavia	United Kingdom	Switzerland	Sweden	Spain	Portugal	Norway	Netherlands	Monaco	Luxembourg	Italy	Ireland	Germany	France	Finland	Belgium	Austria
Portugal	5					3		2										
Netherlands	1											1						
Belgium	8		1			1	1					3			1	1		
Austria	2					2												
Luxembourg	5		1						1	1					1			1
Switzerland	2	2																
Monaco	8		1				1		2		1					3		
Sweden	15		2					6	1				3			1		2
Finland	1							1										
France	20			3	1		1		3		3			2		1	6	
Italy	7	2		2							1			2				
United Kingdom	28			4	3		1		2	5	1	5		6	1			
Norway	2					1					1							
Ireland	18	6			4		1		1		1						1	4
Spain	29			1	2		4	1		4		1	7		4	3		2
Germany	11		5			2					1					1	2	
Yugoslavia	8					1	1				1				3		1	1

Note: Ten jurors from each country each awarded 1 point to their favourite act.

45

1969 Eurovision 14: Madrid, Spain

Rank	Start	Country	Artist	Song	Writer	Composer	POINTS
=1	14	France	Frida Boccara	Un Jour, Un Enfant	Eddy Marnay	Emile Stern	18
=1	7	United Kingdom	Lulu	Boom Bang-a-bang	Peter Warne	Alan Moorhouse	18
=1	8	Netherlands	Lenny Kuhr	De Troubadour	Lenny Kuhr	David Hartsema	18
=1	3	Spain	Salomé	Vivo Cantando	Aniano Alcalde	Maria José de Cerato	18
5	11	Switzerland	Paola del Medico	Bonjour, Bonjour	Jack Stark	Henry Mayer	13
6	4	Monaco	Jean-Jacques	Maman, Maman	Jo Perrier	Jo Perrier	11
7	10	Belgium	Louis Neefs	Jennifer Jennings	Phil van Cauwenbergh	Paul Quintens	10
8	5	Ireland	Muriel Day & the Lindsays	The Wages Of Love	Michael Reade	Michael Reade	10
9	13	Germany	Siw Malmkvist	Primaballerina	Hans Blüm	Hans Blüm	8
10	9	Sweden	Tommy Körberg	Judy, Min Vän	Britt Lindeborg	Roger Wallis	8
11	2	Luxembourg	Romuald	Cathérine	André Pascal	Paul Mauriat, André Borly	7
12	16	Finland	Jarkko & Laura	Kuin Silloin Ennen	Juha Vainio	Toivo Kärki	6
13	1	Yugoslavia	Ivan	Pozdrav Svijetu	Milan Lentic	Milan Lentic	5
14	6	Italy	Iva Zanicchi	Due Grosse Lacrime Bianche	Daiano	Piero Soffici	5
15	15	Portugal	Simone de Oliveira	Desfolhada Portuguesa	José Carlos Ary dos Santos	Nuño Nazareth Fernandes	4
16	12	Norway	Kirsti Sparboe	Oj, Oj, Oj, Så Glad, Jeg Skal Bli	Arne Bendiksen	Arne Bendiksen	1

Note: Four joint winners were declared. A tie-break system was introduced in 1970.

1969 Eurovision 14: Madrid, Spain

29 March 1969

Receiving \ Voting	Yugoslavia	United Kingdom	Switzerland	Sweden	Spain	Portugal	Norway	Netherlands	Monaco	Luxembourg	Italy	Ireland	Germany	France	Finland	Belgium	TOTAL
Yugoslavia					1	3										1	5
Luxembourg	1				2				3				1				7
Spain	1			1		2		2	3	2			3	2		2	18
Monaco				2				2		4	3						11
Ireland			3	1				1			4		1				10
Italy	1					1		1	1				1				5
United Kingdom	2			5		1		1		4	3		1	1			18
Netherlands			4		1		1				3		1	6	1	1	18
Sweden							3						1		3	1	8
Belgium		3	2				2	1						1	1		10
Switzerland		2		1			1	1				3	2		2	1	13
Norway				1													1
Germany					2		1	1	1	1				1		1	8
France		4		1	2	2	1		1	1		4	1			1	18
Portugal	3										1						4
Finland			1	1			1	1		1						1	6

Note: Ten jurors from each country each awarded 1 point to their favourite act.

1970 Eurovision 15: Amsterdam, Netherlands

Rank	Start	Country	Artist	Song	Writer	Composer	POINTS
1	12	Ireland	Dana	All Kinds Of Everything	Derry Lindsay, Jackie Smith	Derry Lindsay, Jackie Smith	32
2	7	United Kingdom	Mary Hopkin	Knock, Knock (who's there?)	John Carter, Geoff Stephens	John Carter, Geoff Stephens	26
3	11	Germany	Katja Ebstein	Wunder Gibt Es Immer Wieder	Günther Loose	Christian Bruhn	12
4	9	Spain	Julio Iglesias	Gwendolyne	Julio Iglesias	Julio Iglesias	8
5	6	France	Guy Bonnet	Marie Blanche	Pierre-André Dousset	Guy Bonnet	8
6	2	Switzerland	Henri Dès	Retour	Henri Dès	Henri Dès	8
7	1	Netherlands	Patricia & Hearts of Soul	Waterman	Pieter Goemans	Pieter Goemans	7
8	10	Monaco	Dominique Dussault	Marlène	Henri Dijan	Eddie Barclay, Jimmy Walter	5
9	3	Italy	Gianni Morandi	Occhi Di Ragazza	Gianfranco Baldazzi, Sergio Bardotti	Lucio Dalla	5
10	5	Belgium	Jean Vallée	Viens L'oublier	Jean Vallée	Jean Vallée	5
11	4	Yugoslavia	Eva Sršen	Pridi, Dala Ti Bom Cvet	Dušan Velkaverh	Mojmir Sepe	4
12	8	Luxembourg	David-Alexandre Winter	Je Suis Tombé Du Ciel	Eddy Marnay	Yves de Vriendt	0

Note: Only 12 countries participated due to a boycott over the voting system used in 1969.

1970 Eurovision 15: Amsterdam, Netherlands

21 March 1970

	Belgium	France	Germany	Ireland	Italy	Luxembourg	Netherlands	Spain	Sweden	Switzerland	United Kingdom	Yugoslavia	TOTAL
Netherlands					3						1	3	**7**
Switzerland		2	2	1			2				1		**8**
Italy			2					2				1	**5**
Yugoslavia											4		**4**
Belgium		3		1		1							**5**
France				3	1				2			2	**8**
United Kingdom		2	4	3	2	2	3		4	2		4	**26**
Luxembourg													**0**
Spain					3	2			3				**8**
Monaco	1	2						1		1			**5**
Germany				2	1	3		4	1	1			**12**
Ireland	9	1	2			2	5	3		6	4		**32**

Note: Ten jurors from each country each awarded 1 point to their favourite act.

49

Rank	Start	Country	Artist	Song	Writer	Composer	POINTS
1	3	Monaco	Séverine	Un Banc, Un Arbre, Une Rue	Yves Dessca	Jean-Pierre Bourtayre	128
2	6	Spain	Karina	En Un Mundo Nuevo	Tony Luz	Rafael Trabucchelli	115
3	5	Germany	Katja Ebstein	Diese Welt	Fred Jay	Dieter Zimmermann	100
4	9	United Kingdom	Clodagh Rodgers	Jack In The Box	David Myers	John Worsley	98
5	11	Italy	Massimo Ranieri	L'amore è Un Attimo	Gaetano Savio, Giancarlo Bigazzi	Federico Polito	91
6	12	Sweden	Family Four	Vita Vidder	Håkan Elmquist	Håkan Elmquist	85
7	14	Netherlands	Saskia & Serge	De Tijd	Gerrit den Braber	Joop Stokkermans	85
8	17	Finland	Markku Aro & the Koivisto Sisters	Tie Uuteen Päivään	Rauno Lehtinen	Rauno Lehtinen	84
9	15	Portugal	Tonicha	Menina Do Alto Da Serra	José Carlos Ary dos Santos	Nuño Nazareth Fernandes	83
10	7	France	Serge Lama	Un Jardin Sur La Terre	Henri Dijan, Jacques Demarny	Alice Dona	83
11	13	Ireland	Angela Farrell	One Day Love	Donald Martin, Ita Flynn	Donald Martin, Ita Flynn	79
12	4	Switzerland	Peter, Sue & Marc	Les Illusions De Nos Vingt Ans	Maurice Tézé	Peter Reber	78
13	8	Luxembourg	Monique Melsen	Pomme, Pomme, Pomme	Pierre Cour	Hubert Giraud	70
14	16	Yugoslavia	Krunoslav Slabinac	Tvoj Djecak Je Tuzan	Zvonimir Golob	Ivica Krajac	68
15	10	Belgium	Lily Castel & Jacques Raymond	Goeie Morgen, Morgen	Phil van Cauwenbergh	Paul Quintens	68
16	1	Austria	Marianne Mendt	Musik	Richard Schönherz, Manuel Rigoni	Richard Schönherz, Manuel Rigoni	66
17	18	Norway	Hanne Krogh	Lykken Er	Arne Bendiksen	Arne Bendiksen	65
18	2	Malta	Joe Grech	Marija L-maltija	Charles Misfud	Joe Grech	52

1971 Eurovision 16: Dublin, Ireland

	Austria	Belgium	Finland	France	Germany	Ireland	Italy	Luxembourg	Malta	Monaco	Netherlands	Norway	Portugal	Spain	Sweden	Switzerland	United Kingdom	Yugoslavia	TOTAL
Austria		3	3	3	7	6	6	2	3	5	3	5	5	2	4	2	3	4	66
Malta	4	4	3	3	3	4	4	2		2	5	2	2	5	2	2	3	2	52
Monaco	4	10	7	8	10	9	4	4	5		9	10	8	2	10	10	8	10	128
Switzerland	5	3	4	6	6	5	7	2	5	4	5	4	6	2	4		6	4	78
Germany	6	7	5	8		5	6	2	5	7	5	4	7	8	6	6	6	7	100
Spain	4	4	9	10	7	9	4	4	8	10	6	8	7		6	5	7	7	115
France	3	3	3		5	6	5	2	2	8	9	5	5	5	4	8	5	5	83
Luxembourg	2	3	5	5	2	5	3		7	6	3	4	6	4	2	3	6	4	70
United Kingdom	4	8	6	8	5	7	3	4	8	8	5	6	7	2	5	6		6	98
Belgium	3		6	5	2	4	3	2	2	5	6	4	6	2	5	4	6	3	68
Italy	4	2	2	9	6	6		2	6	9	2	5	3	6	7	8	6	8	91
Sweden	7	6	4	5	4	3	6	2	4	4	9	6	3	2		9	5	6	85
Ireland	7	3	4	7	4		6	2	6	6	5	4	4	5	2	3	6	5	79
Netherlands	6	2	6	7	4	5	2	2	2	6		8	9	5	6	5	5	5	85
Portugal	4	4	5	8	5	3	4	5	3	6	5	5		10	2	2	6	6	83
Yugoslavia	6	2	3	6	7	5	5	2	2	4	4	5	4	6	2	2	3		68
Finland	4	10		4	2	6	2	2	4	4	3	6	8	3	4	4	10	6	84
Norway	3	6	3	5	2	7	3	2	3	6	2		5	2	2	4	7	4	65

Note: Two jurors from each country both awarded between 1 and 5 points per act.

Rank	Start	Country	Artist	Song	Writer	Composer	POINTS
1	17	Luxembourg	Vicky Leandros	Après Toi	Klaus Munro, Yves Dessca	Mario Panas, Klaus Munro	128
2	5	United Kingdom	The New Seekers	Beg, Steal Or Borrow	Tony Cole, Graeme Hall, Steve Wolfe	Tony Cole, Graeme Hall, Steve Wolfe	114
3	1	Germany	Mary Roos	Nur Die Liebe Läßt Uns Leben	Joachim Relin	Joachim Heider	107
4	18	Netherlands	Sandra & Andres	Als Het Om De Liefde Gaat	Hans van Hemert	Dries Holten	106
5	11	Austria	The Milestones	Falter Im Wind	Heinz Unger	Richard Schönherz, Manuel Rigoni	100
6	12	Italy	Nicola di Bari	I Giorni Dell' Arcobaleno	Dalmazio Masini	Piero Pintucci, Nicola di Bari	92
7	7	Portugal	Carlos Mendes	A Festa Da Vida	José Niza	José Calvário	90
8	8	Switzerland	Véronique Müller	C'est La Chanson De Mon Amour	Catherine Desage	Véronique Müller	88
9	13	Yugoslavia	Tereza	Muzika I Ti	Ivica Krajac	Nikica Kalogjera	87
10	4	Spain	Jaime Morey	Amanece	Ramón Arcusa	Augusto Algueró	83
11	2	France	Betty Mars	Comé-comédie	Frédéric Botton	Frédéric Botton	81
12	10	Finland	Päivi Paunu & Kim Floor	Muistathan	Juha Flinck	Juha Flinck, Nacke Johansson	78
13	14	Sweden	Family Four	Härliga Sommardag	Håkan Elmquist	Håkan Elmquist	75
14	6	Norway	Grethe Kausland & Benny Borg	Småting	Kåre Grøttum, Ivar Børsum	Kåre Grøttum, Ivar Børsum	73
15	3	Ireland	Sandie Jones	Ceol On Ghrá	Liam MacUistin	Joe Burkett	72
16	15	Monaco	Anne-Marie Godart & Peter MacLane	Comme On S'aime	Jean Drejac	Raymond Bernard	65
17	16	Belgium	Serge & Christine Ghisoland	À La Folie Ou Pas Du Tout	Daniël Nelis	Daniël Nelis, Bob Milan	55
18	9	Malta	Helen & Joseph	L-imħabba	Albert Cassola	Charles Camilleri	48

1972 Eurovision 17: Edinburgh, United Kingdom

	Austria	Belgium	Finland	France	Germany	Ireland	Italy	Luxembourg	Malta	Monaco	Netherlands	Norway	Portugal	Spain	Sweden	Switzerland	United Kingdom	Yugoslavia	TOTAL
Germany	5	7	5	8		6	7	7	4	8	6	6	6	9	8	5	5	5	107
France	2	7	4		5	5	3	8	5	6	6	7	2	2	2	3	9	5	81
Ireland	4	4	3	3	4		3	6	6	5	5	6	4	4	5	3	4	3	72
Spain	5	3	4	5	7	5	3	5	4	8	5	8	6		7	3	3	2	83
United Kingdom	7	4	7	9	8	6	7	8	2	9	8	10	4	2	6	8		9	114
Norway	3	4	7	3	4	6	2	6	5	4	4		5	5	4	2	4	5	73
Portugal	4	7	2	4	3	7	9	10	5	4	5	2		7	7	6	4	4	90
Switzerland	8	4	7	5	4	6	5	7	4	6	5	7	2	5	4		4	5	88
Malta	2	2	5	2	3	4	2	2		3	4	2	2	2	3	2	6	2	48
Finland	3	8		3	4	3	3	6	3	5	8	6	4	6	4	3	5	4	78
Austria		4	4	6	6	6	6	5	5	5	9	5	5	6	10	7	3	8	100
Italy	6	6	6	5	4	3		6	6	6	5	6	7	2	8	9	3	4	92
Yugoslavia	3	8	3	4	7	5	2	8	4	9	6	4	5	8	4	2	5		87
Sweden	4	7	5	3	5	5	3	5	4	5	5	5	4	3		2	3	7	75
Monaco	3	4	5	3	4	4	3	4	5		5	6	2	3	3	2	5	4	65
Belgium	2		4	3	2	4	3	6	5	4	3	2	3	2	3	3	5	2	55
Luxembourg	8	8	6	8	9	9	9		4	7	9	8	7	2	8	6	10	10	128
Netherlands	6	2	9	6	6	8	3	7	3	5		8	5	8	6	6	9	9	106

Note: Two jurors from each country both awarded between 1 and 5 points per act.

53

Rank	Start	Country	Artist	Song	Writer	Composer	POINTS
1	11	Luxembourg	Anne-Marie David	Tu Te Reconnaîtras	Vline Buggy	Claude Morgan	129
2	7	Spain	Mocedades	Eres Tú	Juan Carlos Calderón	Juan Carlos Calderón	125
3	15	United Kingdom	Cliff Richard	Power To All Our Friends	Guy Fletcher, Doug Flett	Guy Fletcher, Doug Flett	123
4	17	Israel	Ilanit	Ey-sham	Ehud Manor	Nurit Hirsh	97
5	12	Sweden	The Nova & The Dolls	You're Summer	Lars Forssell	Monica & Carl-Axel Dominique	94
6	1	Finland	Marion Rung	Tom Tom Tom	Rauno Lehtinen	Rauno Lehtinen	93
7	5	Norway	Bendik Singers	It's Just A Game	Arne Bendiksen	Arne Bendiksen	89
8	6	Monaco	Marie	Un Train Qui Part	Boris Bergman	Bernard Liamis	85
9	4	Germany	Gitte	Junger Tag	Stephan Lego	Günther-Eric Thöner	85
10	3	Portugal	Fernando Tordo	Tourada	José Carlos Ary dos Santos	Fernando Tordo	80
11	14	Ireland	Maxi	Do I Dream?	Jack Brierley, George Crosby	Jack Brierley, George Crosby	80
12	8	Switzerland	Patrick Juvet	Je Me Vais Marier, Marie	Pierre Delanoë	Patrick Juvet	79
13	10	Italy	Massimo Ranieri	Chi Sarà Con Te	Giancarlo Bigazzi	Federico Polito, Gaetano Savio	74
14	13	Netherlands	Ben Cramer	De Oude Muzikant	Pierre Kartner	Pierre Kartner	69
15	16	France	Martine Clémenceau	Sans Toi	Anne Gregory	Paul Koulak	65
16	9	Yugoslavia	Zdravko Colic	Gori Vatra	Kemal Monteno	Kemal Monteno	65
17	2	Belgium	Nicole & Hugo	Baby, Baby	Erik Marijsse	Ignace Baert	58

1973 Eurovision 18: Luxembourg

	Belgium	Finland	France	Germany	Ireland	Israel	Italy	Luxembourg	Monaco	Netherlands	Norway	Portugal	Spain	Sweden	Switzerland	United Kingdom	Yugoslavia	TOTAL
Finland	9		4	6	5	5	2	6	5	5	6	5	6	7	6	9	7	93
Belgium		4	2	4	4	2	2	4	6	3	3	3	6	2	4	5	4	58
Portugal	6	4	6	5	4	5	3	4	4	5	5		8	2	8	5	6	80
Germany	5	2	7		6	4	3	7	5	5	4	6	9	6	7	5	4	85
Norway	5	8	6	6	3	9	5	7	7	3		5	6	3	7	3	6	89
Monaco	3	6	5	4	6	4	8	6		5	3	2	6	4	5	9	9	85
Spain	8	3	9	9	10	8	10	8	9	10	4	9		7	8	4	9	125
Switzerland	3	4	2	4	7	3	4	6	5	8	7	3	7	3		7	6	79
Yugoslavia	3	5	4	4	5	4	2	4	5	4	2	3	8	2	6	4		65
Italy	5	2	5	5	4	4		5	5	4	5	3	5	5	7	5	5	74
Luxembourg	6	6	10	7	8	8	9		7	9	8	8	6	8	10	10	9	129
Sweden	4	8	4	5	5	5	5	6	5	6	8	4	7		9	7	6	94
Netherlands	4	4	6	5	5	2	4	7	4		5	2	5	3	5	3	5	69
Ireland	7	3	4	4		4	5	6	6	6	6	6	7	5	5	5	5	80
United Kingdom	6	9	8	7	9	9	5	10	8	10	7	6	4	9	8		8	123
France	3	4		4	5	3	2	2	5	5	4	2	5	5	4	5	7	65
Israel	6	6	5	7	7		7	8	7	6	5	5	4	6	6	5	7	97

Note: Two jurors from each country both awarded between 1 and 5 points per act.

1974 Eurovision 19: Brighton, United Kingdom

Rank	Start	Country	Artist	Song	Writer	Composer	POINTS
1	8	Sweden	ABBA	Waterloo	Stig Anderson	Benny Andersson, Björn Ulvæus	24
2	17	Italy	Gigliola Cinquetti	Si	Mario Panzeri, Daniele Pace, Lorenzo Pilat, Corrado Conti	Mario Panzeri, Daniele Pace, Lorenzo Pilat, Corrado Conti	18
3	12	Netherlands	Mouth & MacNeal	I See A Star	Hans van Hemert	Hans van Hemert	15
4	10	Monaco	Romuald	Celui Qui Reste Et Celui Qui S'en Va	Michael Jourdan	Jean-Pierre Bourtayre	14
5	9	Luxembourg	Ireen Sheer	Bye, Bye, I Love You	Michael Kunze, Humbert Ibach	Ralph Siegel	14
6	2	United Kingdom	Olivia Newton-John	Long Live Love	Valerie Avon, Harold Spiro	Valerie Avon, Harold Spiro	14
7	6	Israel	Poogy	Natati La Khaiai	Dani Sanderson, Alon Oleartchick	Dani Sanderson	11
8	13	Ireland	Tina	Cross Your Heart	Paul Lyttle	Paul Lyttle	11
9	3	Spain	Peret	Canta Y Se Feliz	Pedro Pubill Calaf	Pedro Pubill Calaf	10
10	11	Belgium	Jacques Hustin	Fleur De Liberté	Franck F Gérald	Jacques Hustin	10
11	5	Greece	Marinella	Krassi, Thalassa Ke Tagori Mou	Pythagoras	George Katsaros	7
12	7	Yugoslavia	Korni	Generacija 42	Kornelije Kovac	Kornelije Kovac	6
13	1	Finland	Carita	Âla Mene Pois (Keep Me Warm)	Hector	Eero Koivistoinen	4
14	16	Portugal	Paulo de Carvalho	E Depois Do Adeus	José Niza	José Calvário	3
15	14	Germany	Cindy & Bert	Die Sommermelodie	Kurt Feltz	Werner Scharfenberger	3
16	4	Norway	Anne-Karine Ström & the Bendik Singers	The First Day Of Love	Philip Kruse	Frode Thingnæs	3
17	15	Switzerland	Piera Martell	Mein Ruf Nach Dir	Pepe Ederer	Pepe Ederer	3

1974 Eurovision 19: Brighton, United Kingdom

Receiving \ Voting	Belgium	Finland	Germany	Greece	Ireland	Israel	Italy	Luxembourg	Monaco	Netherlands	Norway	Portugal	Spain	Sweden	Switzerland	United Kingdom	Yugoslavia	TOTAL
Finland					1	2										1		4
United Kingdom			2						3		2	2			1		4	14
Spain			1	1				1	3		2	2						10
Norway			1						1					1				3
Greece						3				4								7
Israel		1					3			2		2		1		2		11
Yugoslavia	1	1					2					1	1					6
Sweden		5	2		1	2	1			3	2	1	1		5		1	24
Luxembourg	1		1	1	3	2	2		1		1	1	1					14
Monaco	2		2	1		1		2			1	1	2	1	1			14
Belgium		1	1	5	1					2								10
Netherlands			1	2	2	1		3			2	1					3	15
Ireland	1		1			1		2	4		2							11
Germany				1									1		1			3
Switzerland			1										1			1		3
Portugal													1		2			3
Italy		2			1	1		1	4				2	2		5		18

Note: 10 jurors from each country awarded 1 point each to their favourite act

1975 Eurovision 20: Stockholm, Sweden

Rank	Start	Country	Artist	Song	Writer	Composer	POINTS
1	1	Netherlands	Teach-In	Teach-In	Will Luikinga, Eddy Ouwens	Dick Bakker	152
2	9	United Kingdom	The Shadows	Let Me Be The One	Paul Curtis	Paul Curtis	138
3	19	Italy	Wess & Dori Ghezzi	Era	Andrea lo Vecchio	Shel Shapiro	115
4	3	France	Nicole Rieu	Et Bonjour à Toi L'artiste	Pierre Delanoë, Jeff Barnel	Pierre Delanoë, Jeff Barnel	91
5	5	Luxembourg	Géraldine	Toi	Pierre Cour, Bill Martin, Phil Coulter	Bill Martin, Phil Coulter	84
6	7	Switzerland	Simone Drexel	Mikado	Simone Drexel	Simone Drexel	77
7	15	Finland	Pihasoittajat	Old Man Fiddle	Hannu Karlsson	Kim Kuusi	74
8	18	Sweden	Lars Berghagen & the Dolls	Jennie, Jennie	Lars Berghagen	Lars Berghagen	72
9	2	Ireland	The Swarbriggs	That's What Friends Are For	Jimmy Swarbrigg, Tommy Swarbrigg	Jimmy Swarbrigg, Tommy Swarbrigg	68
10	17	Spain	Sergio y Estíbaliz	Tú Volverás	Juan Carlos Calderón	Juan Carlos Calderón	53
11	12	Israel	Shlomo Artzi	At Ve'ani	Ehud Manor	Shlomo Artzi	40
12	10	Malta	Renato	Singing This Song	M Idris Misfud	Sammy Galea	32
13	8	Yugoslavia	Pepel In Kri	Dan Ljubezni	Dusan Velkaverh	Tadej Hrusovar	22
14	14	Monaco	Sophie	Une Chanson C'est Une Lettre	Boris Bergman	André Popp	22
15	11	Belgium	Ann Christy	Gelukkig Zijn	Mary Boduin	Mary Boduin	17
16	16	Portugal	Duarte Mendes	Madrugada	José Luis Tinoco	José Luis Tinoco	16
17	4	Germany	Joy Fleming	Ein Lied Kann Eine Brücke Sein	Michael Holm	Rainer Pietsch	15
18	6	Norway	Ellen Nikolaysen	You Touched My Life With Summer	Svein Hundnes	Svein Hundnes	11
19	13	Turkey	Semiha Yanki	Seninle Bir Dakika	Hikmet Munir Ebcioglu	Kemal Ebcioglu	3

Note: 1975 marked the introduction of the current 12, 10, 8, 7, 6, 5, 4, 3, 2 & 1 points system.

1975 Eurovision 20: Stockholm, Sweden

From ↓ / To →	Netherlands	Ireland	France	Germany	Luxembourg	Norway	Switzerland	Yugoslavia	United Kingdom	Malta	Belgium	Israel	Turkey	Monaco	Finland	Portugal	Spain	Sweden	Italy
TOTAL	**152**	**68**	**91**	**15**	**84**	**11**	**77**	**22**	**138**	**32**	**17**	**40**	**3**	**22**	**74**	**16**	**53**	**72**	**115**
Yugoslavia	8	1			7				12	2	3				5		4	6	10
United Kingdom	12	6	8		3		5			1				2	4			7	10
Turkey	4		1		5			7		2		6				12	3	8	10
Switzerland	6	7	3					8		4		2			12		5	1	10
Sweden	12	10	8		4				7		2	6			3		5		1
Spain	12	3	8	4	6				10						1	2		5	7
Portugal	7	4	12		8			2	1	5				3				6	10
Norway	12	4					1		7	2		5			10		3	8	6
Netherlands		6	2		12	5	7	3	4	1		10							8
Monaco	10	5	7	3	4				12	1		8						6	2
Malta	12	4	7	3	5		6					8		1				2	10
Luxembourg	10		12	8				2		5		1		4	6			7	3
Italy	1	6	4		3				10			5		8		7	12	2	
Israel	12	7	6						10	8				2	1		5	4	3
Ireland	8		12		10				3	7		6				1	5	4	2
Germany	8	1	10		4		7	2						3	12			5	6
France	5	6		3	12		1		8					2	4			7	10
Finland	10	1	8		7		6			4				2			5	3	12
Belgium	3	12	2				8	5	10	7		1					6	4	

59

1976 Eurovision 21: The Hague, Netherlands

Rank	Start	Country	Artist	Song	Writer	Composer	POINTS
1	1	United Kingdom	Brotherhood of Man	Save Your Kisses For Me	Tony Hiller, Lee Sheriden, Martin Lee	Tony Hiller, Lee Sheriden, Martin Lee	164
2	17	France	Catherine Ferry	Un, Deux, Trois	Jean Paul Cara	Tony Rallo	147
3	16	Monaco	Mary Christy	Toi, La Musique Et Moi	Gilbert Sinoué	Georges Costa, André Bars	93
4	2	Switzerland	Peter, Sue & Marc	Djambo, Djambo	Peter Reber	Peter Reber	91
5	14	Austria	Waterloo & Robinson	My Little World	Gerhard Heinz	Gerhard Heinz	80
6	4	Israel	Chocolate, Menta, Mastik	Emor Shalom	Ehud Manor	Matti Caspi	77
7	13	Italy	Romina & Al Bano	We'll Live It All Again	Al Bano, Romina Power	Detto Mariano	69
8	6	Belgium	Pierre Rapsat	Judy Et Cie	Eric van Hulse	Pierre Rapsat	68
9	8	Netherlands	Sandra Reemer	The Party's Over Now	Hans van Hemert	Hans van Hemert	56
10	7	Ireland	Red Hurley	When	Brendan J Graham	Brendan J Graham	54
11	11	Finland	Fredi & The Friends	Pump-pump	Matti Siitonen	Vexi Salmi	44
12	15	Portugal	Carlos do Carmo	Uma Flor De Verde Pinho	Manuel Alégre	José Niza	24
13	10	Greece	Mariza Koch	Panaghia Mou, Panaghia Mou	Michael Fotiades	Mariza Koch	20
14	5	Luxembourg	Jürgen Marcus	Chansons Pour Ceux Qui S'aiment	Vline Buggy, Fred Jay	Jack White	17
15	3	Germany	Les Humphries Singers	Sing, Sang, Song	Kurt Hertha	Ralph Siegel	12
16	12	Spain	Braulio	Sobran Las Palabras	Braulio	Braulio	11
17	9	Yugoslavia	Ambasadori	Ne Mogu Skriti Svoju Bol	Slobodan Djurasovic	Slobodan Vujovic	10
18	18	Norway	Anne-Karine Strøm	Mata Hari	Philip Kruse	Frode Thingnæs	7

1976 Eurovision 21: The Hague, Netherlands

	TOTAL	Yugoslavia	United Kingdom	Switzerland	Spain	Portugal	Norway	Netherlands	Monaco	Luxembourg	Italy	Israel	Ireland	Greece	Germany	France	Finland	Belgium	Austria
United Kingdom	164	10		12	12	12	12	10	10	8	4	12	3	12	8	7	10	12	10
Switzerland	91	7	12		4	7	10	6	4	1		4	1	2	5	6	7	7	8
Germany	12	3			2					2	1							1	
Israel	77	8	6	7	1	2	7	2	1	7	10		4		3	5	8		6
Luxembourg	17							5					6					6	
Belgium	68	1		5			6	4	8		8	1		8			12		3
Ireland	54		1					2	6		2	3			12	10		7	7
Netherlands	56	5	6	4		6	1		2	4	2	8	2	7	4		8		12
Norway	7					4		3											
Greece	20			8		1			7		5								
Finland	44			2	4			1	7		3		5		6	10		6	5
Spain	11		3		1		10	6	4	5		2	10			1			
Italy	69	6	7		8				5			10	12	10	10	12	5	6	7
Austria	80	2	10	8	6	4	7	6	7	3	8	7	8	4	12		6	5	
Portugal	24		7	2	1		6	4		12	1	7	8	4	7		3	5	
Monaco	93	4	5	5	7	3	5	8		12	7	7	8	5	7		2	8	5
France	147	12	8	10	10	5	8	12	12	10	6	5	7	5	12		3	10	12
Yugoslavia	10			1										3	2	4			

1977 Eurovision 22: London, United Kingdom **7 May 1977**

Rank	Start	Country	Artist	Song	Writer	Composer	POINTS
1	18	France	Marie Myriam	L'oiseau Et L'enfant	Joe Garcy	Jean-Paul Cara	136
2	9	United Kingdom	Lynsey de Paul & Mike Moran	Rock Bottom	Lynsey de Paul, Mike Moran	Lynsey de Paul, Mike Moran	121
3	1	Ireland	The Swarbriggs Plus Two	It's Nice To Be In Love Again	Tommy Swarbrigg, Jimmy Swarbrigg	Tommy Swarbrigg, Jimmy Swarbrigg	119
4	2	Monaco	Michèle Torr	Une Petite Française	Jean Albertini	Paul de Senneville, Olivier Toussaint	96
5	10	Greece	Pascalis, Marianna, Robert & Bessy	Mathema Solfege	Sevy Tiliakou	Georges Hatzinassios	92
6	12	Switzerland	Pepe Lienhard Band	Swiss Lady	Peter Reber	Peter Reber	71
7	17	Belgium	Dream Express	A Million In One, Two, Three	Luc Smets	Luc Smets	69
8	6	Germany	Silver Convention	Telegram	Michael Kunze	Silvester Levay	55
9	14	Spain	Micky	Enseñame A Cantar	Fernando Arbex	Fernando Arbex	52
10	16	Finland	Monica Aspelund	Lapponia	Monica Aspelund	Aarno Raninen	50
11	11	Israel	Ilanit	Ah-haa-vah Hee Shir Lish-naa-yim	Edna Peleg	Eldad Shrim	49
12	3	Netherlands	Heddy Lester	De Mallemolen	Wim Hogenkamp	Frank Affolter	35
13	15	Italy	Mia Martini	Libera	Luigi Albertelli	Salvatore Fabrizio	33
14	8	Portugal	Os Amigos	Portugal No Coração	José Carlos Ary dos Santos	Fernando Tordo	18
15	5	Norway	Anita Skorgan	Casanova	Dag Nordtomme	Svein Strugstad	18
16	7	Luxembourg	Anne Marie B	Frère Jacques	Guy Béart, Pierre Cour	Guy Béart, Pierre Cour	17
17	4	Austria	Schmetterlinge	Boom Boom Boomerang	E. Lukas Resetarits	Schuri Hernnstadt, Willi Resetarits & Herbert Zöchling-Tampier	11
18	13	Sweden	Forbes	Beatles	Sven-Olof Bagge	Claes Bure	2

1977 Eurovision 22: London, United Kingdom

Voting ↓ / Performer →	Ireland	Monaco	Netherlands	Austria	Norway	Germany	Luxembourg	Portugal	United Kingdom	Greece	Israel	Switzerland	Sweden	Spain	Italy	Finland	Belgium	France
United Kingdom	12	7	1															
Switzerland	8	6	7															
Sweden	12	10																
Spain	4	8	1															
Portugal	1	6																
Norway	12	1		2														
Netherlands	1																	
Monaco	8		3	5														
Luxembourg	8	1																
Italy	8	12																
Israel	12	2	1															
Ireland		5	3															
Greece	10	12	1	3														
Germany	5	6																
France	10	5	8															
Finland		5		1														
Belgium	3	2	10															
Austria	5	8																
TOTAL	**119**	**96**	**35**	**11**	**18**	**55**	**17**	**18**	**121**	**92**	**49**	**71**	**2**	**52**	**33**	**50**	**69**	**136**

Rank	Start	Country	Artist	Song	Writer	Composer	POINTS
1	18	Israel	Izhar Cohen & the Alphabeta	Abanibi	Ehud Manor	Nurit Hirsh	157
2	10	Belgium	Jean Vallée	L'amour ça Fait Chanter La Vie	Jean Vallée	Jean Vallée	125
3	6	France	Joël Prévost	Il Y Aura Toujours Des Violons	Didier Barbelivien	Gérard Stern	119
4	14	Monaco	Caline & Olivier Toussaint	Les Jardins De Monaco	Didier Barbelivien, Jean Albertini	Paul de Senneville, Olivier Toussaint	107
5	1	Ireland	Colm Wilkinson	Born To Sing	Colm Wilkinson	Colm Wilkinson	86
6	13	Germany	Ireen Sheer	Feuer	John Möring	Erich Leissman, Jean Frankfurter	84
7	17	Luxembourg	Baccara	Parlez-vous Français?	Frank Dostal, Peter Zenter	Rolf Soja	73
8	15	Greece	Tania Tsanaklidou	Charlie Chaplin	Yannis Xantoulis	Sakis Tsilikis	66
9	7	Spain	José Vélez	Bailemos Un Vals	Ramón Arcusa, Manuel de la Calva	Ramón Arcusa, Manuel de la Calva	65
10	9	Switzerland	Carole Vinci	Vivre	Pierre Alain	Alain Morisod	65
11	8	United Kingdom	Co-Co	The Bad Old Days	Stephanie de Sykes, Stuart Slater	Stephanie de Sykes, Stuart Slater	61
12	3	Italy	Ricchi e Poveri	Questo Amore	Sergio Bardotti	Dario Farina, Mario Luisini	53
13	11	Netherlands	Harmony	't Is Ok	Toon Gispen, Dick Bakker	Eddy Ouwens	37
14	20	Sweden	Björn Skifs	Det Blir Alltid Värre Framåt Natten	Peter Himmelstrand	Peter Himmelstrand	26
15	19	Austria	Springtime	Mrs Caroline Robinson	Walter Markel, Gerhard Markel, Norbert Niedermayer	Walter Markel, Gerhard Markel	14
16	16	Denmark	Mabel	Boom Boom	Mabel	Mabel	13
17	5	Portugal	Gemini	Dai-li-dou	Carlos Quintas	Victor Maméde	5
18	4	Finland	Seija Simola	Anna Rakkaudelle Tilaisuus	Reijo Karvonen, Seija Simola	Reijo Karvonen	2
19	12	Turkey	Nazar	Sevinçe	Hulki Aktunç	Daghan Baydur, Onno Tunç	2
20	2	Norway	Jahn Teigen	Mil Etter Mil	Kai Eide	Kai Eide	0

1978 Eurovision 23: Paris, France

22 April 1978

Receiving	TOTAL	United Kingdom	Turkey	Switzerland	Sweden	Spain	Portugal	Norway	Netherlands	Monaco	Luxembourg	Italy	Israel	Ireland	Greece	Germany	France	Finland	Denmark	Belgium	Austria
Ireland	86		10	7	8			12			10				10	5	5	3		10	6
Norway	0																				
Italy	53	6	1	1		8		6		8	3			2	2	2	4	3		1	
Finland	2						2														
Portugal	5					1						4									
France	119	8	4	6	10	5	2	3	6	5	1	10	5	6	8	10		2	8	8	12
Spain	65		8	1			1		1	4	2	5	6	3	7	8	7				
United Kingdom	61						6		2	7	5	1		4	3	6	2	8	10		8
Switzerland	65	2	6		3	3	6	3	2	7		1	2		3			1		7	
Belgium	125	12	8	7	4			5	8	2	7		7	12	12	3	8	6			12
Netherlands	37	3			1			7		1	6	5	12	3		4			5		
Turkey	2	1						1													
Germany	84	7	8	3	7		7		10	10				7			10		7	7	1
Monaco	107	10	5	5	12	7	5	4	10		3	7	8	4	4	7	1	7	6	6	3
Greece	66		4		2	7	8				4	2	10	7		1	10	5	4		3
Denmark	13								1				4				6			2	
Luxembourg	73	2	2		6	12	12	8	3	6		12		2	1	12	8		7	3	
Israel	157	7	12	12	6	12	10	8	12	3	12	8		8	5	12	8	10	6	12	8
Austria	14	5	3	3	5										3	1		4		2	
Sweden	26	4						10						5			3				

65

1979 Eurovision 24: Jerusalem, Israel

Rank	Start	Country	Artist	Song	Writer	Composer	POINTS
1	10	Israel	Milk and Honey	Hallelujah	Shimrit Orr	Kobi Oshrat	125
2	19	Spain	Betty Missiego	Su Canción	Fernando Moreno	Fernando Moreno	116
3	11	France	Anne-Marie David	Je Suis L'enfant-soleil	Eddy Marnay	Hubert Giraud	106
4	9	Germany	Dschinghis Khan	Dschinghis Khan	Bernd Meinunger	Ralph Siegel	86
5	4	Ireland	Cathal Dunne	Happy Man	Cathal Dunne	Cathal Dunne	80
6	3	Denmark	Tommy Seebach	Disco Tango	Keld Heick	Tommy Seebach	76
7	17	United Kingdom	Black Lace	Mary Ann	Peter Morris	Peter Morris	73
8	7	Greece	Elpida	Socrates	Sotia Tsotou	Doros Georghiades	69
9	1	Portugal	Manuela Bravo	Sobe, Sobe, Balão Sobe	Carlos Nobrega e Sousa	Carlos Nobrega e Sousa	64
10	8	Switzerland	Peter, Sue, Marc, Pfuri, Gorps &	Trödler Und Co	Peter Reber	Peter Reber	60
11	16	Norway	Anita Skorgan	Oliver	Philip Kruse	Anita Skorgan	57
12	14	Netherlands	Xandra	Colorado	Gerard Cox	Rob Bolland, Ferdi Bolland	51
13	13	Luxembourg	Jeane Manson	J'ai Déjà Vu ça Dans Tes Yeux	Jean Renard	Jean Renard	44
14	5	Finland	Katri-Helena	Katso Sineen Taivaan	Vexi Salmi	Matti Siitonen	38
15	2	Italy	Matia Bazar	Raggio Di Luna	Giancarlo Golzi, Salvatore Stellita	Carlo Marrale, Piero Cassano, Antoniella Ruggiero	27
16	6	Monaco	Laurent Vaguener	Notre Vie, C'est La Musique	Jean Albertini, Didier Barbelivien	P de Senneville, L Vaguener	12
17	15	Sweden	Ted Gärdestad	Satellit	Kenneth Gärdestad, Ted Gärdestad	Kenneth Gärdestad, Ted Gärdestad	8
18	12	Belgium	Micha Marah	Hey Nana	Guy Beyers	Charles Dumolin	5
19	18	Austria	Christina Simon	Heute In Jerusalem	André Heller	Peter Wolf	5

1979 Eurovision 24: Jerusalem, Israel

31 March 1979

	Austria	Belgium	Denmark	Finland	France	Germany	Greece	Ireland	Israel	Italy	Luxembourg	Monaco	Netherlands	Norway	Portugal	Spain	Sweden	Switzerland	United Kingdom	TOTAL
Portugal	7	5		2	10	4				6	3	5	3	6		6	3	4		64
Italy	3	7		8										3	8	8				27
Denmark		10		6	6	10	12	2	12	5	4	3	8			4	1	1	3	76
Ireland	10		5	6		6	10		3	5	7			5	5		8	6	4	80
Finland					5	5	7			7	6						8	8		38
Monaco			4	3	3					2					1	2				12
Greece	2	1	1		4	2		4	10		5	7	7		10	7	2	7		69
Switzerland	12		7	10	7	7	2	1	4			2		8			6			60
Germany		4	12	3	12		5	5	6	1	1	12	2	12	2	12	6		8	86
Israel	8	2	6	12	1			12			8	8	1	7	12	10	12	10	12	125
France	5	6		1		8	8	12	5	10	12	10	12	7	6	3	5	10	6	106
Belgium			2		1													2	2	5
Luxembourg	4	3		4	2	3	5	3		4		4	4	2	7			3	10	44
Netherlands			8	5		10	3	10	7					4			4			51
Sweden							1	6	1											8
Norway	1	8		7		8	8	8	2	3	2	6	6		3	1	10		7	57
United Kingdom	6		10		8		7	7		8	1	1	5	10	4	5		2		73
Austria										4								1	1	5
Spain	10	12	3		8	12	6		8	12	10	7	10	1			7	12	5	116

67

1980 Eurovision 25: The Hague, Netherlands

Rank	Start	Country	Artist	Song	Writer	Composer	POINTS
1	17	Ireland	Johnny Logan	What's Another Year	Shay Healy	Shay Healy	143
2	12	Germany	Katja Ebstein	Theater	Bernd Meinunger	Ralph Siegel	128
3	13	United Kingdom	Prima Donna	Love Enough For Two	Stephanie de Sykes, Stuart Slater	Stephanie de Sykes, Stuart Slater	106
4	9	Switzerland	Paola	Cinéma	Peter Reber, Véronique Müller	Peter Reber	104
5	15	Netherlands	Maggie MacNeal	Amsterdam	Alex Alberts	Frans Smit, Sjoukje Smit, Robert Verwey	93
6	6	Italy	Alan Sorrenti	Non So Che Darei	Alan Sorrenti	Alan Sorrenti	87
7	14	Portugal	José Cid	Um Grande, Grande Amor	José Cid	José Cid	71
8	1	Austria	Blue Danube	Du Bist Musik	Klaus-Peter Sattler	Klaus-Peter Sattler	64
9	4	Luxembourg	Sophie & Magaly	Papa Pingouin	Pierre Delanoë, Jean-Paul Cara	Ralph Siegel, Bernd Meinunger	56
10	8	Sweden	Tomas Ledin	Just Nu!	Tomas Ledin	Tomas Ledin	47
11	16	France	Profil	Hé, Hé M'sieurs Dames	Richard de Bordeaux, Richard Joffo	Sylvano Santorio	45
12	18	Spain	Trigo Limpio	Qué Date Esta Noche	José Antonio Martin	José Antonio Martin	38
13	3	Greece	Anna Vishy & the Epikouri	Autostop	Rony Sofou	Jick Nakassian	30
14	7	Denmark	Bamses Venner	Tænker Altid Pä Dig	Flemming Jørgensen	Bjarne Gren-Jensen	25
15	2	Turkey	Ajda Pekkan	Petr'oil	Sanar Yurdatapan	Atilla Ozdemiroglu	23
16	11	Norway	Sverre Kjellsberg & Mattis Hætta	Sámiid Ædnan	Ragnar Olsen	Sverre Kjellsberg	15
17	19	Belgium	Telex	Euro-vision	Telex	Telex	14
18	5	Morocco	Samira Bensaïd	Bitakat Hob	Malou Rouanne	Abdel Ati Amenna	7
19	10	Finland	Vesa-Matti Loiri	Huilumies	Vexi Salmi	Aarno Raninen	6

19 April 1980

Voting country	Austria	Turkey	Greece	Luxembourg	Morocco	Italy	Denmark	Sweden	Switzerland	Finland	Norway	Germany	United Kingdom	Portugal	Netherlands	France	Ireland	Spain	Belgium
TOTAL	64	23	30	56	7	87	25	47	104	6	15	128	106	71	93	45	143	38	14
United Kingdom	6		3	8		4			7			10			2	5	12		1
Turkey													5	4	12				
Switzerland	4					8		6				7	10	2	3	1	12		
Sweden	1			6		10	7		5			12		8	3		7		
Spain	4		3	3	5	10		3				12	8	8	5	6	7		3
Portugal	3			1		12			6			8	7		4		5	10	
Norway	6			7	4	2	1	1	10	5		6	6	8	12	3	12		
Netherlands	3		8	3		1			10		2	12	7	5		4	6	5	
Morocco	3	12											8					5	5
Luxembourg	1		1		7	12		10	5			3	8	4	12	2	7	6	6
Italy	4	8	2	7			3		3	6		12		10	1		1	6	
Ireland	10		12	8				7	12			6		7	1	3		7	
Greece	1					5		10							6	7	12	8	
Germany	4		3	1		7	5	2	10		6		3	1	12	5	12		
France	4		7	2		5	3	4	8	1		5	8	6	4		8	6	2
Finland	5			3		6	7		12			8	8		10		8		
Denmark	5		2	4		3		7	8		3		10				12		
Belgium	1		1	4			2	5	2			12	6	4	3	5	12	3	
Austria		3		1		2			6			8		4	3				

Rank	Start	Country	Artist	Song	Writer	Composer	POINTS
1	14	United Kingdom	Bucks Fizz	Making Your Mind Up	Andy Hill	John Danter	136
2	3	Germany	Lena Valaitis	Johnny Blue	Bernd Meinunger	Ralph Siegel	132
3	9	France	Jean Gabilou	Humanahum	Joel Gracy	Jean-Paul Cara	125
4	19	Switzerland	Peter, Sue & Marc	Io Senza Tei	Peter Reber, Nella Martinetti	Peter Reber	121
5	12	Ireland	Sheeba	Horoscopes	Joe Burkett	Jim Kelly	105
6	18	Cyprus	Island	Monika	Stavros Sideras	Doros Georghiades	69
7	5	Israel	Habibi	Halaylah	Shlomit Aharon, Yuval Dor	Shuki Levi	56
8	17	Greece	Yiannis Dimitras	Feggari Kalokerino	Yiannis Dimitras	Giorgos Niachros	55
9	11	Netherlands	Linda Williams	Het Is Een Wonder	Bart van de Laar	Cees de Wit	51
10	20	Sweden	Björn Skifs	Fångad I En Dröm	Björn Skifs, Bengt Palmers	Björn Skifs, Bengt Palmers	50
11	4	Luxembourg	Jean-Claude Pascal	C'est Peut-être Pas L'amérique	Sophie Makhno, Jean-Claude Villemino	Sophie Makhno, Jean-Claude Villemino	41
12	6	Denmark	Debbie Cameron & Tommy Seebach	Krøller Eller Ej	Keld Heick	Tommy Seebach	41
13	16	Belgium	Emly Starr	Samson	Kick Dandy, Els van den Abeele	Kick Dandy, Giuseppe Marchese	40
14	10	Spain	Bacchelli	Y Solo Tú	Amado Jaén	Amado Jaén	38
15	7	Yugoslavia	Seid-Memic Vajta	Leila	Ranko Boban	Ranko Boban	35
16	8	Finland	Riki Sorsa	Reggae OK	Olli Ojala	Jim Pembroke	27
17	1	Austria	Marty Brem	Wenn Du Da Bist	Werner Böhmler	Werner Böhmler	20
18	15	Portugal	Carlos Paião	Play-back	Carlos Paião	Carlos Paião	9
19	2	Turkey	Modern Folk Trio & Aysegül	Dönme Dolap	Ali Kocatepe	Ali Kocatepe	9
20	13	Norway	Finn Kalvik	Aldri I Livet	Finn Kalvik	Finn Kalvik	0

1981 Eurovision 26: Dublin, Ireland

	Yugoslavia	United Kingdom	Turkey	Switzerland	Sweden	Spain	Portugal	Norway	Netherlands	Luxembourg	Israel	Ireland	Greece	Germany	France	Finland	Denmark	Cyprus	Belgium	Austria	TOTAL
Austria			6		2	6									5		1		5		20
Turkey	3									1						5					9
Germany	2	7	12		12	12	12	4	3	3	8	6	5		8	7	8	2	10	10	132
Luxembourg				6	5	1	4							5	7	4					41
Israel		4	1	4	3	3	5	8	7	4		8	2	1		6		7			56
Denmark		5			4		2		2	7	3				4			3	12	12	41
Yugoslavia			4	10	6			1	5		2					8				5	35
Finland				5								5					12				27
France	4	1		12	10	2	1	5	6	12	7	4	8	12		10	2	10	3	3	125
Spain			10	2			10	10	4	5		3		8							38
Netherlands	5	6	5		7	7	3				4	2	3	4	2		7	8	2	2	51
Ireland			3	1	1	5		3	10	10	10		6	6	6	3	10	1	8	1	105
Norway																					0
United Kingdom	10		8	8	8	8	6		8		12	10	10	7		2		5		8	136
Portugal																					9
Belgium	8	3	7				8	6		8			1	2			6				40
Greece	1	8		7		10		2	1	6	5	1		5	1		3	12	6	6	55
Cyprus	6	10						7			1	12	12	10	10				7	4	69
Switzerland	12	12			3	4	7	12	12		6	7	4		12	12	4	4	1		121
Sweden	7	2	2	3						2		1	7	3	3	1	5	6	4	7	50

1982 Eurovision 27: Harrogate, United Kingdom

24 April 1982

Rank	Start	Country	Artist	Song	Writer	Composer	POINTS
1	18	Germany	Nicole	Ein bißchen Frieden	Bernd Meinunger	Ralph Siegel	161
2	15	Israel	Avi Toledano	Hora	Yoram Tahar-Lev	Avi Toledano	100
3	7	Switzerland	Arlette Zola	Amour on t'aime	Pierre Alain	Alain Morisod	97
4	11	Belgium	Stella	Si tu aimes ma musique	Jo May	Fred Bekky, Rony Brack, Bobott	96
5	8	Cyprus	Anna Vishy	Mono i agapi	Anna Vishy	Anna Vishy	85
6	2	Luxembourg	Svetlana	Cours après le temps	Cyril Assous	Michel Jouveaux	78
7	4	United Kingdom	Bardo	One step further	Simon Jeffries	Simon Jeffries	76
8	9	Sweden	Chips	Dag efter dag	Monica Forsberg	Lasse Holm	67
9	10	Austria	Mess	Sonntag	Rudolph Leve	Michael Scheikl	57
10	12	Spain	Lucía	Él	Ignacio Román	Francisco Cepero	52
11	17	Ireland	The Duskeys	Here Today, Gone Tomorrow	Sally Keating	Sally Keating	49
12	3	Norway	Jahn Teigen & Anita Skorgan	Adieu	Herodes Falsk	Jahn Teigen	40
13	1	Portugal	Doce	Bem-bom	António Pinho, Tózé Brito, Pedro Brito	António Pinho, Tózé Brito, Pedro Brito	32
14	14	Yugoslavia	Aska	Halo Halo	Miro Zec	Aleksandar Sanja Ilic	21
15	5	Turkey	Neço	Hani	Olcayto Ahmet Tugsuz, Fait Tugsuz	Olcayto Ahmet Tugsuz	20
16	16	Netherlands	Bill van Dijk	Jij En Ik	Liselore Gerritsen	Dick Bakker	8
17	13	Denmark	Brixx	Video-video	Jens Brixtofte	Jens Brixtofte	5
18	6	Finland	Kojo	Nuku Pommiin	Juice Leskinen	Jim Pembroke, Otto Donner	0

72

1982 Eurovision 27: Harrogate, United Kingdom

24 April 1982

	Yugoslavia	United Kingdom	Turkey	Switzerland	Sweden	Spain	Portugal	Norway	Netherlands	Luxembourg	Israel	Ireland	Germany	Finland	Denmark	Cyprus	Belgium	Austria	TOTAL
Portugal		4	5	1	6	5		7	4	7	1	2		2				2	32
Luxembourg	6	6	3	5	4	2		7	7		5	10	8	7	4	3	8		78
Norway			10	3	2	1	4		1	6	2	6	10	4	2	4	2	6	40
United Kingdom	6		2		7	1	4		2	12	2	7	1	1			3	12	76
Turkey				3	1			3										3	20
Finland																			0
Switzerland	10	12	2		8		2	4	10	8	10	8	4	8	7	8	5		97
Cyprus	5	3	7	8	1	7	5	12		8	7	5	6	3	8		6	3	85
Sweden	2	5	6	4		4	3	8	5	2	4	4	2	5	6	2	4	10	67
Austria	4	10		2		8	3			4	6					7			57
Belgium	7	2	8	7	12	10	10	5	12	3	8		7	6	10	5		5	96
Spain	1		4				1		5	5	3		5					8	52
Denmark								1				1					1		5
Yugoslavia					3										3				21
Israel	3	1		10	10	6			3			3	12	12	1	10	7	4	100
Netherlands								2											8
Ireland	8	7	1	6	5	3		10	8	1			3	10	5	1	10	7	49
Germany	12	8	12	12	8	12	12	3	6	10	12	12			12	12	12	1	161

73

Rank	Start	Country	Artist	Song	Writer	Composer	POINTS
1	20	Luxembourg	Corinne Hermès	Si La Vie Est Cadeau	Alain Garcia	Jean-Pierre Millers	142
2	16	Israel	Ofra Haza	Hi	Ehud Manor	Avi Toledano	136
3	4	Sweden	Carola Häggkvist	Främling	Monica Forsberg	Lasse Holm	126
4	12	Yugoslavia	Danijel	Dzuli	Mario Mihaljevic	Danijel Popovic	125
5	14	Germany	Hoffmann & Hoffmann	Rücksicht	Volker Lechtenbrink	Michael Reinecke	94
6	3	United Kingdom	Sweet Dreams	I'm Never Giving Up	Ron Roker, Jan Pulsford, Phil Wigger	Ron Roker, Jan Pulsford, Phil Wigger	79
7	11	Netherlands	Bernadette	Sing Me A Song	Martin Duiser	Piet Souer	66
8	1	France	Guy Bonnet	Vivre	Fulbert Cant	Guy Bonnet	56
9	18	Austria	Westend	Hurricane	Heli Deinboek, Heinz Nessizius	Peter Vieweger	53
10	2	Norway	Jahn Teigen	Do Re Mi	Herodes Falsk, Jahn Teigen	Anita Skorgan, Jahn Teigen	53
11	5	Italy	Riccardo Fogli	Per Lucia	Riccardo Fogli, Vincenzo Spampinato	Maurizio Fabrizio	41
12	9	Finland	Ami Aspelund	Fantasiaa	Kaisu Liuhala	Kari Kuusamo	41
13	17	Portugal	Armando Gama	Esta Balada Que Te Dou	Armando Gama	Armando Gama	33
14	10	Greece	Christie	Mou Les	Sophia Fildissi	Antonis Plessas, Mimis Plessas	32
15	8	Switzerland	Mariella Farré	Io Cosi Non Ci Sto	Nella Martinetti	Thomas Gonzenbach, Remo Kessler	28
16	13	Cyprus	Stavros & Constantina	I Agapi Akoma Zi	Stavros Sideras	Stavros Sideras	26
17	15	Denmark	Gry Johansen	Kloden Drejer	Flemming Gernyx, Christian Jacobsen	Flemming Gernyx, Christian Jacobsen, Lars Christensen	16
18	19	Belgium	Pas de Deux	Rendez-vous	Paul Peyskens	Walter Verdin	13
=19	6	Turkey	Çetin Alp and the Short Wave	Opera	Aysel Gürel	Bugra Ugur	0
=19	7	Spain	Remedios Amaya	¿quién Maneja Mi Barca?	Isidro Muñoz	José Miguel Evóras	0

74

Voting country	TOTAL	France	Norway	United Kingdom	Sweden	Italy	Turkey	Spain	Switzerland	Finland	Greece	Netherlands	Yugoslavia	Cyprus	Germany	Denmark	Israel	Portugal	Austria	Belgium	Luxembourg
TOTAL		56	53	79	126	41	0	0	28	41	32	66	125	26	94	16	136	33	53	13	142
Yugoslavia		3			1	8			7			5		6			10	2	4		12
United Kingdom			5		8	4				6		1	12		7	2	10		3		
Turkey		6		5	7	4				3		2	12		1				10		8
Switzerland		10		8	5					4		12		1	2			7	6		3
Sweden		3	12			2						6			8	7	5	1	4		10
Spain									1		12	2	10		3	4	6	5	7	8	
Portugal		3		6	2	4									8		10		5	1	12
Norway		3		5	12				1			2		4		10	6				8
Netherlands		2	8	5	3										10	12		6	4	1	7
Luxembourg		3	2	6					5			4			12	10		7			8
Italy		10		2	8				7			4	1		6				5		12
Israel		1	4		8	6						3	10	5					2		12
Greece		7		5	10	2			8			3	6		1			4			12
Germany		4	1	3	12					7		2	6	5		10			8		
France						10											12				
Finland		6		10	1				5			3	12		7			8	2		
Denmark			8	5	10							4	12	1	3		7		6		2
Cyprus		4		6	7	1			12			5	8		3		2		10		
Belgium			7		5				1			2	12	4	6		10		3		8
Austria		3	10	8					6		12	4	1		7					5	

1984 Eurovision 29: Luxembourg

Rank	Start	Country	Artist	Song	Writer	Composer	POINTS
1	1	Sweden	Herrey's	Diggi-loo diggy-ley	Britt Lindeborg	Torgny Söderberg	145
2	9	Ireland	Linda Martin	Terminal 3	Sean Sherrard	Sean Sherrard	137
3	4	Spain	Bravo	Lady, lady	Amaya Saizar	Miguel Blasco Larami	106
4	10	Denmark	Hot Eyes	Det' lige det	Keld Heick	Søren Bundgård	101
5	8	Belgium	Jacques Zegers	Avanti la vie	Jacques Zegers	Henri Seroka	70
6	18	Italy	Alice & Battiato	I treni di Tozeur	Rosario Cosentino	Franco Battiato	70
7	6	United Kingdom	Belle & the Devotions	Love games	Paul Curtis, Graham Sacher	Paul Curtis, Graham Sacher	63
8	3	France	Annick Thoumazeau	Autant d'amoureux que d'étoiles	Charel Level	Vladimir Cosma	61
9	16	Finland	Kirka	Hengailaan	Jussi Tuominen	Jukka Siikavire	46
10	2	Luxembourg	Sophie Carle	100% d'amour	Jean-Michel Bériat, Patrick Jaymes	Jean-Pierre Goussaud	39
11	19	Portugal	Maria Guinot	Silêncio e tanta gente	Maria Guinot	Maria Guinot	38
12	15	Turkey	Bes Yil Önce, On Yil Sonra	Halay	Ulku Aker	Selcuk Basar	37
13	14	Germany	Mary Roos	Aufrecht geh'n	Michael Kunze	Michael Reinecke	34
14	11	Netherlands	Maribelle	Ik hou van jou	Peter van Asten, Richard De Bois	Peter van Asten, Richard De Bois	34
15	7	Cyprus	Andy Paul	Anna Mari-Elena	Andy Paul	Andy Paul	31
16	17	Switzerland	Rainy Day	Welche Farbe hat der Sonnenschein	Günther Loose	Günther Loose	30
17	5	Norway	Dollie de Luxe	Lenge leve livet	Ingrid Bjørnov, Benedicte Adrian	Ingrid Bjørnov, Benedicte Adrian	29
18	12	Yugoslavia	Vlado and Isolda	Ciao amore	Milan Peric	Slobodan Bucevac	26
19	13	Austria	Anita	Einfach weg	Walter Müller	Brigitte Seuberth, Ernst Seuberth	5

1984 Eurovision 29: Luxembourg

	Yugoslavia	United Kingdom	Turkey	Switzerland	Sweden	Spain	Portugal	Norway	Netherlands	Luxembourg	Italy	Ireland	Germany	France	Finland	Denmark	Cyprus	Belgium	Austria	TOTAL
Sweden	4	7	3	10		4	4	10	10	6	6	12	12	6	8	12	12	7	12	145
Luxembourg	8		4			7						5		10		5				39
France		6		4	2		7										3	3	6	61
Spain	2	4	12	3	10		12	2	12	8	7	7	2		6	7	6	2	8	106
Norway				2	8						8	3	7	12	4	1				29
United Kingdom	1		1		3		6	6	4	7	10	8		3	10		7	10		63
Cyprus	12				4	3	10				1	4		1		10				31
Belgium			5			2	2	8	8	1	12		4			3	2		2	70
Ireland	6	8	10	12	12	10	1	3	7	12	5		10	8	7		10	12	10	137
Denmark		12	2	1	5	6		4	3	5		10	5	7	5		5	8	4	101
Netherlands	5	1		5		8		12		3		6	3	2			8	6		34
Yugoslavia		3	8						2	2	2				2	6				26
Austria												1	1			4				5
Germany		2			6		5				4			4	3	2		4	3	34
Turkey	10	5		6			3	5	1	10		2		5	1		4	5		37
Finland	3		6		7	1					3		6			8	1	1	7	46
Switzerland		10			1	12	8		5	4					12				1	30
Italy			7	7				7											5	70
Portugal	7			8		5		1	6				8							38

1985 Eurovision 30: Gothenburg, Sweden

3 May 1985

Rank	Start	Country	Artist	Song	Writer	Composer	POINTS
1	13	Norway	Bobbysocks	La Det Swinge	Rolf Løvland	Rolf Løvland	123
2	10	Germany	Wind	Für Alle	Hanne Haller	Hanne Haller	105
3	16	Sweden	Kikki Danielsson	Bra Vibrationer	Ingela "Pling" Forsman	Lasse Holm	103
4	14	United Kingdom	Vikki	Love Is....	Vikki Watson, James Kaleth	Vikki Watson, James Kaleth	100
5	11	Israel	Izhar Cohen	Olé Olé	Hamutal Ben Ze'ev	Kobi Oshrat	93
6	1	Ireland	Maria Christian	Wait Until The Weekend Comes	Brendan J. Graham	Brendan J. Graham	91
7	12	Italy	Al Bano & Romina Power	Magic, Oh Magic	Christiano Minellono	Dario Farina, Michael Hoffmann	78
8	17	Austria	Gary Lux	Kinder Dieser Welt	Michael Kunze	Mick Jackson, Geoff Bastow	60
9	2	Finland	Sonja Lumme	Eläköön Elämä	Veli-Pekka Lehto	Petri Laaksonen	58
10	6	France	Roger Bens	Femme Dans Ses Rêves Aussi	Didier Pascalis	Didier Pascalis	56
11	4	Denmark	Hot Eyes	Sku' Du Spør Fra No'n	Keld Heick	Søren Bundgård	41
12	15	Switzerland	Mariella Farré & Pino Gasparini	Piano Piano	Trudi Müller-Bosshard	Anita Kerr	39
13	18	Luxembourg	Margo, Franck Olivier, Diane Solomon, Ireen Sheer, Malcolm Roberts & Chris Roberts	Children, Kinder, Enfants	Bernd Meinunger, Jean-Michel Bériat	Ralph Siegel	37
14	5	Spain	Paloma San Basilio	La Fiesta Terminó	Juan Carlos Calderón	Juan Carlos Calderón	36
15	7	Turkey	MFÖ	Di Dai Di Dai (a'sik Oldum)	Mazhar Alanson, Fuat Güner, Özkan Ugur	Mazhar Alanson, Fuat Güner, Özkan Ugur	36
16	19	Greece	Takis Biniaris	Miazoume	Maro Bizani	Takis Biniaris	15
17	3	Cyprus	Lia Vishy	To Katalava Arga	Lia Vishy-Piliouri	Lia Vishy-Piliouri	15
18	9	Portugal	Adelaïde	Penso Em Ti, Eu Sei	Adelaïde Ferreira, Luis Fernando	Tózé Brito	9
19	8	Belgium	Linda Lepomme	Laat Me Nu Gaan	Bert Vivier	Pieter Verlinden	7

1985 Eurovision 30: Gothenburg, Sweden

	Ireland	Finland	Cyprus	Denmark	Spain	France	Turkey	Belgium	Portugal	Germany	Israel	Italy	Norway	United Kingdom	Switzerland	Sweden	Austria	Luxembourg	Greece
TOTAL	91	58	15	41	36	56	36	7	9	105	93	78	123	100	39	103	60	37	15
United Kingdom	3	7			4	2	8			1	5		12			6	10		
Turkey	5	3			12	1			7	2		8	10			6	4		
Switzerland	5	2	3			4	12				7		6	10		8	1		
Sweden	7	10		5	6					8	2	12	4	1			3		
Spain	4	6					3			10	8	12	1	5		2		7	
Portugal	8			1		2	3			7	5	12	6	4				10	
Norway	3	6				1				8	10			7	5	12	2	4	
Luxembourg						1	3			10	6	12	7	8	2	5	4		
Italy	12	7		3	2	10					5		6	8		4	1		
Israel	8	1				3				7		12	2	6	4	10	5		
Ireland		6	1		2		7			8	4	5	12	10	3				
Greece		10	8		6	12			7		2	1		4	5		3		
Germany	4	6				2					7		12	5	1	8	10		3
France	3			10						8	12	5	2	6		7	1		4
Finland					8	5	2	7		12	10	4	3	1	6				
Denmark	3	4			8					7	12	5	6	10		1	2		
Cyprus	7	6		3	1	4					12			5	2		10		8
Belgium	8	3				6				10	2	12	5	1		7	4		
Austria	10			5		3	6				7	12	2		1	4		8	

Rank	Start	Country	Artist	Song	Writer	Composer	POINTS
1	13	Belgium	Sandra Kim	J'aime La Vie	Rosario Marino Atria	Jean-Pierre Furnémont, Angelo Crisci	176
2	10	Switzerland	Daniela Simons	Pas Pour Moi	Nella Martinetti	Atilla Sereftug	140
3	1	Luxembourg	Sherisse Laurence	L'amour De Ma Vie	Alain Garcia, Frank Dostal	Rolf Soja	117
4	12	Ireland	Luv Bug	You Can Count On Me	Kevin Sheerin	Kevin Sheerin	96
5	17	Sweden	Lasse Holm & Monica Törnell	E' De' Det Här Du Kallar Kärlek	Lasse Holm	Lasse Holm	78
6	18	Denmark	Lise Haavik & Trax	Du Er Fuld Af Løgn	John Hatting	John Hatting	77
7	5	United Kingdom	Ryder	Runner In The Night	Maureen Darbyshire	Brian Wade	72
8	14	Germany	Ingrid Peters	Über Die Brücke Geh'n	Hans Blüm	Hans Blüm	62
9	8	Turkey	Klips ve Onlar	Halley	Ilhan Irem	Melih Kibar	53
10	9	Spain	Cadillac	Valentino	José Maria Guzmán	José Maria Guzmán	51
11	2	Yugoslavia	Doris Dragovic	Zeljo Moja	Zrinko Tutic	Zrinko Tutic	49
12	4	Norway	Ketil Stokkan	Romeo	Ketil Stokkan	Ketil Stokkan	44
13	7	Netherlands	Frizzle Sizzle	Alles Heeft Ritme	Peter Schön	Peter Schön, Rob ten Bokum	40
14	20	Portugal	Dora	Não Sejas Mau Para Mim	Guilherme Inês, Zé da Ponte, Luis Oliveira	Guilherme Inês, Zé da Ponte, Luis Oliveira	28
15	19	Finland	Kari Kuivalainen	Päivä Kahden Ihmisen	Kari Kuivalainen	Kari Kuivalainen	22
16	6	Iceland	Icy	Gleðibankinn	Magnús Eiríksson	Magnús Eiríksson	19
17	3	France	Cocktail Chic	Européennes	Georges Costa, Michel Costa	Georges Costa, Michel Costa	13
18	16	Austria	Timna Brauer	Die Zeit Ist Einsam	Peter Cornelius	Peter Janda	12
19	11	Israel	Moti Galadi & Sarai Tzuriel	Yavoh Yom	Moti Galadi	Yoram Zadok	7
20	5	Cyprus	Elpida	Tora Zo	Phivos Gavris, Petros Yiannaki	Petros Yiannaki	4

1986 Eurovision 31: Bergen, Norway

Receiving \ Voting	TOTAL	Yugoslavia	United Kingdom	Turkey	Switzerland	Sweden	Spain	Portugal	Norway	Netherlands	Luxembourg	Israel	Ireland	Iceland	Germany	France	Finland	Denmark	Cyprus	Belgium	Austria
Luxembourg	117	5	8	2	2	10	6	6	12	8		4	7	1	12	8	4	2		10	10
Yugoslavia	49		7	3		1	3		3	7			3	5					12	4	1
France	13				7		6														
Norway	44		2			5	2			2		6	6	4	6	4	8	10			
United Kingdom	72			6	6	8	2	2	6			6	6	8	1	3	8	7		1	
Iceland	19			2		2	6			5								6	4		
Netherlands	40	2	7	7	8		1	7		6	1	8	5		10		3			2	
Turkey	53	12	2		1	3		6	2	7	6	3		2	8				4	6	2
Spain	51	4	1	8		3		3	8	7	7	6	5	2					3		1
Switzerland	140	6	4	10		12	4	10	5	12	12	12	10	3		7	7	4	5	10	8
Israel	7			5		7			1												
Ireland	96	8	5		8	7	12	8	2		3	6		8		3		4		12	2
Belgium	176	10	10	12	10	6	10	12	8	10		5	12	10	1	12	12		7		1
Germany	62	1	12				6	4				8	8		10	8	2	7			2
Cyprus	4												1								3
Austria	12							1					2		2		6			1	
Sweden	78	3	3	5	12		7	5	7	3	5	5		12	4	2	5	6	6		5
Denmark	77	7	6	3	3	4	5	5	10	4		10	4	7	7	5		3	7		
Finland	22			1	1		8		4	1				6	3		2			8	3
Portugal	28		4	4	4		8		4			7							1		

81

Rank	Start	Country	Artist	Song	Writer	Composer	POINTS
1	20	Ireland	Johnny Logan	Hold Me Now	Sean Sherrard	Sean Sherrard	172
2	16	Germany	Wind	Laß Die Sonne In Dein Herz	Bernd Meinunger	Ralph Siegel	141
3	7	Italy	Umberto Tozzi & Raf	Gente Di Mare	Giancarlo Bigazzi	Umberto Tozzi, Raffaele Riefoli	103
4	21	Yugoslavia	Novi Fosili	Ja Sam Za Ples	Stevo Cvikic	Rajko Dujmic	92
5	12	Netherlands	Marcha	Rechtop In De Wind	Peter Koelewijn	Peter Koelewijn	83
6	19	Denmark	Anne-Catherine Herdorf & Bandjo	En Lille Melodi	Jacob Jonia	Helga Engelbrecht	83
7	17	Cyprus	Alexia	Aspro Mavro	Maria Papapavlou	Andreas Papapavlou	80
8	2	Israel	Datner & Kushnir	Shir Habatlanim	Zohar Laskov	Zohar Laskov	73
9	1	Norway	Kate Gulbrandsen	Mitt Liv	Hanne Krogh, Rolf Løvland	Rolf Løvland	65
10	11	Greece	Bang	Stop!	Thanos Kalliris, Vassilis Dertilis	Thanos Kalliris, Vassilis Dertilis	64
11	5	Belgium	Liliane Saint-Pierre	Soldiers Of Love	Liliane Keuninckx, Gyuri Spies, Marc de Coen	Liliane Keuninckx, Gyuri Spies, Marc de Coen	56
12	6	Sweden	Lotta Engberg	Boogaloo	Christer Lundh	Mikael Wendt	50
13	14	United Kingdom	Rikki	Only The Light	Richard Peebles	Richard Peebles	47
14	15	France	Christine Minier	Les Mots D'amour N'ont Pas De Dimanche	Gérard Curci	Marc Minier	44
15	18	Finland	Vicky Rosti	Sata Salamaa	Veli-Pekka Lehto	Petri Laaksonen	32
16	4	Iceland	Halla Margarét	Hægt Og Hljótt	Valgeir Guðjónsson	Valgeir Guðjónsson	28
17	22	Switzerland	Carole Rich	Moitié Moitié	Jean-Jacques Egli	Jean-Jacques Egli	26
18	8	Portugal	Nevada	Neste Barco à Vela	Alfredo Azinheira	Alfredo Azinheira, Jorge Mendes	15
19	9	Spain	Patricia Kraus	No Estás Solo	Patricia Kraus	Rafael Martinez, Rafael Trabucchelli	10
20	3	Austria	Gary Lux	Nur Noch Gefühl	Stefanie Werger	Kenneth Westmore	8
21	13	Luxembourg	Plastic Bertrand	Amour Amour	Roger Jouret, Alec Mansion	Roger Jouret, Alec Mansion	4
22	10	Turkey	Seyyal Tanner & Lokomotif	Sarkim Sevgi üstüne	Olcayto Ahmet Tugsuz	Olcayto Ahmet Tugsuz	0

1987 Eurovision 32: Brussels, Belgium

Receiving \ Voting	Yugoslavia	United Kingdom	Turkey	Switzerland	Sweden	Spain	Portugal	Norway	Netherlands	Luxembourg	Italy	Israel	Ireland	Iceland	Greece	Germany	France	Finland	Denmark	Cyprus	Belgium	Austria	TOTAL
Norway				6	10	3			4		7		2	5		7	4	5	3	3	7	4	65
Israel		4		8	4		10	2	3				5	5		8	10	7		6	6	1	73
Austria						4					1				7								8
Iceland					8	4									6	10							28
Belgium		8	4		5	7		3		5	6	2	4	8		4		3		5		4	56
Sweden			2				7	1	12		3		12	8			3	10		7	1		50
Italy	12	1	8	7		12	12		1	4		3	12	3		12		4		3	5	6	103
Portugal						8									5								15
Spain												8			10								10
Turkey																							0
Greece	5	5			6	5		5	5	7	8	5	6	1			7	8	2	6	2	2	64
Netherlands	8	3	7	10	10		2	4		8	10	5			3		12	2	2	12		10	83
Luxembourg		2			5	2		4			1							1				3	4
United Kingdom			3	5	5	4	3		1	12	5	10	3	4		5		1	2	4	3	5	47
France	2	10	6	2	7	1	5	1	10	6	4	8	7	12	4			10	8		8		44
Germany	7	6	1	1			4	3	2		12		6	6	8		5	6	7	3	10	10	141
Cyprus	10			4	2	2	8	6	8	10		4	8		12	3		6	12		6	8	80
Finland		1			3		4	10	6					7	1	1							32
Denmark	1	7		12	8		1	7	6		2	6	4		8	6	8	8		10	5	7	83
Ireland	6	12	10	3	12	10	8	8	12	10	12	4		10	2		1	12	5	8	8	12	172
Yugoslavia			12		1	6	6	12	7	3	12	7	1	2		7	2	6	8	10	8	8	92
Switzerland	3		5						7			1		2					1		4		26

Rank	Start	Country	Artist	Song	Writer	Composer	POINTS
1	9	Switzerland	Céline Dion	Ne Partez Pas Sans Moi	Nella Martinetti	Atilla Sereftug	137
2	4	United Kingdom	Scott Fitzgerald	Go	Julie Forsyth	Julie Forsyth	136
3	13	Denmark	Hot Eyes	Ka' Du Se Hva' Jeg Sa'	Keld Heick	Søren Bundgård	92
4	17	Luxembourg	Lara Fabian	Croire	Alain Garcia	Jacques Cardona	90
5	15	Norway	Karoline Krüger	For Vår Jord	Erik Hillestad	Anita Skorgan	88
6	21	Yugoslavia	Srebrna Krila	Mangup	Stevo Cvikic, Rajko Dujmic	Rajko Dujmic	87
7	8	Israel	Yardena Arazi	Ben Adam	Ehud Manor	Boris Dimitshtein	85
8	10	Ireland	Jump the Gun	Take Him Home	Peter Eades	Peter Eades	79
9	7	Netherlands	Gerard Joling	Shangri-la	Peter de Wijn	Peter de Wijn	70
10	19	France	Gérard Lenorman	Chanteur De Charme	Gérard Lenorman, Claude Lemesle	Gérard Lenorman	64
11	6	Spain	La Década	La Chica Que Yo Quiero (made In Spain)	Francisco Dondiego	Enrique Piero	58
12	2	Sweden	Tommy Körberg	Stad I Ljus	Py Bäckman	Py Bäckman	52
13	18	Italy	Luca Barbarossa	Ti Scrivo	Luca Barbarossa	Luca Barbarossa	52
14	11	Germany	Maxi & Chris Garden	Lied Für Einen Freund	Bernd Meinunger	Ralph Siegel	48
15	5	Turkey	MFÖ	Sufi (hey Ya Hey)	Mazhar Alanson	Mazhar Alanson, Fuat Güner, Özkan Ugu	37
16	1	Iceland	Beathoven	Sókrates	Sverrir Stormsker	Sverrir Stormsker	20
17	14	Greece	Aphroditi Fryda	Kloun	Dimitris Sakislis	Dimitris Sakislis	10
18	20	Portugal	Dora	Voltarei	José Calvário, José Niza	José Calvário, José Niza	5
19	16	Belgium	Reynaert	Laissez Briller Le Soleil	Joseph Reynaerts, Philippe Anciaux	Joseph Reynaerts, Dany Willem	5
20	3	Finland	Boulevard	Nauravat Silmät Muistetaan	Kirsti Willberg	Pepe Willberg	3
21	12	Austria	Wilfried	Lisa Mona Lisa	Wilfried Scheutz, Klaus Kofler, Ronnie Herbholzheimer	Wilfried Scheutz, Klaus Kofler, Ronnie Herbholzheimer	0

1988 Eurovision 33: Dublin, Ireland

30 April 1988

	Austria	Belgium	Denmark	Finland	France	Germany	Greece	Iceland	Ireland	Israel	Italy	Luxembourg	Netherlands	Norway	Portugal	Spain	Sweden	Switzerland	Turkey	United Kingdom	Yugoslavia	TOTAL
Iceland			4		2						1		4		8		1					**20**
Sweden		1	8					3	5		10	3	8	12						2		**52**
Finland										3												**3**
United Kingdom	10	12	10	10		10	6	1	7	10	12	8		5	3	10	5	5	12			**136**
Turkey					6	8				8		4	1			5	4			1		**37**
Spain	8	6	1				8	2		2	8	6		2				6	5		4	**58**
Netherlands						6	12		2	7	5	12						7	6	6	7	**70**
Israel	2	10		6	10	5	3	6	1		3	5	3		10	6		10		4	1	**85**
Switzerland		4		5	1	12	10	7	10	4	7	1	10	8	12	8	12		10	10	6	**137**
Ireland	6	5	7	2	4	7							6	7	5	12	7	4	2	3	2	**79**
Germany			6					8	6	5				4	2	3			1	5	8	**48**
Austria																						**0**
Denmark	12	7		4	12	4		10	4	6			12	10	6	1	3	1				**92**
Greece					7														3			**10**
Norway	3	3	5	7		1	7	5	8	1	4		7		7		8			12	10	**88**
Belgium					5																	**5**
Luxembourg	1	8	2	12			2	4	12		2		5	6	4		10	12		7	3	**90**
Italy	5			8	8	2						2		3		7		8	4		5	**52**
France	7	2	3	3		3	5					10	2	1	1	2	2	3	8		12	**64**
Portugal							1									4						**5**
Yugoslavia	4		12	1	3		4	12	3	12	6	7					6	2	7	8		**87**

Rank	Start	Country	Artist	Song	Writer	Composer	POINTS
1	22	Yugoslavia	Riva	Rock Me	Stevo Cvikic	Rajko Dujmic	137
2	7	United Kingdom	Live Report	Why Do I Always Get It Wrong	Brian Hodgson	John Beeby	130
3	12	Denmark	Birthe Kjær	Vi Maler Byen Rød	Keld Heick	Søren Bundgård	111
4	10	Sweden	Tommy Nilsson	En Dag	Tim Norell, Ola Håkansson	Tim Norell, Ola Håkansson, Alexander Bard	110
5	13	Austria	Thomas Forstner	Nur Ein Lied	Joachim Horn-Bernges	Dieter Bohlen	97
6	16	Spain	Nina	Nacida Para Amar	Juan Carlos Calderón	Juan Carlos Calderón	88
7	14	Finland	Anneli Saaristo	La Dolce Vita	Turkka Mali	Matti Puurtinen	76
8	15	France	Nathalie Pâque	J'ai Volé La Vie	Sylvain Lebel	Guy Matteoni, G G Candy	60
9	1	Italy	Anna Oxa & Fausto Leali	Avrei Voluto	Franco Ciani, Franco Berlincioni	Franco Fasano	56
10	19	Greece	Marianna	To Diko Sou Asteri	Villy Sanianou	Yiannis Kyris, Marianna Efstratiou	56
11	17	Cyprus	Fanny Polymeri & Yiannis Savvidakis	Apopse As Vrethoume	Efi Meletiou	Marios Meletiou	51
12	2	Israel	Gili ve Galit	Derech Ha'melech	Shaike Paikov	Shaike Paikov	50
13	18	Switzerland	Furbaz	Viver Senza Tei	Marie-Louise Werth	Marie-Louise Werth	47
14	21	Germany	Nino de Angelo	Flieger	Joachim Horn-Bernges	Dieter Bohlen	46
15	4	Netherlands	Justine Pelmelay	Blijf Zoals Je Bent	Cees Bergman, Geert-Jan Hessing, Aart Mol, E van Prehn, E Veerhoff	Jan Kisjes	45
16	9	Portugal	Da Vinci	Conquistador	Pedro Luis	Ricardo	39
17	8	Norway	Britt Synnøve Johansen	Venners Nærhet	Leiv N Grøtte	Inge Enoksen	30
18	3	Ireland	Kiev Connolly & the Missing Passengers	The Real Me	Kiev Connolly	Kiev Connolly	21
19	6	Belgium	Ingeborg	Door De Wind	Stef Bos	Stef Bos	13
20	11	Luxembourg	Park Café	Monsieur	Maggie Parke, Bernard Loncheval, Yves Lacomblez	Maggie Parke, Gast Waltzing	8
21	5	Turkey	Pan	Bana Bana	Timur Selçuk	Timur Selçuk	5
22	20	Iceland	Daníel Ágúst Haraldsson	Það Sem Enginn Sér	Valgeir Guðjónsson	Valgeir Guðjónsson	0

1989 Eurovision 34: Lausanne, Switzerland

Voter ↓ / Contestant →	Italy	Israel	Ireland	Netherlands	Turkey	Belgium	United Kingdom	Norway	Portugal	Sweden	Luxembourg	Denmark	Austria	Finland	France	Spain	Cyprus	Switzerland	Greece	Iceland	Germany	Yugoslavia
Yugoslavia	8	7	2		4		6			12		1	5	10	3							
United Kingdom	2			3				4		10			7				6	8	5		1	12
Turkey			7				3	2		5	1			10		6		8			4	12
Switzerland	2	7		3				1					8		10	7	4		3		6	5
Sweden		5					2	3				12	7	4			1				8	8
Spain	12				6		1		8				2	7				10			6	5
Portugal	7						12	12		3	7	2	1				6				5	4
Norway		2			3	2	12		1	8		10		5	4			6			7	8
Netherlands						5	7	2				12	6	4			10		1		8	8
Luxembourg			2		1		12		7			3	4	8		10			5			6
Italy				10			6					5	12		8	2		4			7	
Israel	12				10		7	2				1	8	10	5		3	4			12	12
Ireland		7			3	5	4					10	8	6		1		2			12	12
Iceland		5			1		1					10	8			12	7		4		6	6
Greece	4				1		2	6		8			12		5	10		7			3	3
Germany	7	3	4	6			12		8	5					2	10		1				
France				7			12	4		2		6		10		8	3	1				
Finland	10	5		4			6		2			12	1			8	3				7	
Denmark		5					1	6		12			4				8	2			10	7
Cyprus	6						2	8				10	3	7	4						5	1
Belgium		3						8	2	6		4	12			7		1			10	5
Austria				4			8	1	6	12			7	3	5	2			3		10	10
TOTAL	**56**	**50**	**21**	**45**	**5**	**13**	**130**	**30**	**39**	**110**	**8**	**111**	**97**	**76**	**60**	**88**	**51**	**47**	**56**	**0**	**46**	**137**

Rank	Start	Country	Artist	Song	Writer	Composer	POINTS
1	19	Italy	Toto Cutugno	Insieme: 1992	Toto Cutugno	Toto Cutugno	149
2	14	France	Joelle Ursull	White And Black Blues	Serge Gainsbourg	Georges Ougier de Moussac	132
3	17	Ireland	Liam Reilly	Somewhere In Europe	Liam Reilly	Liam Reilly	132
4	8	Iceland	Stjörnin	Eitt Lag Enn	Aðalsteinn Ásberg Sigurðsson	Hörður G Ólafsson	124
5	1	Spain	Azúcar Moreno	Bandido	José-Luis Abel	Raúl Orellana, Jaime Stinus	96
6	7	United Kingdom	Emma	Give A Little Love Back To The World	Paul Curtis	Paul Curtis	87
7	15	Yugoslavia	Tajci	Hajde Da Ludujemo	Alka Vuica	Zrinko Tutic	81
8	11	Denmark	Lonnie Devantier	Hallo Hallo	Keld Heick	John Hatting, Torben Lendager	64
9	13	Germany	Chris Kempers & Daniel Kovac	Frei Zu Leben	Michael Kunze	Ralph Siegel	60
10	20	Austria	Simone	Keine Mauern Mehr	Mario Botazzi	Wolfgang Berry, Nana Berry	58
11	12	Switzerland	Egon Egemann	Musik Klingt In Die Welt Hinaus	Cornelia Lackner	Cornelia Lackner	51
12	3	Belgium	Philippe Lafontaine	Macédomienne	Philippe Lafontaine	Philippe Lafontaine	46
13	6	Luxembourg	Céline Carzo	Quand Je Te Rêve	Thierry Delianis	Jean-Charles France	38
14	21	Cyprus	Haris Anastasiou	Milas Poli	Haris Anastasiou	John Vickers	36
15	5	Netherlands	Maywood	Ik Wil Alles Met Je Delen	Alice May	Alice May	25
16	18	Sweden	Edin-Ådahl	Som En Vind	Mikael Wendt	Mikael Wendt	24
17	4	Turkey	Kayahan	Gözlerinin Hapsindeyim	Kayahan Acar	Kayahan Acar	21
18	10	Israel	Rita	Shara Barechovot	Tzruya Lahav	Rami Kleinstein	16
19	2	Greece	Christos Callow & Wave	Horis Skopo	Giorgos Papagiannakis	Giorgos Paleokastriris	11
20	16	Portugal	Nucha	Há Sempre Alguém	Francisco Teotonio Pereira	Jan van Dijck, Luis Filipe	9
21	22	Finland	Beat	Fri?	Stina Engblom	Kim & Janne Engblom, Tina Krause	8
22	9	Norway	Ketil Stokkan	Brandenburger Tor	Ketil Stokkan	Ketil Stokkan	8

1990 Eurovision 35: Zagreb, Yugoslavia

Receiving \ Giving	Yugoslavia	United Kingdom	Turkey	Switzerland	Sweden	Spain	Portugal	Norway	Netherlands	Luxembourg	Italy	Israel	Ireland	Iceland	Greece	Germany	France	Finland	Denmark	Cyprus	Belgium	Austria	TOTAL
Spain	3	1	10	6			5	5	2		8			4	8	12	5	10		8	1	8	96
Greece																				6			11
Belgium				4	7			1	7	4		1	1		1	8	8					2	46
Turkey	7							4	3					2		5							21
Netherlands		4	3							1						10		5				2	25
Luxembourg	2	3		2	4						12		5			1	4					5	38
United Kingdom	10		3		6		2		2	3	10		7	12		8			7		12	7	87
Iceland	4	12	2	10	8	7	12	10		3	6	8	7		3		12	7	10				124
Norway	1		4									4	3					5					8
Israel				2					4				7			4	12			5		3	16
Denmark	5			1	3	6	7	7		2	7	7	4	7				12		4	3		64
Switzerland		6			4	1	8			12	5			1	12		5	3	5	7	6	2	51
Germany		7	5		4	8			8	10		6		6			10	8	6		2		60
France	12	3	4	7	5	5	4	12	12	5		12	12	12		10		8	5		4	6	132
Yugoslavia		5	12	10	1	3		3			10		5	10			2	1	7	10			81
Portugal		2								7													9
Ireland		10	5	5	12	10	6	8	10	6				8	7	7	7	4	8		7	12	132
Sweden		6				2		6	6				2		2								24
Italy		8	8	8	10	12	10		8	10		1	12	3	10	6	4	8	6	8		7	149
Austria		8	7		2			2	1	5	12	5	2	6	6		3	2	5	7	2		58
Cyprus					6	12		2		10	4	3		5	6			6	2		5		36
Finland		2										3		5									8

1991 Eurovision 36: Rome, Italy

Rank	Start	Country	Artist	Song	Writer	Composer	POINTS
1	8	Sweden	Carola	Fångad Av En Stormvind	Stephan Berg	Stephan Berg	146
2	9	France	Amina	C'est Le Dernier Qui A Parlé Qui A Raison	Amina Annabi	Wasis Diop	146
3	15	Israel	Duo Datz	Kan	Uzi Chitman	Uzi Chitman	139
4	19	Spain	Sergio Dalma	Bailar Pegados	Luis Gomez Escolar	Julio Seijas	119
5	5	Switzerland	Sandra Simò	Canzone Per Te	Renato Mascetti	Renato Mascetti	118
6	3	Malta	Paul Giordimaina & Georgina	Could It Be	Raymond Mahoney	Paul Abela	106
7	22	Italy	Peppino di Capri	Comme E' Ddoce 'o Mare	Giampiero Artegiani	Marcello Marocchi	89
8	12	Portugal	Dulce	Lusitana Paixão	Fred Micael, Zé da Ponte, J Quintela	Fred Micael, Zé da Ponte, J Quintela	62
9	21	Cyprus	Elena Patroclou	SOS	Andreas Christou	Kypros Charalambous	60
10	20	United Kingdom	Samantha Janus	A Message To Your Heart	Paul Curtis	Paul Curtis	47
11	11	Ireland	Kim Jackson	Could It Be That I'm In Love	Liam Reilly	Liam Reilly	47
12	10	Turkey	Izel Çelíköz, Rayhan Soykarçi & Can Uğurluér	Iki Dakika	Aysel Gürel	Sevket Uğurluér	44
13	4	Greece	Sofia Vossou	I Anixi	Andreas Mikroutsikos	Andreas Mikroutsikos	36
14	7	Luxembourg	Sarah Bray	Un Baiser Volé	Linda Lecomte, Mick Wersant	Patrick Hippert	29
15	2	Iceland	Stefán & Eyfi	Nina	Eyjólfur Kristjánsson	Eyjólfur Kristjánsson	26
16	18	Belgium	Clouseau	Geef Het Op	Bob Savenberg, Koen Wauters, Kris Wauters, Jan Leyers	Bob Savenberg, Koen Wauters, Kris Wauters, Jan Leyers	23
17	14	Norway	Just 4 Fun	Mrs Thompson	P G Roness, Kaare Skevik	Dag Kolsrud	14
18	17	Germany	Atlantis 2000	Dieser Traum Darf Niemals Sterben	Helmut Frey	Alfons Weindorf	10
19	13	Denmark	Anders Frandsen	Lige Der Hvor Hjertet Slår	Michael Elo	Michael Elo	8
20	16	Finland	Kaija	Hullu Yö	Jukka Välimaa	Ile Kallio	6
21	1	Yugoslavia	Baby Doll	Brazil	Dragana Saric	Zoran Vracevic	1
22	6	Austria	Thomas Forstner	Venedig Im Regen	Robby Musenbichler, Hubert Moser, Wolfgang Eltner	Robby Musenbichler, Hubert Moser, Wolfgang Eltner	0

Note: Sweden win on the higher number of '10' votes, after finishing level on total points and number of '12' votes.

1991 Eurovision 36: Rome, Italy

Scoreboard — jury votes (rows = voting juries, columns = contestants). Points awarded by each jury to each contestant, with each contestant's TOTAL.

Contestant	TOTAL	Yug	UK	Tur	Swi	Swe	Spa	Por	Nor	Mal	Lux	Ita	Isr	Irl	Ice	Gre	Ger	Fra	Fin	Den	Cyp	Bel	Aut
Yugoslavia	1									1													
Iceland	26				4	10						7					5						
Malta	106	1	7	7	6	12	6	7	6		10	10		12	2	2	10	2	1		10	1	4
Greece	36					8	5	6	1	5	10	2	4	1	5			4			8		2
Switzerland	118	5	8	2		8		6	3		12	4	8	2	5	7	6	4	5	5	8	12	8
Austria	0																						
Luxembourg	29		3	3		1		2						3	4		3			4	2	2	5
Sweden	146	6	12	6	10		4	10	8	3	7		10	12	12	12	12	8	8	12	6	10	10
France	146	10	6	12	7	5	8	5	12	3		12	12	7	7	8	8		10	1	7	7	12
Turkey	44		5				2			7		8	7					7					
Ireland	47	3	4	4	3	1		8	2	4	8	3	1			4	2			7		5	1
Portugal	62			5	1	7	10		2		2	1			8	4		10	7	2	4		
Denmark	8					3			5													6	
Norway	14	1		1				1		1	1		6	4	6		4			2			
Israel	139	12	10	12	8	6	12	7	7	8	5		1	8	10	5		3	6	10	5	8	
Finland	6												4		1	1						3	
Germany	10		2	3	2	1	1			2		5	3		2	6		4	3	6	3		3
Belgium	23					2	3			6	6	6	5	6	2		7	6	3	3			
Spain	119	8	1	8	12	4		8	4	6	3	6	6	5	3	10		1	4	1	12	6	7
United Kingdom	47				5		2	1	10	10	3	6	5	10		3	3	12		3	1	3	6
Cyprus	60	2	2	10	2		7	3		12	4	6	6	5	3	12		12		3			6
Italy	89	7		10				12		2			3		10	6		8	12				

Rank	Start	Country	Artist	Song	Writer	Composer	POINTS
1	17	Ireland	Linda Martin	Why Me	Johnny Logan	Johnny Logan	155
2	16	United Kingdom	Michael Ball	One Step Out Of Time	Tony Ryan, Paul Davies, Victor Stratton	Tony Ryan, Paul Davies, Victor Stratton	139
3	10	Malta	Mary Spiteri	Little Child	Raymond Mahoney	Georgina Abela	123
4	19	Italy	Mia Martini	Rapsodia	Giancarlo Bigazzi	Giuseppe Dati	111
5	5	Greece	Cleopatra	Olou Tou Kosmou I Elpida	Christos Lagos	Christos Lagos	94
6	3	Israel	Dafna	Ze Rak Sport	Ehud Manor	Kobi Oshrat	85
7	11	Iceland	Heart 2 Heart	Nei Eða Já	Stefán Hilmarsson	Friðrik Karlsson, Grétar Örvarsson	80
8	6	France	Kali	Monté La Riviè	Remy Bellenchombre	Kali	73
9	23	Netherlands	Humphrey Campbell	Wijs Me De Weg	Edwin Schimscheimer	Edwin Schimscheimer	67
10	15	Austria	Tony Wegas	Zusammen Geh'n	Joachim Horn-Bernges	Dieter Bohlen	63
11	9	Cyprus	Evridiki	Teriazoume	George Theophanous	George Theophanous	57
12	18	Denmark	Lotte Nilsson & Kenny Lübcke	Ält Det Som Ingen Ser	Carsten Warming	Carsten Warming	47
13	20	Yugoslavia	Extra Nena	Ljubim Te Pesmama	Gale Jankovic	Radivoje Radivojevic	44
14	1	Spain	Serafin	Todo Esto Es La Música	Luis Miguelez	Luis Miguelez, Alfredo Albuena	37
15	13	Switzerland	Daisy Auvray	Mister Music Man	Gordon Dent	Gordon Dent	32
16	22	Germany	Wind	Träume Sind Für Alle Da	Bernd Meinunger	Ralph Siegel	27
17	8	Portugal	Diná	Amor D'água Fresca	Rosa Lobato de Faria	Nandina Veloso	26
18	21	Norway	Merethe Troan	Visjoner	Eva Jansen	Robert Morley	23
19	4	Turkey	Aylin Vatankos	Yaz Bitti	Aylin Üçanlar	Aldogan Simsekyay	17
20	2	Belgium	Morgane	Nous On Veut Des Violons	Anne-Marie Gaspard	Claude Barzotti	11
21	14	Luxembourg	Marion Welter & Kontinent	Sou Frái	Jang Linster, Ab van Goor	Jang Linster, Ab van Goor	10
22	7	Sweden	Christer Björkmann	I Morgon är En Annan Dag	Niklas Strömstedt	Niklas Strömstedt	9
23	12	Finland	Pave	Yamma Yamma	Hector	Pave Maijanen	4

1992 Eurovision 37: Malmö, Sweden

Voting ↓ / Performer →	Spain	Belgium	Israel	Turkey	Greece	France	Sweden	Portugal	Cyprus	Malta	Iceland	Finland	Switzerland	Luxembourg	Austria	United Kingdom	Ireland	Denmark	Italy	Yugoslavia	Norway	Germany	Netherlands
TOTAL	37	11	85	17	94	73	9	26	57	123	80	4	32	10	63	139	155	47	111	44	23	27	67
Yugoslavia			12	6	7		4	5	8	10		3							2		1		
United Kingdom	1		7			3				12	12		4		10		8			5	6	6	
Turkey	1	4	2		8	3			1							10	12	3					7
Switzerland			4		10	12			2	5	3					8	6	7			7		1
Sweden	4		4		3					12	6				1	5	10	7	8	2			2
Spain		3	10			6			12	12	8				2	5	1	4		3			7
Portugal	3		7		5				2	12	6				3	4	4	1	8			10	
Norway	5		2		8	10			3		1					7	12	6	12				4
Netherlands	1		3		4	6			8	5	2					7	10		12				
Malta	2		7	8					1				10		4	6	12			5	3		
Luxembourg	3	1	8						12	5					7	10	6			2	4		
Italy	7				12	6		1	4	3	5		10		8	2							
Israel					7	12		8	3		4	1			2			6			10		5
Ireland				3		5			6	10		1			12					4		2	8
Iceland					2					8		12			4	7	6	6	10	5	1		3
Greece	4						2		10	7	6				8		12		3	1			5
Germany		4			3		8			6						12	10	5	1	2		7	
France	6	3			7	1			2						10	10	12		12	5			4
Finland	3		5		7		2		8							6	10	12	4	1			
Denmark	1		2			4			5						7	12	10			6	3		
Cyprus			7		12	3				10	1				8	6	5			2			
Belgium			4		5			10	6	8	7				8	12	7	3		2		6	2
Austria	2		1		4				8		7		5			8			12		3	6	5

1993 Eurovision 38: Millstreet, Ireland

15 May 1993

Qualification: 7 new applicant countries took part in a preliminary heat, the top 3 qualified for the main contest.

Rank	Start	Country	Artist	Song	Writer	Composer	POINTS
1	14	Ireland	Niamh Kavanagh	In your eyes	Jimmy Walsh	Jimmy Walsh	187
2	19	United Kingdom	Sonia	Better the devil you know	Dean Collinson, Red	Dean Collinson, Red	164
3	4	Switzerland	Annie Cotton	Moi, tout simplement	Jean-Jacques Egli	Christophe Dúc	148
4	12	France	Patrick Fiori	Mama Corsica	François Valéry	François Valéry	121
5	25	Norway	Silje Vige	Alle mine tankar	Björn-Erik Vige	Björn-Erik Vige	120
6	20	Netherlands	Ruth Jacott	Vrede	Henk Westbroek	Eric van Tijn, Jochem Fluitsma	92
7	13	Sweden	Arvingarna	Eloïse	Gert Lengstrand	Lasse Holm	89
8	8	Malta	William Mangion	This time	William Mangion	William Mangion	69
9	6	Greece	Katerina Garbi	Ellada, hora tou fotos	Dimosthenis	Dimosthenis	64
10	11	Portugal	Anabela	A cidade até ser dia	Paulo Dacosta, Marco Quelhas, Pedro Abrantes	Paulo Dacosta, Marco Quelhas, Pedro Abrantes	60
11	22	Spain	Eva Santamaria	Hombres	Carlos Toro	Carlos Toro	58
12	1	Italy	Enrico Ruggeri	Sole d'Europa	Enrico Ruggeri	Enrico Ruggeri	45
13	9	Iceland	Inga	þá veistu svarið	Friðrik Sturlúson	Jon-Kjell Seljeseth	42
14	10	Austria	Tony Wegas	Maria Magdalena	Thomas Spitzer	Christian Kolonovits, Johann Bertl	32
15	21	Croatia	Put	Don't ever cry	Dorde Novkovic	Andrej Basa	31
16	18	Bosnia & H	Fazla	Sva bol svijeta	Fahrudin Pecikoza	Dino Dervishalidovic	27
17	17	Finland	Katri-Helena	Tule luo	Jukka Saarinen	Matti Puurtinen	20
18	3	Germany	Münchener Freiheit	Viel zu weit	Stefan Zauner	Stefan Zauner	18
19	23	Cyprus	Kyriakos Zymboulakis & Demos Van Beke	Mi stamatas	Rodoula Papalambrianou	Aristos Moschovakis	17
20	15	Luxembourg	Modern Times	Donne-moi une chance	Patrick Hippert, Jimmy Martin	Patrick Hippert, Jimmy Martin	11
21	2	Turkey	Burak Aydos, Öztürk Baybora & Serter	Esmer yarim	Burak Aydos	Burak Aydos	10
22	16	Slovenia	1X Band	Tih dezeven dan	Tomaz Kosec	Cole Moretti	9
23	5	Denmark	Tommy Seebach Band	Under stjernerne på himlen	Keld Heick	Tommy Seebach	9
24	24	Israel	Lakahat Shiru	Shiru	Yoram Tahar-Lev	Shaike Paikov	4
25	7	Belgium	Barbara	Iemand als jij	Tobana	Marc Vliegen	3

Eurosong Qualifier: Ljubliana, Slovenia

3 April 1993

Rank	Start	Country	Artist	Song	Writer	Composer	POINTS
1	6	Slovenia	1X Band	Tih dezeven dan	Tomaz Kosec	Cole Moretti	54
2	1	Bosnia & H	Fazla	Sva bol svijeta	Fahrudin Pecikoza	Dino Dervishalidovic	52
3	2	Croatia	Put	Don't ever cry	Dorde Novkovic	Andrej Basa	51
4	7	Slovakia	Elán	Amnestia na neveru	Jan Baláž	Jožef Ráž	50
5	3	Estonia	Jaanika Sillamaa	Muretut meelt ja südametuld	Leelo Tungal	Andres Valkoneni	47
6	4	Hungary	Andrea Szulák	Arva regel	Petar Ugrin	György Jakob, Emesi Hatvani	44
7	5	Romania	Dida Dragan	Nu pleca	Adrian Ordean	Dida Dragan	38

1993 Eurovision 38: Millstreet, Ireland

15 May 1993

	TOTAL	United Kingdom	Turkey	Switzerland	Sweden	Spain	Slovenia	Portugal	Norway	Netherlands	Malta	Luxembourg	Italy	Israel	Ireland	Iceland	Greece	Germany	France	Finland	Denmark	Cyprus	Croatia	Bosnia & H	Belgium	Austria
Italy	45		1		2	2		10		2	7	10	—						5	8				2		6
Turkey	10					6							8		4											8
Germany	18			2						1	5	3	—					—			3		2		5	
Switzerland	148	10	2	—	6	3	8	1	3	8	5	12	10	4	7	4		12	12	4	10	6	3	8	3	6
Denmark	9				1							3								1	12				10	
Greece	64		2			8			7	5	6	—	2	7				2		7	6	12	7	3	7	
Belgium	3				1				7			—	7	3				5	3							
Malta	69	6	5	7	4	4	5	2	2	7	—			3	2			5	4	2	5	2		4	4	4
Iceland	42	2			7		5		2		1	10	7	2	1			4			4		2	6		1
Austria	32	3	4									—			6		1	3	3					12		
Portugal	60	1		2	2	12		—	5	12	—	4	4		2	2	2	1	8		1	3	8			5
France	121	4	7	4	8		4	12	6	3		6	—		10	8	3		—	7		10	8		7	7
Sweden	89	7		8	—	10	6	4		—	6	5	12	10	10	7		8	8	7	7		6		10	10
Ireland	187	12	1	12	12	10	12	6	12	10	12	—	12	5	—	3	6	5	10	3	6	12	7	8	8	8
Luxembourg	11						1				10		4											1		
Slovenia	9		3		3						1	—		4		5	8								1	
Finland	20			5			2			2	2	—	3	3	3		5			4						
Bosnia & H	27		12	4						—	4	—	3	12			12	6						1	1	
United Kingdom	164	—	8	5	10	5	10	7	8	4		8	1	12	8	12	8	6	6	5	8		10		12	12
Netherlands	92	6	6	3	5	7	7	5	10	—	3	—	6		12	6		7					3	10	7	3
Croatia	31	8		3	1	1	7	5	4	4	—	—		6									—		4	4
Spain	58			6		—			1	2	8	—	5	1				—	5	10			5	6	5	2
Cyprus	17	5								—		—					10				2	—				
Israel	4							3											1							
Norway	120	12	10	10		8	3	8		6		1	10		5	10	12	10		1	12		12	7	6	6

1994 Eurovision 39: Dublin, Ireland

30 April 1994

Qualification: Bottom 6 countries from 1993 relegated, replaced with 7 new applicant countries.

Rank	Start	Country	Artist	Song	Writer	Composer	POINTS
1	3	Ireland	P Harrington & C McGettigan	Rock 'n' roll kids	Brendan J. Graham	Brendan J. Graham	226
2	24	Poland	Edyta Górniak	To nie ja!	Jacek Cygan	Stanislas Syrewicz	166
3	14	Germany	MeKaDo	Wir geben 'ne Party	Bernd Meinunger	Ralph Siegel	128
4	22	Hungary	Friderika Bayer	Kinek mondjam el vétkeimet	Szilveszter Jenei	Szilveszter Jenei	122
5	12	Malta	Moira Stafrace & Christopher	More than love	Moira Stafrace	Christopher Scicluna	97
6	17	Norway	E Andreasson & J W Danielsen	Duett	Hans Olav Mørk	Rolf Løvland	76
7	25	France	Nina Morato	Je suis un vrai garçon	Nina Morato	Bruno Maman	74
8	8	Portugal	Sara Tavares	Chamar a música	Rosa Lobato Faria	João Carlos Mota Oliveira	73
9	23	Russia	Youddiph	Vechni stranik	Youddiph	Lev Zemlinski	70
10	6	United Kingdom	Frances Ruffelle	We will be free (Lonely symphony)	George de Angelis, Mark Dean	George de Angelis, Mark Dean	63
11	4	Cyprus	Evridiki	Ime anthropos ke ego	George Theophanous	George Theophanous	51
12	5	Iceland	Sigga	Nætur	Stefán Hilmarsson	Friðrik Karlsson	49
13	1	Sweden	Marie Bergman & Roger Pontare	Stjärnorna	Mikael Littwold	Peter Bertilsson	48
14	19	Greece	Costas Bigalis & the Sea Lovers	To trehantiri (diri diri)	Costas Bigalis	Costas Bigalis	44
15	18	Bosnia & H	Alma & Dejan	Ostani kraj mene	Edu Mulahalilovic	Adi Mulahalilovic	39
16	7	Croatia	Tony Cetinski	Nek'ti bude ljubav sva	Zeljko Krznaric	Zeljko Klasterka	27
17	20	Austria	Petra Frey	Für den Frieden der Welt	Karl Brunner, Johann Brunner	Alfons Weindorf	19
18	21	Spain	Alejandro Abad	Ella no es ella	Alejandro Abad	Alejandro Abad	17
19	15	Slovakia	Martin Durinda & Tublatanka	Nekovecná piesen	Martin Sarvas	Martin Durinda	15
20	9	Switzerland	Duilio	Sto pregando	Giuseppe Scaramella	Giuseppe Scaramella	15
21	11	Romania	Dan Bittman	Dincolo de nori	Antoniu Furtuna, Dan Bittman	Antoniu Furtuna, Dan Bittman	14
22	2	Finland	CatCat	Bye bye baby	Kari Salli, Markku 'Make' Lentonen	Kari Salli, Markku 'Make' Lentonen	11
23	13	Netherlands	Willeke Alberti	Waar is de zon	Cooth van Doesburgh	Edwin Schimscheimer	4
24	10	Estonia	Silvi Vrait	Nagu merelaine	Leelo Tungal	Ivar Must	2
25	16	Lithuania	Ovidijus Vyšniauskas	Lopšine mylimai	Gintaras Zdebskis	Ovidijus Vyšniauskas	0

1994 Eurovision 39: Dublin, Ireland

30 April 1994

	Austria	Bosnia & H	Croatia	Cyprus	Estonia	Finland	France	Germany	Greece	Hungary	Iceland	Ireland	Lithuania	Malta	Netherlands	Norway	Poland	Portugal	Romania	Russia	Slovakia	Spain	Sweden	Switzerland	United Kingdom	**TOTAL**
Sweden	5				2			5		2	2		5	3	6	10						1		7		**48**
Finland		1							10																	**11**
Ireland	10	10	12	8	10	7	8	12		10	12		10	5	12	12	8	12	8	12	6	10	10	12	10	**226**
Cyprus						10	3		12		3					5	5	5		2		4		2		**51**
Iceland	3					1	4					6	3				4	3		1	1	6	8	3	6	**49**
United Kingdom	1	4	6	5	5			4		3		1			2	2	3	8		5	3	3		8		**63**
Croatia									5					10							12					**27**
Portugal						5	6			7	8	8		1	3		1			4		12	5	5	8	**73**
Switzerland							5							8								2				**15**
Estonia									2																	**2**
Romania									6				2	6												**14**
Malta		12	7	2	7	6		3	7			10	7		1			4	10		10		4	6	1	**97**
Netherlands	4																									**4**
Germany	2	7	10	6	3	3				12	7	5	4		4	1	7	10	12	7	7	8	6		7	**128**
Slovakia									3					12												**15**
Lithuania																										**0**
Norway		6	3	10	8			2	1	5	1	3	1		7				4	8		5	7	1	4	**76**
Bosnia & H			4			2	10			1				7							8	7				**39**
Greece				12		4		1		4				4		4	2		6		5		2			**44**
Austria		5	2	7															1				1		3	**19**
Spain							2		8										5		2					**17**
Hungary	8	3	5		4	12	7	7			10	12			10	8	12	1	2	3			12	4	2	**122**
Russia	6		1	3	1		1	6	4	6	4	4	6		5	3	10	2	3						5	**70**
Poland	12	8	8	1	12	8	12	10		8	6	7	12	2	8	6		7	7	6	4			10	12	**166**
France	7	2		4	6			8			5	2	8			7	6	6		10			3			**74**

1995 Eurovision 40: Dublin, Ireland

Qualification: Bottom 6 countries from 1994 relegated, replaced with the countries relegated in 1993.

Rank	Start	Country	Artist	Song	Writer	Composer	POINTS
1	5	Norway	Secret Garden	Nocturne	Petter Skavlan	Rolf Løvland	148
2	9	Spain	Anabel Conde	Vuelve conmigo	José Maria Purón	José Maria Purón	119
3	18	Sweden	Jan Johansen	Se på mej	Ingela Pling Forsman	Håkan Almqvist, Bobby Ljunggren	100
4	12	France	Nathalie Santamaria	Il me donne rendez-vous	Didier Barbelivien	François Bernheim	94
5	19	Denmark	Aud Wilken	Fra Mols til Skagen	Lise Cabble	Mette Mathiesen, Lise Cabble	92
6	11	Croatia	Magazin & Lidija	Nostalgija	Vjekoslava Huljic	Tonci Huljic	91
7	20	Slovenia	Darja Svajger	Prisluhni mi	Primoz Peterca	Primoz Peterca, Saso Fajon	83
8	21	Israel	Liora	Amen	Hamutal Ben Ze'ev	Moshe Datz	81
9	17	Cyprus	Alexandros Panayi	Sti fotia	Alexandros Panayi	Alexandros Panayi	79
10	22	Malta	Mike Spiteri	Keep me in mind	Alfred Sant	Ray Agius	76
11	15	United Kingdom	Love City Groove	Love City Groove	Paul Hardy, Steven Rudden, Tatsiana Mais, Jay Williams	Paul Hardy, Steven Rudden, Tatsiana Mais, Jay Williams	76
12	23	Greece	Elina Constantopoulou	Pia prosefchi	Antonis Pappas	Nikos Terzis	68
13	8	Austria	Stella Jones	Die Welt dreht sich verkehrt	Mischa Krausz	Mischa Krausz	67
14	2	Ireland	Eddie Friel	Dreamin'	Richard Abbott, Barry Woods	Richard Abbott, Barry Woods	44
15	7	Iceland	Bó Halldórsson	Núna	Jón Örn Marinósson	Bó Halldórsson, Ed Welch	31
16	10	Turkey	Arzu Ece	Sev!	Zeynep Talu	Melih Kibar	21
17	6	Russia	Philipp Kirkorov	Kolybelnaya dlya vulkana	Ilya Bershadsky	Ilya Reznyk	18
18	1	Poland	Justyna	Sama	Wojciech Waglewski	Mateusz Pospieszalski, Wojciech Waglewski	15
19	4	Bosnia & H	Davor Popovic	Dvadeset i prvi vijek	Zlatan Fazlic	Zlatan Fazlic, Sinan Alimanovic	14
20	14	Belgium	Frédéric Etherlinck	La voix est libre	Pierre Theunis	Pierre Theunis	8
21	16	Portugal	Tó Cruz	Baunilha e chocolate	Rosa Lobato De Faria	António Vitorino de Almeida	5
22	13	Hungary	Czaba Szigeti	Új név egy régi ház falan	Attila Horváth	Ferenc Balázs	3
23	3	Germany	Stone & Stone	Verliebt in Dich	Cheyenne Stone	Cheyenne Stone	1

1995 Eurovision 40: Dublin, Ireland

13 May 1995

Voter \ Recipient	Poland	Ireland	Germany	Bosnia & H	Norway	Russia	Iceland	Austria	Spain	Turkey	Croatia	France	Hungary	Belgium	United Kingdom	Portugal	Cyprus	Sweden	Denmark	Slovenia	Israel	Malta	Greece
TOTAL	15	44	1	14	148	18	31	67	119	21	91	94	3	8	76	5	79	100	92	83	81	76	68
United Kingdom		5		3	4		6		8	2	7	1					3	8			10		7
Turkey					5				3		12						8			3	2		
Sweden		10						6		4					5		8		12		2	1	
Spain		3			4			6		2	12						5			10		8	
Slovenia		5			7						12	8			4	1	6			10		2	
Russia		5			12		3				7	6		2	1		4	6	10		8		
Portugal	1				12		2	3	12	7		4			10		8		6			3	
Poland					12		2	2	8		7				5		1	10	3	4		6	
Norway	4	1				10	2	3			7	6			5		8		12				
Malta			1		6				8	7	12				4		3			2	5		10
Israel					10			2	12	1	4	7			5		6		3			8	
Ireland					10		6		2		3	5			1		8	12	7	8		4	
Iceland	6	3			12	1		5	5		10	8			2		4	7	7				
Hungary	1	4			6			2	2			10			7		12	3	8	5			
Greece	3	4			12		7	6	6		5	2				1	8	10			10		
Germany		1			4			8	6		8						3	12		5	10	2	
France	1	1			10	2			7		3				12	4		3		8		6	5
Denmark		1	3		2			10			3	6			7		5	12		7		4	
Cyprus				8	7	1					5							4	3		8	6	12
Croatia			8			6		10	10	5							2	2	3		4	12	7
Bosnia & H		5			1				8		3	10			4			2	3	6	7	12	12
Belgium		10			12				1			6		1	7		8	2	3		4	12	2
Austria	12				4						10	10					8	8	7	3	6	2	5

99

Qualification: 1995 Winner plus 22 from 29 entries based on judged preselection

Rank	Start	Country	Artist	Song	Writer	Composer	POINTS
1	17	Ireland	Eimear Quinn	The voice	Brendan Graham	Brendan Graham	162
2	12	Norway	Elisabeth Andreasson	I evighet	Torhild Nigar	Torhild Nigar	114
3	23	Sweden	One More Time	Den vilda	Nanne Grönvall	Peter Grönvall	100
4	7	Croatia	Maja Blagdan	Sveta ljubav	Zrinko Tutic	Zrinko Tutic	98
5	11	Estonia	Ivo Linna & Maarja-Liis Ilus	Kaelakee hääl	Kaari Sillamaa	Priit Pajusaar	94
6	4	Portugal	Lúcia Moniz	O meu coração não tem cor	José Fanha	Pedro Osório	92
7	15	Netherlands	Maxine & Franklin Brown	De eerste keer	Peter van Asten, Piet Souer	Peter van Asten	78
8	2	United Kingdom	Gina G	Just a little bit	Simon Tauber	Steve Rodway	77
9	5	Cyprus	Constantinos	Mono gia mas	Rodoula Papalambrianou	Andreas Giorgallis	72
10	8	Austria	George Nußbaumer	Weil's Dr Guat Got	Mischa Krausz, George Nußbaumer	Mischa Krausz, George Nußbaumer	68
11	6	Malta	Miriam Christine	In a woman's heart	Alfred Sant	Paul Abela	68
12	1	Turkey	Sebnem Paker	Besinçi mevsim	Dr. Çuhaci	Levent Çoker	57
13	19	Iceland	Anna Mjöll	Sjúbidú	Anna Mjöll Ólafsdóttir, Ólafur Gaukur	Anna Mjöll Ólafsdóttir, Ólafur Gaukur	51
14	10	Greece	Marianna Efstratiou	Emis forame to himona anixiatika	Iro Trigoni	Costas Bigalis	36
15	20	Poland	Kasia Kowalska	Choce znac swój grzech	Kasia Kowalska	Robert Amirian	31
16	9	Switzerland	Cathy Leander	Mon coeur l'aime	Régis Mounir	Régis Mounir	22
17	16	Belgium	Lisa del Bo	Liefde is een kaartspel	Daniel Ditmar	John Terra, Sarah Brogden	22
18	22	Slovakia	Marcel Palonder	Kým nás máš	Jozef Urban	Juraj Burian	19
19	13	France	Dan Ar Braz et l'Héritage des Celtes	Diwanit bugale	Dan Ar Braz	Dan Ar Braz	18
20	3	Spain	Antonio Carbonell	¡Ay, qué deseo!	Ketama	Ketama	17
21	14	Slovenia	Regina	Dan najlepših sanj	Aleksander Kogoj	Aleksander Kogoj	16
22	21	Bosnia & H	Amila Glamocak	Za našu ljubav	Sinan Alimanovic, Aida Frijak, Adnan Bajramovic	Sinan Alimanovic, Aida Frijak, Adnan Bajramovic	13
23	18	Finland	Jasmine	Niin kaunis on taivas	Timo Niemi	Timo Niemi	9

1996 Eurovision 41: Oslo, Norway

	TOTAL	United Kingdom	Turkey	Switzerland	Sweden	Spain	Slovenia	Slovakia	Portugal	Poland	Norway	Netherlands	Malta	Ireland	Iceland	Greece	France	Finland	Estonia	Cyprus	Croatia	Bosnia & H	Belgium	Austria
Turkey	57	6		6		8						7	10				4	5	2		1	5	5	3
United Kingdom	77		3	4	6		6		12				6	3	4	5	8	3	7	1	7	10	12	
Spain	17		5										5			6			2	2	4	3		2
Portugal	92	2	5	10	4	7		4			6	6		1	10	5	5	3	12	12	10	1		1
Cyprus	72	12	10	5	2	10	10	3	3		12		2			12	2	6	5	6	8			2
Malta	68		10				12			6	1					8					12			12
Croatia	98	4	8	1	1	5	5	3	10	2	7	5	7	6	5	1	12			6			4	
Austria	68		4				3	1	5	8			12	8		2			1	7		6		
Switzerland	22	3						2				4		4	3			4					2	
Greece	36	7		2	3		8			1	3	1	1								10			
Estonia	94	10	5		12	4		8		10	8	3		2	12		1	12		7		3	8	5
Norway	114	8	2	7	10			10	2	4		10		7	8	10	7	7	5	3	5		8	8
France	18	1							1		4							2	3			7	
Slovenia	16					1									1						6	8		
Netherlands	78		1	3	8	6		5	7	7		2		5	2		10		4	1	5	2	1	12
Belgium	22	5				12						2							1					
Ireland	162		12	12	7		7	12	8	12		12	4			10	6	10	12	6	12	12	3	7
Finland	9										2				7									
Iceland	51	7			3	3	1	6	6	3	5	5		10		3	3	8	8	8			6	
Poland	31		7				2									7								4
Bosnia & H	13		6		2								3								3		7	
Slovakia	19			8			4	2	4		6		8			4								
Sweden	100			8							6	8		12	6		3	8	10	10			4	10

1997 Eurovision 42: Dublin, Ireland

3 May 1997

Qualification: The 25 countries with the best average scores in the last 5 years qualified.

Rank	Start	Country	Artist	Song	Writer	Composer	POINTS
1	24	United Kingdom	Katrina and The Waves	Love shine a light	Kimberley Rew	Kimberley Rew	227
2	5	Ireland	Marc Roberts	Mysterious woman	John Farry	John Farry	157
3	2	Turkey	Sebnem Paker & Group Etnic	Dinle	Mehtap Alnitemiz	Levent Çoker	121
4	9	Italy	Jalisse	Fiumi di parole	Carmen di Domenico, Alessandra Drusian	Fabio Ricci	114
5	1	Cyprus	Chara & Andreas Konstantinou	Mana mou	Constantina Konstantinou	Constantina Konstantinou	98
6	10	Spain	Marcos Llunas	Sin rencor	Marcos Llunas	Marcos Llunas	96
7	22	France	Fanny	Sentiments songes	Jean-Paul Dreau	Jean-Paul Dreau	95
8	13	Estonia	Maarja-Liis Ilus	Keelatud maa	Kaari Sillamaa	Harmo Kallaste	82
9	18	Malta	Debbie Scerri	Let me fly	Ray Agius	Ray Agius	66
10	6	Slovenia	Tanja Ribic	Zbudi se	Zoran Predin	Sašo Lošic	60
11	12	Poland	Anna Maria Jopek	Ale jestem	Magda Czapinska	Tomasz Lewandowski	54
12	19	Hungary	VIP	Miert kell, hogy elmenj?	Krisztina Bokor Fekete, Attila Kornyei	Viktor Rakonczai, Sandor Jozsa	39
13	17	Greece	Marianna Zorba	Horepse	Manolis Manouselis	Manolis Manouselis	39
14	16	Sweden	Blond	Bara hon älskar mig	Stephan Berg	Stephan Berg	36
15	20	Russia	Alla Pugachova	Primadonna	Alla Pugachova	Alla Pugachova	33
16	21	Denmark	Kølig Kaj	Stemmen i mit liv	Thomas Laegård	Lars Pedersen	25
17	23	Croatia	ENI	Probudi me	Alida Sarar	Davor Tolja	24
18	11	Germany	Bianca Shomburg	Zeit	Bernd Meinunger	Ralph Siegel	22
19	14	Bosnia & H	Alma Cardzic	Goodbye	Milic Vukasinovic	Sinan Alimanovic, Milic Vukasinovic	22
20	25	Iceland	Paul Oscar	Minn hinsti dans	Paul Oscar	Trausti Haraldsson, Paul Oscar	18
21	4	Austria	Bettina Soriat	One step	Ina Siber, Marc Berry	Marc Berry	12
22	7	Switzerland	Barbara Berta	Dentro di me	Barbara Berta	Barbara Berta	5
23	8	Netherlands	Mrs. Einstein	Niemand heeft nog tijd	Ed Hooijmans	Ed Hooijmans	5
24	15	Portugal	Célia Lawson	Antes do adeus	Rosa Lobato de Faria	Thilo Krassmann	0
25	3	Norway	Tor Endresen	San Francisco	Tor Endresen	Tor Endresen, Arne Myksvol	0

	Austria	Bosnia & H	Croatia	Cyprus	Denmark	Estonia	France	Germany	Greece	Hungary	Iceland	Ireland	Italy	Malta	Netherlands	Norway	Poland	Portugal	Russia	Slovenia	Spain	Sweden	Switzerland	Turkey	United Kingdom	**TOTAL**
Cyprus			4		7	1	4	5	12		12	3	4	7	10	2		3	1	4	10		4		5	**98**
Turkey	7	12				6	6	12	7	6	7	2	7	10	2			5	4		12	6	6		4	**121**
Norway																										**0**
Austria										5					3		1		3							**12**
Ireland	10	8	6	8	10	8	10	8		8			10		4	3	7	10	5	1	6	10	7	6	12	**157**
Slovenia		7	3	2		4	7		3		3			5			2	4	10					10		**60**
Switzerland													2								3					**5**
Netherlands														4										1		**5**
Italy	1	6	10	6	4			4	5	3	1	1			7		8	12	7	10	8	3	10	5	3	**114**
Spain				10	2		2	2	6	10		6	3	12	6		4	8	8	5			8	4		**96**
Germany	3		5							1			5	3									5			**22**
Poland	8	4			5	3	3	6	1	7			1		1	4		2		7	2					**54**
Estonia	6	1		1	8		8	7		4	2	8	12				6	1		3	4	1			10	**82**
Bosnia & H	4		1					3														4	2	8		**22**
Portugal																										**0**
Sweden					6						4	5				8				6					7	**36**
Greece			7	12										6		5			2		7					**39**
Malta		5	8	5	3		1		8			7	6			10					1			12		**66**
Hungary			2			5	5				5	4		2			5							3	8	**39**
Russia	5					7									8	1				12						**33**
Denmark									2		6					7						7	1		2	**25**
France		3		3	1	12			4	2	10	10			5	12	12	6	6	2		2	3	2		**95**
Croatia		2		4				1						8			3					5			1	**24**
United Kingdom	12	10	12	7	12	10	12	10	10	12	8	12	8	1	12	6	10	7	12	8	5	12	12	7		**227**
Iceland	2					2																8			6	**18**

1998 Eurovision 43: Birmingham, United Kingdom

Qualification: Four automatic qualifiers (UK, Germany, Spain, France), along with those countries who failed to qualify for 1997 plus FYR Macedonia, the remaining places being given to the countries with the best average scores over the last 5 years.

Rank	Start	Country	Artist	Song	Writer	Composer	POINTS
1	8	Israel	Dana International	Diva	Yoav Ginai	Tzvika Pik	176
2	16	United Kingdom	Imaani	Where are you?	Scott English, Simon Stirling, Phil Manikiza	Scott English, Simon Stirling, Phil Manikiza	166
3	10	Malta	Chiara	The one that I love	Sunny Aquilina	Jason Paul Cassar	165
4	18	Netherlands	Edsilia Rombley	Hemel en aarde	Eric van Tijn, Jochem Fluitsma	Eric van Tijn, Jochem Fluitsma	150
5	1	Croatia	Danijela	Neka mi ne svane	Petar Grašo, Remi Kasinoti	Petar Grašo, Remi Kasinoti	131
6	20	Belgium	Mélanie Cohl	Dis oui	Philippe Swan	Philippe Swan	122
7	9	Germany	Guildo Horn	Guildo hat euch lieb	Stefan Raab	Stefan Raab	86
8	22	Norway	Lars A. Fredriksen	Alltid sommer	Linda Andernach Johannesen	David Eriksen	79
9	13	Ireland	Dawn	Is always over now?	Gerry Morgan	Gerry Morgan	64
10	19	Sweden	Jill Johnson	Kärleken är	Ingela "Pling" Forsman	Bobby Ljunggren, Håkan Almqvist	53
11	17	Cyprus	Michael Hajiyanni	Genesis	Zenon Zindilis	Michael Hajiyanni	37
12	23	Estonia	Koit Toome	Mere lapsed	Peeter Pruuli	Maria and Tomi Rahula	36
13	14	Portugal	Alma Lusa	Se eu te pudesse abraçar	José Cid	José Cid	36
14	24	Turkey	Tüzmen	Unutamazsin	Canan Tunç	Erding Tunç	25
15	21	Finland	Edea	Aava	Tommy Mansikka-Aho	Alexi Ahoniemi	22
16	4	Spain	Mikel Herzog	¿Qué voy a hacer sin ti?	Mikel Herzog	Alberto Estébanez	21
17	7	Poland	Sixteen	To takie proste	Olga Pruszkowska	Jaroslaw Pruszkowski	19
18	12	Slovenia	Vili Resnik	Naj bogovi slišijo	Urša Vlašic	Matjaz Vlašic	17
19	25	FYR Macedonia	Vlado Janevski	Ne zori, zoro	Vlado Janevski	Grigor Koprov	16
20	2	Greece	Dionysia & Thalassa group	Mia krifi evaisthissia	Yiannis Malachias	Yiannis Valvis	12
21	6	Slovakia	Katarína Hasprová	Modlitba	Anna Wepperyová	Gabriel Dušík	8
22	15	Romania	Malina Olinescu	Eu cred	Liliana Stefan	Adrian Romcescu	6
23	11	Hungary	Charlie	A holnap már nem lesz szomorú	Attila Horváth	István Lehr	4
24	3	France	Marie-Line	Où aller	Marie-Line Marolany	Marie-Line Marolany, Jean-Philippe Dary, Micaël Sene, Moïse Crespy	3
25	5	Switzerland	Gunvor	Lass ihn	Gunvor Guggisberg	Gunvor Guggisberg, Egon Egemann	0

1998 Eurovision 43: Birmingham, United Kingdom

Voting country ↓ / Points to →	Croatia	Greece	France	Spain	Switzerland	Slovakia	Poland	Israel	Germany	Malta	Hungary	Slovenia	Ireland	Portugal	Romania	United Kingdom	Cyprus	Netherlands	Sweden	Belgium	Finland	Norway	Estonia	Turkey	FYR Macedonia
TOTAL	131	12	3	21	0	8	19	172	86	165	4	17	64	36	6	166	37	150	53	122	22	79	36	25	16
United Kingdom	2							5	6	12			8				3	10	1	7		4			
Turkey	4							5	12	10		3	8	6				7	2	1					
Switzerland	5			6				10	12	8		2					3	4		7		1			
Sweden	3							5		6			1			7		8		2	10	12	4		
Spain	1							10	12	5		6				3		4		7		8	2		
Slovenia	10							5	3	12			4	1		6		8		7		2			
Slovakia	12							7	8	3			1			5				6		10	2		4
Romania							10	7	6	5	1		8			12	4						2		3
Portugal	2							12	10	5			1			6	4	7		8		3			
Poland	6							10	8				2			7	5	3		12		4			1
Norway	6							3	12		2		4			5		8	10	7	1				
Netherlands	4							6	12	8						7			5	10		3	2		1
Malta	10							12	6			2				8	1	7	4	3		5			
Israel	10			3										2	6	12	1	8	4	5		7			
Ireland	3							6	8	12						5		2	10	7		4	1		
Hungary							2		7				6			10	1	12	8	3		5	4		
Greece	5							10	3	6		2		1		7	12	8		4					
Germany	10						5	7		8			2			1		6	3	4				12	
FYR Macedonia	12		2					8					7	4		10	3		6	1				5	
France	8			4			2	12		6		1		10		3	5			7					
Finland	3							10	1	5		4				8		7		6		2	12		
Estonia	3							7	1	5			2			8		10		6	12	4			
Cyprus	7	12	1	4				10	5							8		2		6		3			
Croatia				1		8		10		7		3	2			12		4						5	6
Belgium	5			3				7		8			1			6	2	12	10			4			

1999 Eurovision 44: Jerusalem, Israel

Qualification: Four automatic qualifiers (UK, Germany, Spain, France), along with those countries who failed to qualify for 1998, the remaining places being given to the countries with the best average scores over the last 5 years.

Rank	Start	Country	Artist	Song	Writer	Composer	POINTS
1	15	Sweden	Charlotte Nilsson	Take me to your heaven	Gert Lengstrand	Lars Diedricson	163
2	13	Iceland	Selma Björnsdóttir	All out of luck	Thorvaldur B. Thorvaldsson	S Björnsdóttir, T B. Thorvaldsson, S I. Baldvinsson	146
3	21	Germany	Sürpriz	Reise nach Jerusalem - Kudüs'e seyahat	Bernd Meinunger	Ralph Siegel	140
4	4	Croatia	Doris Dragovic	Marija Magdalena	Vjekoslava Huljic	Tonci Huljic	118
5	19	Israel	Eden	Yom huledeth	Moshe Datz, Gabriel Batler, Yaacov Lymay, Jacky Oved	Moshe Datz, Gabriel Batler, Yaacov Lymay, Jacky Oved	93
6	23	Estonia	Evelin Samuel and Camille	Diamond of night	Marian-Anna Kärmas & Kaari Sillamaa	Priit Pajusaar and Glen Pilvr	90
7	22	Bosnia & H	Dino and Beatrice	Putnici	Dino Dervišhalidovic	Dino Dervišhalidovic	86
8	9	Denmark	Trine Jepsen & Michael Teschl	This time (I mean it)	Ebbe Ravn	Ebbe Ravn	71
9	11	Netherlands	Marlayne	One good reason	Tjeerd Van Zanen and Alan Michael	Tjeerd Van Zanen and Alan Michael	71
10	18	Austria	Bobbie Singer	Reflection	Dave Moskin	Dave Moskin	65
11	6	Slovenia	Darja Svajger	For a thousand years	Primoz Peterca	Primoz Peterca	50
12	2	Belgium	Venessa Chinitor	Like the wind	Wim Claes, Emma Phillipa, Ilia Beyers, John Terra	Wim Claes, Emma Phillipa, Ilia Beyers, John Terra	38
13	5	United Kingdom	Precious	Say it again	Paul Varney	Paul Varney	38
14	8	Norway	Stig André Van Eijk	Living my life without you	Sem & Stig Van Eijk & Peter Brandt	Sem & Stig Van Eijk & Peter Brandt	35
15	20	Malta	Times 3	Believe 'n peace	Moira Stafrace	Chris Scicluna	32
16	7	Turkey	Tuba Önal & Grup Mystik	Dön artik	Canan Tunç	Erdinç Tunç	21
17	17	Ireland	The Mullans	When you need me	Bronagh Mullan	Bronagh Mullan	18
18	12	Poland	Mietek (Mieczyslaw) Szczesniak	Przytul mnie mocno	Wojciech Ziembicki	Seweryn Krajewski	17
19	10	France	Nayah	Je veux donner ma voix	Gilles Arcens & Luigi Rutigliano	Pascal Graczyk & René Colombies	14
20	1	Lithuania	Aiste Smilgeviciute	Strazdas	Sigitas Geda	Linas Rimša	13
21	14	Portugal	Marlain Angelidou	Tha'nai erotas	Andreas Karanikolas	George Kallis	13
22	16	Cyprus	Rui Bandeira	Como tudo começou	Tó Andrade	Jorge do Carmo	12
23	3	Spain	Lydia	No quiero escuchar	F R Fernández, A P Ramírez, A C Zamarreno, C L González	Fernando Rodriguez Fernández & Alejandro Piqueras Ramírez	1

1999 Eurovision 44: Jerusalem, Israel

29 May 1999

Final scoreboard — total points by country:

Country	TOTAL
Lithuania	13
Belgium	38
Spain	1
Croatia	118
United Kingdom	38
Slovenia	50
Turkey	21
Norway	35
Denmark	71
France	14
Netherlands	71
Poland	17
Iceland	146
Cyprus	2
Sweden	163
Portugal	12
Ireland	18
Austria	65
Israel	93
Malta	32
Germany	140
Bosnia & H	86
Estonia	90

2000 Eurovision 45: Stockholm, Sweden

13 May 2000

Qualification: Four automatic qualifiers (UK, Germany, Spain, France), along with those countries who failed to qualify for 1999, the remaining places being given to the countries with the best average scores over the last 5 years.

Rank	Start	Country	Artist	Song	Writer	Composer	POINTS
1	14	Denmark	Olsen Brothers	Fly on the wings of love	Jørgen Olsen	Jørgen Olsen	195
2	9	Russia	Alsou	Solo	Andrew Lane, Brandon Barnes	Andrew Lane, Brandon Barnes	155
3	21	Latvia	BrainStorm	My star	Renars Kaupers	Renars Kaupers	136
4	4	Estonia	Ines	Once in a lifetime	Jana Hallas	Pearu Paulus, Ilmar Laisaar, Alar Kotkas	98
5	15	Germany	Stefan Raab	Wadde hadde dudde da	Stefan Raab	Stefan Raab	96
6	23	Ireland	Eamonn Toal	Millennium of love	Raymond J. Smyth, Gerry Simpson	Raymond J. Smyth, Gerry Simpson	92
7	18	Sweden	Roger Pontare	When spirits are calling my name	Thomas Holmstrand, Linda Jansson, Peter Dahl	Thomas Holmstrand, Linda Jansson, Peter Dahl	88
8	7	Malta	Claudette Pace	Desire	Gerard James Borg	Philip Vella	73
9	17	Croatia	Goran Karan	Kada zaspu andeli	Nenad Nincevic	Zdenko Runjic	70
10	22	Turkey	Pınar Ayhan & S.O.S. band	Yorgunum anla	Sühan Ayhan, Pınar Ayhan, Orkun Yazgan	Sühan Ayhan, Pınar Ayhan, Orkun Yazgan	59
11	8	Norway	Charmed	My heart goes boom	Tore Madsen	Morten Henriksen	57
12	12	Iceland	Einar Ágúst Víðisson & Telma Ágústdóttir	Tell me! (Hvert sem er)	Sigurður Örn Jónsson	Örlygur Smári	45
13	2	Netherlands	Linda Wagenmakers	No goodbyes	John O'Hare	Ellert Driessen	40
14	24	Austria	The rounder girls	All to you	Dave Moskin	Dave Moskin	34
15	19	FYC Macedonia	XXL	100% te ljubam	Orce Zafirofski, Dragan Karanfilovski	Dragan Karanfilovski	29
16	3	United Kingdom	Nicki French	Don't play that song again	John Springate, Gary Shephard	John Springate, Gary Shephard	28
17	6	Romania	Taxi	The moon	Dan Teodorescu	Dan Teodorescu	25
18	13	Spain	Serafín Zubiri	Colgado de un sueño	José María Purón	José María Purón	18
19	20	Finland	Nina Åström	A little bit	Gerrit aan 't Goor	Luca Genta	18
20	16	Switzerland	Jane Bogaert	La vita cos'è?	Thomas Marin	Bernie Staub	14
21	11	Cyprus	Voice	Nomiza	Alexandros Panayi	Alexandros Panayi	8
22	1	Israel	Ping Pong	Same'akh	Roi Arad, Guy Asif, Ronen Ben Tal	Roi Arad, Guy Asif	7
23	5	France	Sofia Mestari	On aura le ciel	Pierre Legay	Benoît Heinrich	5
24	10	Belgium	Nathalie Sorce	Envie de vivre	Silvio Pezzuto	Silvio Pezzuto	2

13 May 2000

Receiving country	TOTAL	United Kingdom	Turkey	Switzerland	Sweden	Spain	Russia	Romania	Norway	Netherlands	Malta	Latvia	Israel	Ireland	Iceland	Germany	FYR Macedonia	France	Finland	Estonia	Denmark	Cyprus	Croatia	Belgium	Austria
Israel	7																1	6							
Netherlands	40		3			4					5	3	8	1	1	1		2				5		10	
United Kingdom	28		6					3			6	10	6							2		6	6		
Estonia	98	4	2		6			6	4	7	7			7	5	5			8		4	6			3
France	5						3			2							12						7		
Romania	25						6																		
Malta	73		5		3	1	8	7	2	1		4	3	3	7	3	8		6	1	3	8	8	1	2
Norway	57	3	10		7		8				3	6	7	4					7	3	7	12			
Russia	155	8	8	2	5	5		12	8		12	8	10	10	8	4	7	5	5	10	6	12	12	7	7
Belgium	2																2								
Cyprus	8										1						4			7			3		
Iceland	45			1	8		2	5	7	10	8	7	5		12					6	12				
Spain	18		1	10							8	12	12	12	12	12			12	8					
Denmark	195	12		10	12	10	12	1	10	10	8	8	12	12	12	7	3	7	10	8		1	1	10	8
Germany	96	5		12	2	12	10	8	3	8							3	1	2	12				6	2
Switzerland	14						5			6		2												1	
Croatia	70		8	6		2	10	8			4			6	4		6	8	6		10	4		5	6
Sweden	88	6	12	10		6		10	5				5				12	1	7	5	10			5	
FYR Macedonia	29						7	10												7		2	10		
Finland	18							4		5													7		
Latvia	136		1	7	10	7	1	1	12	12	8		4	8	10	7	3	3	12	12	8	1	1	12	8
Turkey	59	7		5	4		12		1	12		1	2	5		10	5	12	4		1	7	7	3	5
Ireland	92	10	7	8		3	4	2	6	3	10	5	2		2	2	3	4	1	4	5		5	4	4
Austria	34	1	4	4		8					2	5		2	3	2		4	3						

2001 Eurovision 46: Copenhagen, Denmark

12 May 2001

Qualification: Four automatic qualifiers (UK, Germany, Spain, France), along with those countries who failed to qualify for 2000, the remaining places being given to the countries with the best average scores over the last 5 years.

Rank	Start	Country	Artist	Song	Writer	Composer	POINTS
1	20	Estonia	Tanel Padar, Dave Benton & 2XL	Everybody	Maian-Anna Kärmas	Ivar Must	198
2	23	Denmark	Rollo & King	Never ever let you go	Stefan Nielsen	Søren Poppe	177
3	22	Greece	Antique	Die for you	Antonis Papas	Antonis Papas	147
4	14	France	Natasha Saint-Pier	Je n'ai que mon âme	Jill Kapler	Jill Kapler	142
5	7	Sweden	Friends	Listen to your heartbeat	Thomas G:son, Henrik Sethsson	Thomas G:son, Henrik Sethsson	100
6	13	Spain	David Civera	Dile que la quiero	Alejandro Abad	Alejandro Abad	76
7	17	Slovenia	Nuša Derenda	Energy	Lucienne Lonchina	Matjaz Vlasic	70
8	19	Germany	Michelle	Wer Liebe lebt	Eva Richter	Gino Trovatello, Matthias Stingl	66
9	21	Malta	Fabrizio Faniello	Another summer night	Georgina Abela	Paul Abela	48
10	10	Croatia	Vanna	Strings of my heart	Vjekoslava Huljic	Tonci Huljic	42
11	15	Turkey	Sedat Yüce	Sevgiliye son	Nurdan Güneri	Semih Güneri	41
12	6	Russia	Mumiy troll	Lady alpine blue	Ilia Lagoutenko	Ilia Lagoutenko	37
13	8	Lithuania	Skamp	You got style	Erica Quinn Jennings, Vilius Alesius, Viktoras Diawara	Viktoras Diawara, Linas Rimša	35
14	3	Bosnia & H	Nino	Hano	Nino Pršeš	Nino Pršeš	29
15	16	United Kingdom	Lindsay D.	No dream impossible	Russ Ballard, Chris Winter	Russ Ballard, Chris Winter	28
16	5	Israel	Tal Sondak	Ein davar	Shimrit Orr	Yair Klinger	25
17	11	Portugal	MTM	Só sei ser feliz assim	Marco Quelhas	Marco Quelhas	18
18	9	Latvia	Arnis Mednis	Too much	Gustavs Terzens, Arnis Mednis	Arnis Mednis	16
19	1	Netherlands	Michelle	Out on my own	André Remkes, Dirk Jan Vermeij	André Remkes, Dirk Jan Vermeij	16
20	18	Poland	Piasek	2 long	Andrzej Piaseczny	Robert Chojnacki	11
21	12	Ireland	Gary O'Shaughnessy	Without your love	Pat Sheridan	Pat Sheridan	6
22	2	Iceland	TwoTricky	Angel (Birta)	Einar Bárðarson	Einar Bárðarson, Magnus Thor Sigmundsson	3
23	4	Norway	Haldor Lægreid	On my own	Ole Henrik Antonsen, Tom-Steinar Hanssen, Ole Jørgen Olsen	Ole Henrik Antonsen, Tom-Steinar Hanssen	3

2001 Eurovision 46: Copenhagen, Denmark

12 May 2001

Receiving ↓ / Voting →	TOTAL	United Kingdom	Turkey	Sweden	Spain	Slovenia	Russia	Portugal	Poland	Norway	Netherlands	Malta	Lithuania	Latvia	Israel	Ireland	Iceland	Greece	Germany	France	Estonia	Denmark	Croatia	Bosnia & H
Netherlands	16					4	1	6							5									
Iceland	3									1												2		
Bosnia & H	29			4		7						1									7		10	
Norway	3							3																
Israel	25		7								6	2						5		10	4			
Russia	37			5									10	8	3	8	5		6	2	4	7		
Sweden	100	8	8		5		2	5	5	2		8	2	6	8	1	7		6	8	2	7	10	
Lithuania	35	4		1		2	10		10		5			5	4	1						2		
Latvia	16				6								8							5				8
Croatia	42		10			5						10							7	3				7
Portugal	18				6			1													12			
Ireland	6	5				1		7		4												1		
Spain	76	3	6	5		1		7	1	3	7	5		1	12		2	8		6		3	6	5
France	142	6	1	6	3	6	12	12	10	10	8	12	12	7	2	7	4	4			8	10	7	12
Turkey	41				1					7	3	4	1				4	3	10	7				
United Kingdom	28			7	1		3	2	2	2	2	3	3	3	3	6		6		2		5	3	10
Slovenia	70	8		2	2		4	2	6	6	4	4	5	4	4	1	2			4	4	6	8
Poland	11	2				3														5		1		
Germany	66	2	3		10	1	8	10	4	4	3	1	5	1	1		6		1		6	4	1	1
Estonia	198	12	12	8	8	12	6	6	12	10	12	12	12	12	6	10	10	12	8	10		12	2	8
Malta	48	1	2	3	4	8	7	7	8	5	8	7			2	7	5	3	3	1		6	6	1
Greece	147	7	5	12	12	8	10	5	8	8	12	6	7	6	10	5	12	8	6	8	3	5	5	12
Denmark	177	10	4	10	7	7	10	5	12	8	12	10	6	6	10	7	12	12	6	12	8		12	8

111

2002 Eurovision 47: Tallinn, Estonia   **25 May 2002**

Qualification: Four automatic qualifiers (UK, Germany, Spain, France), along with the top 15 from the other participants in 2001, plus those countries which failed to qualify for the 2001 contest and Israel and Latvia by invitation.

Rank	Start	Country	Artist	Song	Writer	Composer	POINTS
1	23	Latvia	Marie N	I wanna	Marija Naumova, Marats Samauskis	Marija Naumova	176
2	20	Malta	Ira Losco	7th wonder	Gerard James Borg	Philip Vella	164
3	2	United Kingdom	Jessica Garlick	Come back	Martyn Baylay	Martyn Baylay	111
4	8	Estonia	Sahléne	Runaway	Jana Hallas	Pearu Paulus, Ilmar Laisaar, Alar Kotkas	111
5	17	France	Sandrine François	Il faut du temps	Patrick Bruel, Marie-Florence Gros	Rick Allison	104
6	1	Cyprus	One	Gimme	George Theophanous	George Theophanous	85
7	5	Spain	Rosa	Europe's living a celebration	Xasqui Ten	Toni Ten	81
8	21	Romania	Monica Anghel & Marcel Pavel	Tell me why	Mirela Fugaru	Ionel Tudor	72
9	12	Sweden	Afro-dite	Never let it go	Marcos Ubeda	Marcos Ubeda	72
10	7	Russia	Prime minister	Northern girl	Karen Kavaleryan, Evgene Fridlyand, Irina Antonyan	Kim Breitburg	55
11	6	Croatia	Vesna Pisarovic	Everything I want	Milana Vlaovic	Milana Vlaovic	44
12	10	Israel	Sarit Hadad	Light a candle	Yoav Ginai	Tzvika Pik	37
13	15	Bosnia & H	Maja Tatic	Na jastuku za dvoje	Ružica Cavic, Stevo Cvikic	Dragan Mijatovic	33
14	16	Belgium	Sergio & the Ladies	Sister	Dirk Paelinck	Mark Paelinck	33
15	22	Slovenia	Sestre	Samo Ijubezen	Barbara Pešut	Robert Pešut	32
16	19	Turkey	Buket Bengisu & Saphire	Leylaklar soldu kalbinde	Sami Hodara, Figen Cakmak	Fani Hodara	29
17	4	Greece	Michalis Rakintzis	S.A.G.A.P.O.	Michalis Rakintzis	Michalis Rakintzis	27
18	3	Austria	Manuel Ortega	Say a word	Robert Pflugler	Alexander Kahr	26
19	9	FYR Macedonia	Karolina	Od nas zavisi	Vladimir Krstevski	Nikola Perevski	25
20	13	Finland	Laura	Addicted to you	Janina Frostell, Tracy Lipp	Maki Kolehmainen	24
21	18	Germany	Corinna May	I can't live without music	Bernd Meinunger	Ralph Siegel	17
22	11	Switzerland	Francine Jordi	Dans le jardin de mon âme	Francine Lehmann	Francine Lehmann	15
23	24	Lithuania	Aivaras	Happy You	Aivaras Stepukonis	Aivaras Stepukonis	12
24	14	Denmark	Malene	Tell me who you are	Michael Ronson	Michael Ronson	7

2002 Eurovision 47: Tallinn, Estonia

Receiving \ Voting	TOTAL	United Kingdom	Turkey	Switzerland	Sweden	Spain	Slovenia	Russia	Romania	Malta	Lithuania	Latvia	Israel	Greece	Germany	FYR Macedonia	France	Finland	Estonia	Denmark	Cyprus	Croatia	Bosnia & H	Belgium	Austria
Cyprus	**85**	3	2	6	1	6	4	6	8	12	4	8		12	8	4	1	4	4	6		10	7	3	12
United Kingdom	**111**		6	6	2		8	6		10		5	5	7	8	4	1	8	6				7	6	
Austria	**26**		12	7				1													1			5	
Greece	**27**			12				8	6												12		1		
Spain	**81**	2		5	7		12						6	4	7		12		10				6	12	
Croatia	**44**					12								5	3	5		3					2		
Russia	**55**	7	8		12		6		2		6	10	1	2	4			10	8		5	6	10		
Estonia	**111**		8				6		10	8	7	12	2			6		1	10	8		5	5	10	
FYR Macedonia	**25**		12				1		12	5									1			3	4		
Israel	**37**	5	1	1					5			3		5	5	5	10		5	1				2	
Switzerland	**15**	1				1	1		3			1			2		3								5
Sweden	**72**		4	7		7				1	10	4		1				7	7	10			12		4
Finland	**24**			10						1			4	3		1	10			5	3	2	3		
Denmark	**7**	1								1			4								1				
Bosnia & H	**33**				6	3	2	7		3	2			3	6	3				2		7			7
Belgium	**33**	4	10	10	3	1	3	7			2						2			4			8	10	
France	**104**	10		10	8	8	8	10	4	4	5	2	7	3	6	10		12	3	5	8	12	8		
Germany	**17**	3	3	3	2	2			1							12	2		1					1	
Turkey	**29**				4	4			7	7						8	7					3	3		
Malta	**164**	12	5	4	4	10	10	5	12	6	3	12	10	6	10	10	6	2	7	12	10	12		7	8
Romania	**72**		7	2		5	5	12		12	12	12	8	8	1	12	5				8		1		
Slovenia	**32**	6		2			7									2	4					8			2
Latvia	**176**	8	6	8	5	12	5	10	7	7	12		12	10	12	7	8	6	12	7	4	2	5	8	10
Lithuania	**12**							4				6							2						

Qualification: Four automatic qualifiers (UK, Germany, Spain, France), along with the top 15 from the other participants in 2002, plus those countries which failed to qualify for the 2002 contest and new entrant Ukraine.

Rank	Start	Country	Artist	Song	Writer	Composer	POINTS
1	4	Turkey	Sertab Erener	Everyway that I can	Demir Demirkan	Sertab Erener, Demir Demirkan	167
2	22	Belgium	Urban Trad	Sanomi	Yves Barbieux	Yves Barbieux	165
3	11	Russia	t.A.T.u.	Ne ver', ne boisia	Valeriy Polienko	Mars Lasar, Ivan Pogomalov	164
4	18	Norway	Jostein Hasselgård	I'm not afraid to move on	Arve Furset	Arve Furset	123
5	25	Sweden	Fame	Give me your love	Calle Kindbom, Carl Lösnitz	Calle Kindbom, Carl Lösnitz	107
6	2	Austria	Alf Poier	Weil der Mensch zählt	Alf Poier	Alf Poier	101
7	20	Poland	Ich Troje	Keine Grenzen - Zadnych granic	André Franke, J Horn-Bernges, Michal Wisniewski, Jacek Lagwa	André Franke, J Horn-Bernges, Michal Wisniewski, Jacek Lagwa	90
8	1	Iceland	Birgitta	Open your heart (Segðu mér allt)	Sveinbjörn Baldvinsson, Birgitta Haukdal	Hallgrímur Óskarsson	81
9	12	Spain	Beth	Dime	Amaya Martinez	Jesús-María Pérez	81
10	24	Romania	Nicola	Don't break my heart	Nicola	Mihai Alexandru	73
11	10	Germany	Lou	Let's get happy	Bernd Meinunger	Ralph Siegel	53
12	3	Ireland	Mickey Harte	We've got the world	Keith Molloy, Martin Brannigan	Keith Molloy, Martin Brannigan	53
13	14	Netherlands	Esther Hart	One more night	Alan Michael, Tjeerd van Zanen	Alan Michael, Tjeerd van Zanen	45
14	16	Ukraine	Olexandr	Hasta la vista	Mirit Shem-Ur	Tzvika Pik	30
15	8	Croatia	Claudia Beni	Više nisam tvoja	Andrej Babich	Andrej Babich	29
16	6	Bosnia & H	Mija Martina	Ne brini	Arjana Kunštek	Ines Prajo	27
17	17	Greece	Mando	Never let you go	Terry Siganos	Mando	25
18	19	France	Louisa Baileche	Monts et merveilles	Hocine Hallaf	Hocine Hallaf	19
19	13	Israel	Lior Narkis	Words for love	Yossi Gispan	Yoni Ro'en	17
20	9	Cyprus	Stelios Constantas	Feeling alive	Stelios Constantas	Stelios Constantas	15
21	23	Estonia	Ruffus	Eighties coming back	Vaiko Eplik	Vaiko Eplik	14
22	7	Portugal	Rita Guerra	Deixa-me sonhar	Paulo Martins	Paulo Martins	13
23	26	Slovenia	Karmen	Nanana	Karmen Stavec	Martin Stibernik	7
24	21	Latvia	F.L.Y.	Hello from Mars	Martin Freiman, Lauris Raynix	Martin Freiman, Lauris Raynix	5
25	5	Malta	Lynn Chirchop	To dream again	Cynthia Sammut	Alfred Zammit	4
26	15	United Kingdom	Jemini	Cry baby	Martin Isherwood	Martin Isherwood	0

2003 Eurovision 48: Riga, Latvia

24 May 2003

The table below records the points awarded by each voting country (columns) to each participating country (rows), together with each country's TOTAL score.

Contestant	TOTAL	United Kingdom	Ukraine	Turkey	Sweden	Spain	Slovenia	Russia	Romania	Portugal	Poland	Norway	Netherlands	Malta	Latvia	Israel	Ireland	Iceland	Greece	Germany	France	Estonia	Cyprus	Croatia	Bosnia & H	Belgium	Austria
Iceland	81	8	4	8	7	8	4	7		10	1	12	6	12	3	7	7		1	1	1	1	5	6	5	3	12
Austria	101	8		6	6	8	7	6	1	7	2	8	8	5	4	1	2	10	12	2	10	6	4	5	12	2	7
Ireland	53	12	1	5	8	3	2	5	5	8	5	6	12	4	1	10	6	2	7	10	6	12	7	4	12	1	5
Turkey	167	7	2	12	8	3	10	10	2	1	4	10	12	2	2	7	4	3	7	10	7	10	8	7	10	12	8
Malta	4								10	1				4			3										
Bosnia & H	27		3	12															8				6				7
Portugal	13					2					5			7			2	6	1		6						
Croatia	29			3			8										6		12				1	6			5
Cyprus	15	4			10	4		7	1					2		1			5				12				
Germany	53		7	10	2	6	12	1	7	4	4	2	1	3	2	10	4	8	8	8	4	7	2	10	3	7	1
Russia	164		12	2	4	1		6	5	4	4	5	1	1	12	12	12	4	10	8	5	7	12	6	7	10	8
Spain	81		2		4	5	1	6	12	12		10	5	7	8	12	2	6	5		3	8	1				10
Israel	17	1			5	1	10	5				5		7			5		3						2	8	
Netherlands	45																5	5								
United Kingdom	0																										
Ukraine	30			4				8			10		10		5	4					3			2	8	
Greece	25							1	2								1		12	5			12	12		
Norway	123	4	7		12	4	5	4	3	5	6	1	7	6	7	3	1	12	7	7	3	10		10		6	2
France	19								6	2	3						8					4			8		
Poland	90	2	8		3	5			4	8	12	4	4	10	8	8		7	8	6	12	5	4	6		5	10
Latvia	5																	1				5				
Belgium	165	5	10	7		12	3	3	8	6	12	3	10	6	10	8	10	7	8	6	5	12	3	10	10	4	4
Estonia	14	3		1				2			8	1	3			1	8	1		4					7		
Romania	73		6	1	1	10	6	12	12	3	7			8		6				4	1	2	2	1	1	7	6
Sweden	107	10	5			7	6		12	3	7	7	3	8	6		5	5		3			7	2	3	5	3
Slovenia	7																							3	4		

115

Rank	Start	Country	Artist	Song	Writer	Composer	POINTS
1Q	20	Serbia & Mont	Željko Joksimović	Lane moje	Leontina Vukmanoviæ	Željko Joksimović	263
2Q	11	Ukraine	Ruslana	Wild dances	Alexander Ksenofontov	Ruslana Lyzchicko	256
3Q	10	Greece	Sakis Rouvas	Shake it	Nektarios Tirakis	Nikos Terzis	238
4Q	13	Albania	Anjeza Shahini	The image of you	Agim Doçit	Edmon Zhulali	167
5Q	14	Cyprus	Lisa Andreas	Stronger every minute	Mike Konnaris	Mike Konnaris	149
6Q	22	Netherlands	Re-union	Without you	Angeline van Otterdijk	Ed van Otterdijk	146
7Q	21	Bosnia & H	Deen	In the Disco	Vesna Pisarovic	Vesna Pisarovic	133
8Q	8	Malta	Julie & Ludwig	On again...off again	Gerard James Borg	Philip Vella	74
9Q	18	Croatia	Ivan Mikulic	You are the only one	Duško Gruborovic & Marina Madrinic	Ivan Mikulic	72
10Q	15	FYR Macedonia	Tose Proeski	Life	Tose Proeski	Tose Proeski	71
11	5	Israel	David D'or	Le'ha'amin	David D'or	David D'or	57
12	17	Estonia	Neiokõsõ	Tii	Aapo Ilves	Priit Pajusaar, Glen Pilvre	57
13	19	Denmark	Tomas Thordarson	Shame on you	Ivar Lind Greiner	Ivar Lind Greiner	56
14	1	Finland	Jari Sillanpää	Takes 2 to tango	Jari Sillanpää	Mika Toivanen	51
15	7	Portugal	Sofia	Foi Magia	Paulo Neves	Paulo Neves	38
16	12	Lithuania	Linas ir Simona	What's happened to your love	Camden MS	Michalis Antonio, Linas Adomaitis	26
17	4	Latvia	Fomins & Kleins	Dziesma par laimi	Tomass Kleins	Guntars Racs	23
18	6	Andorra	Marta Roure	Jugarem a estimar-nos	Jofre Bardagí	Jofre Bardagí	12
19	2	Belarus	Aleksandra & Konstantin	My Galileo	Aleksey Solomaha	Aleksandra & Konstantin	10
20	9	Monaco	Maryon	Notre planète	Philippe Bosco	Philippe Bosco	10
21	16	Slovenia	Platin	Stay forever	Diana Lecnik	Simon Gomilsek	5
22	3	Switzerland	Piero Esteriore & the Music Stars	Celebrate	Greg Manning	Greg Manning	0

2004 Eurovision 49: Istanbul, Turkey

Semi-final: 12 May 2004

Receiving country	TOTAL	United Kingdom	Ukraine	Turkey	Switzerland	Sweden	Spain	Slovenia	Serbia & Mont	Russia	Romania	Portugal	Poland	Norway	Netherlands	Monaco	Malta	Lithuania	Latvia	Israel	Ireland	Iceland	Greece	Germany	FYR Macedonia	France	Finland	Estonia	Denmark	Cyprus	Croatia	Bosnia & H	Belgium	Belarus	Austria	Andorra	Albania
Finland	51					8								3		6						3	5		2			7		6			1		3		7
Belarus	10		5																2			1						2									
Switzerland	0																																				
Latvia	23															2		6		2	4							5						4			
Israel	57	2		4					3		5	7			2	6	6													8		7	2	3	1		
Andorra	12						12																														
Portugal	38				7	6	6				8					1				6		2	1		4					5			4			12	
Malta	74	5	2			4		1				4			3			7	7	6	1	2	1		4			10	4		2	4	1		1	5	
Monaco	10				7																									4				2	4		2
Greece	238	12	10	12	3	4	7	4	10		8	8		5	6	4	12	8	6	12	2	6		7	7			4	3	12	6	6	8	8	5	8	12
Ukraine	256	7		8	2	6	8	8	8		7	12		7	7	5	10	12	10	10	10	10		6	8		8	12	6	10	8	7	8	12	12	10	3
Lithuania	26																3		8	1	3		2							7			2	2			
Albania	167	6	1	6	10	7	2	5	6		2	2		8	5	3	8		5	8	5	4	8	12	12		6	1		1	7	6	5		7	6	
Cyprus	149	10	7	5	1		1	3	2		3	3		4	10	12	5	4	3	3	8	8	12	4			7	6			2	2	6	6	6	10	2
FYR Macedonia	71		3	3	2	2	5	6	12		4			1	1		1		4		12		4						1	5	5	8			2		8
Slovenia	5																								1						3						
Estonia	57	1	3	1		1		7	4		5	5		1	4		7	3	12		7			5	6		12		3	5			5	7		1	1
Croatia	72	8	8	6	6				5		1	1				10		1	1			5	5				1		3	10		10	12	7	8		
Denmark	56			1	2	5					2	10		6	12		4			8		12		5			4	3		10	3			10			
Serbia & Mont	263	8	12	7	12	12	8	12			10	10		12	12	7	4	1	4	8	6	12	12	7	10		10		4	10	12	12	5	10	12	12	4
Bosnia & H	133	4	12	10	8	10		10	7					8	8	8	7		2	4	7	5		2	5		10		12	5	10		12	3	10	10	10
Netherlands	146	3	4	2			5	2	1		3	6		2		8	8	5		2	12	5	6	3	3			8		8	5	4	12	5	5	2	7

Note: France, Poland & Russia chose not to vote in the semi-final

117

2004 Eurovision 49: Istanbul, Turkey

Final: 12 May 2004

Final qualification rules:
Top 10 countries from the 2003 Final
Top 10 countries from the 2004 Semi-Final

Automatic qualification:
United Kingdom, France, Germany, Spain

Rank	Start	Country	Artist	Song	Writer	Composer	POINTS
1	10	Ukraine	Ruslana	Wild dances	Alexander Ksenofontov	Ruslana Lyzchicko	280
2	5	Serbia & Mont	Željko Joksimović	Lane moje	Leontina Vukmanoviæ	Željko Joksimoviæ	263
3	16	Greece	Sakis Rouvas	Shake it	Nektarios Tirakis	Nikos Terzis	252
4	22	Turkey	Athena	For Real	Gökhan & Hakan Özoğuz	Gökhan & Hakan Özoğuz	195
5	21	Cyprus	Lisa Andreas	Stronger every minute	Mike Konnaris	Mike Konnaris	170
6	24	Sweden	Lena Philipsson	It Hurts	Thomas Orup Eriksson	Thomas Orup Eriksson	170
7	9	Albania	Anjeza Shahini	The image of you	Agim Doçit	Edmon Zhulali	106
8	8	Germany	Max (Maximilian Mutzke)	Can't Wait Until Tonight	Stefan Raab	Stefan Raab	93
9	12	Bosnia & H	Deen	In the Disco	Vesna Pisarovic	Vesna Pisarovic	91
10	1	Spain	Ramón	Para Llenarme De Ti	Kike Santander	Kike Santander	87
11	14	Russia	Julia Savicheva	Believe Me	Brenda Loring	Maxim Fadeev	67
12	6	Malta	Julie & Ludwig	On again...off again	Gerard James Borg	Philip Vella	50
13	11	Croatia	Ivan Mikulic	You are the only one	Duško Gruborovic &	Ivan Mikulic	50
14	15	FYR Macedonia	Tose Proeski	Life	Tose Proeski	Tose Proeski	47
15	4	France	Jonatan Cerrada	A Chaque Pas	Jonatan Cerrada, Benjamin Robbins, Steve Balsamo	Jonatan Cerrada, Benjamin Robbins, Steve Balsamo	40
16	20	United Kingdom	James Fox	Hold On To Our Love	Gary Miller and Tim Woodcock	Gary Miller and Tim Woodcock	29
17	19	Poland	Blue Cafe	Love Song	Tatiana Okupnik	Pawel Rurak-Sokal	27
18	23	Romania	Sanda Ladosi	I Admit	Irina Gligor	George Popa	18
19	17	Iceland	Jónsi	Heaven	Magnús Þór Sigmundsson	Sveinn Rúnar Sigurðsson	16
20	7	Netherlands	Re-union	Without you	Angeline van Otterdijk	Ed van Otterdijk	11
21	2	Austria	Tie Break	Du Bist	Peter Zimmermann	Peter Zimmermann	9
22	13	Belgium	Xandee	1 Life	Dirk Paelinck	Marc Paelinck	7
23	18	Ireland	Chris Doran	If My World Stopped Turning	Brian McFadden, Jonathan Shorten	Brian McFadden, Jonathan Shorten	7
24	3	Norway	Knut Anders Sørum	High	Dan Attlerud	Thomas Thörnholm, Lars Andersson	3

2004 Eurovision 49: Istanbul, Turkey

Final: 12 May 2004

The table below records the points each voting country (columns) awarded to each receiving country (rows). The small italic figure beside each voting country is its *Order votes announced*. Blank cells indicate no points awarded.

Receiving \ Voting	UK (16)	Ukraine (36)	Turkey (35)	Switzerland (7)	Sweden (33)	Spain (13)	Slovenia (34)	Serbia & Mont (8)	Russia (32)	Romania (31)	Portugal (30)	Poland (29)	Norway (28)	Netherlands (27)	Monaco (24)	Malta (26)	Lithuania (22)	Latvia (23)	Israel (20)	Ireland (19)	Iceland (21)	Greece (17)	Germany (10)	FYR Macedonia (25)	France (15)	Finland (14)	Estonia (12)	Denmark (11)	Cyprus (9)	Croatia (18)	Bosnia & H (4)	Belgium (5)	Belarus (6)	Austria (3)	Andorra (1)	Albania (2)	TOTAL
Spain			2	6			12		4	5	12	1		4	3	3			8		1		2	1	8				7			7	2		12		87
Austria																																7	2				9
Norway					3																																3
France			4		4				4		2				12					4			7									10			7		40
Serbia & Mont	7	12	8	12	12	6	12		10	8	7	5	6	10	1	6	2	5	7	3	7	8	10	10	10	10	1	7	12	7	12	3	7	12	2	12	263
Malta			2								1	3						6	6					3		6	3			8	1	8	6	8	6	3	50
Netherlands		2														2																					11
Germany	2			10											7		1		4						7		2			3		1	8	2	10	2	93
Albania		12					3	8		1		6	3	1		10		1	2	4	4		5	12	1	3		4		6	4	1		5		5	106
Ukraine	5		6	7	10	8	4	10	12	6	10	12	7	7	6	8	12	12	12	2	12	7	5	8	2	8	12	5	8	8	6	5	10	4	10	10	280
Croatia		7		3	8	8	5	10	5														1	5			10	12			10	5	5		3		50
Bosnia & H			7	5	8	10	5	5					2	5	4		6	6	6			6		4		1	8									10	91
Belgium													10																1					12			7
Russia		10	4	1		1										1	8	10				2							6			12					67
FYR Macedonia	6	3	12	4				12		12																				5	8	8				12	47
Greece	12	8	10	4	4	7	6	7	7	6	6	7	2	6	10	12	5	7	10	5	6		7	7	5	6	7	6	12	12	5	8	6	2	8	12	252
Iceland		12							2			8	5	12	5										12	2		2									16
Ireland																					7																7
Poland		5			1	1	3	6	1	2	2	4	4	8	2	4	7	8	3	8	2	4	4	8			4		2				1				27
United Kingdom		4	1	7	2	3	1	3	1	3		2	4		1	5	3	3	2	10	2	4	8	2	3	5	4	6					1				29
Cyprus	4	1	12	2	6	1	3	3	6	3	3	4	8	8	2	7	4	4	3	10	2	12	8	2	5	12	6	6			5	4	4	6	4	2	170
Turkey	6	4		8	5	2	1	10	8	10		8	8	12	8	5	6	2	5	1	5	6	12	6	12	5		10	3	7	12	2	3	8	6	8	195
Romania	6	6				10	2				4								1									3								3	18
Sweden	8	2	3			5	2	4	3	7	5	10	12			5	6	8		12	8		3	3	3	12		12	5		2	2	4	1	5	4	170

119

2005 Eurovision 50: Kiev, Ukraine

Semi-final: 19 May 2005

Rank	Start	Country	Artist	Song	Writer	Composer	POINTS
1Q	14	Romania	Luminita Anghel & Sistem	Let me try	Cristian Faur	Cristian Faur	235
2Q	4	Moldova	Zdob si Zdub	Boonika bate toba	Zdob si Zdub	Zdob si Zdub	207
3Q	24	Denmark	Jakob Sveistrup	Talking to you	Jacob Launbjerg & Andreas Mørck	Jacob Launbjerg & Andreas Mørck	185
4Q	20	Croatia	Boris Novkovic & Lado members	Vukovi umiru sami	Boris Novkoviæ	Franjo Valentiæ	169
5Q	15	Hungary	NOX	Forogj világ	Attila Valla	Szabolcs Harmath	167
6Q	13	Norway	Wig Wam	In my dreams	Trond "Teeny" Holter	Trond "Teeny" Holter	164
7Q	7	Israel	Shiri Maymon	Hasheket shenish'ar	Eyal Shachar & Pini Aronbayev	Pini Aronbayev	158
8Q	19	Switzerland	Vanilla Ninja	Cool vibes	David Brandes	David Brandes	114
9Q	17	FYR Macedonia	Martin Vucic	Make my day	Ognen Nedelkovski	Dragan Vucić	97
10Q	5	Latvia	Walter & Kazha	The war is not over	Martins Freimanis	Martins Freimanis	85
11	25	Poland	Ivan & Delfin	Czarna dziewczyna	Ivan Komarenko & Pawel Radziszewski	Lukasz Lazer	81
12	23	Slovenia	Omar Naber	Stop	Ursa Vlašič	Omar Naber	69
13	8	Belarus	Angelica Agurbash	Love me tonight	Nektarios Tyrakis	Nikos Terzis	67
14	22	Ireland	Donna and Joseph McCaul	Love?	Karl Broderick	Karl Broderick	53
15	9	Netherlands	Glennis Grace	My impossible dream	Bruce Smith	Robert D. Fisher	53
16	10	Iceland	Selma	If I had your love	Linda Thompson	Thorvaldur Bjarni Thorvaldsson, Vignir Snær Vigfússon	52
17	3	Portugal	2B	Amar	Jose da Ponte, Alexandre Honrado, Ernesto Leite	Jose da Ponte, Alexandre Honrado, Ernesto Leite	51
18	16	Finland	Geir Rönning	Why	Steven Stewart	Mika Toivanen	50
19	21	Bulgaria	Kaffe	Lorraine	Vesselin Ivanov, Orlin Pavlov	Vesselin Ivanov	49
20	12	Estonia	Suntribe	Let's get loud	Sven Lõhmus	Sven Lõhmus	31
21	1	Austria	Global.Kryner	Y así	Christof Spörk	Christof Spörk, Edi Köhldorfer	30
22	11	Belgium	Nuno Resende	Le grand soir	Alec Mansion & Frédéric Zeitoun	Alec Mansion & Frédéric Zeitoun	29
23	18	Andorra	Marian van de Wal	La mirada interior	Rafah Tanit, Daniel Aragay & Rafa Fernández	Rafah Tanit	27
24	6	Monaco	Lise Darly	Tout de moi	Phil Bosco	Didier Fabre	22
25	2	Lithuania	Laura and the Lovers	Little by little	Billy Butt	Bobby Ljunggren	17

	Albania	Andorra	Austria	Belarus	Belgium	Bosnia & H	Bulgaria	Croatia	Cyprus	Denmark	Estonia	Finland	France	FYR Macedonia	Germany	Greece	Hungary	Iceland	Ireland	Israel	Latvia	Lithuania	Malta	Moldova	Monaco	Netherlands	Norway	Poland	Portugal	Romania	Russia	Serbia & Mont	Slovenia	Spain	Sweden	Switzerland	Turkey	Ukraine	United Kingdom	**TOTAL**
Austria	5	7													1	1																	10			6				**30**
Lithuania																			5		8																		4	**17**
Portugal					10								12		12																			5		12				**51**
Moldova	3		8	10	4	6	6	4	8		5	3	5	10		6	6	8	3	10	10	10					1	6	8	12	12	6	7	1			12	12	5	**207**
Latvia				7				7	2	5	10							2	6	6		12	12				3		4		1		6					2		**85**
Monaco		10											10											2																**22**
Israel	7	12		12	3		4		3	4		1	8	1	3		5		7			2	6	5	12	10		4	6	8	8	3		4		3	6	5	6	**158**
Belarus							12		7					6		8				2	3	3	7		1			1			10						3	4		**67**
Netherlands		5			12					6									4	5			8		8					1						2			2	**53**
Iceland		6								10			2							4				10			8							2	7				3	**52**
Belgium	1												7											3		6			12											**29**
Estonia										3		6					1		1		12	5		1									2							**31**
Norway	2		2	5	2	7	2		4	12	6	12		2		4		12	10	7	6	6	3	8		2		7	1	7		4	3		8	5	2	6	7	**164**
Romania		4	10	3	8	5	5	1	12	7	1	4	6	5	7	12	12	5	8	12			10	12	7	8	7	8	10		3	5	1	12	5	4	7	1	8	**235**
Hungary		1	7	4	6	3	7	8	6	1	4	5	4	4		5		7		8	5		2				6	12	7	10	7	8	4	3	3	1	8	10	1	**167**
Finland		3								8	8				4										6	1	10								10					**50**
FYR Macedonia	12		4			10	10	12							2										3	3				4		10	8		1	8	10			**97**
Andorra	6																							4		7								10						**27**
Switzerland			1	8		2	3	3	5	2	12	10		3	6	3	3	6	2	3	7	8	1		2		2	5	2	2	2	2	5		4					**114**
Croatia	10		12	1	1	12	8				3	2		12	10		8	4			4	4		6	5	4	4	3	3	6		12	12		6	10		7		**169**
Bulgaria	4					1			10					8		7								7								1		6			5			**49**
Ireland		2				4	1	5	1		2						10						5					2		5							4		12	**53**
Slovenia	8		3	2		8		10				7		7			2	1		1					4						6	7						3		**69**
Denmark		8	6		7			6			7	8	1		5	2	7	10	12		2	7	4		10	12	12	10	5	3	4			8	12	7			10	**185**
Poland			5		5			2					3		8	10	4	3			1	1				5	5				5			7	2		1	8		**75**

Final qualification rules:
Top 10 countries from the 2004 Final
Top 10 countries from the 2005 Semi-Final

Automatic qualification:
United Kingdom, France, Germany, Spain

Rank	Start	Country	Artist	Song	Writer	Composer	POINTS
1	19	Greece	Helena Paparizou	My number one	Christos Dantis & Natalia Germanou	Christos Dantis	230
2	3	Malta	Chiara	Angel	Chiara Siracusa	Chiara Siracusa	192
3	4	Romania	Luminita Anghel & Sistem	Let me try	Cristian Faur	Cristian Faur	158
4	11	Israel	Shiri Maymon	Hasheket shenish'ar	Eyal Shachar & Pini Aronbayev	Pini Aronbayev	154
5	23	Latvia	Walter & Kazha	The war is not over	Martins Freimanis	Martins Freimanis	153
6	7	Moldova	Zdob si Zdub	Boonika bate toba	Zdob si Zdub	Zdob si Zdub	148
7	12	Serbia & Mont	No Name	Zauvijek moja	Milan Peric	Slaven Knezovic	137
8	22	Switzerland	Vanilla Ninja	Cool vibes	David Brandes	David Brandes	128
9	5	Norway	Wig Wam	In my dreams	Trond "Teeny" Holter	Trond "Teeny" Holter	125
10	13	Denmark	Jakob Sveistrup	Talking to you	Jacob Launbjerg & Andreas Mørck	Jacob Launbjerg & Andreas Mørck	125
11	18	Croatia	Boris Novkovic & Lado members	Vukovi umiru sami	Boris Novkoviæ	Franjo Valentiæ	115
12	1	Hungary	NOX	Forogj világ	Attila Valla	Szabolcs Harmath	97
13	6	Turkey	Gülseren	Rimi rimi ley	Göksan Arman	Erdinç Tunç	92
14	21	Bosnia & H	Feminnem	Call me	Andrej Babic	Andrej Babic	79
15	20	Russia	Natalia Podolskaya	Nobody hurt no one	M.S. Applegate, J.P. Chase	Victor Drobysh	57
16	8	Albania	Ledina Celo	Tomorrow I go	Pandi Laço	Adi Hila	53
17	15	FYR Macedonia	Martin Vucic	Make my day	Ognen Nedelkovski	Dragan Vucic	52
18	9	Cyprus	Constantinos Christoforou	Ela ela	Constantinos Christoforou	Constantinos Christoforou	46
19	16	Ukraine	Greenjolly	Razom nas bahato	Greenjolly	Greenjolly	30
20	14	Sweden	Martin Stenmarck	Las Vegas	Niklas Edberger, Johan Fransson, Tim Larsson & Tobias Lundgren	Niklas Edberger, Johan Fransson, Tim Larsson & Tobias Lundgren	30
21	10	Spain	Son de sol	Brujería	Alfredo Panebianco	Alfredo Panebianco	28
22	2	United Kingdom	Javine	Touch my fire	Javine Hilton & John Themis	Javine Hilton & John Themis	18
23	24	France	Ortal	Chacun pense à soi	Saad Tabainet, Ortal	Saad Tabainet, Ortal	11
24	17	Germany	Gracia	Run & hide	John O'Flynn	David Brandes, Jane Tempest	4

Final: 21 May 2005

Results (finalists, in the order shown, with total points):

Country	TOTAL
Hungary	97
United Kingdom	18
Malta	192
Romania	158
Norway	125
Turkey	92
Moldova	148
Albania	53
Cyprus	46
Spain	28
Israel	154
Serbia & Mont	137
Denmark	125
Sweden	30
FYR Macedonia	52
Ukraine	30
Germany	4
Croatia	115
Greece	230
Russia	57
Bosnia & H	79
Switzerland	128
Latvia	153
France	11

Voting countries and order votes announced:

Country	Order votes announced
United Kingdom	17
Ukraine	31
Turkey	21
Switzerland	37
Sweden	29
Spain	25
Slovenia	14
Serbia & Mont	27
Russia	35
Romania	19
Portugal	3
Poland	15
Norway	20
Netherlands	6
Monaco	4
Moldova	22
Malta	18
Lithuania	2
Latvia	38
Israel	26
Ireland	13
Iceland	7
Hungary	16
Greece	34
Germany	32
FYR Macedonia	30
France	39
Finland	10
Estonia	9
Denmark	28
Cyprus	24
Croatia	33
Bulgaria	12
Bosnia & H	36
Belgium	8
Belarus	5
Austria	1
Andorra	11
Albania	23

2006 Eurovision 51: Athens, Greece

Semi-final: 18 May 2006

Rank	Start	Country	Artist	Song	Writer	Composer	POINTS
1Q	16	Finland	Lordi	Hard rock hallelujah	Mr. Lordi	Mr. Lordi	292
2Q	22	Bosnia & H	Hari Mata Hari	Lejla	Fahrudin Pecikoza & Dejan Ivanović	Željko Joksimović	267
3Q	13	Russia	Dima Bilan	Never let you go	Karen Kavaleryan, Irina Antonyan	Alexandr Lunyov	217
4Q	20	Sweden	Carola	Invincible	Thomas G:son, Carola Häggkvist	Thomas G:son, Bobby Ljunggren, Henrik Wikström	214
5Q	18	Lithuania	LT United	We are the winners	Andrius Mamontovas, Viktoras Diawara	Andrius Mamontovas, Saulius Urbonavicius	163
6Q	1	Armenia	André	Without your love	Catherine Bekian	Armen Martirosyan	150
7Q	15	Ukraine	Tina Karol	Show me your love	Tina Karol	Tina Karol	146
8Q	14	Turkey	Sibel Tüzün	Superstar	Sibel Tüzün	Sibel Tüzün	91
9Q	8	Ireland	Brian Kennedy	Every song is a cry for love	Brian Kennedy	Brian Kennedy	79
10Q	11	FYR Macedonia	Elena Risteska	Ninanajna	Rade Vrcakovski	Darko Dimitrov	76
11	12	Poland	Ich Troje	Follow my heart	Michael Wisnieski, Real McCoy, William Lennox	André Franke	70
12	7	Belgium	Kate Ryan	Je t'adore	Kate Ryan, Niklas Bergwall, Niclas Kings, Lisa Greene	Kate Ryan, Niklas Bergwall, Niclas Kings, Lisa Greene	69
13	23	Iceland	Silvia Night	Congratulations	Ágústa Eva Erlendsdóttir & Gaukur Úlfarsson	Þorvaldur Bjarni Þorvaldsson	62
14	6	Albania	Luiz Ejlli	Zjarr e ftohtë	Floran Kondi	Klodian Qafoku	58
15	9	Cyprus	Annet Artani	Why angels cry	Peter Yiannakis	Peter Yiannakis	57
16	3	Slovenia	Anžej Dežan	Mr. Nobody	Ursa Vlašić	Matjaz Vlašić	49
17	2	Bulgaria	Mariana Popova	Let me cry	Elina Gavrilova	Dani Milev	36
18	21	Estonia	Sandra	Through my window	Jana Hallas	Pearu Paulus, Ilmar Laisaar, Alar Kotkas	28
19	19	Portugal	Nonstop	Coisas de nada	José Manuel Afonso, Elvis Veiguinha	José Manuel Afonso, Elvis Veiguinha	26
20	17	Netherlands	Treble	Amambanda	Treble	Treble	22
21	10	Monaco	Séverine Ferrer	La coco-dance	J. Woodfeel, Iren Bo	J. Woodfeel, Iren Bo	14
22	5	Belarus	Polina Smolova	Mum	Andrey Kostiugov	Sergey Sukhomlin	10
23	4	Andorra	Jennifer	Sense tu	Joan Antoni Rechi	Rafael Artesero Herrero	8

Giving country	Armenia	Bulgaria	Slovenia	Andorra	Belarus	Albania	Belgium	Ireland	Cyprus	Monaco	FYR Macedonia	Poland	Russia	Turkey	Ukraine	Finland	Netherlands	Lithuania	Portugal	Sweden	Estonia	Bosnia & H	Iceland
United Kingdom	3					2		8	7			1			12		10		6	4		4	5
Ukraine	7		2		1			8					10	12		6	6	5		4		8	
Turkey	10	1		3		3					8		4			7	6	5	2		12	12	
Switzerland	3			8		10	2		1		6			8			5			7		12	
Sweden	3	5				2	5	1			8		7			12		4			8	10	6
Spain	12			8		2					4				3	10	10	7	1			6	6
Slovenia						1	5	3			8	4			2	10	6				12	2	
Serbia & Mont	12	7				6	1	1			10		6	4	5	8	8	3			12	2	
Russia	12					6	2	1			5				8	10	8	4			7		
Romania	2								4		1		7	10	8	5	3	6		12			
Portugal	3	1					2	4		1		7			10	8	5	12		6	3		
Poland	3						4	2					2	4	8	12	10	7	5	5			
Norway						3			6		2	2	1	4	1	8	5	5	10	12		7	
Netherlands	12						6	7	3		2		1	10		6	4	4	5	8		8	
Monaco			3				6	7	10		2		4			8		5	12			1	
Moldova	2					3		1	10		4		12			5	6	7		8	2		1
Malta			5				7	6	4		1		8		3	10	3	2	2				
Lithuania							2	4			8	12	6	6	10		1	3					7
Latvia							4				3	12	3	12	6	8		10		5	1	2	7
Israel	10					4		5			2	12	2	3	8	7		6	1	6	7		1
Ireland							5				7		3		10	3	12	1	12	8		6	2
Iceland							4	2			3	6	6		5	12	1	8		10		7	
Greece	10	3				7		12			2	2	5		4	8	1	1		6		2	
Germany	7					3		12			6	5	5	8	7	12	1	4		10			
FYR Macedonia							12					5	8	8	2	7		1			1		
France	12	4				3		8		8		2		10	5	6	6		7	1			
Finland			1			4						6			2		8	5		12	5	7	
Estonia					2									6			8	7		1	12	5	1
Denmark					2	3	6	5				1	10		6	7	4	10	4		2	7	
Cyprus	12	8				1					10				2	4	3	5		4		7	
Croatia			6			7					8	3	2	10		5	4	4		12		1	1
Bulgaria	8						1			2	5	4	12	1	7		6	6		10		3	
Bosnia & H				5				3			10	2	4	8	3	8	2	7		4		6	1
Belgium	12						7					1		8	10	10	4	5	5	5		6	
Belarus	7	2						3	1					8	10	8	6	5		3			
Armenia			2				1	7			8	3	12		10	10	4	6		5		3	5
Andorra	2					7				3						10			12				
Albania	3	8	7		6			1	4		12		4	6		10	2	5		5	7	10	
TOTAL	**150**	**36**	**49**	**8**	**10**	**58**	**69**	**79**	**57**	**14**	**76**	**70**	**217**	**91**	**146**	**292**	**22**	**163**	**26**	**214**	**28**	**267**	**62**

Final qualification rules:
Top 10 countries from the 2005 Final
Top 10 countries from the 2006 Semi-Final

Automatic qualification:
United Kingdom, France, Germany, Spain

Rank	Start	Country	Artist	Song	Writer	Composer	POINTS
1	17	Finland	Lordi	Hard rock hallelujah	Mr. Lordi	Mr. Lordi	292
2	10	Russia	Dima Bilan	Never let you go	Karen Kavaleryan, Irina Antonyan	Alexandr Lunyov	248
3	13	Bosnia & H	Hari Mata Hari	Lejla	Fahrudin Pecikoza & Dejan Ivanović	Željko Joksimović	229
4	12	Romania	Mihai Traistariu	Tornero	Cristian Hriscu, Mihaela Deac	Eduard Circotă	172
5	22	Sweden	Carola	Invincible	Thomas G:son, Carola Häggkvist	Thomas G:son, Bobby Ljunggren, Henrik Wikström	170
6	14	Lithuania	LT United	We are the winners	Andrius Mamontovas, Viktoras Diawara	Andrius Mamontovas, Saulius Urbonavicius	162
7	18	Ukraine	Tina Karol	Show me your love	Tina Karol	Tina Karol	145
8	24	Armenia	André	Without your love	Catherine Bekian	Armen Martirosyan	129
9	16	Greece	Anna Vissi	Everything	Anna Vissi	Nikos Karvelas	128
10	21	Ireland	Brian Kennedy	Every song is a cry for love	Brian Kennedy	Brian Kennedy	93
11	23	Turkey	Sibel Tüzün	Superstar	Sibel Tüzün	Sibel Tüzün	91
12	20	Croatia	Severina	Moja štikla	Severina Vučković	Boris Novković, Franjo Valentić	56
13	11	FYR Macedonia	Elena Risteska	Ninanajna	Rade Vrcakovski	Darko Dimitrov	56
14	8	Germany	Texas Lightning	No, no, never	Jane Comerford	Jane Comerford	36
15	5	Norway	Christine Guldbrandsen	Alvedansen	Kjetil Fluge, Christine Guldbrandsen	Kjetil Fluge, Atle Halstensen, Christine Guldbrandsen	36
16	1	Switzerland	Six4One	If we all give a little	Bernd Meinunger	Ralph Siegel	30
17	4	Latvia	Cosmos	I hear your heart	Molly-Ann Leikin, Guntars Raēs	Reinis Sējāns, Andris Sējāns	30
18	9	Denmark	Sidsel Ben Semmane	Twist of love	Niels Drevsholt	Niels Drevsholt	26
19	15	United Kingdom	Daz Sampson	Teenage life	Daz Sampson, John Matthews	Daz Sampson, John Matthews	25
20	2	Moldova	Arsenium & Natalia Gordienko	Loca	Arsenium	Arsenium	22
21	6	Spain	Las Ketchup	Bloody Mary	Manuel Ruiz Gómez (Queco)	Manuel Ruiz Gómez (Queco)	18
22	19	France	Virginie Pouchin	Il était temps	Corneille	Corneille	5
23	3	Israel	Eddie Butler	Ze hazman	Osnat Tsabag, Orly Burg	Eddie Butler	4
24	7	Malta	Fabrizio Faniello	I do	Aldo Spiteri, Fabrizio Faniello	Aldo Spiteri, Fabrizio Faniello	1

2006 Eurovision 51: Athens, Greece

The table below shows the scoreboard for the Final. Rows are the contestant countries (with the points total they received); columns are the voting countries (with the order in which their votes were announced).

Contestant	TOTAL	UK (15)	Ukraine (18)	Turkey (23)	Switzerland (1)	Sweden (22)	Spain (6)	Slovenia (25)	Serbia & Mont (29)	Russia (10)	Romania (12)	Portugal (27)	Poland (33)	Norway (5)	Netherlands (32)	Monaco (36)	Moldova (2)	Malta (7)	Lithuania (14)	Latvia (4)	Israel (3)	Ireland (21)	Iceland (35)	Greece (16)	Germany (8)	FYR Macedonia (11)	France (19)	Finland (17)	Estonia (30)	Denmark (9)	Cyprus (31)	Croatia (20)	Bulgaria (38)	Bosnia & H (13)	Belgium (28)	Belarus (34)	Armenia (24)	Andorra (26)	Albania (37)
Switzerland	30															6	6	12													3			4					
Moldova	22									3	12	3				8											4												
Israel	4		4																																				
Latvia	30	2	4																8			4							3										
Norway	36		3			2				7						1	3			6			4					5			1					1	1		
Spain	18																																					12	6
Malta	1																																						1
Germany	36	5		1			5								3					3		3						5		3					1				5
Denmark	26					8			8					6									8						1						1			8	
Russia	248	1	12	5		7	7	4	5		8	7	10	3	2		10	5	12	12	12	5	5	8	6	8	2	12	2	2	8	7	6	6	3	2	12	1	4
FYR Macedonia	56	6	1	6	4	2	12	6	8	4			3			8		1	12	6	10		7	8	5		2	6	10		10	8	6	8	2	5	7	8	3
Romania	172		3	3	1		12	5	4	6		10	4	4			12	10	1	2	10	2	2	7	7	12	7		6	6	10	5	2	2	2	3	4	3	2
Bosnia & H	229	10	10	12	12	10	1	12	12	6	7	8	8	8	8	12	1		4	4	3	2	3	6	10	12	6	10	8	8	2	12	7	7	6	4	5		12
Lithuania	162		5	12		3	1	3	3	5		4	8	5	6	7	4	1			10	12	10	1	3	3		8		7	4	6	1	5	4	6	8		1
United Kingdom	25												2	1				3			1	8			2		5		2	4	1	1	12	1	10	2		2	
Greece	128	7	4	4	5	4	5	8	6			5	2	2	5		1	8	3	8	7	8	7		8	7	5	1	1	5	12		12	1	10	2	1	1	8
Finland	292	12	12	7	1	10	10	8	7	8	4	8	12	12	7	5	6	7	10	8	5	12	7	12	10	6	8		6	12	5	10	5	7	10	7	8	10	
Ukraine	145		7	8	8	1	3	2	2	10	3	8	6	10	1		2	2	7	5	1	6	6	5	3	5		7	5	2	6	4	3	5	5	10		5	
France	5														12	3									2												2		
Croatia	56		5	2	6			10	10							4							1	10	10	10	12	4			2			12					
Ireland	93	8	7	4	3	5	7	1	7	2	5	5	2	7	4	10	2	4	4	4	4			1	1	4	1	6	4	5	2	2	2	3	2	3	3	4	4
Sweden	170	4	6	7	2	12	6	7	1	2	5	8	7	10	12	5		6	5		7	7	7		3		1		6	10			5	3	5	5	6	8	
Turkey	91	3			10					12	1	6	5		10		7		2		8			3	12	4	12			10		3	4	10	7				7
Armenia	129		8	10		8	8			12		1	5		10		7							10	3		10		7		7		8		12	8		6	

Notes: Serbia-Montenegro withdrew due to a dispute over the representing act. Croatia were awarded an automatic place in the Final

Rank	Start	Country	Artist	Song	Writer	Composer	POINTS
1Q	15	Serbia	Marija Šerifović	Molitva	Saša Milošević Mare	Vladimir Graić	298
2Q	22	Hungary	Magdi Rúzsa	Unsubstantial Blues	Imre Mózsik	Magdi Rúzsa	224
3Q	26	Turkey	Kenan Doğulu	Shake it up shekerim	Kenan Doğulu	Kenan Doğulu	197
4Q	4	Belarus	Dmitry Koldun	Work your magic	Karen Kavaleryan	Philip Kirkorov	176
5Q	28	Latvia	Bonaparti.lv	Questa Notte	Kjell Jennstig, Torbjörn Wassenius, Francesca Russo	Kjell Jennstig	168
6Q	1	Bulgaria	Elitsa Todorova, Stoyan Yankoulov	Water	Elitsa Todorova	Elitsa Todorova, Stoyan Yankoulov	146
7Q	25	Slovenia	Alenka Gotar	Cvet z juga	Andrej Babiæ	Andrej Babiæ	140
8Q	6	Georgia	Sopho	My Story	Bibi Kvachadze	Beqa Jafaridze	123
9Q	18	FYR Macedonia	Karolina	Mojot Svet	Grigor Koprov, O Nedelkovski, V Dojcinovski	Grigor Koprov, O Nedelkovski, V Dojcinovski	97
10Q	9	Moldova	Natalia Barbu	Fight	Buga	Brasoveanu	91
11	17	Portugal	Sabrina	Dança comigo (vem ser feliz)	Emanuel, Tó Maria Vinhas	Emanuel	88
12	21	Andorra	Anonymous	Salvem el món	Anonymous	Anonymous	80
13	5	Iceland	Eiríkur Hauksson	Valentine lost	Kristján Hreinsson	Sveinn Rúnar Sigurðsson	77
14	14	Poland	The Jet Set	Time to party	Kamil Varen, David Junior Serame	Mateusz Krezan	75
15	3	Cyprus	Evridiki	Comme ci, comme ça	Poseidonas Giannopoulos	Dimitris Korgialas	65
16	13	Croatia	Dragonfly feat. Dado Topic	Vjerujem u ljubav	Dado Topic	Dado Topic	54
17	11	Albania	Aida & Frederik Ndoci	Hear my plea	Pandi Laço	Adrian Hila	49
18	19	Norway	Guri Schanke	Ven a bailar conmigo	Thomas G:son	Thomas G:son	48
19	12	Denmark	DQ	Drama Queen	Peter Andersen, Claus Christensen	Peter Andersen, Simon Munk	45
20	8	Switzerland	DJ BoBo	Vampires are alive	DJ BoBo	DJ BoBo	40
21	10	Netherlands	Edsilia Rombley	On top of the world	Tjeerd Oosterhuis, Martin Gijzemijter	Tjeerd Oosterhuis	38
22	23	Estonia	Gerli Padar	Partners in crime	Hendrik Sal-Saller	Berit Vaher	33
23	7	Montenegro	Stevan Faddy	Ajde kroci	Milan Periæ	Slaven Knezoviæ	33
24	2	Israel	Teapacks	Push the button	Kobi Oz	Kobi Oz	17
25	20	Malta	Olivia Lewis	Vertigo	Gerald James Borg	Philip Vella	15
26	24	Belgium	The KMG's	Love power	Paul Curtiz, Sexyfire	Paul Curtiz	14
27	27	Austria	Eric Papilaya	Get a life - Get alive	Austin Howard	Gerg Usek	4
28	16	Czech Rep	Kabát	Malá dáma	Kabát	Kabát	1

	Bulgaria	Israel	Cyprus	Belarus	Iceland	Georgia	Montenegro	Switzerland	Moldova	Netherlands	Albania	Denmark	Croatia	Poland	Serbia	Czech Rep	Portugal	FYR Macedonia	Norway	Malta	Andorra	Hungary	Estonia	Belgium	Slovenia	Turkey	Austria	Latvia
TOTAL	**146**	**17**	**65**	**176**	**77**	**123**	**33**	**40**	**91**	**38**	**49**	**45**	**54**	**75**	**298**	**1**	**88**	**97**	**48**	**15**	**80**	**224**	**33**	**14**	**140**	**197**	**4**	**168**
United Kingdom	6		10								1	7			5							4			3	3		8
Ukraine	2	2		5	12	10			6						8							4			7	1		3
Turkey	12		5	6		10			8		4		5	2	8				6		7	2	1		3			
Switzerland											7	7	5		12		8	6	6			4					3	2
Sweden	3			12		3	5			5		4			10				5	6		8			7	1		
Spain	10					3							8	2	5		8		4		12	1			7	2		
Slovenia	3						5	2					8		12		1	10			4	6				7		
Serbia	5		4			8	2		3		3		6	2				10				12			7	2	3	
Russia		1	12		10				6						8						4	3	5		5	7	2	
Romania	1		7	3				12							6		2				10	10			4	8	5	
Portugal	5		1		3		12	12	6	3					4				2		6	10	3		7	8		
Poland				4	3								5		5		10		2		6	6			7	1	12	
Norway				12			1	4		5			8		8						2	10	6	2	5	7	7	4
Netherlands						5					1		10	8	12		4	3			8		12		6	7		7
Montenegro	5		4		12	8					6		7	1	12				10			4	4		8	3		
Moldova	5		12								8	6			6		7				2	2			3	10	2	
Malta	3		7		10				8		8			1	1				2		5	12	12					
Lithuania			4		10	5								3	1						2	8	7					
Latvia			12		6	7		4						1	2		3					8	12	6	5			
Israel	6		4		8		2	3	1	5	8	5		7	7						2					12	10	
Ireland			6				2	5		8	10	5	10	8							6	4	3		1	7		12
Iceland			1	4							8	2	10				7				12	12	3		6	5		
Hungary	8		2	10				5				6			12						7				7	6	4	
Greece	10		12		6		2	3	8		5				5						4					1		
Germany	4		3	12		6	8	2	5				2		10		7							12				
Georgia	3		4	4	1				7				6	8	8						10	6		12	5		
FYR Macedonia	7		4			3			10			6	2	12					1			5						
France	8	6	5		4								3	7	8		10				1	12					3	
Finland	2			12	4								5	10	8						7	6					12	
Estonia			5	7		10	3					4			6	1					5	8					12	3
Denmark			1		6		3		4				2		6				7	4		12			8		5	
Czech Republic	10		5				2		6						12		6				7	8			4	1	3	
Cyprus	12			10		7		2	6				3		8		1				4					5		
Croatia	6				5		5		1	2	3		10		8				2		7		10		4			
Bulgaria									1		2				8		7	12	8						5			10
Bosnia & H	3		2	10		5			12		4		10		12			7	6		6	8			6	8		
Belgium	2		5		1			10							4		3		7		6	12			7	8		
Belarus		3		8					12						10		7				4	6	1		2	6		8
Austria	6		4	5							3	7			12			5			8	8	1		2	10		
Armenia	10	5		12				7			3	3			10		6	5				2	10		3	2		1
Andorra	12	7					5						7					10	3			4			8	2	3	
Albania	1	8		4		8	7		12			3	6	2		1		5	10	6		5			5	12	1	

Final qualification rules:
Top 10 countries from the 2006 Final
Top 10 countries from the 2007 Semi-Final

Automatic qualification:
United Kingdom, France, Germany, Spain, Finland

Rank	Start	Country	Artist	Song	Writer	Composer	POINTS
1	17	Serbia	Marija Šerifovic	Molitva	Saša Milošević Mare	Vladimir Graić	268
2	18	Ukraine	Verka Serduchka	Dancing Lasha Tumbai	Andrei Danilko	Andrei Danilko	235
3	15	Russia	Serebro	Song # 1	Daniil Babichev	Maxim Fadeev	207
4	22	Turkey	Kenan Dogulu	Shake it up shekerim	Kenan Dogulu	Kenan Dogulu	163
5	21	Bulgaria	Elitsa Todorova, Stoyan Yankulov	Water	Elitsa Todorova	Elitsa Todorova, Stoyan Yankoulov	157
6	3	Belarus	Dmitry Koldun	Work your magic	Karen Kavaleryan	Philip Kirkorov	145
7	10	Greece	Sarbel	Yassou Maria	Mack	Alex Papakonstantinou, Marcus Englöf	139
8	23	Armenia	Hayko	Anytime you need	Karen Kavaleryan	Hayko	138
9	8	Hungary	Magdi Rúzsa	Unsubstantial Blues	Imre Mózsik	Magdi Rúzsa	128
10	24	Moldova	Natalia Barbu	Fight	Buga	Brasoveanu	109
11	1	Bosnia & H	Marija Sestic	Rijeka bez imena	Aleksandra Milutinovic, Goran Kovacic	Aleksandra Milutinovic, Goran Kovacic	106
12	11	Georgia	Sopho	My Story	Bibi Kvachadze	Beqa Jafaridze	97
13	20	Romania	Todomondo	Liubi, liubi, I love you	Mister M, Vlad Crepu, Ghedi Kamara	Mister M	84
14	6	FYR Macedonia	Karolina	Mojot Svet	Grigor Koprov, O Nedelkovski, V Dojcinovski	Grigor Koprov, O Nedelkovski, V Dojcinovski	73
15	7	Slovenia	Alenka Gotar	Cvet z juga	Andrej Babiœ	Andrej Babiœ	66
16	14	Latvia	Bonaparti.lv	Questa Notte	Kjell Jennstig, Torbjörn Wassenius, Francesca Russo	Kjell Jennstig	54
17	5	Finland	Hanna Pakarinen	Leave me alone	Martti Vuorinen, Hanna Pakarinen	Martti Vuorinen, Miikka Huttunen	53
18	12	Sweden	The Ark	The worrying kind	The Ark	The Ark	51
19	16	Germany	Roger Cicero	Frauen regieren die Welt	Frank Ramond, Matthias Hass	Frank Ramond, Matthias Hass	49
20	2	Spain	NASH	I love you mi vida	Tony Sanchez-Ohlsson, Rebeca Pous del Toro	Thomas G:son, Andreas Rickstrand	43
21	9	Lithuania	4Fun	Love or leave	Julija Ritčik	Julija Ritčik	28
22	13	France	Les Fatals Picards	L'amour à la Française	I Callot, L Honel, P Léger, J-M Sauvagnargues, Y Giraud	I Callot, L Honel, P Léger, J-M Sauvagnargues, Y Giraud	19
23	19	United Kingdom	Scooch	Flying the flag (for you)	Andrew Hill, Morten Schjolin, Russ Spencer, Paul Tarry	Andrew Hill, Morten Schjolin, Russ Spencer, Paul Tarry	19
24	4	Ireland	Dervish	They can't stop the spring	John Waters, Tommy Moran	John Waters, Tommy Moran	5

2007 Eurovision 52: Helsinki, Finland

Final: 12 May 2007

Scoreboard matrix. Columns are the contestant countries (with their overall **TOTAL**); rows are the voting countries together with their vote-announcement order number ("Order votes announced").

Voting country (order)	BiH 106	Spain 43	Belarus 145	Ireland 5	Finland 53	FYR Mac. 73	Slovenia 66	Hungary 128	Lithuania 28	Greece 139	Georgia 97	Sweden 51	France 19	Latvia 54	Russia 207	Germany 49	Serbia 268	Ukraine 235	UK 19	Romania 84	Bulgaria 157	Turkey 163	Armenia 138	Moldova 109
United Kingdom (40)	8		12				8		10	8		6			6		10	4			6		5	7
Ukraine (34)			12								8						5		10		3	6	1	7
Turkey (12)	10					1	3			4					12		5	8		2	6		7	7
Switzerland (25)	8	5			1	6		3	4	4		7			2		12	3			10	12		2
Sweden (33)	6				12		8	4		8	2			5	1	10	3		12		7		6	
Spain (38)							3	2				12			5	1	4	7	10		8		6	
Slovenia (20)	8					10			5		2		6		3		12	4		7		10	1	1
Serbia (10)	8		2			10	5	12		4				7	3			6		4	5	2	1
Russia (35)			12					8		10	7			6		8		2		4		3	1	5
Romania (17)	6		1				6	8		10			2	3		5	4	12			5	7		
Portugal (15)		8	7	1	12		2	2			5			3	4		7	12			6		10	
Poland (31)		7				4	2				5		1		8	5	10	12			6		10	
Norway (24)	6				4		3	8			12		3	5	10	2	1			7				1
Netherlands (27)	7	7						4		5	2		6	3	10	8	1	2		12	7		10	
Montenegro (1)	7				10			8			4			6	6	12	2		1	5	3	1		
Moldova (39)	4		10	3				6			4			8	6	5	3	7	12	1	2			
Malta (29)	2	2	10			5	1						4	6	8	3	7		12	7	3	5		
Lithuania (23)			7		5		4	1					3	10	8	8	3	7		12	1	1	2	
Latvia (36)	8					4	5	10		1	6		10	4	3	12	2	7	3	5		7	2	
Israel (21)	12	2												8	4	10	3	7		5	1		4	
Ireland (28)			10			12		5	12	1				6	4	8	8		7	3	2		4	
Iceland (37)			4		12					5		10		1	7	6	6	3	2		1	3	2	
Hungary (42)			4			4		7			2			6	12	7	3	8		2	8	1	10	5
Greece (8)	1		4		5	6				3	3			6	8	4	12	10		2	10	12	5	
Germany (22)	3		7		1			10						6	6	4	8	5		4	12	2	10	5
Georgia (9)	8					1		5		4				7	7	5	10		2	3	12	2	1	3
FYR Macedonia (41)	4		1			6		3						5	6	2	12	8		10	2	7		
France (6)	1	6				5				3				2	8	8	12	4		7	5	12	10	3
Finland (11)		6						8	10	5	7	8		3	12	6	6	4		1	5	4	2	
Estonia (30)		7	2		6			4			5	12	10	2	2	8	8	3				1		
Denmark (7)	7		2		4			8	1			12		5	2	6	6	3			10			
Czech Republic (26)	4	5						3			2			7	6	8	8	12		6	7		8	10
Cyprus (18)			6			5		12	11	12				3	7	4	6	4		2	10	8		2
Croatia (19)	10			8		7	4			2	1		1	3	5	6	12	5		6	6			
Bulgaria (32)			4	1	8	10	7	8	12	1				2	5	3	2	12			3	7	4	
Bosnia & H (13)			4		8	7		8	3	6	1				2	6	5	3		1	6	10	5	4
Belgium (14)		3	2	5				8		6	6		1	7	7	1					4	6	12	10
Belarus (2)			4		1				2		6	6			7	7	12	10	1			5	5	8
Austria (5)	8		10		1		2				5				12	7		4		3	6	10	5	
Armenia (3)							5			8	5	2	8		12			6			4		3	3
Andorra (4)		12	3		7		6	2	1	7		2	8		3	5		10	10	10		10	4	
Albania (16)	8	12	2	5	3	3			7	7				4	6	5	1	12		10		10	6	4

131

2008 Eurovision 53: Belgrade, Serbia

Semi-final 1: 20 May 2008

Votes are cast by countries participating in each semi-final plus two of the four automatically qualifying countries decided by draw: Germany & Spain in semi-final 1, United Kingdom & France in semi-final 2. The hosts, Serbia, were drawn to vote in semi-final 2. The top 9 countries ranked by televoting in each semi-final qualify for the final. The back-up jury also chose an additional act that finished outside the top 9 in each semi-final.

Rank	Start	Country	Artist	Song	Writer	Composer	POINTS
1Q	19	Greece	Kalomira	Secret Combination	Poseidon Yannopoulos	Konstantinos Pantzis	156
2Q	14	Armenia	Sirusho	Qele, Qele	Sirusho	H A Der-Hovagimian	139
3Q	18	Russia	Dima Bilan	Believe	Dima Bilan & Jim Beanz	Dima Bilan & Jim Beanz	135
4Q	9	Norway	Maria	Hold On Be Strong	Mira Craig	Mira Craig	106
5Q	2	Israel	Boaz	The Fire In Your Eyes	Dana International & Shai Kerem	Dana International	104
6Q	7	Azerbaijan	Elnur & Samir	Day After Day	Zahra Badalbeyli	Govher Hasanzadeh	96
7Q	17	Romania	Nico & Vlad	Pe-o Margine De Lume	Andreea Andrei & Adina Şuteu	Andrei Tudor	94
8Q	16	Finland	Teräsbetoni	Missä Miehet Ratsastaa	J Ahola	J Ahola	79
9Q	13	Bosnia & H	Laka	Pokušaj	Elvir Lakovic Laka	Elvir Lakovic Laka	72
10J	10	Poland	Isis Gee	For Life	Isis Gee	Isis Gee	42
12	4	Moldova	Geta Burlacu	A Century Of Love	Viorica Demici	Oleg Baraliuc	36
11	8	Slovenia	Rebeka Dremelj	Vrag Naj Vzame	Amon	Josip Miani-Pipi	36
13	15	Netherlands	Hind	Your Heart Belongs To Me	Hind Laroussi Tahiri & Tjeerd van Zanen	Hind Laroussi Tahiri, Tjeerd van Zanen & Bas van den Heuvel	27
14	1	Montenegro	Stefan Filipović	Zauvijek Volim Te	Ognen Nedelkovski	Grigor Koprov	23
15	11	Ireland	Dustin the Turkey	Irelande Douze Pointe	Darren Smith, Simon Fine & Dustin The Turkey	Darren Smith, Simon Fine & Dustin The Turkey	22
16	12	Andorra	Gisela	Casanova	Jordi Cubino	Jordi Cubino	22
17	6	Belgium	Ishtar	O Julissi	Michel Vangheluwe	Michel Vangheluwe	16
18	3	Estonia	Kreisiraadio	Leto Svet	Priit Pajusaar, Glen Pilvre, Peeter Oja, Hannes Võrno & Tarmo Leinatamm	Priit Pajusaar, Glen Pilvre, Peeter Oja, Hannes Võrno & Tarmo Leinatamm	8
19	5	San Marino	Miodio	Complice	Nicola Della Valle	Francesco Sancisi	5

2008 Eurovision 53: Belgrade, Serbia

Semi-final 1: 20 May 2008

	TOTAL	Spain	Slovenia	San Marino	Russia	Romania	Poland	Norway	Netherlands	Montenegro	Moldova	Israel	Ireland	Greece	Germany	Finland	Estonia	Bosnia & H	Belgium	Azerbaijan	Armenia	Andorra
Montenegro	23		10	1						5				5				12	7			7
Israel	104	4	4	2	8	6	4	10	6	5				2	4	10		5	7	10	7	7
Estonia	8			5							1					7	6					
Moldova	36			5	5	10								4							6	1
San Marino	5													3								2
Belgium	16								10								6					
Azerbaijan	96		3	4	10	7	10		4	3	10	5	5	7	8	5	4	3	5	2	2	8
Slovenia	36				2	1	2			10	2	2		2				10		1	4	
Norway	106	2		7	7	4	7		5	4	3	6	8		1	12	8	4	1	7	8	10
Poland	42	3		10	3	2		2	1				12		5		2		3		1	
Ireland	22	1					1	1	1	1		3	1			2	7	2	4			
Andorra	22	12	1					1		1		4					3					
Bosnia & H	72		12		12	5	12	12	7	12	6	3	2	3	7	8	1				3	
Armenia	139	10	5	8	12	8	3	6	12	5	5	10	2	2	10	4	2	12	6	12		3
Netherlands	27		2	3		3	3	7			1	1	1				12		3	8	2	
Finland	79	6	3	4	4	5	5	6	3	2	8	8	6	6	2	4		1	6	2	6	5
Romania	94	8	6	6	1		3	5	3	5	12	7		7	3	1	6	6	3	1	6	8
Russia	135	5	7		8	8	8	8	2	8	7	12	8	4	6	6	10	5	8	3	8	7
Greece	156	7	8	12	6	12	6	4	8	7	4	7	7	10	12	3	5	5	8	10	12	5

2008 Eurovision 53: Belgrade, Serbia

Votes are cast by countries participating in each semi-final plus two of the four automatically qualifying countries decided by draw: Germany & Spain in semi-final 1, United Kingdom & France in semi-final 2. The hosts, Serbia, were drawn to vote in semi-final 2. The top 9 countries ranked by televoting in each semi-final qualify for the final. The back-up jury also chose an additional act that finished outside the top 9 in each semi-final.

Rank	Start	Country	Song	Artist	Writer	Composer	POINTS
1Q	4	Ukraine	Shady Lady	Ani Lorak	Karen Kavaleryan	Philip Kirkorov	152
2Q	19	Portugal	Senhora Do Mar (Negras Águas)	Vânia Fernandes	Carlos Coelho	Andrej Babić	120
3Q	13	Denmark	All Night Long	Simon Mathew	Jacob Launbjerg, Svend Gudiksen & Nis Bøgvad	Jacob Launbjerg, Svend Gudiksen & Nis Bøgvad	112
4Q	11	Croatia	Romanca	Kraljevi Ulice & 75 Cents	Miran Hadži Veljković	Miran Hadži Veljković	112
5Q	14	Georgia	Peace Will Come	Diana Gurtskaya	Karen Kavaleryan	Kim Breitburg	107
6Q	10	Latvia	Wolves Of The Sea	Pirates Of The Sea	Jonas Liberg, Johan Sahlen, Claes Andreasson, Torbjorn Wassenius	Jonas Liberg, Johan Sahlen, Claes Andreasson, Torbjorn Wassenius	86
7Q	3	Turkey	Deli	Mor ve Ötesi	Mor ve Ötesi	Mor ve Ötesi	85
8Q	1	Iceland	This Is My Life	Euroband	Paul Oscar & Peter Fenner	Örlygur Smári	68
9Q	6	Albania	Zemrën E Lamë Peng	Olta Boka	Pandi Laço	Adrian Hila	67
10	18	FYR Macedonia	Let Me Love You	Tamara, Vrčak & Adrijan	Rade Vrchakovski-Vrcak	Rade Vrchakovski-Vrcak	64
11	12	Bulgaria	DJ, Take Me Away	Deep Zone & Balthazar	Dian Savov	Dian Savov	56
12J	2	Sweden	Hero	Charlotte Perrelli	Fredrik Kempe	Fredrik Kempe & Bobby Ljunggren	54
13	7	Switzerland	Era Stupendo	Paolo Meneguzzi	Pablo Meneguzzo & Vincenzo Incenzo	Pablo Meneguzzo	47
14	16	Malta	Vodka	Morena	Gerard James Borg	Philip Vella	38
15	17	Cyprus	Femme Fatale	Evdokia Kadi	Vangelis Evangelou	Nicos Evagelou	36
16	5	Lithuania	Nomads In The Night	Jeronimas Milius	Jeronimas Milius	Vytautas Diškevičius	30
17	9	Belarus	Hasta La Vista	Ruslan Alehno	Eleonora Melnik	Taras Demchuk	27
18	8	Czech Republic	Have Some Fun	Tereza Kerndlová	Gordon Pogoda	Gordon Pogoda & Stano Simor	9
19	15	Hungary	Candlelight	Csézy	Imre Mózsik	Viktor Rakonczai	6

Semi-final 2: 22 May 2008

Receiving ↓ \ Voting →	TOTAL	United Kingdom	Ukraine	Turkey	Switzerland	Sweden	Serbia	Portugal	Malta	Lithuania	Latvia	Iceland	Hungary	Georgia	FYR Macedonia	France	Denmark	Czech Republic	Cyprus	Croatia	Bulgaria	Belarus	Albania
Iceland	68	4	1	3	4	10	3	5	5	2	2		7			8	10		1		12	1	5
Sweden	54	6		2	3		3	3	7	3		8	1			1	12		4			3	1
Turkey	85	10	5		7	6	3	12	8	7	6	6	4	5		10	8	12	10	7	7	3	12
Ukraine	152	8		12	1	3	8	12	8	7	6	6	8	12	6	3	7	1	10	7	12	10	8
Lithuania	30	8			10						12	1		10									
Albania	67	3	3	8	10	7		2				1				5	5	1		10		5	
Switzerland	47			1					12						12	7			7	2			
Czech Republic	9								1						5								
Belarus	27	10	10				2			6	5			4					2				
Latvia	86	5	2	5	6	8	2	10	6	12	5	7	10	6	4	2	6	5	6	6	1	6	3
Croatia	112	112	7	6	6	4	10	6	2	5	7	4	3	8	10	2	3	3	6	1	6	7	8
Bulgaria	56		6	6	5		5	1	4	1	1	5	3	7	7	6		2	8	1	2	2	5
Denmark	112	1	4	6	5	12		8	4	8	8	12	12	3	3	4		10	5	3	2	4	4
Georgia	107	12	12	10		1	7	7	10	10	10	2	2	2	2		1	8	12	12	8	4	10
Hungary	6						4							1			1						
Malta	38	2	2	3	3			4			4	3	5				4	6		4	3		8
Cyprus	36	12	7	4	2	2	1						5	2						12	8		2
FYR Macedonia	64		7	7	8	2	12									12	2	4	3	8	10		7
Portugal	120	7	8		12	5	6		3	4	3	10	6	7		12		7	3	8	5	8	6

2008 Eurovision 53: Belgrade, Serbia

Final qualification rules:
Top 9 countries from each semi-final decided by televoting,
plus one from each semi-final decided by a back-up jury.

Automatic qualification:
United Kingdom, France, Germany, Spain, Serbia

Rank	Start	Country	Artist	Song	Writer	Composer	POINTS
1	24	Russia	Dima Bilan	Believe	Dima Bilan & Jim Beanz	Dima Bilan & Jim Beanz	272
2	18	Ukraine	Ani Lorak	Shady Lady	Karen Kavaleryan	Philip Kirkorov	230
3	21	Greece	Kalomira	Secret Combination	Poseidon Yannopoulos	Konstantinos Pantzis	218
4	5	Armenia	Sirusho	Qele, Qele	Sirusho	H A Der-Hovagimian	199
5	25	Norway	Maria	Hold On Be Strong	Mira Craig	Mira Craig	182
6	23	Serbia	Jelena Tomašević & Bora Dugic	Oro	Dejan Ivanović	Željko Joksimović	160
7	12	Turkey	Mor ve Ötesi	Deli	Mor ve Ötesi	Mor ve Ötesi	138
8	20	Azerbaijan	Elnur & Samir	Day After Day	Zahra Badalbeyli	Govher Hasanzadeh	132
9	7	Israel	Boaz	The Fire In Your Eyes	Dana International & Shai Kerem	Dana International	124
10	6	Bosnia & H	Laka	Pokušaj	Elvir Lakovic Laka	Elvir Lakovic Laka	110
11	17	Georgia	Diana Gurtskaya	Peace Will Come	Karen Kavaleryan	Kim Breitburg	83
12	14	Latvia	Pirates Of The Sea	Wolves Of The Sea	Jonas Liberg, Johan Sahlen, Claes Andreasson, Torbjorn Wassenius	Jonas Liberg, Johan Sahlen, Claes Andreasson, Torbjorn Wassenius	83
13	13	Portugal	Vânia Fernandes	Senhora Do Mar (Negras Águas)	Carlos Coelho	Andrej Babić	69
14	11	Iceland	Euroband	This Is My Life	Paul Oscar & Peter Fenner	Örlygur Smári	64
15	16	Denmark	Simon Mathew	All Night Long	Jacob Launbjerg, Svend Gudiksen & Nis Bøgvad	Jacob Launbjerg, Svend Gudiksen & Nis Bøgvad	60
16	22	Spain	Rodolfo Chikilicuatre	Baila El Chiki Chiki	Rodolfo Chikilicuatre	Rodolfo Chikilicuatre	55
17	3	Albania	Olta Boka	Zemrën E Lamë Peng	Pandi Laço	Adrian Hila	55
18	15	Sweden	Charlotte Perrelli	Hero	Fredrik Kempe	Fredrik Kempe & Bobby Ljunggren	47
19	19	France	Sébastien Tellier	Divine	Sébastien Tellier, Amandine de La Richardière	Sebastien Tellier	47
20	1	Romania	Nico & Vlad	Pe-o Margine De Lume	Andreea Andrei & Adina Şuteu	Andrei Tudor	45
21	9	Croatia	Kraljevi Ulice & 75 Cents	Romanca	Miran Hadži Veljković	Miran Hadži Veljković	44
22	8	Finland	Teräsbetoni	Missä Miehet Ratsastaa	J Ahola	J Ahola	35
23	4	Germany	No Angels	Disappear	Remee, Hanne Sorvaag & Thomas Troelsen	Remee, Hanne Sorvaag & Thomas Troelsen	14
24	10	Poland	Isis Gee	For Life	Isis Gee	Isis Gee	14
25	2	United Kingdom	Andy Abraham	Even If	Andy Abraham, Andy Watkins & Paul Wilson	Andy Abraham, Andy Watkins & Paul Wilson	14

Scoreboard of the 2008 Eurovision Song Contest Final (cross-tabulation of points given by each voting country to each finalist).

Finalists and total points

Finalist	TOTAL
Romania	45
United Kingdom	14
Albania	55
Germany	14
Armenia	199
Bosnia & H	110
Israel	124
Finland	35
Croatia	44
Poland	14
Iceland	64
Turkey	138
Portugal	69
Latvia	83
Sweden	47
Denmark	60
Georgia	83
Ukraine	230
France	47
Azerbaijan	132
Greece	218
Spain	55
Serbia	160
Russia	272
Norway	182

Order votes announced (voting countries)

Voting country	Order
United Kingdom	1
Ukraine	3
Turkey	29
Switzerland	32
Sweden	37
Spain	27
Slovenia	24
Serbia	12
San Marino	9
Russia	40
Romania	18
Portugal	19
Poland	23
Norway	20
Netherlands	28
Montenegro	41
Moldova	15
Malta	30
Lithuania	39
Latvia	10
Israel	13
Ireland	31
Iceland	16
Hungary	21
Greece	34
Germany	4
Georgia	42
FYR Macedonia	2
France	17
Finland	35
Estonia	5
Denmark	43
Czech Republic	26
Cyprus	14
Croatia	36
Bulgaria	11
Bosnia & H	6
Belgium	8
Belarus	38
Azerbaijan	33
Armenia	25
Andorra	22
Albania	7

Votes are cast by countries participating in each semi-final plus two of the four automatically qualifying countries decided by draw: Germany & United Kingdom in semi-final 1, Spain & France in semi-final 2. The hosts, Russia, were drawn to vote in semi-final 2. The top 9 countries ranked by televoting in each semi-final qualify for the final. The back-up jury also chose an additional act that finished outside the top 9 in each semi-final.

Rank	Start	Country	Artist	Song	Writer	Composer	POINTS
1Q	12	Iceland	Yohanna	Is It True?	Óskar Páll Sveinsson, Chris Neil, Tinatin Japaridze	Óskar Páll Sveinsson, Chris Neil, Tinatin Japaridze	174
2Q	9	Turkey	Hadise	Düm Tek Tek	Sinan Akçıl, Hadise Açıkgöz, Stefaan Fernande	Sinan Akçıl	172
3Q	18	Bosnia & H	Regina	Bistra Voda	Aleksandar Čović	Aleksandar Čović	125
4Q	5	Sweden	Malena Ernman	La Voix	Fredrik Kempe and Malena Ernman	Fredrik Kempe	105
5Q	6	Armenia	Inga & Anush	Jan Jan	Vardan Zadoyan & Avet Barseghyan	Mane Hakobyan	99
6Q	17	Malta	Chiara	What If We	Gregory Bilsen	Marc Paelinck	86
7Q	10	Israel	Noa & Mira Awad	There Must Be Another Way	Noa, Mira Awad, Gil Dor	Noa, Mira Awad, Gil Dor	75
8Q	16	Portugal	Flor-de-lis	Todas As Ruas Do Amor	Pedro Marques	Pedro Marques, Paulo Pereira	70
9Q	14	Romania	Elena	The Balkan Girls	Laurenţiu Duţă, Alexandru Pelin	Laurenţiu Duţă, Ovidiu Bistriceanu, Daris Mangal	67
10	13	FYR Macedonia	Next Time	Neshto Shto Ke Ostane	Elvir Mekic	Jovan Jovanov & Damjan Lazarov	45
11	1	Montenegro	Andrea Demirovic	Just Get Out of My Life	Bernd Meinunger & Jose Juan Santana Rodriguez	Ralph Siegel	44
12J	15	Finland	Waldo's People	Lose Control	Waldo, A. Lehtonen, Karima, A. Kratz Gutã	A. Lehtonen, Karima	42
13	4	Belarus	Petr Elfimov	Eyes That Never Lie	Valery Prokhozhy	Petr Elfimov	25
14	8	Switzerland	Lovebugs	The Highest Heights	Adrian Sieber, Thomas Rechberger, Florian Senn, Lovebugs	Adrian Sieber, Thomas Rechberger, Florian Senn, Lovebugs	15
15	7	Andorra	Susanne Georgi	La Teva Decisió (Get A Life)	Rune Braager, Lene Dissing, Marcus Winther-John, Pernille Georgi, Susanne Georgi	Rune Braager, Lene Dissing, Marcus Winther-John, Pernille Georgi, Susanne Georgi	8
16	11	Bulgaria	Krassimir Avramov	Illusion	Krassimir Avramov, William Tabanau, Casie Tabanau	Krassimir Avramov, William Tabanau	7
17	3	Belgium	Copycat	Copycat	Jacques Duvall	Benjamin Schoos	1
18	2	Czech Republic	Gipsy.cz	Aven Romale	Radoslav Gipsy Bang	Radoslav Gipsy Bang	0

2009 Eurovision 54: Moscow, Russia

Semi-final 1: 12 May 2009

Receiving ↓ / Voting →	Andorra	Armenia	Belarus	Belgium	Bosnia & H	Bulgaria	Czech Republic	Finland	FYR Macedonia	Germany	Iceland	Israel	Malta	Montenegro	Portugal	Romania	Sweden	Switzerland	Turkey	United Kingdom	TOTAL
Montenegro	1	5	3		10				8	2		1	6		1			2	5		44
Czech Republic																					0
Belgium		1																			1
Belarus					1	1	1	4	6	4			1	2			1		4		25
Sweden	7	8	7	4	4	8	6	10	3	5	12	12	8	7	3	12			4	7	105
Armenia	8		10	10	2		12	7	7	10	10	7		10	6	8		4	10	5	99
Andorra	1																				8
Switzerland	2	7	4	5				2			6			5	10	1	2		3		15
Turkey	5	10	12	12	12	2	5	6	12	6	7	6	7	8	12	4		1		12	172
Israel		4						5			3		—	6?	2	3		12	6	1	75
Bulgaria									5										2		7
Iceland	10	12		7	7	10	10	12	4	1	—	3	12	1	8	10	12	7	8	8	174
FYR Macedonia			1			5	3											6	6		45
Romania	4	2		2	6	6		1	2		5	4	2	6	7	—	3	6	7	2	67
Finland	3		2	1	8	4	2	—	7	3	12?	5		3		2	10	2		4	42
Portugal	12		6	6	3	3	7	3	1	7	8	2	5	4	—	7	3	10		6	70
Malta	6	3	8	8	5	2	4	5	5	12	4	10	—	3	6	6	4	3	12	10	86
Bosnia & H	—	6	5	3	—	7	8	8	10	8	3	3	7	12	5	5	8	8	12	3	125

139

Votes are cast by countries participating in each semi-final plus two of the four automatically qualifying countries decided by draw: Germany & United Kingdom in semi-final 1, Spain & France in semi-final 2. The hosts, Russia, were drawn to vote in semi-final 2. The top 9 countries ranked by televoting in each semi-final qualify for the final. The back-up jury also chose an additional act that finished outside the top 9 in each semi-final.

Rank	Start	Country	Artist	Song	Writer	Composer	POINTS
1Q	6	Norway	Alexander Rybak	Fairytale	Alexander Rybak	Alexander Rybak	201
2Q	12	Azerbaijan	AySel & Arash	Always	Arash Labaf, Robert Uhlmann, Elin Wrethov, Anderz Wrethov	A Labaf, R Uhlmann, J Bejerholm, M Englof, A Papaconstantinou	180
3Q	18	Estonia	Urban Symphony	Rändajad	Sven Löhmus	Sven Löhmus	115
4Q	13	Greece	Sakis Rouvas	This Is Our Night	Graig Porteils & Cameron Giles-Webb	Dimitris Kontopoulos	110
5Q	15	Moldova	Nelly Ciobanu	Hora Din Moldova	Nelly Ciobanu	Veaceslav Daniliuc	106
6Q	17	Ukraine	Svetlana Loboda	Be my Valentine! (Anti-crisis Girl)	Yevgeny Matyushenko	Svetlana Loboda	80
7Q	16	Albania	Kejsi Tola	Carry Me In Your Dreams	Agim Doçi	Edmond Zhulali	73
8Q	9	Denmark	Brinck	Believe Again	Lars Halvor Jensen, Martin Michael Larsson, Ronan Keating	Lars Halvor Jensen, Martin Michael Larsson, Ronan Keating	69
9Q	14	Lithuania	Sasha Son	Love	Dmitrij Šavrov (Sasha Son)	Dmitrij Šavrov (Sasha Son)	66
10	4	Serbia	Marko Kon & Milaan	Cipela	Marko Kon, Aleksandar Kobac	Marko Kon, Aleksandar Kobac, Milan Nikolic	60
11	2	Ireland	Sinéad Mulvey & Black Daisy	Et Cetera	Niall Mooney, Jonas Gladnikoff, Daniele Moretti & Christina Schilling	Niall Mooney, Jonas Gladnikoff, Daniele Moretti & Christina Schilling	52
12	5	Poland	Lidia Kopania	I Don't Wanna Leave	Alex Geringas, Bernd Klimpel, Rike Boomgaarden, Dee Adam	Alex Geringas, Bernd Klimpel, Rike Boomgaarden, Dee Adam	43
13J	1	Croatia	Igor Cukrov featuring Andrea	Lijepa Tena	Vjekoslava Huljić	Tonči Huljić	33
14	7	Cyprus	Christina Metaxa	Firefly	Nikolas Metaxas	Nikolas Metaxas	32
15	11	Hungary	Zoli Ádok	Dance With Me	Kasai	Szabó Zé	16
16	10	Slovenia	Quartissimo featuring Martina	Love Symphony	Andrej Babić	Andrej Babić	14
17	19	Netherlands	The Toppers	Shine	Gordon Heuckeroth	Gordon Heuckeroth	11
18	8	Slovakia	Kamil Mikulčík & Nela Pocisková	Let' Tmou	Anna Žigová, Petronela Kolevská	Rastislav Dubovský	8
19	3	Latvia	Intars Busulis	Probka	Janis Elsbergs, Sergej Timofejev	Karlis Lacis	7

Semi-final 2: 14 May 2009

Voting countries (columns, left to right): Albania, Azerbaijan, Croatia, Cyprus, Denmark, Estonia, France, Greece, Hungary, Ireland, Latvia, Lithuania, Moldova, Netherlands, Norway, Poland, Russia, Serbia, Slovakia, Slovenia, Spain, Ukraine.

Country (receiving)	TOTAL
Croatia	33
Ireland	52
Latvia	7
Serbia	60
Poland	43
Norway	201
Cyprus	32
Slovakia	8
Denmark	69
Slovenia	14
Hungary	16
Azerbaijan	180
Greece	110
Lithuania	66
Moldova	106
Albania	73
Ukraine	80
Estonia	115
Netherlands	11

Selected clearly-readable entries (giver → receiver, points):

- Croatia (33): Ukraine 1, Slovenia 10, Serbia 12, Russia 3, Moldova 3, Hungary 1, Cyprus 2, Albania 1
- Albania received 12 from Greece; Greece received 12 from Cyprus; Norway and Azerbaijan received the highest scores (Norway 201, Azerbaijan 180).

Final qualification rules: Top 9 countries from each semi-final decided by televoting, plus one from each semi-final decided by a back-up jury.
Automatic qualification: United Kingdom, France, Germany, Spain, Russia

Final points scoring system: televoting by all countries participating in semi-finals/final equals 50% of points awarded, 50% also determined by a jury from each country.

Rank	Start	Country	Artist	Song	Writer	Composer	POINTS
1	20	Norway	Alexander Rybak	Fairytale	Alexander Rybak	Alexander Rybak	387
2	7	Iceland	Yohanna	Is It True?	Óskar Páll Sveinsson, Chris Neil, Tinatin Japaridze	Óskar Páll Sveinsson, Chris Neil, Tinatin Japaridze	218
3	11	Azerbaijan	AySel & Arash	Always	Arash Labaf, Robert Uhlmann, Elin Wrethov, Anderz Wrethov	A Labaf, R Uhlmann, J Bejerholm, M Englof, A Papaconstantinou	207
4	18	Turkey	Hadise	Düm Tek Tek	Sinan Akçil, Hadise Açıkgöz, Stefaan Fernande	Sinan Akçil	177
5	23	United Kingdom	Jade Ewen	It's My Time	Andrew Lloyd Webber & Diane Warren	Andrew Lloyd Webber & Diane Warren	173
6	15	Estonia	Urban Symphony	Rändajad	Sven Lõhmus	Sven Lõhmus	129
7	8	Greece	Sakis Rouvas	This Is Our Night	Graig Porteils & Cameron Giles-Webb	Dimitris Kontopoulos	120
8	3	France	Patricia Kaas	Et S'il Fallait Le Faire	Anse Lazio	Fred Blondin	107
9	12	Bosnia & H	Regina	Bistra Voda	Aleksandar Čović	Aleksandar Čović	106
10	9	Armenia	Inga & Anush	Jan Jan	Vardan Zadoyan, Avet Barseghyan	Mane Hakobyan	92
11	10	Russia	Anastasia Prikhodko	Mamo	Konstantin Meladzé, Diana Golde	Konstantin Meladzé	91
12	21	Ukraine	Svetlana Loboda	Be my Valentine! (Anti-crisis Girl)	Yevgeny Matyushenko	Svetlana Loboda	76
13	16	Denmark	Brinck	Believe Again	Lars Halvor Jensen, Martin Michael Larsson, Ronan Keating	Lars Halvor Jensen, Martin Michael Larsson, Ronan Keating	74
14	13	Moldova	Nelly Ciobanu	Hora Din Moldova	Nelly Ciobanu	Veaceslav Daniliuc	69
15	6	Portugal	Flor-de-lis	Todas As Ruas Do Amor	Pedro Marques	Pedro Marques, Paulo Pereira	57
16	2	Israel	Noa & Mira Awad	There Must Be Another Way	Noa, Mira Awad, Gil Dor	Noa, Mira Awad, Gil Dor	53
17	19	Albania	Kejsi Tola	Carry Me In Your Dreams	Agim Doçi	Edmond Zhulali	48
18	5	Croatia	Igor Cukrov featuring Andrea	Lijepa Tena	Vjekoslava Huljić	Tonči Huljić	45
19	22	Romania	Elena	The Balkan Girls	Laurenţiu Duţă, Alexandru Pelin	Laurenţiu Duţă, Ovidiu Bistriceanu, Daris Mangal	40
20	17	Germany	Alex Swings Oscar Sings!	Miss Kiss Kiss Bang	Alex Christensen, Steffen Haefeliger	Alex Christensen, Steffen Haefeliger	35
21	4	Sweden	Malena Ernman	La Voix	Fredrik Kempe & Malena Ernman	Fredrik Kempe	33
22	14	Malta	Chiara	What If We	Gregory Bilsen	Marc Paelinck	31
23	1	Lithuania	Sasha Son	Love	Dmitrij Šavrov (Sasha Son)	Dmitrij Šavrov (Sasha Son)	23
24	25	Spain	Soraya	La Noche Es Para Mí (The Night Is For Me)	Felipe Pedroso	Jason Gill, Dimitri Stassos, Irini Michas	23
25	24	Finland	Waldo's People	Lose Control	Waldo, A. Lehtonen, Karima, Kratz Gutá	A. A. Lehtonen, Karima	22

Voting countries (Order votes announced): United Kingdom 19, Ukraine 24, Turkey 25, Switzerland 16, Sweden 7, Spain 1, Slovenia 38, Slovakia 21, Serbia 27, Russia 11, Romania 34, Portugal 33, Poland 29, Norway 42, Netherlands 30, Montenegro 13, Moldova 37, Malta 4, Lithuania 18, Latvia 12, Israel 10, Ireland 35, Iceland 8, Hungary 40, Greece 22, Germany 5, FYR Macedonia 20, France 9, Finland 15, Estonia 31, Denmark 36, Czech Republic 6, Cyprus 28, Croatia 32, Bulgaria 17, Bosnia & H 23, Belgium 2, Belarus 3, Azerbaijan 41, Armenia 39, Andorra 14, Albania 26

Scoreboard (receiving country — TOTAL):

Country	TOTAL
Lithuania	23
Israel	53
France	107
Sweden	33
Croatia	45
Portugal	57
Iceland	218
Greece	120
Armenia	92
Russia	91
Azerbaijan	207
Bosnia & H	106
Moldova	69
Malta	31
Estonia	129
Denmark	74
Germany	35
Turkey	177
Albania	48
Norway	387
Ukraine	76
Romania	40
United Kingdom	173
Finland	22
Spain	23

2010 Eurovision 55: Oslo, Norway

Semi-final 1: 25 May 2010

Votes are cast by countries participating in each semi-final plus the four automatically qualifying countries decided by draw: Germany, France & Spain in semi-final 1, United Kingdom in semi-final 2. The hosts, Norway, were drawn to vote in semi-final 2. Points awarded are the combined totals of the televoting and jury votes. The top 10 countries in each semi-final qualify for the final.

Rank	Start	Country	Artist	Song	Writer	Composer	POINTS
1Q	10	Belgium	Tom Dice	Me And My Guitar	Tom Dice, Jeroen Swinnen & Ashley Hicklin	Tom Dice, Jeroen Swinnen & Ashley Hicklin	167
2Q	13	Greece	Giorgos Alkaios & Friends	OPA	Giannis Antoniou & Friends	Giorgos Alkaios	133
3Q	17	Iceland	Hera Björk	Je Ne Sais Quoi	Örlygur Smári & Hera Björk	Örlygur Smári & Hera Björk	123
4Q	14	Portugal	Filipa Azevedo	Há Dias Assim	Augusto Madureira	Augusto Madureira	89
5Q	7	Serbia	Milan Stanković	Ovo Je Balkan	Goran Bregović, Marina Tucaković & Ljiljana Jorgovanović	Goran Bregović	79
6Q	12	Albania	Juliana Pasha	It's All About You	Pirro Çako	Ardit Gjebrea	76
7Q	2	Russia	Peter Nalitch & Friends	Lost And Forgotten	Peter Nalitch	Peter Nalitch	74
8Q	8	Bosnia & H	Vukašin Brajić	Thunder And Lightning	Dino Šaran	Dino Šaran	59
9Q	16	Belarus	3+2	Butterflies	Malka Chaplin	Maxim Fadeev	59
10Q	1	Moldova	Sunstroke Project & Olia Tira	Run Away	Alina Galetskaya	Anton Ragoza & Sergey Stepanov	52
11	5	Finland	Kuunkuiskaajat	Työlki Ellää	Timo Kiiskinen	Timo Kiiskinen	49
12	11	Malta	Thea Garrett	My Dream	Sunny Aquilina	Jason Cassar	45
13	9	Poland	Marcin Mroziński	Legenda	Marcin Mroziński	Marcin Nierubiec	44
14	3	Estonia	Malcolm Lincoln	Siren	Robin Juhkental	Robin Juhkental	39
15	15	FYR Macedonia	Gjoko Taneski	Jas Ja Imam Silata	Kristijan Gabroski	Kristijan Gabroski	37
16	4	Slovakia	Kristina Pelakova	Horehronie	Kamil Peteraj	Martin Kavulic	24
17	6	Latvia	Aisha	What For?	Guntars Racs	Janis Lusens	11

	TOTAL	Spain	Slovakia	Serbia	Russia	Portugal	Poland	Moldova	Malta	Latvia	Iceland	Greece	Germany	FYR Macedonia	France	Finland	Estonia	Bosnia & Herzegovina	Belgium	Belarus	Albania
Moldova	52	5		1	5	8			7			4		7	3				2	10	
Russia	74			4		1	8	12	1	10		3	1			3	12	2	5	12	
Estonia	39					4	5			12	2	1				12		1		1	1
Slovakia	24			6		5					5					2			1		
Finland	49	2		6		5			2	6	6		3				10		7	7	
Latvia	11															5	6				
Serbia	79	6	6		4	2		3	3	3	3	7	4	10	12	8	1	12	3		3
Bosnia & Herzegovina	59		5	12	2		6	1	3			5		8	6					4	7
Poland	44	3			6			2		4			7		7	6	5	4	6	3	6
Belgium	167	8	10	7	10	12	12	6	12	8	12	10	12	4	10	10	8	4		4	4
Malta	45	1	12			3				1	4	2	2	6	2	1	3	6	8	2	2
Albania	76	4		2			4		6		10	12	5		2	4		7	8		
Greece	133	10	8	10	7	10	7	7	8	8	8		8	3	4	8	2	8	10	5	10
Portugal	89	12	4	5	5	10	2	5	4	7	7	5	10	2	8	6	5	3	4		5
FYR Macedonia	37		1	8	1			4			1				1		4	10	3		12
Belarus	59		3	3	12	7	3	8	5	5		6	6	5	1	7					
Iceland	123	7	7	3	8	6	10	10	10	2		8	6	1	5	7	7		12	6	8

Votes are cast by countries participating in each semi-final plus the four automatically qualifying countries decided by draw: Germany, France & Spain in semi-final 1, United Kingdom in semi-final 2. The hosts, Norway, were drawn to vote in semi-final 2. Points awarded are the combined totals of the televoting and jury votes. The top 10 countries in each semi-final qualify for the final.

Rank	Start	Country	Artist	Song	Writer	Composer	POINTS
1Q	17	Turkey	maNga	We Could Be The Same	Evren Özdemir, maNga, Fiona Movery Akıncı	maNga	118
2Q	7	Azerbaijan	Safura	Drip Drop	Sandra Bjurman	Anders Bagge, Stefan Örn	113
3Q	16	Georgia	Sofia Nizharadze	Shine	Hanne Sorvaag, Harry Sommerdahl & Christian Leuzzi	Hanne Sorvaag, Harry Sommerdahl & Christian Leuzzi	106
4Q	10	Romania	Paula Seling & Ovi	Playing With Fire	Ovidiu Cernăuţeanu	Ovidiu Cernăuţeanu	104
5Q	4	Denmark	Chanée & N'evergreen	In A Moment Like This	Thomas G:son, Henrik Sethsson & Erik Bernholm	Thomas G:son, Henrik Sethsson & Erik Bernholm	101
6Q	2	Armenia	Eva Rivas	Apricot Stone	Karen Kavaleryan	Armen Martirosyan	83
7Q	8	Ukraine	Alyosha	Sweet People	Olena Kucher	Olena Kucher, Borys Kukoba & Vadim Lisitsa	77
8Q	3	Israel	Harel Skaat	Milim	Noam Horev	Tomer Adaddi	71
9Q	12	Ireland	Niamh Kavanagh	It's For You	Niall Mooney, Mårten Eriksson, Jonas Gladnikoff & Lina Eriksson	Niall Mooney, Mårten Eriksson, Jonas Gladnikoff & Lina Eriksson	67
10Q	14	Cyprus	Jon Lilygreen & The Islanders	Life Looks Better In Spring	Nasos Lambrianides	Nasos Lambrianides, Melis Konstantinou	67
11	6	Sweden	Anna Bergendahl	This Is My Life	Kristian Lagerström	Bobby Ljunggren	62
12	1	Lithuania	InCulto	East European Funk	InCulto	InCulto	44
13	15	Croatia	Feminnem	Lako Je Sve	Neda Parmać, Pamela Ramljak	Branimir Mihaljević	33
14	9	Netherlands	Sieneke	Ik Ben Verliefd (Sha-la-lie)	Pierre Kartner	Pierre Kartner	29
15	13	Bulgaria	Miro	Angel Si Ti	Miroslav Kostadinov	Miroslav Kostadinov	19
16	11	Slovenia	Ansambel Žlindra & Kalamari	Narodnozabavni Rock	Leon Oblak	Marino Legovič	6
17	5	Switzerland	Michael von der Heide	Il Pleut de L'Or	Michael von der Heide, Heike Kospach, André Grüter	Michael von der Heide, Pele Loriano	2

	TOTAL	United Kingdom	Ukraine	Turkey	Switzerland	Sweden	Slovenia	Romania	Netherlands	Lithuania	Ireland	Iceland	Greece	Georgia	Denmark	Cyprus	Croatia	Bulgaria	Azerbaijan	Armenia
Lithuania	44	7	2			4					12	5		8	1	2	1			2
Armenia	83		8	4	3	5	10	10		1			12	10		12		8		
Israel	71	5	6	6	5	8	5	3	12	5	4	8	7	5	3	4	2	1	6	8
Denmark	101		5			12		12	4					3		3		2	4	5
Switzerland	2													2						
Sweden	62	3		2	10			1	6	3	5	12			12				7	
Azerbaijan	113		12	12	6	3	8	8	1	2	10	2	5	12		10	10			6
Ukraine	77	2		3			1	5	2	10	2	4	2	7		6	6	6	8	10
Netherlands	29			5	2	1	6	1				3	4	1	4		4		1	
Romania	104	12	3	8	4	7	4		3	6	6	10	8	4	8	10	3	4	2	4
Slovenia	6												1							
Ireland	67	10		1	12		2	4	8	7			3				12		5	
Bulgaria	19	6		7				6			3					5	5		3	
Cyprus	67	4				6			5	4	1		10		2					
Croatia	33		4		7		12	2							7			12		7
Georgia	106	1	7	10	1	2	7	7	7	12	7	1	6		6	7	7	10	10	12
Turkey	118	8	10		8	10	3		10	8	8	7		6	10	8	8	3	12	3

2010 Eurovision 55: Oslo, Norway

Final qualification rules: Top 10 placed countries from each semi-final. Automatic qualification: United Kingdom, France, Germany, Spain, Norway.
Points awarded are the combined totals of the televoting and jury votes from each of the 39 participating countries.

Rank	Start	Country	Artist	Song	Writer	Composer	POINTS
1	22	Germany	Lena Meyer-Landrut	Satellite	Julie Frost & John Gordon	Julie Frost & John Gordon	246
2	14	Turkey	maNga	We Could Be The Same	Evren Özdemir, maNga, Fiona Movery Akıncı	maNga	170
3	19	Romania	Paula Seling & Ovi	Playing With Fire	Ovidiu Cernăuțeanu	Ovidiu Cernăuțeanu	162
4	25	Denmark	Chanée & N'evergreen	In A Moment Like This	Thomas G:son, Henrik Sethsson & Erik Bernholm	Thomas G:son, Henrik Sethsson & Erik Bernholm	149
5	1	Azerbaijan	Safura	Drip Drop	Sandra Bjurman	Anders Bagge, Stefan Örn	145
6	7	Belgium	Tom Dice	Me And My Guitar	Tom Dice, Jeroen Swinnen & Ashley Hicklin	Tom Dice, Jeroen Swinnen & Ashley Hicklin	143
7	21	Armenia	Eva Rivas	Apricot Stone	Karen Kavaleryan	Armen Martirosyan	141
8	11	Greece	Giorgos Alkaios & Friends	OPA	Giannis Antoniou & Friends	Giorgos Alkaios	140
9	13	Georgia	Sofia Nizharadze	Shine	Hanne Sorvaag, Harry Sommerdahl & Christian Leuzzi	Hanne Sorvaag, Harry Sommerdahl & Christian Leuzzi	136
10	17	Ukraine	Alyosha	Sweet People	Olena Kucher	Olena Kucher, Borys Kukoba & Vadim Lisitsa	108
11	20	Russia	Peter Nalitch & Friends	Lost And Forgotten	Peter Nalitch	Peter Nalitch	90
12	18	France	Jessy Matador	Allez Ola Olé	H Ducamin & J Ballue	H Ducamin & J Ballue	82
13	8	Serbia	Milan Stanković	Ovo Je Balkan	Goran Bregović, Marina Tucaković & Liljana Jorgovanović	Goran Bregović	72
14	24	Israel	Harel Skaat	Milim	Noam Horev	Tomer Adaddi	71
15	2	Spain	Daniel Diges	Algo Pequeñito (Something Tiny)	Jesús Cañadilla, Luis Miguel de la Varga, Alberto Jodar, Daniel Diges	Jesús Cañadilla, Luis Miguel de la Varga, Alberto Jodar, Daniel Diges	68
16	15	Albania	Juliana Pasha	It's All About You	Pirro Çako	Ardit Gjebrea	62
17	6	Bosnia & H	Vukašin Brajić	Thunder And Lightning	Dino Šaran	Dino Šaran	51
18	23	Portugal	Filipa Azevedo	Há Dias Assim	Augusto Madureira	Augusto Madureira	43
19	16	Iceland	Hera Björk	Je Ne Sais Quoi	Örlygur Smári & Hera Björk	Örlygur Smári & Hera Björk	41
20	3	Norway	Didrik Solli-Tangen	My Heart Is Yours	Hanne Sørvaag & Fredrik Kempe	Hanne Sørvaag & Fredrik Kempe	35
21	5	Cyprus	Jon Lilygreen & The Islanders	Life Looks Better In Spring	Nasos Lambrianides	Nasos Lambrianides, Melis Konstantinou	27
22	4	Moldova	Sunstroke Project & Olia Tira	Run Away	Alina Galetskaya	Anton Ragoza & Sergey Stepanov	27
23	10	Ireland	Niamh Kavanagh	It's For You	Niall Mooney, Mårten Eriksson, Jonas Gladnikoff & Lina Eriksson	Niall Mooney, Mårten Eriksson, Jonas Gladnikoff & Lina Eriksson	25
24	9	Belarus	3+2	Butterflies	Malka Chaplin	Maxim Fadeev	18
25	12	United Kingdom	Josh Dubovie	That Sounds Good To Me	Pete Waterman, Mike Stock, Steve Crosby	Pete Waterman, Mike Stock, Steve Crosby	10

Scoreboard — points awarded by each voting country (rows) to each finalist (columns).

Finalists (columns), with TOTAL points:

Finalist	TOTAL
Azerbaijan	145
Spain	68
Norway	35
Moldova	27
Cyprus	27
Bosnia & Herzegovina	51
Belgium	143
Serbia	72
Belarus	18
Ireland	25
Greece	140
United Kingdom	10
Georgia	136
Turkey	170
Albania	62
Iceland	41
Ukraine	108
France	82
Romania	162
Russia	90
Armenia	141
Germany	246
Portugal	43
Israel	71
Denmark	149

Voting countries (rows), with voting-announcement order:

United Kingdom (32), Ukraine (23), Turkey (6), Switzerland (30), Sweden (38), Spain (20), Slovenia (11), Slovakia (21), Serbia (4), Russia (13), Romania (1), Portugal (14), Poland (8), Norway (26), Netherlands (33), Moldova (36), Malta (25), Lithuania (28), Latvia (24), Israel (34), Ireland (2), Iceland (17), Greece (16), Germany (3), Georgia (37), FYR Macedonia (35), France (19), Finland (10), Estonia (12), Denmark (18), Cyprus (27), Croatia (7), Bulgaria (22), Bosnia & Herzegovina (9), Belgium (31), Belarus (29), Azerbaijan (15), Armenia (39), Albania (5).

Voting announcement order (finalists, bottom axis): Azerbaijan 15, Spain 20, Norway 26, Moldova 36, Cyprus 27, Bosnia & Herzegovina 9, Belgium 31, Serbia 4, Belarus 29, Ireland 2, Greece 16, United Kingdom 32, Georgia 37, Turkey 6, Albania 5, Iceland 17, Ukraine 23, France 19, Romania 1, Russia 13, Armenia 39, Germany 3, Portugal 14, Israel 34, Denmark 18.

Votes are cast by countries participating in each semi-final plus the five automatically qualifying countries decided by draw: United Kingdom and Spain in semi-final 1, France, Germany and Italy in semi-final 2. Points awarded are based on the combined votes of the viewers and jury from each country voting in this semi-final. The top 10 countries in each semi-final qualify for the final.

Rank	Start	Country	Artist	Song	Writer	Composer	POINTS
1Q	19	Greece	Loucas Yiorkas feat Stereo Mike	Watch My Dance	Eleana Vrachali	Giannis Christodoulopoulos	133
2Q	18	Azerbaijan	Ell/Nikki	Running Scared	Stefan Örn, Sandra Bjurman	Stefan Örn, Sandra Bjurman, Iain Farquharson	122
3Q	10	Finland	Paradise Oskar	Da Da Dam	Axel Ehnström	Axel Ehnström	103
4Q	14	Iceland	Sjonni's Friends	Coming Home	Thorunn Clausen & Sjonni Brink	Sjonni Brink	100
5Q	17	Lithuania	Evelina Sašenko	C'est Ma Vie	Andrius Kairys	Paulius Zdanavičius	81
6Q	9	Georgia	Eldrine	One More Day	DJ Rock, Mikheil Chelidze	Beso Tsikhelashvili	74
7Q	15	Hungary	Kati Wolf	What About My Dreams?	Péter Geszti, Johnny K Palmer	Viktor Rakonczai; Gergő Rácz	72
8Q	6	Serbia	Nina	Čaroban	Kristina Kovač	Kristina Kovač	67
9Q	7	Russia	Alexej Vorobjov	Get You	Alexej Vorobjov, Nadir Khayat, AJ Junior, Bilal Hajji, Eric Sanicola	Alexej Vorobjov, Nadir Khayat, AJ Junior, Bilal Hajji, Eric Sanicola	64
10Q	8	Switzerland	Anna Rossinelli	In Love For A While	David Klein	David Klein	55
11	11	Malta	Glen Vella	One Life	Fleur Balzan	Paul Giordimaina	54
12	4	Armenia	Emmy	Boom Boom	Sosi Khanikyan	Hayk Harutyunyan, Hayk Hovhannisyan	54
13	5	Turkey	Yüksek Sadakat	Live It Up	Ergün Arsal	Kutlu Özmakinaci	47
14	3	Albania	Aurela Gaçe	Feel The Passion	Sokol Marsi	Shpetim Saraci	47
15	13	Croatia	Daria	Celebrate	Boris Djurdjevic & Marina Mudrinic	Boris Djurdjevic	41
16	12	San Marino	Senit	Stand By	Radiosa Romani	Radiosa Romani	34
17	2	Norway	Stella Mwangi	Haba Haba	Stella Mwangi	Big City/Beyond51	30
18	16	Portugal	Homens Da Luta	Luta É Alegria	Nuno Duarte	Vasco Duarte	22
19	1	Poland	Magdalena Tul	Jestem	Magdalena Tul	Magdalena Tul	18

2011 Eurovision 56: Düsseldorf, Germany

Semi-final 1: 10 May 2011

Points awarded to each entrant (row) by each voting country (column).

Entrant	TOTAL	United Kingdom	Turkey	Switzerland	Spain	Serbia	San Marino	Russia	Portugal	Poland	Norway	Malta	Lithuania	Iceland	Hungary	Greece	Georgia	Finland	Croatia	Azerbaijan	Armenia	Albania
Poland	18	5									3		2		4		4				1	1
Norway	30		2	2					2	1		4		10				8		1		
Albania	47		8	6			8		4							12	8		7	2		
Armenia	54		7		3		7	8		2			5	4		8			4	4		
Turkey	47	1		5			10	2		6		7	3		6		3			12	2	12
Serbia	67		3	12	2		3	4	1	3	7	3	8	5	3	3	5	3	12	5	12	2
Russia	64					6	1		3	5	4		6	3	8		2	6	3		8	3
Switzerland	55	2			6	2			5		6			7	1				2	8	3	
Georgia	74		10			4	2	5	8	10		8	12	6		10		1	5	3	8	5
Finland	103	6	1	10	4	3	12	12			12	2	7	12	6		1			6	6	8
Malta	54		2			5				4			1		2	2	6				4	7
San Marino	34		5	8							12									6		7
Croatia	41				10	12	4	1		4	1			1	12	6				10	5	8
Iceland	100	7		8		8		3	10		1	10	2			5		12	6			
Hungary	72	10	6		12	10			6		8						10	2		7		
Portugal	22	3		4	8							6				1		10				
Lithuania	81	12		3	5	1		7	7	12	10	6		2	5	4	12	7		7	5	4
Azerbaijan	122	4	12	1	1		5	10		8	2	1	10	8	7	7	7	5	10		7	10
Greece	133	8	4	7	7	7	6	6	12	7	5	5	4		10		10	4	8	10	10	6

Votes are cast by countries participating in each semi-final plus the five automatically qualifying countries decided by draw: United Kingdom and Spain in semi-final 1, France, Germany and Italy in semi-final 2. Points awarded are based on the combined votes of the viewers and jury from each country voting in this semi-final. The top 10 countries in each semi-final qualify for the final.

Rank	Start	Country	Artist	Song	Writer	Composer	POINTS
1Q	8	Sweden	Eric Saade	Popular	Fredrik Kempe	Fredrik Kempe	155
2Q	18	Denmark	A Friend in London	New Tomorrow	Lise Cabble, Jakob Schack Glæsner	Lise Cabble, Jakob Schack Glæsner	135
3Q	13	Slovenia	Maja Keuc	No One	Urša Vlašič	Matjaž Vlašič	112
4Q	14	Romania	Hotel FM	Change	Alexandra Ivan, Gabriel Băruţa	Gabriel Băruţa	111
5Q	1	Bosnia & H	Dino Merlin	Love in Rewind	Dino Merlin	Dino Merlin	109
6Q	6	Ukraine	Mika Newton	Angel	Maryna Skomorohova	Ruslan Kvinta	81
7Q	2	Austria	Nadine Beiler	The Secret is Love	Nadine Beiler	Thomas Rabitsch	69
8Q	19	Ireland	Jedward	Lipstick	Daniel Priddy, Lars Halvor Jensen, Martin Michael Larsson	Daniel Priddy, Lars Halvor Jensen, Martin Michael Larsson	68
9Q	15	Estonia	Getter Jaani	Rockefeller Street	Sven Lõhmus	Sven Lõhmus	60
10Q	7	Moldova	Zdob şi Zdub	So Lucky	Andy Schuman, Marc Elsner	Mihai Gincu, Marc Elsner	54
11	4	Belgium	Witloof Bay	With Love Baby	Benoît Giaux, RoxorLoops	Benoît Giaux, RoxorLoops	53
12	10	Bulgaria	Poli Genova	Na Inat	Sebastian Arman, David Bronner, Borislav Milanov, Poli Genova	Sebastian Arman, David Bronner, Borislav Milanov, Poli Genova	48
13	5	Slovakia	TWiiNS	I'm Still Alive	Bryan Todd, Sandra Nordstrom, Branislav Jancich	Bryan Todd, Sandra Nordstrom, Branislav Jancich	48
14	16	Belarus	Anastasiya Vinnikova	I Love Belarus	Eugene Oleinik, Svetlana Geraskova	Eugene Oleinik	45
15	12	Israel	Dana International	Ding Dong	Dana International	Dana International	38
16	11	FYR Macedonia	Vlatko Ilievski	Rusinka	Marko Marinkovikj-Slatkaristika, Jovan Jovanov	Grigor Koprov, Vladimir Dojchinovski	36
17	17	Latvia	Musiqq	Angel in Disguise	Marats Ogleznevs	Marats Ogleznevs	25
18	9	Cyprus	Christos Mylordos	San Aggelos S'Agapisa	Mihalis Antoniou	Andreas Anastasiou	16
19	3	The Netherlands	3JS	Never Alone ˉ	Jaap Kwakman, Jan Dulles, Jaap de Witte	Jaap Kwakman, Jan Dulles, Jaap de Witte	13

2011 Eurovision 56: Düsseldorf, Germany

	TOTAL	Ukraine	Sweden	Slovenia	Slovakia	Romania	Netherlands	Moldova	Latvia	Italy	Israel	Ireland	Germany	FYR Macedonia	France	Estonia	Denmark	Cyprus	Bulgaria	Bosnia & H	Belgium	Belarus	Austria
Bosnia & Herzegovina	109	4	8	12	12		10		2	4			7	12	10		7				4	5	12
Austria	69	1	4	7	5		3			5		2	12		1	2	5	4	10	7	1		
Netherlands	13																		5		8		
Belgium	53			2		8	6		3	2	2					6	1	8	2	6	8		
Slovakia	48	12				3		7	4			5				5	3		3	6		3	5
Ukraine	81		3	3		2				6	8						7	5		4	3	12	
Moldova	54			6	10	12				7	4	4	4			12				5		10	6
Sweden	155	5		5	4	7	12	8	1	3	12	8	5	6	12	6	12	12	1		12	8	8
Cyprus	16	6								8	1			5	3		4						
Bulgaria	48			4			2			10		7		10				10					10
FYR Macedonia	36	7		8				5		1										10	2		2
Israel	38		5			4		1							7							6	
Slovenia	112		1		8	10	5	4	5		6		3	4	5	4	6	8	8	12	6		3
Romania	111		7		7		4	12			7	3	6	2	8		1			1			
Estonia	60	8			6		8	10	8		5	10		8	4		10	3	4	3	10	1	4
Belarus	45	10			1	1			6				1	1			2						1
Latvia	25		2					2			10	6	2			8		6				2	
Denmark	135	3	12	10	3	5	7	3	12	12	3	12	10	3		10		7	12	2	5	4	7
Ireland	68	2	10	1	2	6	1		10				8	7	2	3			7		7	7	

2011 Eurovision 56: Düsseldorf, Germany

Final qualification rules: Top 10 placed countries from each semi-final. Automatic qualification: United Kingdom, France, Germany, Spain, Italy. Points awarded are based on the combined votes of the viewers and jury from each of the 43 participating countries.

Rank	Start	Country	Artist	Song	Writer	Composer	POINTS
1	19	Azerbaijan	Ell/Nikki	Running Scared	Stefan Örn, Sandra Bjurman	Stefan Örn, Sandra Bjurman, Iain Farquharson	221
2	12	Italy	Raphael Gualazzi	Madness of Love	Raphael Gualazzi	Raphael Gualazzi	189
3	7	Sweden	Eric Saade	Popular	Fredrik Kempe	Fredrik Kempe	185
4	23	Ukraine	Mika Newton	Angel	Maryna Skomorohova	Ruslan Kvinta	159
5	3	Denmark	A Friend in London	New Tomorrow	Lise Cabble, Jakob Schack Glæsner	Lise Cabble, Jakob Schack Glæsner	134
6	2	Bosnia & H	Dino Merlin	Love in Rewind	Dino Merlin	Dino Merlin	125
7	9	Greece	Loucas Yiorkas feat Stereo Mike	Watch My Dance	Eleana Vrachali	Giannis Christodoulopoulos	120
8	6	Ireland	Jedward	Lipstick	Daniel Priddy, Lars Halvor Jensen, Martin Michael Larsson	Daniel Priddy, Lars Halvor Jensen, Martin Michael Larsson	119
9	25	Georgia	Eldrine	One More Day	DJ Rock, Mikheil Chelidze	Beso Tsikhelashvili	110
10	16	Germany	Lena Meyer-Landrut	Taken by a Stranger	Gus Seyffert, Nicole Morier, Monica Birkenes	Gus Seyffert, Nicole Morier, Monica Birkenes	107
11	14	United Kingdom	Blue	I Can	Ciaron Bell, Ben Collier, Ian Hope, Duncan James, Liam Keenan, Lee Ryan, StarSign	Ciaron Bell, Ben Collier, Ian Hope, Duncan James, Liam Keenan, Lee Ryan, StarSign	100
12	15	Moldova	Zdob și Zdub	So Lucky	Andy Schuman, Marc Elsner	Mihai Gincu, Marc Elsner	97
13	20	Slovenia	Maja Keuc	No One	Urša Vlašič	Matjaž Vlašič	96
14	24	Serbia	Nina	Čaroban	Kristina Kovač	Kristina Kovač	85
15	11	France	Amaury Vassili	Sognu	Jean-Pierre Marcellesi, Julie Miller	Daniel Moyne, Quentin Bachelet	82
16	10	Russia	Alexej Vorobjov	Get You	Alexej Vorobjov, Nadir Khayat, AJ Junior, Bilal Hajji, Eric Sanicola	Alexej Vorobjov, Nadir Khayat, AJ Junior, Bilal Hajji, Eric Sanicola	77
17	17	Romania	Hotel FM	Change	Alexandra Ivan, Gabriel Băruţa	Gabriel Băruţa	77
18	18	Austria	Nadine Beiler	The Secret is Love	Nadine Beiler	Thomas Rabitsch	64
19	4	Lithuania	Evelina Sašenko	C'est Ma Vie	Andrius Kairys	Paulius Zdanavičius	63
20	21	Iceland	Sjonni's Friends	Coming Home	Thorunn Clausen & Sjonni Brink	Sjonni Brink	61
21	1	Finland	Paradise Oskar	Da Da Dam	Axel Ehnström	Axel Ehnström	57
22	5	Hungary	Kati Wolf	What About My Dreams?	Péter Geszti, Johnny K Palmer	Viktor Rakonczai, Gergő Rácz	53
23	22	Spain	Lucía Pérez	Que Me Quiten Lo Bailao	Rafael Artesero	Rafael Artesero	50
24	8	Estonia	Getter Jaani	Rockefeller Street	Sven Lõhmus	Sven Lõhmus	44
25	13	Switzerland	Anna Rossinelli	In Love For A While	David Klein	David Klein	19

This scoreboard is a cross-tabulation. Columns (across the top, read downward) are the voting countries with their order of announcement; rows (along the bottom) are the 25 finalists receiving points, each with its TOTAL.

Receiving countries (rows) and TOTAL points:

Receiving country	TOTAL
Finland	57
Bosnia & Herzegovina	125
Denmark	134
Lithuania	63
Hungary	53
Ireland	119
Sweden	185
Estonia	44
Greece	120
Russia	77
France	82
Italy	189
Switzerland	19
United Kingdom	100
Moldova	97
Germany	107
Romania	77
Austria	64
Azerbaijan	221
Slovenia	96
Iceland	61
Spain	50
Ukraine	159
Serbia	85
Georgia	110

Voting countries (columns) and order votes announced:

Voting country	Order votes announced
United Kingdom	13
Ukraine	6
Turkey	22
Switzerland	23
Sweden	17
Spain	38
Slovenia	21
Slovakia	12
Serbia	27
San Marino	18
Russia	1
Romania	30
Portugal	33
Poland	16
Norway	8
Netherlands	3
Moldova	41
Malta	32
Lithuania	35
Latvia	43
Italy	4
Israel	39
Ireland	37
Iceland	11
Hungary	34
Greece	24
Germany	19
Georgia	25
FYR Macedonia	10
France	26
Finland	7
Estonia	40
Denmark	14
Cyprus	5
Croatia	28
Bulgaria	2
Bosnia & Herzegovina	36
Belgium	42
Belarus	29
Azerbaijan	20
Austria	15
Armenia	9
Albania	31

2012 Eurovision 57: Baku, Azerbaijan

Semi-final 1: 22 May 2012

Votes are cast by countries participating in each semi-final plus the five automatically qualifying countries decided by draw: Italy and Spain in semi-final 1, France, Germany and the United Kingdom in semi-final 2. Host Azerbaijan voted in semi-final 1. Points awarded are based on the combined votes of the viewers and jury from each of the countries voting in this semi-final. The top 10 countries in each semi-final qualify for the final.

Rank	Start	Country	Artist	Song	Writer	Composer	POINTS
1Q	14	Russia	Buranovskiye Babushki	Party for Everybody	Olga Tuktareva, Mary S Applegate	Viktor Drobysh, Timofei Leontiev	152
2Q	5	Albania	Rona Nishliu	Suus	Rona Nishliu	Florent Boshnjaku	146
3Q	6	Romania	Mandinga	Zaleilah	Elena Ionescu, Dihigo Omar Secada, Costi Ionita	Costi Ionita	120
4Q	3	Greece	Eleftheria Eleftheriou	Aphrodisiac	Dimitri Stassos, Mikaela Stenström, Dajana Lööf	Dimitri Stassos, Mikaela Stenström, Dajana Lööf	116
5Q	17	Moldova	Pasha Parfeny	Lăutar	Pasha Parfeny	Pasha Parfeny, Alex Brashovean	100
6Q	18	Ireland	Jedward	Waterline	Nick Jarl & Sharon Vaughn	Nick Jarl & Sharon Vaughn	92
7Q	12	Cyprus	Ivi Adamou	La La Love	Alex Papaconstantinou, Bjorn Djupström, Alexandra Zakka &	Alex Papaconstantinou, Bjorn Djupström, Alexandra Zakka &	91
8Q	2	Iceland	Greta Salóme & Jónsi	Never Forget	Gréta Salóme	Gréta Salóme	75
9Q	13	Denmark	Soluna Samay	Should've Known Better	Chief 1, Remee & Isam B	Chief 1 & Remee	63
10Q	15	Hungary	Compact Disco	Sound of Our Hearts	Behnam Lotfi, Gábor Pál	Behnam Lotfi, Gábor Pál	52
11	7	Switzerland	Sinplus	Unbreakable	Attila Sándor, Csaba Walkó, Gabriel Broggini, Ivan Broggini	Attila Sándor, Csaba Walkó, Gabriel Broggini, Ivan Broggini	45
12	9	Finland	Pernilla	När Jag Blundar	Jonas Karlsson	Jonas Karlsson	41
13	10	Israel	Izabo	Time	Ran Shem-Tov & Shiri Hadar	Ran Shem-Tov & Shiri Hadar	33
14	11	San Marino	Valentina Monetta	The Social Network Song (Oh Oh - Uh - Oh Oh)	Timothy Touchton & José Santana Rodriguez	Ralph Siegel	31
15	1	Montenegro	Rambo Amadeus	Euro Neuro	Rambo Amadeus	Rambo Amadeus	20
16	4	Latvia	Anmary	Beautiful Song	Rolands Üdris	Ivars Makstnieks	17
17	8	Belgium	Iris	Would You?	Nina Sampermans, Jean Bosco Safari, Walter Mannaerts	Nina Sampermans, Jean Bosco Safari, Walter Mannaerts	16
18	16	Austria	Trackshittaz	Woki Mit Deim Popo	Lukas Plöchl, Manuel Hoffelner	Lukas Plöchl	8

Semi-final 1: 22 May 2012

	TOTAL	Switzerland	Spain	San Marino	Russia	Romania	Montenegro	Moldova	Latvia	Italy	Israel	Ireland	Iceland	Hungary	Greece	Finland	Denmark	Cyprus	Belgium	Azerbaijan	Austria	Albania
Montenegro	20	8		8				2	5	1	4			4	5	10	10	8	5		2	12
Iceland	75	4	6	3	1		5				3										1	
Greece	116	3	3	7	5	12	10	10	3	5		10	5	10			4	12	8	10		8
Latvia	17				4		2	4				4								3		
Albania	146	12	4	10	2	4	12	1	4	12	5	1	3	1	10	5	7	10	10	12	12	
Romania	120	2	12	6	8		7	12		10	8	12	4	3	8	1	1		4	7	5	5
Switzerland	45			1		2		8	7	8	1	6	2	8	4			2			3	3
Belgium	16	1	1			1										2		6				
Finland	41													12	2		8	1				1
Israel	33		2						1							3				5	7	
San Marino	31						4	7	6		2	3	7	5					1	8		10
Cyprus	91		8		7	5	6	3	8	3	10	5	12	7	12	4	5			1	4	6
Denmark	63	10		4	3	3				7	12	7	8		7	8		7	12			
Russia	152		7	2		7	8	6	12	6		8	6		3	12	12	5	6	2	10	7
Hungary	52	6			6	6										7	3					
Austria	8	5											1						2			
Moldova	100	7	10	5	12	10	3		2	4	6	2	10	2	6	6	6	3	3	6	6	4
Ireland	92		5	12	10	8	1	5	10	2	7			6	1		2	4	7	4	8	

Votes are cast by countries participating in each semi-final plus the five automatically qualifying countries decided by draw: Italy and Spain in semi-final 1, France, Germany and the United Kingdom in semi-final 2. Host Azerbaijan voted in semi-final 1. Points awarded are based on the combined votes of the viewers and jury from each of the countries voting in this semi-final. The top 10 countries in each semi-final qualify for the final.

Rank	Start	Country	Artist	Song	Writer	Composer	POINTS
1Q	11	Sweden	Loreen	Euphoria	Thomas G:son & Peter Boström	Thomas G:son & Peter Boström	181
2Q	1	Serbia	Željko Joksimović	Nije Ljubav Stvar	Marina Tucaković & Miloš Roganović	Željko Joksimović	159
3Q	18	Lithuania	Donny Montell	Love is Blind	Brandon Stone & Jodie Rose	Brandon Stone	107
4Q	14	Estonia	Ott Lepland	Kuula	Aapo Ilves	Ott Lepland	100
5Q	13	Turkey	Can Bonomo	Love Me Back	Can Bonomo	Can Bonomo	80
6Q	17	Bosnia & H	MayaSar	Korake Ti Znam	Maja Sarihodžić	Maja Sarihodžić	77
7Q	4	Malta	Kurt Calleja	This Is The Night	Johan Jämtberg, Mikael Gunnerås & Kurt Calleja	Johan Jämtberg, Mikael Gunnerås & Kurt Calleja	70
8Q	7	Ukraine	Gaitana	Be My Guest	Gaitana	Gaitana and KIWI Project	64
9Q	2	FYR Macedonia	Kaliopi	Crno I Belo	Kaliopi	Romeo Grill	53
10Q	16	Norway	Tooji	Stay	Tooji; Figge Boström & Peter Boström	Tooji; Figge Boström & Peter Boström	45
11	8	Bulgaria	Sofi Marinova	Love Unlimited	Donka Vasileva	Krum Geopriev & Iasen Kozev	45
12	10	Croatia	Nina Badrić	Nebo	Nina Badrić	Nina Badrić	42
13	6	Portugal	Filipa Sousa	Vida Minha	Carlos Coelho	Andrej Babic	39
14	12	Georgia	Anri Jokhadze	I'm A Joker	Bibi Kvachadze	Rusudan Chkhaidze	36
15	3	Netherlands	Joan Franka	You And Me	Joan Franka	Joan Franka, Jessica Hoogenboom	35
16	5	Belarus	Litesound	We Are The Heroes	Dmitry Kariakin, Vladimir Kariakin	Dmitry Kariakin, Vladimir Kariakin	35
17	9	Slovenia	Eva Boto	Verjamem	Igor Pirković	Vladimir Graić, Hari Mata Hari	31
18	15	Slovakia	Max Jason Mai	Don't Close Your Eyes	Max Jason Mai	Max Jason Mai	22

	United Kingdom	Ukraine	Turkey	Sweden	Slovenia	Slovakia	Serbia	Portugal	Norway	Netherlands	Malta	Lithuania	Germany	Georgia	FYR Macedonia	France	Estonia	Croatia	Bulgaria	Bosnia & Herzegovina	Belarus	TOTAL
Serbia	3	8	8	8	12	8		8	10	10	5	2	10	10	12	12	1	10	12	10	8	**159**
FYR Macedonia		5		1	6		8		3		1	3	8	1				7	7	8	2	**53**
Netherlands	4		7		2	2						6			2			5				**35**
Malta	12	6	6	4	4		3			2				4	1			2	6		5	**70**
Belarus		12								1		7		8			8			1		**35**
Portugal			1		3	5			5		4	1	3		3	8	7	3				**39**
Ukraine	2			6		1	4	2	2	6	6	5		6	6	2	5	1	5	5	12	**64**
Bulgaria	5		10				2	3	6		2		2			3	3			6		**45**
Slovenia							10						4		4			8				**31**
Croatia		1		10	8										7				10			**42**
Sweden	8	7	5		10	12		6	12	12	8	10	12	12	8	6	12	6	8	12	7	**181**
Georgia		10	3	12			12	10		7		12				10	10				6	**36**
Turkey	6	2		7		3	7	7	1		12	8	6	3		7	2			7		**80**
Estonia	7	3		3	1	10	1	1	8	8	7		1	7		1			3		1	**100**
Slovakia				2									5						2	2	4	**22**
Norway			4			4		4		3	3	4	7			4	6		3	4	3	**45**
Bosnia & Herzegovina	1		12	5	5	6	5	12	4	5				2	10			12	1			**77**
Lithuania	10	4	2		7	7	6	5	7	4	10			5	5	5	4	4	4	3	10	**104**

2012 Eurovision 57: Baku, Azerbaijan

Final qualification rules: Top 10 placed countries from each semi-final. Automatic qualification: United Kingdom, France, Germany, Spain, Italy & hosts Azerbaijan.
Points awarded are based on the combined votes of the viewers and jury from each of the 42 participating countries.

Rank	Start	Country	Artist	Song	Writer	Composer	POINTS
1	17	Sweden	Loreen	Euphoria	Thomas G:son & Peter Boström	Thomas G:son & Peter Boström	372
2	6	Russia	Buranovskiye Babushki	Party For Everybody	Olga Tuktareva, Mary S Applegate	Viktor Drobysh, Timofei Leontiev	259
3	24	Serbia	Željko Joksimović	Nije Ljubav Stvar	Marina Tucaković & Miloš Roganović	Željko Joksimović	214
4	13	Azerbaijan	Sabina Babayeva	When The Music Dies	Anders Bagge, Sandra Bjurman, Stefan Örn, Johan Kronlund	Anders Bagge, Johan Kronlund, Sandra Bjurman, Stefan Örn	150
5	3	Albania	Rona Nishliu	Suus	Rona Nishliu	Florent Boshnjaku	146
6	11	Estonia	Ott Lepland	Kuula	Aapo Ilves	Ott Lepland	120
7	18	Turkey	Can Bonomo	Love Me Back	Can Bonomo	Can Bonomo	112
8	20	Germany	Roman Lob	Standing Still	Wayne Hector, Jamie Cullum, Steve Robson	Wayne Hector, Jamie Cullum, Steve Robson	110
9	10	Italy	Nina Zilli	L'Amore È Femmina (Out Of Love)	Nina Zilli, Christian Rabb, Kristoffer Sjökvist, Frida Molander & Charlie Mason	Christian Rabb, Kristoffer Sjökvist, Frida Molander & Charlie Mason	101
10	19	Spain	Pastora Soler	Quédate Conmigo (Stay With Me)	Antonio Sánchez	Antonio Sánchez, Thomas G:son & Erik Bernholm	97
11	26	Moldova	Pasha Parfeny	Lăutar	Pasha Parfeny	Pasha Parfeny, Alex Brashovean	81
12	14	Romania	Mandinga	Zaleilah	Elena Ionescu, Dihigo Omar Secada, Costi Ionita	Costi Ionita	71
13	22	FYR Macedonia	Kaliopi	Crno I Belo	Kaliopi	Romeo Grill	71
14	4	Lithuania	Donny Martell	Love Is Blind	Brandon Stone & Jodie Rose	Brandon Stone	70
15	25	Ukraine	Gaitana	Be My Guest	Gaitana	Gaitana and KIWI Project	65
16	8	Cyprus	Ivi Adamou	La La Love	A Papaconstantinou, B Djupström, A Zakka & V Svensson	A Papaconstantinou, B Djupström, A Zakka & V Svensson	65
17	16	Greece	Eleftheria Eleftheriou	Aphrodisiac	Dimitri Stassos, Mikaela Stenström, Dajana Lööf	Dimitri Stassos, Mikaela Stenström, Dajana Lööf	64
18	5	Bosnia & H	MayaSar	Korake Ti Znam	Maja Sarihodžić	Maja Sarihodžić	55
19	23	Ireland	Jedward	Waterline	Nick Jarl & Sharon Vaughn	Nick Jarl & Sharon Vaughn	46
20	7	Iceland	Greta Salóme & Jónsi	Never Forget	Gréta Salóme	Gréta Salóme	46
21	21	Malta	Kurt Calleja	This Is The Night	Johan Jämtberg, Mikael Gunnerås & Kurt Calleja	Johan Jämtberg, Mikael Gunnerås & Kurt Calleja	41
22	9	France	Anggun	Echo (You And I)	William Rousseau & Anggun	Jean Pierre Pilot & William Rousseau	21
23	15	Denmark	Soluna Samay	Should've Known Better	Chief 1, Remee & Isam B	Chief 1 & Remee	21
24	2	Hungary	Compact Disco	Sound Of Our Hearts	Behnam Lotfi, Gábor Pál, Attila Sándor, Csaba Walkó	Behnam Lotfi, Gábor Pál, Attila Sándor, Csaba Walkó	19
25	1	United Kingdom	Engelbert Humperdinck	Love Will Set You Free	Martin Terefe & Sacha Skarbek	Martin Terefe & Sacha Skarbek	12
26	12	Norway	Tooji	Stay	Tooji, Figge Boström & Peter Boström	Tooji, Figge Boström & Peter Boström	7

Order votes announced	TOTAL	United Kingdom (12)	Ukraine (5)	Turkey (13)	Switzerland (18)	Sweden (27)	Spain (33)	Slovenia (19)	Slovakia (22)	Serbia (37)	San Marino (10)	Russia (39)	Romania (3)	Portugal (25)	Norway (28)	Netherlands (24)	Montenegro (2)	Moldova (16)	Malta (9)	Lithuania (29)	Latvia (32)	Italy (36)	Israel (41)	Ireland (42)	Iceland (26)	Hungary (40)	Greece (14)	Germany (38)	Georgia (35)	FYR Macedonia (23)	France (11)	Finland (34)	Estonia (30)	Denmark (31)	Cyprus (20)	Croatia (21)	Bulgaria (17)	Bosnia & Herzegovina (15)	Belgium (7)	Belarus (6)	Azerbaijan (8)	Austria (4)	Albania (1)
United Kingdom	12																																											
Hungary	19			1						2			7					1			2			4														1				8	
Albania	146	8			1	1		3	8	1	12		1				10		1	12	1	12					10 8	6 10	12 3		12		6			4	5	4 7	6	10			4	
Lithuania	70	7		5	12 5			7				5		4	6	1 1			1	4	4			7			8	10		12		3 3	4	3			5	1	3			8	
Bosnia & Herzegovina	55			10	1		7		2	5				8			6		4												7			2			10		3	4		7	
Russia	259		7 10 3	7		8	8	8	3	7	10 7			8	5	4	4	6	3	6	10 10	10	7	6	7	7	7 7	7	5	8	4	4	8	8		5	6	6		6 12	12	7	5	3
Iceland	46					7	4	4	4					8	5			4					3				6		3	5	4	6	7	6 7		5	6	7 3		6 5				
Cyprus	65				6	5 12	5			8	2 2		2									5		3	8		12						1									2	6	
France	21				2 6	2															3			4	6			2						7			2	2	2	6			2	2
Italy	101	7	4		5		1	5 5	5		7			4 2	4		2	5	4 10	4			2 4	2	4	2	3 5	3	2	4	5	1		7		2 2	2 2						2	7
Estonia	120		1			6 8	6	7	10		6	6		7 7	7 7	7	2	2		8 8	8 8			8	10 8				4			10 10		10 10	3				2	4	4			
Norway	7					3										3									1																			
Azerbaijan	150	4	12 12	12			10		6	3 6	10 4	10							12 12 10 5	12 12	12		1 8	1	1		5			2 10	2					8		7 7	7	7		6		12
Romania	71			4				7			1	1		4								6 7	6	5 6			7						4	1		3 1		1	3	3				
Denmark	21				1										2							2	2			5		1	5		10		2 5	2 5					2 1					
Greece	64	12	3 5	3					4	4		3	8					4						2		5			1 1	1			4		12				2	2	5			12
Sweden	372	12	6 6	7 6	1 7	1	12	12 10	10 12	10 7	3	10 12	10	3	12 12	12 12	4	6 7 7	6 7	12 10	12	6	12 12	12 12	12 12	12 12	12 12	6	12 8	8 8 7	6 8	12 12	12 12	12 12	10 12	10 7	8 7	8 8	8	6 12	6	5 12 7	5 12	5
Turkey	112	1	7 10	7		6 3	8	8	12		5	12 3	3		12 12	8	4	7	8	1 8	1		1			12	1 2	8		8 7	5	5 6	3 6		2	6	12 7	7	5 3	7	10 3 12		
Spain	97	8	6	6 3	4 8	6	5 12	2 3	4 4	8	1	5	6	12 6		6	4		2	8		10			1 2		3		6	5	6	6	3 6	4 6	10	6		3	6 5	6		6		
Germany	110	6			4		3			8				10	2 3	2 3				2	8 7	8	10		10	2		5	2			7	4 3 6	4			6	4	6 5 3	6	2		6	2 4
Malta	41	5	2 7	2 6	4	2 6		5 5	5		2								2												1										8 3			
FYR Macedonia	71	10	8 3	8 3	12			6	12 1	12 1		8	5 5	5	10 10	5	8			7	5			5	4						1		4				3	12 2	12 2	1 1	1 1	1 1	1	
Ireland	46		2		10 10	5		7 12			6	4	5 5	5	1 1				5						3	4					3 6		2	1				5 10 12	5 10	5	3 10		1 10	
Serbia	214	10	2	10 10		10 10	2	7 12	7	7	6	4	5	5	11	5	3		5	2 7 8	2	3 6			3		2 2	8 1	10 8	3 6	3 6	2 8	2	1			10 12 7	10 12	5 10 12 7	5	1	3	1 10	
Ukraine	65		2		2		2				7	8	12 7		1									5											7		1				3 10			
Moldova	81		8	8	2		7	1				12 7 8	6 12 7		3			3									2 2	2						1						1	5		1	

Votes are cast by countries participating in each semi-final plus the five automatically qualifying countries decided by draw: Italy and United Kingdom in semi-final 1, France, Germany and Spain in semi-final 2. Host Sweden voted in semi-final 1. Points awarded are based on the combined votes of the viewers and jury from each of the countries voting in this semi-final. The top 10 countries in each semi-final qualify for the final.

Rank	Start	Country	Artist	Song	Writer	Composer	POINTS
1Q	5	Denmark	Emmelie de Forest	Only Teardrops	Lise Cabble, Julia Fabrin Jakobsen, Thomas Stengaard	Lise Cabble, Julia Fabrin Jakobsen, Thomas Stengaard	167
2Q	6	Russia	Dina Garipova	What If	Gabriel Alares, Joakim Björnberg, Leonid Gutkin	Gabriel Alares, Joakim Björnberg, Leonid Gutkin	156
3Q	7	Ukraine	Zlata Ognevich	Gravity	Karen Kavaleryan	Mikhail Nekrasov	140
4Q	12	Moldova	Aliona Moon	O Mie	Yuliana Scutaru	Pasha Parfeny	95
5Q	15	Belgium	Roberto Bellarosa	Love Kills	Iain James, Jukka Immonen	Iain James, Jukka Immonen	75
6Q	8	Netherlands	Anouk	Birds	Anouk Teeuwe	Tore Johansson, Martin Gjerstad	75
7Q	11	Belarus	Alyona Lanskaya	Solayoh	Martin King	Marc Paelinck	64
8Q	13	Ireland	Ryan Dolan	Only Love Survives	Wez Devine, Ryan Dolan	Wez Devine, Ryan Dolan	54
9Q	10	Lithuania	Andrius Pojavis	Something	Andrius Pojavis	Andrius Pojavis	53
10Q	2	Estonia	Birgit Õigemeel	Et Uus Saaks Alguse	Mihkel Mattisen & Silvia Soro	Mihkel Mattisen	52
11	16	Serbia	Moje 3	Ljubav Je Svuda	Marina Tucaković	Saša Milošević Mare	46
12	9	Montenegro	Who See	Igranka	Dejan Dedovic, Mario Djordjevic, Djordje Miljenovic	Djordje Miljenovic	41
13	4	Croatia	Klapa s mora	Mižerja	Goran Topolovac	Goran Topolovac	38
14	1	Austria	Natália Kelly	Shine	Andreas Grass, Nikola Paryla, Alexander Kahr	Andreas Grass, Nikola Paryla, Alexander Kahr	27
15	14	Cyprus	Despina Olympiou	An Me Thimasai	Zenon Zintilis	Andreas Giorgallis	11
16	3	Slovenia	Hannah	Straight Into Love	Hannah Mancini, Marko Primuzak	Hannah Mancini, Gregor Zemljic, Erik Margan, Matija Rodic	8

	TOTAL	United Kingdom	Ukraine	Sweden	Slovenia	Serbia	Russia	Netherlands	Montenegro	Moldova	Lithuania	Italy	Ireland	Estonia	Denmark	Cyprus	Croatia	Belgium	Belarus	Austria
Austria	27	1			1	2				3		2	4	1	4	2	4	3		
Estonia	52	4	1	6			5	4		5	4	5	8		1			1	5	3
Slovenia	8								3								5			
Croatia	38		6		2	10	4	3			1					1				5
Denmark	167	12	4	12	8	8	10	12		7	6	6	1	12		8	12	10	8	12
Russia	156	10	7	10	10	6		7	5	8	10	4	12	10	12	10	8	7	10	10
Ukraine	140	2		1	12	5	7	8	8	12	12	12	10	6	8	12	7	8	12	2
Netherlands	75	8		8	3	1	3		7		7	1	2	7	10					8
Montenegro	41		8	2		12		2		6	8	10	5		5		6	12	2	
Lithuania	53	7	5		4		1	6	12	2			6	4	2	3			7	
Belarus	64		12			4	2		2	10	3	7	3	8		6	1	4		
Moldova	95			5	7	7	12		6		5	8		3	6	5	2	6	6	7
Ireland	54	6	3	3			6	5	4	1				5	3	7		5	4	
Cyprus	11	3																		
Belgium	75	5		7	6	3	8	10	1	4	2	3	7	2	7	4	3		3	
Serbia	46		2	4	5			1	10								10	2	1	

Votes are cast by countries participating in each semi-final plus the five automatically qualifying countries decided by draw: Italy and United Kingdom in semi-final 1, France, Germany and Spain in semi-final 2. Host Sweden voted in semi-final 1. Points awarded are based on the combined votes of the viewers and jury from each of the countries voting in this semi-final. The top 10 countries in each semi-final qualify for the final.

Rank	Start	Country	Artist	Song	Writer	Composer	POINTS
1Q	4	Azerbaijan	Farid Mammadov	Hold Me	John Ballard & Ralph Charlie Al Fahel	Dimitrios Kontopoulos	139
2Q	9	Greece	Koza Mostra feat. Agathon Iakovidis	Alcohol is Free	Stathis Pachidis, Ilias Kozas	Ilias Kozas	121
3Q	13	Norway	Margaret Berger	I Feed You My Love	Karin Park, Robin Lynch, Niklas Olovson	Karin Park, Robin Lynch, Niklas Olovson	120
4Q	6	Malta	Gianluca	Tomorrow	Boris Cezek & Dean Muscat	Boris Cezek & Dean Muscat	118
5Q	17	Romania	Cezar	It's My Life	Cristian Faur	Cristian Faur	83
6Q	8	Iceland	Eythor Ingi	Ég Á Líf	Örlygur Smári & Pétur Örn Gudmundsson	Örlygur Smári & Pétur Örn Gudmundsson	72
7Q	11	Armenia	Dorians	Lonely Planet	Vardan Zadoyan	Tony Iommi	69
8Q	12	Hungary	ByeAlex	Kedvesem (Zoohacker Remix)	Alex Márta	Alex Márta, Zoltán Palásti Kovács	66
9Q	5	Finland	Krista Siegfrids	Marry Me	Krista Siegfrids, Erik Nyholm, Kristoffer Karlsson, Jessica Lundström	Krista Siegfrids, Erik Nyholm, Kristoffer Karlsson, Jessica Lundström	64
10Q	15	Georgia	Nodi Tatishvili & Sophie Gelovani	Waterfall	Thomas G:son	Thomas G:son & Erik Bernholm	63
11	2	San Marino	Valentina Monetta	Crisalide (Vola)	Mauro Balestri	Ralph Siegel	47
12	7	Bulgaria	Elitsa Todorova feat. Stoyan Yankulov	Samo Shampioni (Only Champions)	Elitsa Todorova, Christian Talev	Elitsa Todorova, Christian Talev	45
13	16	Switzerland	Takasa	You And Me	Georg Schlunegger, Roman Camenzind, Fred Herrmann	Georg Schlunegger, Roman Camenzind, Fred Herrmann	41
14	10	Israel	Moran Mazor	Rak Bishvilo	Gal Sarig	Han Harari	40
15	14	Albania	Adrian Lulgjuraj & Bledar Sejko	Identitet	Eda Sejko	Bledar Sejko	31
16	3	FYR Macedonia	Esma & Lozano	Pred Da Se Razdeni	Magdalena Cvetkovska	Darko Dimitrov, Lazar Cvetkovski, Simeon Atanasov	28
17	1	Latvia	PeR	Here We Go	Ralfs Eilands	Ralfs Eilands, Arturas Burke	13

	Switzerland	Spain	San Marino	Romania	Norway	Malta	Latvia	Israel	Iceland	Hungary	Greece	Germany	Georgia	FYR Macedonia	France	Finland	Bulgaria	Azerbaijan	Armenia	Albania	TOTAL
Latvia	1								3				7	2						12	13
San Marino		10		4		6	3	4		2			1	5	5	1		1	4		47
FYR Macedonia				12	5	5	7	12		12						1	5				28
Azerbaijan	3	2		12		12	8	12	8	12	12		12	8	8	3	12		7	8	139
Finland	2	8	7	3	8	1	8	1	7	5		3	6	12	7		6	12		1	64
Malta	7	8	10	7	12		6	2	6	8	5	5	4	3	2		5	4	7	6	118
Bulgaria		6		1	1					1	2		4	3	1	12			10	4	45
Iceland	10	7	8	10	10		10			10		12	2					1			72
Greece	6	5	12		7	7	5	6	2	3		8	2	6	12	7	8	7	8	10	121
Israel		3		2					1			4	5		4	2	4	6	6	3	40
Armenia				5	4	8	1	8			7	6	10	6	12		8				69
Hungary	12		4	6	2		2	3				10	3		3	8	6	5	5		66
Norway	8	12	5	8		3	12	5	12	7	4	2	8	7		10	7	5			120
Albania	5		6						5		8			10				2			31
Georgia	6	4	1			4	4	7	4	4	6	1		4			3	10	12	2	63
Switzerland					3	2			5	6					10	4	2		2	2	41
Romania		1			6	10		10	10		10	7		1	6		2	8	3	5	83

2013 Eurovision 58: Malmö, Sweden

Final: 18 May 2013

Final qualification rules: Top 10 placed countries from each semi-final. Automatic qualification: United Kingdom, France, Germany, Spain, Italy & hosts Sweden.
Points awarded are based on the combined votes of the viewers and jury from each of the 39 participating countries.

Rank	Start	Country	Artist	Song	Writer	Composer	POINTS
1	18	Denmark	Emmelie de Forest	Only Teardrops	Lise Cabble, Julia Fabrin Jakobsen, Thomas Stengaard	Lise Cabble, Julia Fabrin Jakobsen, Thomas Stengaard	281
2	20	Azerbaijan	Farid Mammadov	Hold Me	John Ballard & Ralph Charlie Al Fahel	Dimitrios Kontopoulos	234
3	22	Ukraine	Zlata Ognevich	Gravity	Karen Kavaleryan	Mikhail Nekrasov	214
4	24	Norway	Margaret Berger	I Feed You My Love	Karin Park, Robin Lynch, Niklas Olovson	Karin Park, Robin Lynch, Niklas Olovson	191
5	10	Russia	Dina Garipova	What If	Gabriel Alares, Joakim Björnberg, Leonid Gutkin	Gabriel Alares, Joakim Björnberg, Leonid Gutkin	174
6	21	Greece	Koza Mostra feat. Agathon Iakovidis	Alcohol is Free	Stathis Pachidis, Ilias Kozas	Ilias Kozas	152
7	23	Italy	Marco Mengoni	L'Essenziale	Roberto Casalino	Francesco De Benedittis, Roberto Casalino, Marco Mengoni	126
8	9	Malta	Gianluca	Tomorrow	Boris Cezek & Dean Muscat	Boris Cezek & Dean Muscat	120
9	13	Netherlands	Anouk	Birds	Anouk Teeuwe	Tore Johansson, Martin Gjerstad	114
10	17	Hungary	ByeAlex	Kedvesem (Zoohacker Remix)	Alex Márta	Alex Márta, Zoltán Palásti Kovács	84
11	3	Moldova	Aliona Moon	O Mie	Yuliana Scutaru	Pasha Parfeny	71
12	6	Belgium	Roberto Bellarosa	Love Kills	Iain James, Jukka Immonen	Iain James, Jukka Immonen	71
13	14	Romania	Cezar	It's My Life	Cristian Faur	Cristian Faur	65
14	16	Sweden	Robin Stjernberg	You	Robin Stjernberg, Joy Deb, Linnea Deb, Joakim Harestad Haukaas	Robin Stjernberg, Joy Deb, Linnea Deb, Joakim Harestad Haukaas	62
15	25	Georgia	Nodi Tatishvili & Sophie Gelovani	Waterfall	Thomas G:son	Thomas G:son & Erik Bernholm	50
16	8	Belarus	Alyona Lanskaya	Solayoh	Martin King	Marc Paelinck	48
17	19	Iceland	Eyþor Ingi	Ég Á Líf	Örlygur Smári & Pétur Örn Gudmundsson	Örlygur Smári & Pétur Örn Gudmundsson	47
18	12	Armenia	Dorians	Lonely Planet	Vardan Zadoyan	Tony Iommi	41
19	15	United Kingdom	Bonnie Tyler	Believe in Me	Desmond Child, Lauren Christy, Christopher Braide	Desmond Child, Lauren Christy, Christopher Braide	23
20	7	Estonia	Birgit Õigemeel	Et Uus Saaks Alguse	Mihkel Mattisen & Silvia Soro	Mihkel Mattisen	19
21	11	Germany	Cascada	Glorious	Yann Peifer, Manuel Reuter, Andres Ballinas, Tony Cornelissen	Yann Peifer, Manuel Reuter, Andres Ballinas, Tony Cornelissen	18
22	2	Lithuania	Andrius Pojavis	Something	Andrius Pojavis	Andrius Pojavis	17
23	1	France	Amandine Bourgeois	L'enfer Et Moi	Boris Bergman	David Salkin	14
24	4	Finland	Krista Siegfrids	Marry Me	Krista Siegfrids, Erik Nyholm, Kristoffer Karlsson, Jessica Lundström	Krista Siegfrids, Erik Nyholm, Kristoffer Karlsson, Jessica Lundström	13
25	5	Spain	ESDM	Contigo Hasta El Final (With You Until The End)	Raquel del Rosario, David Feito, Juan Suárez	Raquel del Rosario, David Feito, Juan Suárez	8
26	26	Ireland	Ryan Dolan	Only Love Survives	Wez Devine, Ryan Dolan	Wez Devine, Ryan Dolan	5

	Albania	Armenia	Austria	Azerbaijan	Belarus	Belgium	Bulgaria	Croatia	Cyprus	Denmark	Estonia	Finland	France	FYR Macedonia	Georgia	Germany	Greece	Hungary	Iceland	Ireland	Israel	Italy	Latvia	Lithuania	Malta	Moldova	Montenegro	Netherlands	Norway	Romania	Russia	San Marino	Serbia	Slovenia	Spain	Sweden	Switzerland	Ukraine	United Kingdom	TOTAL
France		2							1						1			2															8							14
Lithuania			3	5										1					1		6																	1		17
Moldova			2	1	4	3	3						4	7				3	1	4						5			12	6			6		2			8		71
Finland										2			3		1			4														3								13
Spain	6												2																											8
Belgium			3					5	2	3	5					4		4		2						12	3		8	5	3	2		7				3		71
Estonia										6								10	3																					19
Belarus		5		7							5	5		1			3		1	2	4	3																12		48
Malta		6		8	7			3	4	5		2	3	3	5	3	8	5		10	5				8	10	5		10			1					2	7		120
Russia		7		8	4	5	6	5	7	12	2	6	6	6	2		1	10	7		12	7		7	7	4			8	10	6	5		4	10					174
Germany	3		6												5																	3		1						18
Armenia				2		8							7	10		3							1	1					2	1				6						41
Netherlands	4		8			12		2		10	7	8	2			5	8	6		4								8	2	3		7		8	4		6			114
Romania	5		4	6					1					10		6		1		7	10	1		6					4					4			4			65
United Kingdom													7				5							3				1	4	1	2									23
Sweden				1	4	1		8	1	4			3			4	5		4			5	3	12				1	6											62
Hungary	8			6	4			4	10		12	2				3		5			7	2			6	2			3	10										84
Denmark	1	4	5	5	1	10	2	10	7		8	7	12	12	7	10	7	10	12	12	8	12	6	2	6	6	10	10	7	6	4		12	12	8	10	3	5	12	281
Iceland									1	6	5					8	6									4				4		6	5		2				47
Azerbaijan	7		12		10	5	12	7	8				8		12	4	12	12	7	2	12		3	12	12	8	12	2		10	12	2	5	3	7		6	10		234
Greece	10	8	7	4	6	2	7	5	12	6		1		4		6		1			2	7	1		4		8	1	5	7	10	12				8		8		152
Ukraine		12	1	12	12	8	10	12	10	3	10			8		8	7	3	8	10	5	7	10	10	12		5	1	4	1		10		10				5		214
Italy	12	1	10			6		8	6				10	10	2		6								8		6			1		4	4	8	12		12			126
Norway	2	3		2	3	7	1	3	4	12	3	12		8	4	7	4	2	10		6	8	8	6	3	2	4	6		8	7	7	7	5	5	12	7	3		191
Georgia		10		10												5							8		3	2			5								7			50
Ireland								2																								2					1			5

Votes are cast by countries participating in each semi-final plus the five automatically qualifying countries decided by draw: Spain and France in semi-final 1, Italy, Germany and the UK in semi-final 2. Host Denmark voted in semi-final 1. Points awarded are based on the combined votes of the viewers and jury from each of the countries voting in this semi-final. The top 10 countries in each semi-final qualify for the final.

Rank	Start	Country	Artist	Song	Writer	Composer	POINTS
1Q	14	Netherlands	The Common Linnets	Calm After the Storm	Ilse DeLange, JB Meijers, Rob Crosby, Matthew Crosby, Jake Etheridge	Ilse DeLange, JB Meijers, Rob Crosby, Matthew Crosby, Jake Etheridge	150
2Q	4	Sweden	Sanna Nielsen	Undo	Fredrik Kempe, David Kreuger, Hamed "K-One" Pirouzpanah	Fredrik Kempe, David Kreuger, Hamed "K-One" Pirouzpanah	131
3Q	16	Hungary	András Kállay-Saunders	Running	András Kállay-Saunders	András Kállay-Saunders & Krisztián Szakos	127
4Q	1	Armenia	Aram MP3	Not Alone	Garik Papoyan	Aram MP3	121
5Q	9	Ukraine	Mariya Yaremchuk	Tick-Tock	Mariya Yaremchuk & Sandra Bjurman	Mariya Yaremchuk	118
6Q	7	Russia	Tolmachevy Sisters	Shine	John Ballard, Ralph Charlie, Gerard James Borg	Philipp Kirkorov & Dimitris Kontopoulos	63
7Q	15	Montenegro	Sergej Ćetković	Moj Svijet	Sergej Ćetković & Emina Sandal	Sergej Ćetković	63
8Q	5	Iceland	Pollapönk	No Prejudice	Heidar Orn Kristjansson, Haraldur Freyr Gislason, John Grant	Heidar Orn Kristjansson	61
9Q	8	Azerbaijan	Dilara Kazimova	Start a Fire	Stefan Örn, Johan Kronlund, Alessandra Günthardt	Stefan Örn, Johan Kronlund, Alessandra Günthardt	57
10Q	12	San Marino	Valentina Monetta	Maybe (Forse)	Mauro Balestri	Ralph Siegel	40
11	13	Portugal	Suzy	Quero Ser Tua	Emanuel	Emanuel	39
12	3	Estonia	Tanja	Amazing	Tanja	Timo Vendt, Tanja	36
13	2	Latvia	Aarzemnieki	Cake to Bake	Guntis Veilands	Guntis Veilands	33
14	10	Belgium	Axel Hirsoux	Mother	Rafael Artesero & Ashley Hicklin	Rafael Artesero & Ashley Hicklin	28
15	6	Albania	Hersi	One Night's Anger	Jorgo Papingji	Gentian Lako	22
16	11	Moldova	Cristina Scarlat	Wild Soul	Lidia Scarlat	Ivan Akulov	13

2014 Eurovision 59: Copenhagen, Denmark

Semi-final 1: 10 May 2014

Voter ↓ / Contestant →	Armenia	Latvia	Estonia	Sweden	Iceland	Albania	Russia	Azerbaijan	Ukraine	Belgium	Moldova	San Marino	Portugal	Netherlands	Montenegro	Hungary
TOTAL	121	33	36	131	61	22	63	57	118	28	13	40	39	150	63	127
Ukraine	12			10	3		6	5			2	4		7	1	8
Sweden	8	1	5		7		2		6				4	12	3	10
Spain	6		2	12	3			5				1	8	7	4	10
San Marino	10	2		3	7	5	6		4	1				12		8
Russia	12			6				10	7	4	1	3		2	5	8
Portugal	4	3		8	1		5	2	7				12	6		10
Netherlands	12			8	7	1	4	5	3				2		6	10
Montenegro	10			5		12	4	7	8	2	6		3	1		
Moldova				10			12	6	8	7		1	3	2	5	4
Latvia	6		10	8	5		4	2	7			1	12	3		
Iceland	3	6	5	10			2	1	7				12		4	8
Hungary	8	2		10	6		5	1	3			7		12	4	
France	12		4	6	8		2		1		5	10	7	3		
Estonia	5	6		7	2		1	4	10		3		12	8		
Denmark	5	1		10	8	2	4		7				3	12	6	
Belgium	3	5		8	4	2	1		7				6	10		12
Azerbaijan		7	5				10		12	4		6	1	3	2	8
Armenia		5		4			7		12	6		2	3	10	8	1
Albania	5		4	6			7	8	3				1	2	12	10

2014 Eurovision 59: Copenhagen, Denmark

Semi-final 2: 8 May 2014

Votes are cast by countries participating in each semi-final plus the five automatically qualifying countries decided by draw: Spain and France in semi-final 1, Italy, Germany and the UK in semi-final 2. Host Denmark voted in semi-final 1. Points awarded are based on the combined votes of the viewers and jury from each of the countries voting in this semi-final. The top 10 countries in each semi-final qualify for the final.

Rank	Start	Country	Artist	Song	Writer	Composer	POINTS
1Q	6	Austria	Conchita Wurst	Rise Like a Phoenix	Charly Mason, Joey Patulka, Ali Zuckowski, Julian Maas	Charly Mason, Joey Patulka, Ali Zuckowski, Julian Maas	169
2Q	15	Romania	Paul Seling & Ovi	Miracle	Ovi, Philip Halloun, Frida Amundsen, Beyond51	Ovi, Philip Halloun, Frida Amundsen, Beyond51	125
3Q	8	Finland	Softengine	Something Better	Henri Oskár, Topi Latukka	Topi Latukka	97
4Q	12	Switzerland	Sebalter	Hunter of Stars	Sebastiano Paù-Lessi	Sebastiano Paù-Lessi	92
5Q	10	Belarus	Teo	Cheesecake	Dmitry Novik	Yury Vashchuk (Teo)	87
6Q	3	Norway	Carl Espen	Silent Storm	Josefin Winther	Josefin Winther	77
7Q	13	Greece	Freaky Fortune feat. RiskyKidd	Rise Up	Freaky Fortune & RiskyKidd	Freaky Fortune	74
8Q	5	Poland	Donatan & Cleo	My Słowianie - We Are Slavic	Cleo	Donatan	70
9Q	1	Malta	Firelight	Coming Home	Richard Edwards Micallef	Richard Edwards Micallef	63
10Q	14	Slovenia	Tinkara Kovač	Round and Round	Tinkara Kovač, Hannah Mancini, Tina Piš	Raay	52
11	7	Lithuania	Vilija Matačiūnaitė	Attention	Vilija Matačiūnaitė	Vilija Matačiūnaitė & Viktoras Vaupšas	36
12	9	Ireland	Can-Linn (feat. Kasey Smith)	Heartbeat	Jonas Gladnikoff, Rasmus Palmgren, Patrizia Helander	Hazel Kaneswaran, Jonas Gladnikoff, Rasmus Palmgren, Patrizia Helander	35
13	11	FYR Macedonia	Tijana	To The Sky	Elena Risteska Ivanovska, Darko Dimitrov	Darko Dimitrov, Lazar Cvetkoski	33
14	2	Israel	Mei Finegold	Same Heart	Rami Talmid	Rami Talmid	19
15	4	Georgia	The Shin and Mariko	Three Minutes to Earth	Eugen Eiiu	Zaza Miminoshvii	15

2014 Eurovision 59: Copenhagen, Denmark

Semi-final 2: 10 May 2014

	Austria	Belarus	Finland	F.Y.R. Macedonia	Georgia	Germany	Greece	Ireland	Israel	Italy	Lithuania	Malta	Norway	Poland	Romania	Slovenia	Switzerland	United Kingdom	TOTAL
Austria		7	12	6	10	4	12	12	10	12	10	10	8	10	12	10	12	12	169
Belarus	10		7	2	12		8	1	7	2	12	6	1	7	8	6			87
F.Y.R. Macedonia		1	1		2				2	2		3				12	10		33
Finland	8			10	1	5	4	10	3	8	5		12	8	5	2	8	8	97
Georgia		5				1	1				6	2							15
Greece	3	12	4	3	3	6		4	6	6		8	6	1	7	3	4		74
Ireland	4		5	7	3		2		1			4	3	5	2	1		5	35
Israel		2				2	6			4	1		4						19
Lithuania	6	4			7			5					5	2				7	36
Malta	5			3	8	7	7	8		5	8					5	2	7	63
Norway	8	1	10	2		7	6	8			8	7		7		4	2	7	77
Poland	12	10				12	3	2	12	10	4	1	7			3		4	70
Romania	12	8	6	8	6	8	10	7	12	4	2	12	10			7	7	6	125
Slovenia	7	2	2	5	4	3				7	3		4	3	6		6	2	52
Switzerland	6	3	8	1		10	5	6	5	3	7	5	3	12	7	8		3	92

2014 Eurovision 59: Copenhagen, Denmark

Final: 10 May 2014

Final qualification rules: Top 10 placed countries from each semi-final. Automatic qualification: United Kingdom, France, Germany, Spain, Italy & hosts Denmark. Points awarded are based on the combined votes of the viewers and jury from each of the 37 participating countries.

Rank	Start	Country	Artist	Song	Writer	Composer	POINTS
1	11	Austria	Conchita Wurst	Rise Like a Phoenix	Charly Mason, Joey Patulka, Ali Zuckowski, Julian Maas	Charly Mason, Joey Patulka, Ali Zuckowski, Julian Maas	290
2	24	The Netherlands	The Common Linnets	Calm After the Storm	Ilse DeLange, JB Meijers, Rob Crosby, Matthew Crosby, Jake Etheridge	Ilse DeLange, JB Meijers, Rob Crosby, Matthew Crosby, Jake Etheridge	238
3	13	Sweden	Sanna Nielsen	Undo	Fredrik Kempe, David Kreuger,	Fredrik Kempe, David Kreuger,	218
4	7	Armenia	Aram MP3	Not Alone	Hamed "K-One" Pirouzpanah, Garik Papoyan	Hamed "K-One" Pirouzpanah Aram MP3	174
5	21	Hungary	András Kállay-Saunders	Running	András Kállay-Saunders	András Kállay-Saunders, Krisztián Szakos	143
6	1	Ukraine	Mariya Yaremchuk	Tick-Tock	Mariya Yaremchuk & Sandra Bjurman	Mariya Yaremchuk	113
7	15	Russia	Tolmachevy Sisters	Shine	John Ballard, Ralph Charlie, Gerard James Borg	Philipp Kirkorov & Dimitris Kontopoulos	89
8	5	Norway	Carl Espen	Silent Storm	Josefin Winther	Josefin Winther	88
9	23	Denmark	Basim	Cliché Love Song	Lasse Lindorff, Daniel Fält, Basim Moujahid, Kim Novak-Zorde	Lasse Lindorff, Daniel Fält, Basim Moujahid, Kim Novak-Zorde	74
10	19	Spain	Ruth Lorenzo	Dancing in the Rain	Ruth Lorenzo, Julian Emery, James Lawrence Irvin	Ruth Lorenzo, Julian Emery, James Lawrence Irvin	74
11	18	Finland	Softengine	Something Better	Henri Oskár, Topi Latukka	Topi Latukka	72
12	6	Romania	Paul Seling & Ovi	Miracle	Ovi, Philip Halloun, Frida Amundsen, Beyond51	Ovi, Philip Halloun, Frida Amundsen, Beyond51	72
13	20	Switzerland	Sebalter	Hunter of Stars	Sebastiano Paù-Lessi	Sebastiano Paù-Lessi	64
14	9	Poland	Donatan & Cleo	My Słowianie - We Are Slavic	Cleo	Donatan	62
15	4	Iceland	Pollapönk	No Prejudice	Heidar Orn Kristjansson, Haraldur Freyr Gislason, John Grant	Heidar Orn Kristjansson	58
16	2	Belarus	Teo	Cheesecake	Dmitry Novik	Yury Vashchuk (Teo)	43
17	26	United Kingdom	Molly	Children of the Universe	Molly Smitten-Downes, Anders Hansson	Molly Smitten-Downes, Anders Hansson	40
18	12	Germany	Elaiza	Is it Right?	Elzbieta Steinmetz, Adam Kesselhaut	Elzbieta Steinmetz, Frank Kretschmer	39
19	8	Montenegro	Sergej Ćetković	Moj Svijet	Sergej Ćetković & Emina Sandal	Sergej Ćetković	37
20	10	Greece	Freaky Fortune feat. RiskyKidd	Rise Up	Freaky Fortune & RiskyKidd	Freaky Fortune	35
21	16	Italy	Emma	La Mia Città	Emma Marrone	Emma Marrone	33
22	3	Azerbaijan	Dilara Kazimova	Start a Fire	Stefan Örn, Johan Kronlund, Alessandra Günthardt	Stefan Örn, Johan Kronlund, Alessandra Günthardt	33
23	22	Malta	Firelight	Coming Home	Richard Edwards Micallef	Richard Edwards Micallef	32
24	25	San Marino	Valentina Monetta	Maybe (Forse)	Mauro Balestri	Ralph Siegel	14
25	17	Slovenia	Tinkara Kovač	Round and Round	Tinkara Kovač, Hannah Mancini, Tina Piš	Raay	9
26	14	France	Twin Twin	Moustache	Lorent Ardouvin, François Ardouvin	Pierre Beyres, Kim N'Guyen	2

2014 Eurovision 59: Copenhagen, Denmark

Final: 10 May 2014

This page is a full voting-results matrix. The voting (jury) countries are listed as rows; the participating countries that received points are listed as columns. The "TOTAL" column gives each participant's final score.

Receiving country	TOTAL
Ukraine	113
Belarus	43
Azerbaijan	33
Iceland	58
Norway	88
Romania	72
Armenia	174
Montenegro	37
Poland	62
Greece	35
Austria	290
Germany	39
Sweden	218
France	2
Russia	89
Italy	33
Slovenia	9
Finland	72
Spain	74
Switzerland	64
Hungary	143
Malta	32
Denmark	74
Netherlands	238
San Marino	14
United Kingdom	40

Voting countries (appearing as row labels, top to bottom): United Kingdom, Ukraine, Switzerland, Sweden, Spain, Slovenia, San Marino, Russia, Romania, Portugal, Poland, Norway, Netherlands, Montenegro, Moldova, Malta, Lithuania, Latvia, Italy, Israel, Ireland, Iceland, Hungary, Greece, Germany, Georgia, Finland, France, FYR Macedonia, Estonia, Denmark, Belgium, Belarus, Azerbaijan, Austria, Armenia, Albania.

Eurovision 2014 - Voting Order & National Spokespersons

Order	Country	Spokesperson
1	Azerbaijan	Sabina Babayeva
2	Greece	Andrianna Maggania
3	Poland	Paulina Chylewska
4	Albania	Andri Xhahu
5	San Marino	Michele Perniola
6	Denmark	Sofie Lassen-Kahlke
7	Montenegro	Tijana Mišković
8	Romania	Sonia Argint-Ionescu
9	Russia	Alsou
10	Netherlands	Tim Douwsma
11	Malta	Valentina Rossi
12	France	Elodie Suigo
13	United Kingdom	Scott Mills
14	Latvia	Ralfs Eilands
15	Armenia	Anna Avanesyan
16	Iceland	Benedict Valsson
17	FYR Macedonia	Marko Mark
18	Sweden	Alcazar
19	Belarus	Alyona Lanskaya
20	Germany	Helene Fischer
21	Israel	Ofer Nachson
22	Portugal	Joana Teles
23	Norway	Margrethe Røed
24	Estonia	Lauri Pihlap
25	Hungary	Éva Novodomszky
26	Moldova	Olivia Furtuna
27	Ireland	Nicky Byrne
28	Finland	Redrama
29	Lithuania	Ignas Krupavičius
30	Austria	Kati Bellowitsch
31	Spain	Carolina Casado
32	Belgium	Angelique Vlieghe
33	Italy	Linus
34	Ukraine	Zlata Ognevich
35	Switzerland	Kurt Aeschbacher
36	Georgia	Sophie Gelovani & Nodi Tatishvili
37	Slovenia	Ula Furlan

Eurovision 2014 Final - Round by Round Leaderboard

Voting round:

Posn	1 Azerbaijan	Pts	Lead	2 Greece	Pts	Lead	3 Poland	Pts	Lead	4 Albania	Pts	Lead	5 San Marino	Pts	Lead
1st	Russia	12	2	Russia	22	7	Russia	22	2	Hungary	22	0	Hungary	29	6
2nd	Ukraine	10	2	Ukraine	15	1	Ukraine	20	0	Russia	22	2	Sweden	23	1
3rd	Hungary	8	1	Hungary	14	1	Netherlands	20	6	Ukraine	20	0	Netherlands	22	0
4th	Belarus	7	1	Austria	13	5	Switzerland	14	0	Netherlands	20	2	Russia	22	2
5th	Romania	6	1	Netherlands	8	1	Hungary	14	1	Austria	18	4	Ukraine	20	2
6th	Malta	5	1	Belarus	7	0	Austria	13	3	Spain	14	0	Austria	18	4
7th	Greece	4	1	Armenia	7	1	Norway	10	2	Switzerland	14	1	Armenia	14	0
8th	San Marino	3	1	Romania	6	1	Armenia	8	0	Sweden	13	1	Spain	14	0
9th	Poland	2	1	Malta	5	1	Germany	8	1	Germany	12	2	Switzerland	14	2
10th	Austria	1	1	Greece	4	0	Belarus	7	1	Norway	10	0	Germany	12	0
11th	Azerbaijan	0	0	Switzerland	4	1	Sweden	6	0	Italy	10	2	Azerbaijan	12	2
12th	Iceland	0	0	Poland	3	0	Romania	6	0	Armenia	8	1	Malta	10	0
13th	Norway	0	0	Norway	3	0	Denmark	6	1	Belarus	7	1	Norway	10	0
14th	Armenia	0	0	San Marino	3	1	Malta	5	1	Malta	6	0	Italy	10	2
15th	Montenegro	0	0	Azerbaijan	2	2	Greece	4	1	Greece	6	0	Iceland	8	1
16th	Germany	0	0	Sweden	0	0	Poland	3	0	San Marino	6	0	Denmark	7	0
17th	Sweden	0	0	Iceland	0	0	Finland	3	0	Romania	6	0	Belarus	7	1
18th	France	0	0	Montenegro	0	0	San Marino	3	1	Montenegro	6	0	Greece	6	0
19th	Italy	0	0	Germany	0	0	Spain	2	2	Denmark	6	3	Finland	6	0
20th	Slovenia	0	0	France	0	0	Azerbaijan	0	0	Poland	3	0	San Marino	6	0
21st	Finland	0	0	Italy	0	0	Iceland	0	0	Finland	3	3	Romania	6	0
22nd	Spain	0	0	Slovenia	0	0	Montenegro	0	0	Azerbaijan	0	0	Montenegro	6	1
23rd	Switzerland	0	0	Finland	0	0	France	0	0	Iceland	0	0	United Kingdom	5	2
24th	Denmark	0	0	Spain	0	0	Italy	0	0	France	0	0	Poland	3	3
25th	Netherlands	0	0	Denmark	0	0	Slovenia	0	0	Slovenia	0	0	France	0	0
26th	United Kingdom	0		United Kingdom	0		United Kingdom	0		United Kingdom	0		Slovenia	0	

Voting round:

Posn	6 Denmark	Pts	Lead	7 Montenegro	Pts	Lead	8 Romania	Pts	Lead	9 Russia	Pts	Lead	10 Netherlands	Pts	Lead
1st	Sweden	35	3	Hungary	44	6	Hungary	54	4	Hungary	60	8	Hungary	64	4
2nd	Hungary	32	0	Sweden	38	6	Sweden	50	14	Sweden	52	11	Sweden	60	7
3rd	Netherlands	32	6	Netherlands	32	4	Austria	36	1	Austria	41	0	Austria	53	5
4th	Austria	26	4	Austria	28	0	Netherlands	35	2	Armenia	41	3	Armenia	48	10
5th	Russia	22	1	Ukraine	28	2	Armenia	33	5	Netherlands	38	3	Netherlands	38	3
6th	Ukraine	21	5	Armenia	26	4	Ukraine	28	3	Ukraine	35	10	Ukraine	35	7
7th	Armenia	16	0	Russia	22	3	Switzerland	25	3	Switzerland	25	3	Switzerland	28	1
8th	Norway	16	2	Switzerland	19	3	Russia	22	3	Azerbaijan	22	0	Norway	27	5
9th	Spain	14	0	Norway	16	0	Spain	19	2	Russia	22	2	Azerbaijan	22	0
10th	Switzerland	14	1	Italy	16	2	Norway	17	1	Belarus	20	1	Russia	22	2
11th	Iceland	13	1	Spain	14	1	Italy	16	2	Spain	19	2	Iceland	20	0
12th	Germany	12	0	Iceland	13	1	Germany	14	1	Norway	17	1	Belarus	20	1
13th	United Kingdom	12	0	Germany	12	0	Iceland	13	1	Italy	16	2	Spain	19	3
14th	Azerbaijan	12	2	United Kingdom	12	0	United Kingdom	12	0	Iceland	14	0	Italy	16	1
15th	Malta	10	0	Azerbaijan	12	2	Azerbaijan	12	1	Germany	14	2	Malta	15	1
16th	Finland	10	0	Malta	10	0	Denmark	11	1	United Kingdom	12	1	Germany	14	2
17th	Italy	10	3	Finland	10	2	Malta	10	0	Denmark	11	1	Denmark	12	0
18th	Denmark	7	0	Belarus	8	0	Finland	10	2	Malta	10	0	Finland	12	0
19th	Belarus	7	1	Slovenia	8	1	Belarus	8	0	Greece	10	0	United Kingdom	12	2
20th	Greece	6	0	Poland	7	0	Slovenia	8	1	Finland	10	2	Greece	10	2
21st	San Marino	6	0	Denmark	7	1	Poland	7	1	Slovenia	8	1	Slovenia	8	1
22nd	Romania	6	0	Greece	6	0	Greece	6	0	Poland	7	1	Poland	7	1
23rd	Montenegro	6	3	San Marino	6	0	San Marino	6	0	San Marino	6	0	San Marino	6	0
24th	Poland	3	3	Romania	6	0	Romania	6	0	Romania	6	0	Romania	6	0
25th	France	0	0	Montenegro	6	6	Montenegro	6	6	Montenegro	6	6	Montenegro	6	6
26th	Slovenia	0		France	0		France	0		France	0		France	0	

Eurovision 2014 Final - Round by Round Leaderboard

Voting round:

Posn	11 Malta	Pts	Lead	12 France	Pts	Lead	13 United Kingdom	Pts	Lead	14 Latvia	Pts	Lead	15 Armenia	Pts	Lead
1st	Sweden	67	3	Austria	73	2	Austria	85	7	Austria	91	5	Austria	91	5
2nd	Hungary	64	1	Sweden	71	5	Sweden	78	12	Sweden	86	10	Sweden	86	10
3rd	Austria	63	9	Armenia	66	2	Armenia	66	2	Armenia	76	10	Armenia	76	6
4th	Armenia	54	16	Hungary	64	18	Hungary	64	18	Netherlands	66	1	Netherlands	70	5
5th	Netherlands	38	3	Netherlands	46	11	Netherlands	54	19	Hungary	65	23	Hungary	65	23
6th	Ukraine	35	4	Ukraine	35	4	Ukraine	35	3	Ukraine	42	6	Ukraine	42	3
7th	Switzerland	31	2	Norway	31	0	Switzerland	32	1	Norway	36	2	Russia	39	2
8th	Norway	29	1	Switzerland	31	2	Norway	31	0	Spain	34	2	Switzerland	37	1
9th	Italy	28	1	Italy	29	2	Iceland	31	1	Switzerland	32	1	Norway	36	0
10th	Russia	27	5	Iceland	27	0	Spain	30	1	Iceland	31	2	Spain	36	5
11th	Azerbaijan	22	2	Russia	27	2	Italy	29	2	Italy	29	0	Iceland	31	2
12th	Iceland	20	0	Spain	25	3	Russia	27	2	Russia	29	4	Italy	29	1
13th	Belarus	20	1	Azerbaijan	22	2	Malta	25	3	Malta	25	3	Belarus	28	3
14th	Spain	19	3	Belarus	20	4	Azerbaijan	22	2	Azerbaijan	22	1	Malta	25	3
15th	United Kingdom	16	1	United Kingdom	16	1	Belarus	20	2	Finland	21	1	Azerbaijan	22	1
16th	Malta	15	1	Denmark	15	0	Denmark	18	0	Belarus	20	2	Finland	21	1
17th	Germany	14	0	Malta	15	1	Finland	18	2	Denmark	18	2	Greece	20	0
18th	Romania	14	2	Germany	14	0	United Kingdom	16	2	United Kingdom	16	2	Germany	20	1
19th	Denmark	12	0	Romania	14	2	Germany	14	0	Germany	14	0	Denmark	19	1
20th	Finland	12	1	Poland	12	0	Romania	14	1	Romania	14	1	Montenegro	18	2
21st	Greece	11	3	Finland	12	1	Greece	13	1	Greece	13	1	United Kingdom	16	2
22nd	Slovenia	8	1	Greece	11	3	Poland	12	4	Poland	12	4	Romania	14	2
23rd	Poland	7	1	Slovenia	8	2	Slovenia	8	2	Slovenia	8	2	Poland	12	3
24th	San Marino	6	0	San Marino	6	0	San Marino	6	0	San Marino	6	0	San Marino	9	1
25th	Montenegro	6	6	Montenegro	6	6	Montenegro	6	6	Montenegro	6	6	Slovenia	8	8
26th	France	0		France	0		France	0		France	0		France	0	

Voting round:

Posn	16 Iceland	Pts	Lead	17 FYR Macedonia	Pts	Lead	18 Sweden	Pts	Lead	19 Belarus	Pts	Lead	20 Germany	Pts	Lead
1st	Austria	101	8	Austria	104	11	Austria	116	17	Austria	116	15	Austria	123	10
2nd	Sweden	93	11	Sweden	93	4	Netherlands	99	6	Armenia	101	0	Netherlands	113	6
3rd	Netherlands	82	4	Netherlands	89	3	Sweden	93	2	Netherlands	101	8	Armenia	107	14
4th	Armenia	78	7	Armenia	86	5	Armenia	91	3	Sweden	93	0	Sweden	93	0
5th	Hungary	71	29	Hungary	81	36	Hungary	88	43	Hungary	93	36	Hungary	93	36
6th	Ukraine	42	3	Russia	45	3	Russia	45	3	Russia	57	7	Russia	57	7
7th	Russia	39	2	Ukraine	42	5	Ukraine	42	5	Ukraine	50	6	Ukraine	50	1
8th	Norway	37	0	Norway	37	0	Norway	40	3	Norway	44	7	Norway	49	6
9th	Switzerland	37	1	Switzerland	37	1	Switzerland	37	1	Switzerland	37	1	Denmark	43	3
10th	Spain	36	5	Spain	36	5	Spain	36	1	Spain	36	1	Switzerland	40	1
11th	Iceland	31	2	Iceland	31	0	Denmark	35	0	Denmark	35	0	Poland	39	2
12th	Italy	29	1	Italy	31	1	Iceland	35	3	Iceland	35	3	Spain	37	0
13th	Belarus	28	1	Montenegro	30	2	Finland	32	1	Finland	32	1	Iceland	37	1
14th	Denmark	27	1	Belarus	28	1	Italy	31	1	Italy	31	1	Finland	36	5
15th	Finland	26	1	Denmark	27	1	Montenegro	30	2	Montenegro	30	1	Italy	31	1
16th	Malta	25	3	Finland	26	1	Belarus	28	3	Poland	29	1	Montenegro	30	2
17th	Azerbaijan	22	2	Malta	25	3	Malta	25	3	Belarus	28	2	Belarus	28	2
18th	Greece	20	0	Azerbaijan	22	2	Poland	22	0	Greece	26	1	Greece	26	1
19th	Germany	20	0	Greece	20	0	Azerbaijan	22	2	Malta	25	0	Malta	25	0
20th	United Kingdom	20	2	Poland	20	0	Greece	20	0	Azerbaijan	25	5	Azerbaijan	25	5
21st	Montenegro	18	3	Germany	20	0	Germany	20	0	Germany	20	0	Germany	20	0
22nd	Poland	15	1	United Kingdom	20	2	United Kingdom	20	2	United Kingdom	20	1	United Kingdom	20	1
23rd	Romania	14	5	Romania	18	9	Romania	18	9	Romania	19	10	Romania	19	10
24th	San Marino	9	1	San Marino	9	0	San Marino	9	0	San Marino	9	0	San Marino	9	0
25th	Slovenia	8	8	Slovenia	9	9	Slovenia	9	9	Slovenia	9	8	Slovenia	9	8
26th	France	0		France	0		France	1		France	1		France	1	

176

Eurovision 2014 Final - Round by Round Leaderboard

Voting round:

21 Israel · 22 Portugal · 23 Norway · 24 Estonia · 25 Hungary

Posn	21 Israel Country	Pts	Lead	22 Portugal Country	Pts	Lead	23 Norway Country	Pts	Lead	24 Estonia Country	Pts	Lead	25 Hungary Country	Pts	Lead
1st	Austria	135	22	Austria	147	24	Austria	157	22	Austria	161	14	Austria	171	12
2nd	Armenia	113	0	Netherlands	123	6	Netherlands	135	16	Netherlands	147	18	Netherlands	159	22
3rd	Netherlands	113	10	Armenia	117	6	Sweden	119	2	Sweden	129	7	Sweden	137	8
4th	Sweden	103	3	Sweden	111	5	Armenia	117	11	Armenia	122	9	Armenia	129	16
5th	Hungary	100	40	Hungary	106	44	Hungary	106	44	Hungary	113	50	Hungary	113	48
6th	Russia	60	5	Russia	62	7	Russia	62	7	Russia	63	0	Ukraine	65	2
7th	Ukraine	55	6	Ukraine	55	3	Ukraine	55	3	Ukraine	63	8	Russia	63	8
8th	Norway	49	6	Norway	52	4	Norway	52	3	Norway	55	6	Norway	55	0
9th	Denmark	43	2	Denmark	48	1	Denmark	49	2	Denmark	49	0	Finland	55	6
10th	Spain	41	1	Switzerland	47	6	Switzerland	47	1	Finland	49	1	Denmark	49	1
11th	Switzerland	40	1	Spain	41	1	Spain	46	3	Spain	48	1	Spain	48	0
12th	Poland	39	2	Poland	39	2	Finland	43	0	Switzerland	47	4	Switzerland	48	0
13th	Iceland	37	1	Iceland	37	1	Iceland	43	2	Iceland	43	2	Iceland	48	4
14th	Finland	36	5	Finland	36	5	Poland	41	9	Poland	41	9	Poland	44	12
15th	Italy	31	1	Italy	31	1	Romania	32	1	Romania	32	1	Romania	32	1
16th	Montenegro	30	1	Montenegro	30	1	Italy	31	1	Italy	31	1	Italy	31	1
17th	Belarus	29	1	Belarus	29	1	Montenegro	30	1	Montenegro	30	1	Montenegro	30	1
18th	Greece	28	1	Greece	28	0	Belarus	29	1	Belarus	29	1	Belarus	29	1
19th	Romania	27	2	Romania	28	3	Greece	28	3	Greece	28	3	Greece	28	3
20th	Malta	25	0	Malta	25	0	Malta	25	0	Malta	25	0	Malta	25	0
21st	Azerbaijan	25	5	Azerbaijan	25	5	Azerbaijan	25	2	Azerbaijan	25	2	Azerbaijan	25	2
22nd	Germany	20	0	Germany	20	0	United Kingdom	23	3	United Kingdom	23	3	United Kingdom	23	3
23rd	United Kingdom	20	11	United Kingdom	20	11	Germany	20	11	Germany	20	11	Germany	20	7
24th	San Marino	9	0	San Marino	9	0	San Marino	9	0	San Marino	9	0	San Marino	13	4
25th	Slovenia	9	8	Slovenia	9	8	Slovenia	9	8	Slovenia	9	8	Slovenia	9	8
26th	France	1		France	1		France	1		France	1		France	1	

Voting round:

26 Moldova · 27 Ireland · 28 Finland · 29 Lithuania · 30 Austria

Posn	26 Moldova Country	Pts	Lead	27 Ireland Country	Pts	Lead	28 Finland Country	Pts	Lead	29 Lithuania Country	Pts	Lead	30 Austria Country	Pts	Lead
1st	Austria	178	19	Austria	190	21	Austria	202	25	Austria	212	23	Austria	212	13
2nd	Netherlands	159	16	Netherlands	169	22	Netherlands	177	20	Netherlands	189	25	Netherlands	199	29
3rd	Sweden	143	11	Sweden	147	15	Sweden	157	21	Sweden	164	28	Sweden	170	22
4th	Armenia	132	15	Armenia	132	14	Armenia	136	13	Armenia	136	13	Armenia	148	18
5th	Hungary	117	42	Hungary	118	43	Hungary	123	46	Hungary	123	41	Hungary	130	43
6th	Ukraine	75	4	Ukraine	75	4	Ukraine	77	6	Ukraine	82	5	Ukraine	87	9
7th	Russia	71	16	Russia	71	9	Russia	71	2	Norway	77	0	Norway	78	9
8th	Norway	55	0	Norway	62	7	Norway	69	14	Russia	77	19	Russia	77	18
9th	Finland	55	6	Finland	55	1	Denmark	55	0	Spain	58	2	Finland	59	1
10th	Denmark	49	1	Spain	54	1	Finland	55	1	Denmark	56	1	Switzerland	58	0
11th	Spain	48	0	Switzerland	53	4	Spain	54	1	Switzerland	55	0	Spain	58	2
12th	Switzerland	48	0	Denmark	49	1	Switzerland	53	5	Finland	55	7	Denmark	56	2
13th	Iceland	48	2	Iceland	48	2	Iceland	48	2	Iceland	48	2	Romania	54	2
14th	Poland	46	2	Poland	46	0	Poland	46	0	Poland	46	0	Iceland	50	4
15th	Romania	44	10	Romania	46	12	Romania	46	12	Romania	46	9	Poland	46	9
16th	Belarus	34	3	Belarus	34	3	Belarus	34	3	Belarus	37	6	Belarus	37	6
17th	Italy	31	1	United Kingdom	31	0	Malta	31	0	Malta	31	0	Malta	31	0
18th	Montenegro	30	2	Italy	31	1	United Kingdom	31	0	United Kingdom	31	0	United Kingdom	31	0
19th	Greece	28	3	Montenegro	30	2	Italy	31	1	Italy	31	1	Italy	31	1
20th	Malta	25	0	Greece	28	0	Montenegro	30	2	Montenegro	30	2	Montenegro	30	2
21st	Azerbaijan	25	2	Malta	28	3	Greece	28	3	Greece	28	3	Greece	28	3
22nd	United Kingdom	23	3	Azerbaijan	25	5	Azerbaijan	25	5	Azerbaijan	25	5	Azerbaijan	25	5
23rd	Germany	20	6	Germany	20	6	Germany	20	6	Germany	20	6	Germany	20	6
24th	San Marino	14	5	San Marino	14	5	San Marino	14	5	San Marino	14	5	San Marino	14	5
25th	Slovenia	9	8	Slovenia	9	8	Slovenia	9	7	Slovenia	9	7	Slovenia	9	7
26th	France	1		France	1		France	2		France	2		France	2	

Eurovision 2014 Final - Round by Round Leaderboard

Voting round:

Posn	31 Spain	Pts	Lead	32 Belgium	Pts	Lead	33 Italy	Pts	Lead	34 Ukraine	Pts	Lead	35 Switzerland	Pts	Lead
1st	Austria	223	17	Austria	234	20	Austria	243	25	Austria	256	38	Austria	268	40
2nd	Netherlands	206	26	Netherlands	214	24	Netherlands	218	28	Netherlands	218	16	Netherlands	228	20
3rd	Sweden	180	28	Sweden	190	38	Sweden	190	38	Sweden	202	40	Sweden	208	46
4th	Armenia	152	20	Armenia	152	13	Armenia	152	13	Armenia	162	20	Armenia	162	19
5th	Hungary	132	39	Hungary	139	42	Hungary	139	32	Hungary	142	35	Hungary	143	36
6th	Ukraine	93	15	Ukraine	97	19	Ukraine	107	29	Ukraine	107	26	Ukraine	107	24
7th	Norway	78	1	Norway	78	1	Norway	78	1	Russia	81	3	Norway	83	2
8th	Russia	77	15	Russia	77	10	Russia	77	5	Norway	78	6	Russia	81	9
9th	Romania	62	3	Romania	67	2	Romania	72	4	Romania	72	4	Finland	72	0
10th	Denmark	59	0	Denmark	65	3	Finland	68	3	Finland	68	3	Romania	72	2
11th	Finland	59	1	Finland	62	2	Denmark	65	5	Denmark	65	3	Spain	70	2
12th	Switzerland	58	0	Spain	60	2	Switzerland	60	0	Spain	62	1	Denmark	68	7
13th	Spain	58	7	Switzerland	58	7	Spain	60	2	Poland	61	1	Poland	61	1
14th	Iceland	51	5	Iceland	51	5	Iceland	58	4	Switzerland	60	2	Switzerland	60	2
15th	Poland	46	9	Poland	46	9	Poland	54	17	Iceland	58	15	Iceland	58	15
16th	Belarus	37	1	United Kingdom	37	0	United Kingdom	37	0	Belarus	43	6	Belarus	43	6
17th	United Kingdom	36	1	Belarus	37	6	Belarus	37	6	United Kingdom	37	5	United Kingdom	37	4
18th	Malta	31	0	Malta	31	0	Malta	32	1	Malta	32	1	Italy	33	1
19th	Italy	31	1	Italy	31	1	Greece	31	0	Greece	31	0	Malta	32	0
20th	Montenegro	30	2	Montenegro	30	2	Italy	31	1	Italy	31	1	Germany	32	1
21st	Greece	28	3	Greece	28	3	Montenegro	30	5	Montenegro	30	4	Greece	31	1
22nd	Azerbaijan	25	5	Azerbaijan	25	5	Azerbaijan	25	5	Azerbaijan	26	1	Montenegro	30	4
23rd	Germany	20	5	Germany	20	6	Germany	20	6	Germany	25	11	Azerbaijan	26	12
24th	San Marino	14	5	San Marino	14	5	San Marino	14	5	San Marino	14	5	San Marino	14	5
25th	Slovenia	9	7	Slovenia	9	7	Slovenia	9	7	Slovenia	9	7	Slovenia	9	7
26th	France	2		France	2		France	2		France	2		France	2	

Voting round:

Posn	36 Georgia	Pts	Lead	37 Slovenia	Pts	Lead
1st	Austria	278	50	Austria	290	52
2nd	Netherlands	228	18	Netherlands	238	20
3rd	Sweden	210	36	Sweden	218	44
4th	Armenia	174	31	Armenia	174	31
5th	Hungary	143	30	Hungary	143	30
6th	Ukraine	113	24	Ukraine	113	24
7th	Russia	89	6	Russia	89	1
8th	Norway	83	11	Norway	88	14
9th	Finland	72	0	Denmark	74	0
10th	Romania	72	2	Spain	74	2
11th	Spain	70	2	Finland	72	0
12th	Denmark	68	7	Romania	72	8
13th	Switzerland	61	0	Switzerland	64	2
14th	Poland	61	3	Poland	62	4
15th	Iceland	58	15	Iceland	58	15
16th	Belarus	43	3	Belarus	43	3
17th	United Kingdom	40	3	United Kingdom	40	1
18th	Germany	37	2	Germany	39	2
19th	Greece	35	2	Montenegro	37	2
20th	Italy	33	0	Greece	35	2
21st	Azerbaijan	33	1	Italy	33	0
22nd	Malta	32	2	Azerbaijan	33	1
23rd	Montenegro	30	16	Malta	32	18
24th	San Marino	14	5	San Marino	14	5
25th	Slovenia	9	7	Slovenia	9	7
26th	France	2		France	2	

Eurovision 2014 - Jury and Televoting Split Results

Semi-final 1

Country	Televote				Country	Jury			
	Points	Position	Actual SF	Difference		Points	Position	Actual SF	Difference
Netherlands	147	1	1	-	Netherlands	130	1	1	-
Hungary	125	2	3	+1	Sweden	125	2	2	-
Sweden	122	3	2	-1	Hungary	122	3	3	-
Armenia	121	4	4	-	Armenia	102	4	4	-
Ukraine	119	5	5	-	Azerbaijan	94	5	9	-4
Russia	73	6	6	-	Ukraine	88	6	5	+1
Portugal	72	7	11	+4	Montenegro	74	7	7	-
San Marino	58	8	10	+2	Iceland	68	8	8	-
Iceland	50	9	8	-1	Albania	64	9	15	-6
Montenegro	43	10	7	-3	Estonia	61	10	12	-2
Azerbaijan	41	11	9	-2	Russia	57	11	6	+5
Belgium	41	12	14	+2	Latvia	27	12	13	-1
Latvia	40	13	13	-	San Marino	25	13	10	'+3
Albania	23	14	15	+1	Belgium	24	14	14	-
Moldova	14	15	16	+1	Moldova	24	15	16	-1
Estonia	13	16	12	-4	Portugal	17	16	11	+5

In the first semi-final, both the juries and the voting public agreed on the best four songs. Portugal would have benefitted the most if the rankings were based on televoting alone, and Estonia would have suffered the most. The juries liked Albania a lot more than more than the public did, but not so when it came to Portugal and Russia - the latter would not have qualified for the final if only the juries made the decision, even though the combined votes placed them sixth.

Semi-final 2

Country	Televote				Country	Jury			
	Points	Position	Actual SF	Difference		Points	Position	Actual SF	Difference
Austria	165	1	1	-	Austria	138	1	1	-
Romania	126	2	2	-	Finland	117	2	3	+1
Poland	116	3	8	+5	Malta	113	3	9	+6
Switzerland	98	4	4	-	Norway	100	4	6	+2
Greece	91	5	7	+2	Romania	99	5	2	-3
Belarus	86	6	5	-1	Belarus	71	6	5	-1
Finland	63	7	3	-4	Macedonia	70	7	13	+6
Norway	55	8	6	-2	Slovenia	60	8	10	+2
Slovenia	48	9	10	+1	Greece	52	9	7	-2
Ireland	47	10	12	+2	Switzerland	51	10	4	-6
Lithuania	44	11	11	-	Lithuania	41	11	11	-
Malta	36	12	9	-3	Poland	34	12	8	-4
Macedonia	28	13	13	-	Georgia	33	13	15	+2
Israel	26	14	14	-	Ireland	33	14	12	-2
Georgia	15	15	15	-	Israel	32	15	14	-1

In the second semi-final the public voted for Poland in big numbers but the juries were less impressed. Malta qualified for the final despite the public placing it 12th, thanks to the level of jury votes. The juries were also much less keen on Switzerland than the public.

Eurovision 2014 - Jury and Televoting Split Results

FINAL

Country	Televote				Country	Jury			
	Points	Position	Actual Final	Difference		Points	Position	Actual Final	Difference
Austria	311	1	1	-	Austria	224	1	1	-
Netherlands	222	2	2	-	Sweden	201	2	3	+1
Armenia	193	3	4	+1	Netherlands	200	3	2	-1
Sweden	190	4	3	-1	Hungary	138	4	5	+1
Poland	162	5	14	+9	Armenia	125	5	4	-1
Russia	132	6	7	+1	Malta	119	6	23	+17
Switzerland	114	7	13	+6	Finland	114	7	11	+4
Ukraine	112	8	6	-2	Azerbaijan	108	8	22	+14
Romania	103	9	12	+3	Norway	102	9	8	-1
Hungary	98	10	5	-5	Denmark	85	10	9	-1
Belarus	56	11	16	+5	Spain	83	11	10	-1
Iceland	46	12	15	+3	Ukraine	78	12	6	-6
Denmark	43	13	9	-4	Russia	70	13	7	-6
Greece	43	14	20	+6	Germany	61	14	18	+4
Spain	41	15	10	-5	Iceland	59	15	15	-
Norway	39	16	8	-8	United Kingdom	52	16	17	+1
Finland	39	17	11	-6	Romania	51	17	12	-5
Montenegro	33	18	19	+1	Belarus	50	18	16	-2
Italy	32	19	21	+2	Greece	49	19	20	+1
Germany	31	20	18	-2	Montenegro	48	20	19	-1
United Kingdom	29	21	17	-4	Italy	37	21	21	-
Azerbaijan	26	22	22	-	Switzerland	27	22	13	-9
San Marino	18	23	24	+1	Poland	23	23	14	-9
Malta	17	24	23	-1	Slovenia	21	24	25	+1
Slovenia	15	25	25	-	San Marino	16	25	24	-1
France	1	26	26	-	France	5	26	26	-

In the Grand Final there were some spectacular differences between the jury votes and the public televoting. Poland would have finished 5th if just the public voted, but then again, Norway were trashed in the public vote. This was nothing compared to the positions if only the juries had been making the decisions. Malta would have finished 6th yet when the televotes were taken into account they actually ended up fourth from last. Azerbaijan had a similar fate, their public vote collapsed compared to earlier years.

Eurovision 2014 - Country-by-country history: points scored and final positions for each act.

Albania

Year	Artist	Song	Semi-Final		Final	
			Points	Position	Points	Position
2004	Anjeza Shahini	The Image Of You	167	4	106	7
2005	Ledina Celo	Tomorrow I Go	-	-	53	16
2006	Luiz Ejlli	Zjarr E Ftohtë	58	15	-	-
2007	Aida & Frederik Ndoci	Hear My Plea	49	17	-	-
2008	Olta Boka	Zemrën E Lamë Peng	67	9	55	17
2009	Kejsi Tola	Carry Me In Your Dreams	73	7	48	17
2010	Juliana Pasha	It's All About You	76	6	62	16
2011	Aurela Gaçe	Feel The Passion	47	14	-	-
2012	Rona Nishliu	Suus	146	2	146	5
2013	Adrian Lulgjuraj & Bledar Sejko	Identitet	31	15	-	-
2014	Hersi	One Night's Anger	22	15	-	-

Andorra

Year	Artist	Song	Semi-Final		Final	
			Points	Position	Points	Position
2004	Marta Roure	Jugarem A Estimar-nos	12	18	-	-
2005	Marian van de Wal	La Mirada Interior	27	23	-	-
2006	Jennifer	Sense Tu	8	23	-	-
2007	Anonymous	Salvem El Món	80	12	-	-
2008	Gisela	Casanova	22	16	-	-
2009	Susanne Georgi	La Teva Decisió (Get A Life)	8	15	-	-

Armenia

Year	Artist	Song	Semi-Final		Final	
			Points	Position	Points	Position
2006	André	Without Your Love	150	7	129	8
2007	Hayko	Anytime You Need	-	-	138	8
2008	Sirusho	Qele, Qele	139	2	199	4
2009	Inga & Anush	Jan Jan	99	5	92	10
2010	Eva Rivas	Apricot Stone	76	6	141	7
2011	Emmy	Boom Boom	54	12	-	-
2012	-	-	-	-	-	-
2013	Dorians	Lonely Planet	69	7	41	18
2014	Aram MP3	Not Alone	121	4	174	4

Austria

Year	Artist	Song	Semi-Final		Final	
			Points	Position	Points	Position
1957	Bob Martin	Wohin, Kleines Pony			3	10
1958	Liane Augustin	Die Ganze Welt Braucht Liebe			8	5
1959	Ferry Graf	Der K. Und K. Kalypso Aus Wien			4	9
1960	Harry Winter	Du Hast Mich So Fasziniert			6	7
1961	Jimmy Makulis	Sehnsucht			1	15
1962	Eleonore Schwarz	Nur In Der Wiener Luft			0	13
1963	Carmela Corren	Vielleicht Geschieht Ein Wunder			16	7
1964	Udo Jürgens	Warum Nur, Warum?			11	6
1965	Udo Jürgens	Sag Ihr, Ich Lass' Sie Grüßen			16	4
1966	Udo Jürgens	Merci Chérie			31	1
1967	Peter Horten	Warum Es Hunderttausend Sterne Gibt			2	14
1968	Karel Gott	Tausend Fenster			2	13
1969	-	-			-	-
1970	-	-			-	-
1971	Marianne Mendt	Musik			66	6

Austria (continued)

Year	Artist	Song	Semi-Final Points	Semi-Final Position	Final Points	Final Position
1972	The Milestones	Falter Im Wind			100	5
1973	-	-			-	-
1974	-	-			-	-
1975	-	-			-	-
1976	Waterloo and Robinson	My Little World			80	5
1977	Schmetterlinge	Boom Boom Boomerang			11	17
1978	Springtime	Mrs. Caroline Robinson			14	15
1979	Christina Simon	Heute In Jerusalem			5	18
1980	Blue Danube	Du Bist Musik			64	8
1981	Marty Brem	Wenn Du Da Bist			20	17
1982	Mess	Sonntag			57	9
1983	Westend	Hurricane			53	9
1984	Anita	Einfach Weg			5	19
1985	Gary Lux	Kinder Dieser Welt			60	8
1986	Timna Brauer	Die Zeit Ist Einsam			12	18
1987	Gary Lux	Nur Noch Gefühl			8	20
1988	Wilfried	Lisa Mona Lisa			0	21
1989	Thomas Forstner	Nur Ein Lied			97	5
1990	Simone	Keine Mauern Mehr			58	10
1991	Thomas Forstner	Venedig Im Regen			0	22
1992	Tony Wegas	Zusammen Geh'n			63	9
1993	Tony Wegas	Maria Magdalena			32	14
1994	Petra Frey	Für Den Frieden Der Welt			19	17
1995	Stella Jones	Die Welt Dreht Sich Verkehrt			67	13
1996	George Nußbaumer	Weil's Dr Guat Got			68	10
1997	Bettina Soriat	One Step			12	21
1998	-	-			-	-
1999	Bobbie Singer	Reflection			65	9
2000	The Rounder Girls	All To You			34	14
2001	-	-			-	-
2002	Manuel Ortega	Say A Word			26	18
2003	Alf Poier	Weil Der Mensch Zählt			101	6
2004	Tie Break	Du Bist	-	-	9	21
2005	Global.Kryner	Y Así	30	21	-	-
2006	-	-	-	-	-	-
2007	Eric Papilaya	Get A Life - Get Alive	4	27	-	-
2008	-	-	-	-	-	-
2009	-	-	-	-	-	-
2010	-	-	-	-	-	-
2011	Nadine Beiler	The Secret is Love	69	7	64	18
2012	Trackshittaz	Woki Mit Deim Popo	8	18	-	-
2013	Natália Kelly	Shine	27	14	-	-
2014	Conchita Wurst	Rise Like a Phoenix	169	1	290	1

Azerbaijan

Year	Artist	Song	Semi-Final Points	Semi-Final Position	Final Points	Final Position
2008	Elnur & Samir	Day After Day	96	6	132	8
2009	AySel & Arash	Always	180	2	207	3
2010	Safura	Drip Drop	113	2	145	5
2011	Ell/Nikki	Running Scared	122	2	221	1
2012	Sabina Babayeva	When The Music Dies	-	-	150	4
2013	Farid Mammadov	Hold Me	139	1	234	2
2014	Dilara Kazimova	Start a Fire	57	9	33	22

Belarus

Year	Artist	Song	Semi-Final Points	Semi-Final Position	Final Points	Final Position
2004	Aleksandra & Konstantin	My Galileo	10	19	-	-
2005	Angelica Agurbash	Love Me Tonight	67	13	-	-
2006	Polina Smolova	Mum	10	22	-	-
2007	Dmitry Koldun	Work Your Magic	176	4	143	6
2008	Ruslan Alenho	Hasta La Vista	27	17	-	-
2009	Petr Elfimov	Eyes That Never Lie	25	13	-	-
2010	3+2	Butterflies	59	9	18	24
2011	Anastasiya Vinnikova	I Love Belarus	45	14	-	-
2012	Litesound	We Are The Heroes	35	16	-	-
2013	Alyona Lanskaya	Solayoh	64	7	48	16
2014	Teo	Cheesecake	87	5	43	16

Belgium

Year	Artist	Song	Semi-Final Points	Semi-Final Position	Final Points	Final Position
1956	(1) Mony Marc	Le Plus Beau Jour De Ma Vie			-	2
1956	(2) Fud Leclerc	Messieurs Les Noyés De La Seine			-	2
1957	Bobbejaan Schoepen	Straatdeuntje			5	8
1958	Fud Leclerc	Ma Petite Chatte			8	5
1959	Bob Benny	Hou Toch Van Mij			9	6
1960	Fud Leclerc	Mon Amour Pour Toi			9	6
1961	Bob Benny	September, Gouden Roos			1	15
1962	Fud Leclerc	Ton Nom			0	13
1963	Jacques Raymond	Waarom			4	10
1964	Robert Cogoi	Près De Ma Rivière			2	10
1965	Lize Marke	Als Het Weer Lente Is			0	15
1966	Tonia	Un Peu De Poivre, Un Peu De Sel			14	4
1967	Louis Neefs	Ik Heb Zorgen			8	7
1968	Claude Lombard	Quand Tu Reviendras			8	7
1969	Louis Neefs	Jennifer Jennings			10	7
1970	Jean Vallée	Viens L'oublier			5	8
1971	Lily Castel and Jacques Raymond	Goeie Morgen, Morgen			68	14
1972	Serge and Christine Ghisoland	À La Folie Ou Pas Du Tout			55	17
1973	Nicole and Hugo	Baby, Baby			58	17
1974	Jacques Hustin	Fleur De Liberté			10	9
1975	Ann Christy	Gelukkig Zijn			17	15
1976	Pierre Rapsat	Judy Et Cie.			68	8
1977	Dream Express	A Million In One, Two, Three			69	7
1978	Jean Vallée	L'amour ça Fait Chanter La Vie			125	2
1979	Micha Marah	Hey Nana			5	18
1980	Telex	Euro-vision			14	17
1981	Emly Starr	Samson			40	13
1982	Stella	Si Tu Aimes Ma Musique			96	4
1983	Pas de Deux	Rendez-vous			13	18
1984	Jacques Zegers	Avanti La Vie			70	5
1985	Linda Lepomme	Laat Me Nu Gaan			7	19
1986	Sandra Kim	J'aime La Vie			176	1
1987	Liliane Saint-Pierre	Soldiers Of Love			56	11
1988	Reynaert	Laissez Briller Le Soleil			5	18
1989	Ingeborg	Door De Wind			13	19
1990	Philippe Lafontaine	Macédomienne			46	12
1991	Clouseau	Geef Het Op			23	16
1992	Morgane	Nous On Veut Des Violons			11	20
1993	Barbara	Iemand Als Jij			3	25
1994	-	-			-	-
1995	Frédéric Etherlinck	La Voix Est Libre			8	20
1996	Lisa del Bo	Liefde Is Een Kaartspel			22	16

Belgium (continued)

Year	Artist	Song	Semi-Final Points	Semi-Final Position	Final Points	Final Position
1997	-	-			-	-
1998	Mélanie Cohl	Dis Oui			122	6
1999	Venessa Chinitor	Like The Wind			38	12
2000	Nathalie Sorce	Envie De Vivre			2	24
2001	-	-			-	-
2002	Sergio & the Ladies	Sister			33	13
2003	Urban Trad	Sanomi			165	2
2004	Xandee	1 Life	-	-	7	22
2005	Nuno Resende	Le Grand Soir	29	22	-	-
2006	Kate Ryan	Je T'adore	69	12	-	-
2007	The KMG's	Love Power	14	26	-	-
2008	Ishtar	O Julissi	16	17	-	-
2009	Copycat	Copycat	1	17	-	-
2010	Tom Dice	Me and My Guitar	167	1	143	6
2011	Witloof Bay	With Love Baby	53	11	-	-
2012	Iris	Would You?	16	17	-	-
2013	Roberto Bellarosa	Love Kills	75	5	71	12
2014	Axel Hirsoux	Mother	28	14	-	-

Bosnia & Herzegovina

Year	Artist	Song	Semi-Final Points	Semi-Final Position	Final Points	Final Position
1993	Fazla	Sva Bol Svijeta			27	16
1994	Alma & Dejan	Ostani Kraj Mene			39	15
1995	Davor Popovic	Dvadeset I Prvi Vijek			14	19
1996	Amila Glamocak	Za Našu Ljubav			13	22
1997	Alma Cardzic	Goodbye			22	18
1998	-	-			-	-
1999	Dino & Beatrice	Putnici			86	7
2000	-	-			-	-
2001	Nino	Hano			29	14
2002	Maja	Na Jastuku Za Dvoje			33	13
2003	Mija Martina	Ne Brini			27	16
2004	Deen	In The Disco	133	7	91	9
2005	Feminnem	Call Me	-	-	79	14
2006	Hari Mata Hari	Lejla	267	2	229	3
2007	Marija Sestic	Rijeka Bez Imena	-	-	106	11
2008	Laka	Pokušaj	72	9	110	10
2009	Regina	Bistra Voda	125	3	106	9
2010	Vukašin Brajić	Thunder And Lightning	58	8	51	17
2011	Dino Merlin	Love in Rewind	109	5	125	6
2012	MayaSar	Korake Ti Znam	77	6	55	18

Bulgaria

Year	Artist	Song	Semi-Final Points	Semi-Final Position	Final Points	Final Position
2005	Kaffe	Lorraine	49	19	-	-
2006	Mariana Popova	Let Me Cry	36	17	-	-
2007	Elitsa Todorova & Stoyan Yankulov	Water	146	6	157	5
2008	Deep Zone & Balthazar	DJ, Take Me Away	56	11	-	-
2009	Krassimir Avramov	Illusion	7	16	-	-
2010	Miro	Angel Si Ti	19	15	-	-
2011	Poli Genova	Na Inat	48	12	-	-
2012	Sofi Marinova	Love Unlimited	45	11	-	-
2013	Elitsa Todorova feat. Stoyan Yankulov	Samo Shampioni (Only Champions)	45	12	-	-

Croatia

Year	Artist	Song	Semi-Final Points	Semi-Final Position	Final Points	Final Position
1993	Put	Don't Ever Cry			31	15
1994	Tony Cetinski	Nek'ti Bude Ljubav Sva			27	16
1995	Magazin & Lidija	Nostalgija			91	6
1996	Maja Blagdan	Sveta Ljubav			98	4
1997	ENI	Probudi Me			24	17
1998	Danijela	Neka Mi Ne Svane			131	5
1999	Doris Dragovic	Marija Magdalena			118	4
2000	Goran Karan	Kada Zaspu Andeli			70	9
2001	Vanna	Strings Of My Heart			42	10
2002	Vesna Pisarovic	Everything I Want			44	11
2003	Claudia Beni	Više Nisam Tvoja			29	15
2004	Ivan Mikulic	You Are The Only One	72	9	50	12
2005	Boris Novkovic feat. Lado members	Vukovi Umiru Sami	169	4	115	11
2006	Severina	Moja štikla	-	-	56	12
2007	Dragonfly feat. Dado Topic	Vjerujem U Ljubav	54	16	-	-
2008	Kraljevi Ulice & 75 Cents	Romanca	112	4	44	21
2009	Igor Cukrov featuring Andrea	Lijepa Tena	33	13	45	18
2010	Feminnem	Lako Je Sve	33	13	-	-
2011	Daria	Celebrate	41	15	-	-
2012	Nina Badrić	Nebo	42	12	-	-
2013	Klapa s mora	Mižerja	38	13	-	-

Cyprus

Year	Artist	Song	Semi-Final Points	Semi-Final Position	Final Points	Final Position
1981	Island	Monika			69	6
1982	Anna Vishy	Mono I Agapi			85	5
1983	Stavros & Constantina	I Agapi Akoma Zi			26	16
1984	Andy Paul	Anna Mari-elena			31	15
1985	Lia Vishy	To Katalava Arga			15	16
1986	Elpida	Tora Zo			4	20
1987	Alexia	Aspro Mavro			80	7
1988	-				-	-
1989	Fanny Polymeri & Yiannis Savvidakis	Apopse As Vrethoume			51	11
1990	Haris Anastasiou	Milas Poli			36	14
1991	Elena Patroclou	SOS			60	9
1992	Evridiki	Teriazoume			57	10
1993	Kyriakos Zymboulakis & Demos Van Beke	Mi Stamatas			17	19
1994	Evridiki	Ime Anthropos Ke Ego			51	11
1995	Alexandros Panayi	Sti Fotia			79	9
1996	Constantinos	Mono Gia Mas			72	9
1997	Chara & Andreas Konstantinou	Mana Mou			98	5
1998	Michael Hajiyanni	Genesis			37	11
1999	Marlain Angelidou	Tha'nai Erotas			2	22
2000	Voice	Nomiza			8	21
2001	-	-			-	-
2002	One	Gimme			85	6
2003	Stelios Constantas	Feeling Alive			15	20
2004	Lisa Andreas	Stronger Every Minute	149	5	170	5
2005	Constantinos Christoforou	Ela Ela	-	-	46	18
2006	Annet Artani	Why Angels Cry	57	13	-	-
2007	Evridiki	Comme Ci, Comme ça	65	15	-	-
2008	Evdokia Kadi	Femme Fatale	36	15	-	-
2009	Christina Metaxa	Firefly	32	14	-	-
2010	Jon Lilygreen & The Islanders	Life Looks Better In Spring	67	10	27	21
2011	Christos Mylordos	San Aggelos S'Agapisa	16	18	-	-

Cyprus (continued)

Year	Artist	Song	Semi-Final Points	Semi-Final Position	Final Points	Final Position
2012	Ivi Adamou	La La Love	91	7	65	16
2013	Despina Olympiou	An Me Thimasai	11	15	-	-

Czech Republic

Year	Artist	Song	Semi-Final Points	Semi-Final Position	Final Points	Final Position
2007	Kabát	Malá Dáma	1	28	-	-
2008	Tereza Kerndlová	Have Some Fun	9	18	-	-
2009	Gipsy.cz	Aven Romale	0	18	-	-

Denmark

Year	Artist	Song	Semi-Final Points	Semi-Final Position	Final Points	Final Position
1957	Birthe Wilke & Gustav Winckler	Skibet Skal Sejle I Nat			10	3
1958	Raquel Rastenni	Jeg Rev Et Blad Ud Af Min Dagbog			3	8
1959	Birthe Wilke	Uh-jeg Ville Ønske Jeg Var Dig			12	5
1960	Katy Bødtger	Det Var En Yndig Tid			4	10
1961	Dario Campeotto	Angelique			12	5
1962	Ellen Winther	Vuggevise			2	10
1963	Grethe & Jørgen Ingmann	Dansevise			42	1
1964	Bjørn Tidmand	Sangen Om Dig			4	9
1965	Birgit Brüel	For Din Skyld			10	7
1966	Ulla Pia	Stop, Ja Stop - Ja Stop, Mens Legen Er Go			4	14
1967	-	-			-	-
1968	-	-			-	-
1969	-	-			-	-
1970	-	-			-	-
1971	-	-			-	-
1972	-	-			-	-
1973	-	-			-	-
1974	-	-			-	-
1975	-	-			-	-
1976	-	-			-	-
1977	-	-			-	-
1978	Mabel	Boom Boom			13	16
1979	Tommy Seebach	Disco Tango			76	6
1980	Bamses Venner	Tænker Altid På Dig			25	14
1981	Debbie Cameron & Tommy Seebach	Krøller Eller Ej			41	11
1982	Brixx	Video-video			5	17
1983	Gry Johansen	Kloden Drejer			16	17
1984	Hot Eyes	Det' Lige Det			101	4
1985	Hot Eyes	Sku' Du Spør Fra No'n			41	11
1986	Lise Haavik & Trax	Du Er Fuld Af Løgn			77	6
1987	Anne-Catherine Herdorf & Bandjo	En Lille Melodi			83	5
1988	Hot Eyes	Ka' Du Se Hva' Jeg Sa'			92	3
1989	Birthe Kjær	Vi Maler Byen Rød			111	3
1990	Lonnie Devantier	Hallo Hallo			64	8
1991	Anders Frandsen	Lige Der Hvor Hjertet Slår			8	19
1992	Lotte Nilsson & Kenny Lübcke	Ålt Det Som Ingen Ser			47	11
1993	Tommy Seebach Band	Under Stjernerne På Himlen			9	22
1994	-	-			-	-
1995	Aud Wilken	Fra Mols Til Skagen			92	5
1996	-	-			-	-
1997	Kølig Kaj	Stemmen I Mit Liv			25	16
1998	-	-			-	-
1999	Trine Jepsen & Michael Teschl	This Time (I Mean It)			71	8

Denmark (continued)

Year	Artist	Song	Semi-Final Points	Semi-Final Position	Final Points	Final Position
2000	Olsen brothers	Fly On The Wings Of Love			195	1
2001	Rollo & King	Never Ever Let You Go			177	2
2002	Malene	Tell Me Who You Are			7	24
2003	-	-			-	-
2004	Tomas Thordarson	Shame On You	56	13	-	-
2005	Jakob Sveistrup	Talking To You	185	3	125	9
2006	Sidsel Ben Semmane	Twist Of Love	-	-	26	18
2007	DQ	Drama Queen	45	19	-	-
2008	Simon Mathew	All Night Long	112	3	60	15
2009	Brinck	Believe Again	69	8	74	13
2010	Chanée & N'evergreen	In A Moment Like This	101	5	149	4
2011	A Friend in London	New Tomorrow	135	2	134	5
2012	Soluna Samay	Should've Known Better	65	9	21	23
2013	Emmelie de Forest	Only Teardrops	167	1	281	1
2014	Basim	Cliché Love Song	-	-	74	9

Estonia

Year	Artist	Song	Semi-Final Points	Semi-Final Position	Final Points	Final Position
1994	Silvi Vrait	Nagu Merelaine			2	24
1995	-	-			-	-
1996	Ivo Linna & Maarja-Liis Ilus	Kaelakee Hääl			94	5
1997	Maarja-Liis Ilus	Keelatud Maa			82	8
1998	Koit Toome	Mere Lapsed			36	12
1999	Evelin Samuel & Camille	Diamond Of Night			90	6
2000	Ines	Once In A Lifetime			98	4
2001	Tanel Padar, Dave Benton & 2XL	Everybody			198	1
2002	Sahléne	Runaway			111	3
2003	Ruffus	Eighties Coming Back			14	21
2004	Neiokõsõ	Tii	57	11	-	-
2005	Suntribe	Let's Get Loud	31	20	-	-
2006	Sandra	Through My Window	28	18	-	-
2007	Gerli Padar	Partners In Crime	33	22	-	-
2008	Kreisiraadio	Leto Svet	8	18	-	-
2009	Urban Symphony	Rändajad	115	3	129	6
2010	Malcolm Lincoln	Siren	39	14	-	-
2011	Getter Jaani	Rockefeller Street	60	9	44	24
2012	Ott Lepland	Kuula	100	4	120	6
2013	Birgit Õigemeel	Et Uus Saaks Alguse	52	10	19	20
2014	Tanja	Amazing	36	12	-	-

Finland

Year	Artist	Song	Semi-Final Points	Semi-Final Position	Final Points	Final Position
1961	Laila Kinnunen	Valoa Ikkunassa			6	10
1962	Marion Rung	Tipi-tii			4	7
1963	Laila Halme	Muistojeni Laulu			0	13
1964	Lasse Mårtenson	Laiskotellen			9	7
1965	Viktor Klimenko	Aurinko Laskee Länteen			0	15
1966	Ann-Christine Nyström	Play-boy			7	10
1967	Fredi	Varjoon-suojaan			3	12
1968	Kristina Hautala	Kun Kello Käy			1	16
1969	Jarkko & Laura	Kuin Silloin Ennen			6	12
1970	-	-			-	-
1971	Markku Aro & Koivisto Sisters	Tie Uuteen Päivään			84	8
1972	Päivi Paunu & Kim Floor	Muistathan			78	12

Finland (continued)

Year	Artist	Song	Semi-Final Points	Semi-Final Position	Final Points	Final Position
1973	Marion Rung	Tom Tom Tom			93	6
1974	Carita	Äla Mene Pois (Keep Me Warm)			4	13
1975	Pihasoittajat	Old Man Fiddle			74	7
1976	Fredi & The Friends	Pump-pump			44	11
1977	Monica Aspelund	Lapponia			50	10
1978	Seija Simola	Anna Rakkaudelle Tilaisuus			2	18
1979	Katri-Helena	Katso Sineen Taivaan			38	14
1980	Vesa-Matti Loiri	Huilumies			6	19
1981	Riki Sorsa	Reggae OK			27	16
1982	Kojo	Nuku Pommiin			0	18
1983	Ami Aspelund	Fantasiaa			41	11
1984	Kirka	Hengaillaan			46	9
1985	Sonja Lumme	Eläköön Elämä			58	9
1986	Kari Kuivalainen	Päivä Kahden Ihmisen			22	15
1987	Vicky Rosti	Sata Salamaa			32	15
1988	Boulevard	Nauravat Silmät Muistetaan			3	20
1989	Anneli Saaristo	La Dolce Vita			76	7
1990	Beat	Fri?			8	21
1991	Kaija	Hullu Yö			6	20
1992	Pave	Yamma Yamma			4	23
1993	Katri-Helena	Tule Luo			20	17
1994	CatCat	Bye Bye Baby			11	22
1995	-	-			-	-
1996	Jasmine	Niin Kaunis On Taivas			9	23
1997	-	-			-	-
1998	Edea	Aava			22	15
1999	-	-			-	-
2000	Nina Åström	A Little Bit			18	18
2001	-	-			-	-
2002	Laura	Addicted To You			24	20
2003	-	-			-	-
2004	Jari Sillanpää	Takes 2 To Tango	51	14	-	-
2005	Geir Rönning	Why?	50	18	-	-
2006	Lordi	Hard Rock Hallelujah	292	1	292	1
2007	Hanna Pakarinen	Leave Me Alone	-	-	53	17
2008	Teräsbetoni	Missä Miehet Ratsastaa	79	8	35	22
2009	Waldo's People	Lose Control	42	12	22	25
2010	Kuunkuiskaajat	Työlki Ellää	49	11	-	-
2011	Paradise Oskar	Da Da Dam	103	3	57	21
2012	Pernilla	När Jag Blundar	41	12	-	-
2013	Krista Siegfrids	Marry Me	64	9	13	24
2014	Softengine	Something Better	97	3	72	11

France

Year	Artist	Song	Semi-Final Points	Semi-Final Position	Final Points	Final Position
1956	(1) Mathé Altéry	Le Temps Perdu			-	2
1956	(2) Dany Dauberson	Il Est Là			-	2
1957	Paule Desjardins	La Belle Amour			17	2
1958	André Claveau	Dors Mon Amour			27	1
1959	Jean Philippe	Oui, Oui, Oui, Oui			15	3
1960	Jacqueline Boyer	Tom Pillibi			32	1
1961	Jean-Paul Mauric	Printemps (avril Carillonne)			13	4
1962	Isabelle Aubret	Un Premier Amour			26	1
1963	Alain Barrière	Elle était Si Jolie			25	5
1964	Rachel	Le Chant De Mallory			14	4
1965	Guy Mardel	N'avoue Jamais			22	3

Year	Artist	Song	Semi-Final Points	Semi-Final Position	Final Points	Final Position
1966	Dominique Walter	Chez Nous			1	16
1967	Noëlle Cordier	Il Doit Faire Beau Là-bas			20	3
1968	Isabelle Aubret	La Source			20	3
1969	Frida Boccara	Un Jour, Un Enfant			18	1
1970	Guy Bonnet	Marie Blanche			8	4
1971	Serge Lama	Un Jardin Sur La Terre			83	9
1972	Betty Mars	Comé-comédie			81	11
1973	Martine Clémenceau	Sans Toi			65	15
1974	-	-			-	-
1975	Nicole Rieu	Et Bonjour à Toi L'artiste			91	4
1976	Catherine Ferry	Un, Deux, Trois			147	2
1977	Marie Myriam	L'oiseau Et L'enfant			136	1
1978	Joël Prévost	Il Y Aura Toujours Des Violons			119	3
1979	Anne-Marie David	Je Suis L'enfant-soleil			106	3
1980	Profil	Hé, Hé M'sieurs Dames			45	11
1981	Jean Gabilou	Humanahum			125	3
1982	-	-			-	-
1983	Guy Bonnet	Vivre			56	8
1984	Annick Thoumazeau	Autant D'amoureux Que D'étoiles			61	8
1985	Roger Bens	Femme Dans Ses Rêves Aussi			56	10
1986	Cocktail Chic	Européennes			13	17
1987	Christine Minier	Les Mots D'amour N'ont Pas De Dimanche			44	14
1988	Gérard Lenorman	Chanteur De Charme			64	10
1989	Nathalie Pâque	J'ai Volé La Vie			60	8
1990	Joelle Ursull	White And Black Blues			132	2
1991	Amina	C'est Le Dernier Qui A Parlé Qui A Raison			146	1
1992	Kali	Monté La Riviè			73	8
1993	Patrick Fiori	Mama Corsica			121	5
1994	Nina Morato	Je Suis Un Vrai Garçon			74	7
1995	Nathalie Santamaria	Il Me Donne Rendez-vous			94	4
1996	Dan Ar Braz & l'Héritage des Celtes	Diwanit Bugale			18	19
1997	Fanny	Sentiments Songes			95	7
1998	Marie-Line	Où Aller			3	24
1999	Nayah	Je Veux Donner Ma Voix			14	17
2000	Sofia Mestari	On Aura Le Ciel			5	23
2001	Natasha Saint-Pier	Je N'ai Que Mon âme			142	4
2002	Sandrine François	Il Faut Du Temps			104	5
2003	Louisa Baileche	Monts Et Merveilles			19	18
2004	Jonatan Cerrada	A Chaque Pas	-	-	40	15
2005	Ortal	Chacun Pense à Soi	-	-	11	23
2006	Virginie Pouchin	Il était Temps	-	-	5	22
2007	Les Fatals Picards	L'amour à La Française	-	-	19	22
2008	Sébastien Tellier	Divine	-	-	47	19
2009	Patricia Kaas	Et S'il Fallait Le Faire	-	-	107	8
2010	Jessy Matador	Allez Olla Olé	-	-	82	12
2011	Amaury Vassili	Sognu	-	-	82	15
2012	Anggun	Echo (You And I)	-	-	21	22
2013	Amandine Bourgeois	L'enfer Et Moi	-	-	14	23
2014	Twin Twin	Moustache	-	-	2	26

FYR Macedonia

Year	Artist	Song	Semi-Final Points	Semi-Final Position	Final Points	Final Position
1998	Vlado Janevski	Ne Zori, Zoro			16	19
1999	-	-			-	-
2000	XXL	100% Te Ljubam			29	15
2001	-	-			-	-
2002	Karolina	Od Nas Zavisi			25	19
2003	-	-			-	-
2004	Tose Proeski	Life	71	10	47	14
2005	Martin Vucic	Make My Day	97	9	52	17
2006	Elena Risteska	Ninanajna	76	8	56	12
2007	Karolina	Mojot Svet	97	9	73	14
2008	Tamara, Vrčak & Adrijan	Let Me Love You	64	10	-	-
2009	Next Time	Neshto Shto Ke Ostane	45	10	-	-
2010	Gjoko Taneski	Jas Ja Imam Silata	37	15	-	-
2011	Vlatko Ilievski	Rusinka	36	16	-	-
2012	Kaliopi	Crno I Belo	53	9	71	13
2013	Esma & Lozano	Pred Da Se Razdeni	28	16	-	-
2014	Tijana	To The Sky	33	13	-	-

Georgia

Year	Artist	Song	Semi-Final Points	Semi-Final Position	Final Points	Final Position
2007	Sopho	My Story	123	8	97	12
2008	Diana Gurtskaya	Peace Will Come	107	5	83	11
2009	-	-	-	-	-	-
2010	Sofia Nizharadze	Shine	106	3	136	9
2011	Eldrine	One More Day	74	6	110	9
2012	Anri Jokhadze	I'm A Joker	36	14	-	-
2013	Nodi Tatishvili & Sophie Gelovani	Waterfall	63	10	50	15
2014	The Shin and Mariko	Three Minutes to Earth	15	15	-	-

Germany

Year	Artist	Song	Semi-Final Points	Semi-Final Position	Final Points	Final Position
1956	(1) Walter Andreas Schwarz	Im Wartesaal Zum Großen Glück			-	2
1956	(2) Freddy Quinn	So Geht Das Jede Nacht			-	2
1957	Margot Hielscher	Telefon, Telefon			8	4
1958	Margot Hielscher	Für Zwei Groschen Musik			5	7
1959	Alice & Ellen Kessler	Heut' Woll'n Wir Tanzen Geh'n			5	8
1960	Wyn Hoop	Bonne Nuit, Ma Chérie!			11	4
1961	Lale Andersen	Einmal Sehen Wir Uns Wieder			3	13
1962	Conny Froboess	Zwei Kleine Italiener			9	6
1963	Heidi Brühl	Marcel			5	9
1964	Nora Nova	Man Gewöhnt Sich So Schnell An Das Schöne			0	13
1965	Ulla Wiesner	Paradies, Wo Bist Du?			0	15
1966	Margot Eskens	Die Zeiger Der Uhr			7	10
1967	Inge Brück	Anouschka			7	8
1968	Wencke Myhre	Ein Hoch Der Liebe			11	6
1969	Siw Malmkvist	Primaballerina			8	9
1970	Katja Ebstein	Wunder Gibt Es Immer Wieder			12	3
1971	Katja Ebstein	Diese Welt			100	3
1972	Mary Roos	Nur Die Liebe Läßt Uns Leben			107	3
1973	Gitte	Junger Tag			85	8
1974	Cindy & Bert	Die Sommermelodie			3	14
1975	Joy Fleming	Ein Lied Kann Eine Brücke Sein			15	17
1976	Les Humphries Singers	Sing, Sang, Song			12	15

Germany (continued)

Year	Artist	Song	Semi-Final Points	Semi-Final Position	Final Points	Final Position
1977	Silver Convention	Telegram			55	8
1978	Ireen Sheer	Feuer			84	6
1979	Dschinghis Khan	Dschinghis Khan			86	4
1980	Katja Ebstein	Theater			128	2
1981	Lena Valaitis	Johnny Blue			132	2
1982	Nicole	Ein Bißchen Frieden			161	1
1983	Hoffmann & Hoffmann	Rücksicht			94	5
1984	Mary Roos	Aufrecht Geh'n			34	13
1985	Wind	Für Alle			105	2
1986	Ingrid Peters	Über Die Brücke Geh'n			62	8
1987	Wind	Laß Die Sonne In Dein Herz			141	2
1988	Maxi & Chris Garden	Lied Für Einen Freund			48	14
1989	Nino de Angelo	Flieger			46	14
1990	Chris Kempers & Daniel Kovac	Frei Zu Leben			60	9
1991	Atlantis 2000	Dieser Traum Darf Niemals Sterben			10	18
1992	Wind	Träume Sind Für Alle Da			27	16
1993	Münchener Freiheit	Viel Zu Weit			18	18
1994	MeKaDo	Wir Geben 'ne Party			128	3
1995	Stone & Stone	Verliebt In Dich			1	23
1996	-	-			-	-
1997	Bianca Shomburg	Zeit			22	18
1998	Guildo Horn	Guildo Hat Euch Lieb			86	7
1999	Sürpriz	Reise Nach Jerusalem - Kudüs'e Seyahat			140	3
2000	Stefan Raab	Wadde Hadde Dudde Da			96	5
2001	Michelle	Wer Liebe Lebt			66	8
2002	Corinna May	I Can't Live Without Music			17	21
2003	Lou	Let's Get Happy			53	11
2004	Max (Maximilian Mutzke)	Can't Wait Until Tonight	-	-	93	8
2005	Gracia	Run & Hide	-	-	4	24
2006	Texas Lightning	No, No, Never	-	-	36	14
2007	Roger Cicero	Frauen Regieren Die Welt	-	-	49	19
2008	No Angels	Disappear	-	-	14	23
2009	Alex Swings Oscar Sings!	Miss Kiss Kiss Bang	-	-	35	20
2010	Lena Meyer-Landrut	Satellite	-	-	246	1
2011	Lena Meyer-Landrut	Taken by a Stranger	-	-	107	10
2012	Roman Lob	Standing Still	-	-	110	8
2013	Cascada	Glorious	-	-	18	21
2014	Elaiza	Is it Right?	-	-	39	18

Greece

Year	Artist	Song	Semi-Final Points	Semi-Final Position	Final Points	Final Position
1974	Marinella	Krassi, Thalassa Ke T'agori Mou			7	11
1975	-	-			-	-
1976	Mariza Koch	Panaghia Mou, Panaghia Mou			20	13
1977	Pascalis, Marianna, Robert & Bessy	Mathema Solfege			92	5
1978	Tania Tsanaklidou	Charlie Chaplin			66	8
1979	Elpida	Socrates			69	8
1980	Anna Vishy & the Epikouri	Autostop			30	13
1981	Yiannis Dimitras	Feggari Kalokerino			55	8
1982	-	-			-	-
1983	Christie	Mou Les			32	14
1984	-	-			-	-
1985	Takis Biniaris	Miazoume			15	16
1986	-	-			-	-
1987	Bang	Stop!			64	10
1988	Aphroditi Fryda	Kloun			10	17

Greece (continued)

Year	Artist	Song	Semi-Final Points	Semi-Final Position	Final Points	Final Position
1989	Marianna	To Diko Sou Asteri			56	9
1990	Christos Callow & Wave	Horis Skopo			11	9
1991	Sofia Vossou	I Anixi			36	13
1992	Cleopatra	Olou Tou Kosmou I Elpida			94	5
1993	Katerina Garbi	Ellada, Hora Tou Fotos			64	9
1994	Costas Bigalis & the Sea Lovers	To Trehantiri (Diri Diri)			44	14
1995	Elina Constantopoulou	Pia Prossefchi			68	12
1996	Marianna Efstratiou	Emis Forame To Himona Anixiatika			36	14
1997	Marianna Zorba	Horepse			39	12
1998	Dionysia & Thalassa Group	Mia Krifi Evaisthissia			12	20
1999	-	-			-	-
2000	-	-			-	-
2001	Antique	Die For You			147	3
2002	Michalis Rakintzis	SAGAPO			27	17
2003	Mando	Never Let You Go			25	17
2004	Sakis Rouvas	Shake It	238	3	252	3
2005	Helena Paparizou	My Number One	-	-	230	1
2006	Anna Vissi	Everything	-	-	128	9
2007	Sarbel	Yassou Maria	-	-	139	7
2008	Kalomira	Secret Combination	156	1	218	3
2009	Sakis Rouvas	This Is Our Night	110	4	120	7
2010	Giorgos Alkaios & Friends	OPA	133	2	140	8
2011	Loucas Yiorkas feat Stereo Mike	Watch My Dance	133	1	120	7
2012	Eleftheria Eleftheriou	Aphrodisiac	116	4	64	17
2013	Koza Mostra feat. Agathon Iakovidis	Alcohol is Free	121	2	152	6
2014	Freaky Fortune feat. RiskyKidd	Rise Up	74	7	35	20

Hungary

Year	Artist	Song	Semi-Final Points	Semi-Final Position	Final Points	Final Position
1994	Friderika Bayer	Kinek Mondjam El Vétkeimet			122	4
1995	Czaba Szigeti	Ùj Nèv Egy Règi Hàz Fàlan			3	22
1996	-	-			-	-
1997	VIP	Miert Kell, Hogy Elmenj?			39	12
1998	Charlie	A Holnap Már Ném Lesz Szomorú			4	23
1999	-	-			-	-
2000	-	-			-	-
2001	-	-			-	-
2002	-	-			-	-
2003	-	-			-	-
2004	-	-			-	-
2005	NOX	Forogj Világ			97	12
2006	-	-			-	-
2007	Magdi Rúzsa	Unsubstantial Blues			128	9
2008	Csézy	Candlelight	6	19	-	-
2009	Zoli Ádok	Dance With Me	16	15	-	-
2010	-	-	-	-	-	-
2011	Kati Wolf	What About My Dreams?	72	7	53	22
2012	Compact Disco	Sound of Our Hearts	52	10	19	24
2013	ByeAlex	Kedvesem (Zoohacker Remix)	66	8	84	10
2014	András Kállay-Saunders	Running	127	3	143	5

Iceland

Year	Artist	Song	Semi-Final Points	Semi-Final Position	Final Points	Final Position
1986	Icy	Gleðibankinn			19	16
1987	Halla Margarét	Hægt Og Hljótt			28	16
1988	Beathoven	Sókrates			20	16
1989	Daníel Ágúst Haraldsson	Það Sem Enginn Sér			0	22
1990	Stjórnin	Eitt Lag Enn			124	4
1991	Stefán & Eyfi	Nina			26	15
1992	Heart 2 Heart	Nei Eða Já			80	7
1993	Inga	Þá Veistu Svarið			42	13
1994	Sigga	Nætur			49	12
1995	Bó Halldórsson	Núna			31	15
1996	Anna Mjöll	Sjúbídú			51	13
1997	Paul Oscar	Minn Hinsti Dans			18	20
1998	-	-			-	-
1999	Selma Björnsdóttir	All Out Of Luck			146	2
2000	Einer Ágúst Víðisson & Telma Ágústdóttir	Tell Me!			45	12
2001	TwoTricky	Angel			3	22
2002	-	-			-	-
2003	Birgitta	Open Your Heart			81	8
2004	Jónsi	Heaven			16	19
2005	Selma	If I Had Your Love	52	16	-	-
2006	Silvia Night	Congratulations	62	13	-	-
2007	Eiríkur Hauksson	Valentine Lost	77	13	-	-
2008	Euroband	This Is My Life	68	8	64	14
2009	Yohanna	Is It True?	174	1	218	2
2010	Hera Björk	Je Ne Sais Quoi	123	3	41	19
2011	Sjonni's Friends	Coming Home	100	4	61	20
2012	Greta Salóme & Jónsi	Never Forget	75	8	46	20
2013	Eythor Ingi	Ég Á Líf	72	6	47	17
2014	Pollapönk	No Prejudice	61	8	58	15

Ireland

Year	Artist	Song	Semi-Final Points	Semi-Final Position	Final Points	Final Position
1965	Butch Moore	I'm Walking The Streets In The Rain			11	6
1966	Dickie Rock	Come Back To Stay			14	4
1967	Sean Dunphy	If I Could Choose			22	2
1968	Pat McGeegan	Chance Of A Lifetime			18	4
1969	Muriel Day & the Lindsays	The Wages Of Love			10	7
1970	Dana	All Kinds Of Everything			32	1
1971	Angela Farrell	One Day Love			79	11
1972	Sandie Jones	Ceol On Ghrá			72	15
1973	Maxi	Do I Dream?			80	10
1974	Tina	Cross Your Heart			11	7
1975	The Swarbriggs	That's What Friends Are For			68	9
1976	Red Hurley	When			54	10
1977	The Swarbriggs Plus Two	It's Nice To Be In Love Again			119	3
1978	Colm Wilkinson	Born To Sing			86	5
1979	Cathal Dunne	Happy Man			80	5
1980	Johnny Logan	What's Another Year			143	1
1981	Sheeba	Horoscopes			105	5
1982	The Duskeys	Here Today, Gone Tomorrow			49	11
1983	-	-			-	-
1984	Linda Martin	Terminal 3			137	2
1985	Maria Christian	Wait Until The Weekend Comes			91	6
1986	Luv Bug	You Can Count On Me			96	4
1987	Johnny Logan	Hold Me Now			172	1
1988	Jump the Gun	Take Him Home			79	8

Ireland (continued)

Year	Artist	Song	Semi-Final Points	Position	Final Points	Position
1989	Kiev Connolly & the Missing Passengers	The Real Me			21	18
1990	Liam Reilly	Somewhere In Europe			132	2
1991	Kim Jackson	Could It Be That I'm In Love			47	10
1992	Linda Martin	Why Me			155	1
1993	Niamh Kavanagh	In Your Eyes			187	1
1994	Paul Harrington & Charlie McGettigan	Rock 'n' Roll Kids			226	1
1995	Eddie Friel	Dreamin'			44	14
1996	Eimear Quinn	The Voice			162	1
1997	Marc Roberts	Mysterious Woman			157	2
1998	Dawn	Is Always Over Now?			64	9
1999	The Mullans	When You Need Me			18	18
2000	Eamonn Toal	Millennium Of Love			92	6
2001	Gary O'Shaughnessy	Without Your Love			6	21
2002	-	-			-	-
2003	Mickey Harte	We've Got The World			53	11
2004	Chris Doran	If My World Stopped Turning	-	-	7	22
2005	Donna & Joseph McCaul	Love?	53	14	-	-
2006	Brian Kennedy	Every Song Is A Cry For Love	79	10	93	10
2007	Dervish	They Can't Stop The Spring	-	-	5	24
2008	Dustin the Turkey	Irelande Douze Pointe	22	15	-	-
2009	Sinéad Mulvey & Black Daisy	Et Cetera	52	11	-	-
2010	Niamh Kavanagh	It's For You	67	9	25	23
2011	Jedward	Lipstick	68	8	119	8
2012	Jedward	Waterline	92	6	46	19
2013	Ryan Dolan	Only Love Survives	54	8	5	26
2014	Can-Linn (feat. Kasey Smith)	Heartbeat	35	12	-	-

Israel

Year	Artist	Song	Semi-Final Points	Position	Final Points	Position
1973	Ilanit	Ey-sham			97	4
1974	Poogy	Natati La Khaiai			11	7
1975	Shlomo Artzi	At Ve'ani			40	11
1976	Chocolate, Menta, Mastik	Emor Shalom			77	6
1977	Ilanit	Ah-haa-vah Hee Shir Lish-naa-yim			49	11
1978	Izhar Cohen & the Alphabeta	Abanibi			157	1
1979	Milk & Honey	Hallelujah			125	1
1980	-	-			-	-
1981	Habibi	Halaylah			56	7
1982	Avi Toledano	Hora			100	2
1983	Ofra Haza	Hi			136	2
1984	-	-			-	-
1985	Izhar Cohen	Olé Olé			93	5
1986	Moti Galadi & Sarai Tzuriel	Yavoh Yom			7	19
1987	Datner & Kushnir	Shir Habatlanim			73	8
1988	Yardena Arazi	Ben Adam			85	7
1989	Gili ve Galit	Derech Ha'melech			50	12
1990	Rita	Shara Barechovot			16	18
1991	Duo Datz	Kan			139	3
1992	Dafna	Ze Rak Sport			85	6
1993	Lakahat Shiru	Shiru			4	24
1994	-	-			-	-
1995	Liora	Amen			81	8
1996	-	-			-	-
1997	-	-			-	-
1998	Dana International	Diva			172	1
1999	Eden	Yom Huledeth			93	5

Israel (continued)

Year	Artist	Song	Semi-Final Points	Semi-Final Position	Final Points	Final Position
2000	Ping Pong	Sa'me'akh			7	22
2001	Tal Sondak	Ein Davar			25	16
2002	Sarit Hadad	Light A Candle			37	12
2003	Lior Narkis	Words For Love			17	19
2004	David D'or	Le'ha'amin	57	11	-	-
2005	Shiri Maymon	Hasheket Shenish'ar	158	7	154	4
2006	Eddie Butler	Ze Hazman	-	-	4	23
2007	Teapacks	Push The Button	17	24	-	-
2008	Boaz	The Fire In Your Eyes	104	5	124	9
2009	Noa & Mira Awad	There Must Be Another Way	75	7	53	16
2010	Harel Skaat	Milim	71	8	71	14
2011	Dana International	Ding Dong	38	15	-	-
2012	Izabo	Time	33	13	-	-
2013	Moran Mazor	Rak Bishvilo	40	14	-	-
2014	Mei Finegold	Same Heart	19	14	-	-

Italy

Year	Artist	Song	Semi-Final Points	Semi-Final Position	Final Points	Final Position
1956	(1) Tonina Torielli	Amami Se Vuoi			-	2
1956	(2) Franca Raimondi	Aprite Le Finestre			-	2
1957	Nunzio Gallo	Corde Della Mia Chitarra			7	6
1958	Domenico Modugno	Nel Blu Dipinto Di Blu			13	3
1959	Domenico Modugno	Piove			9	6
1960	Renato Rascel	Romantica			5	8
1961	Betty Curtis	Al Di Là			12	5
1962	Claudio Villa	Addio, Addio			3	9
1963	Emilio Pericoli	Uno Per Tutte			37	3
1964	Gigliola Cinquetti	Non Ho L'étà			49	1
1965	Bobby Solo	Se Piangi, Se Ridi			15	5
1966	Domenico Modugno	Dio Come Ti Amo			0	17
1967	Claudio Villa	Non Andare Più Lontano			4	11
1968	Sergio Endrigo	Marianne			7	10
1969	Iva Zanicchi	Due Grosse Lacrime Bianche			5	13
1970	Gianni Morandi	Occhi Di Ragazza			5	8
1971	Massimo Ranieri	L'amore è Un Attimo			91	5
1972	Nicola di Bari	I Giorni Dell' Arcobaleno			92	6
1973	Massimo Ranieri	Chi Sarà Con Te			74	13
1974	Gigliola Cinquetti	Si			18	2
1975	Wess & Dori Ghezzi	Era			115	3
1976	Romina & Al Bano	We'll Live It All Again			69	7
1977	Mia Martini	Liberà			33	13
1978	Ricchi e Poveri	Questo Amore			53	12
1979	Matia Bazar	Raggio Di Luna			27	15
1980	Alan Sorrenti	Non So Che Darei			87	6
1981	-	-			-	-
1982	-	-			-	-
1983	Riccardo Fogli	Per Lucia			41	11
1984	Alice & Battiato	I Treni Di Tozeur			70	5
1985	Al Bano & Romina Power	Magic, Oh Magic			78	7
1986	-	-			-	-
1987	Umberto Tozzi & Raf	Gente Di Mare			103	3
1988	Luca Barbarossa	Ti Scrivo			52	12
1989	Anna Oxa & Fausto Leali	Avrei Voluto			56	9
1990	Toto Cutugno	Insieme: 1992			149	1
1991	Peppino di Capri	Comme E' Ddoce 'o Mare			89	7
1992	Mia Martini	Rapsodia			111	4

Italy (continued)

Year	Artist	Song	Semi-Final Points	Semi-Final Position	Final Points	Final Position
1993	Enrico Ruggeri	Sole D'europa			45	12
1994	-	-			-	-
1995	-	-			-	-
1996	-	-			-	-
1997	Jalisse	Fiumi Di Parole			114	4
1998	-	-			-	-
1999	-	-			-	-
2000	-	-			-	-
2001	-	-			-	-
2002	-	-			-	-
2003	-	-			-	-
2004	-	-	-	-	-	-
2005	-	-	-	-	-	-
2006	-	-	-	-	-	-
2007	-	-	-	-	-	-
2008	-	-	-	-	-	-
2009	-	-	-	-	-	-
2010	-	-	-	-	-	-
2011	Raphael Gualazzi	Madness of Love	-	-	189	2
2012	Nina Zilli	L'Amore È Femmina (Out Of Love)	-	-	101	9
2013	Marco Mengoni	L'Essenziale	-	-	126	7
2014	Emma	La Mia Città	-	-	33	21

Latvia

Year	Artist	Song	Semi-Final Points	Semi-Final Position	Final Points	Final Position
2001	Arnis Mednis	Too Much	-		16	18
2002	Marie N	I Wanna			176	1
2003	FLY	Hello from Mars			5	24
2004	Fomins & Kleins	Dziesma Par Laimi	23	17	-	-
2005	Walter & Kazha	The War Is Not Over	85	10	153	5
2006	Cosmos	I Hear Your Heart	-	-	30	16
2007	Bonaparti.lv	Questa Notte	168	5	54	16
2008	Pirates Of The Sea	Wolves Of The Sea	86	6	83	12
2009	Intars Busulis	Probka	7	19	-	-
2010	Aisha	What For?	11	17	-	-
2011	Musiqq	Angel in Disguise	25	17	-	-
2012	Anmary	Beautiful Song	17	16	-	-
2013	PeR	Here We Go	13	17	-	-
2014	Aarzemnieki	Cake to Bake	33	13	-	-

Lithuania

Year	Artist	Song	Semi-Final Points	Semi-Final Position	Final Points	Final Position
1994	Ovidijus Vyšniauskas	Lopšine mylimai			0	25
1995	-	-			-	-
1996	-	-			-	-
1997	-	-			-	-
1998	-	-			-	-
1999	Aiste Smilgeviciute	Strazdas			13	20
2000	-	-			-	-
2001	Skamp	You Got Style			35	13
2002	Aivaras	Happy You			12	23
2003	-	-			-	-
2004	Linas ir Simona	What's Happened To Your Love?	26	16	-	-
2005	Laura & the Lovers	Little By Little	17	25	-	-

Lithuania (continued)

Year	Artist	Song	Semi-Final Points	Semi-Final Position	Final Points	Final Position
2006	LT United	We Are The Winners	163	5	162	6
2007	4Fun	Love Or Leave	-	-	28	21
2008	Jeronimas Milius	Nomads In The Night	30	16	-	-
2009	Sasha Son	Love	66	9	23	23
2010	InCulto	East European Funk	44	12	-	-
2011	Evelina Sašenko	C'est Ma Vie	81	5	63	19
2012	Donny Montell	Love is Blind	107	3	70	14
2013	Andrius Pojavis	Something	53	9	17	22
2014	Vilija Matačiūnaitė	Attention	36	11	-	-

Luxembourg

Year	Artist	Song	Semi-Final Points	Semi-Final Position	Final Points	Final Position
1956	(1) Michèle Arnaud	Les Amants De Minuit			-	2
1956	(2) Michèle Arnaud	Ne Crois Pas			-	2
1957	Danièle Dupré	Tant De Peine			8	4
1958	Solange Berry	Un Grand Amour			1	9
1959	-	-			-	-
1960	Camillo Felgen	So Laang We's Du Do Bast			1	13
1961	Jean-Claude Pascal	Nous Les Amoureux			31	1
1962	Camillo Felgen	Petit Bonhomme			11	3
1963	Nana Mouskouri	A Force De Prier			13	8
1964	Hugues Aufray	Dès Que Le Printemps Revient			14	4
1965	France Gall	Poupée De Cire, Poupée De Son			32	1
1966	Michèle Torr	Ce Soir Je T'attendais			7	10
1967	Vicky	L'amour Est Bleu			17	4
1968	Chris Baldo & Sophie Garel	Nous Vivrons D'amour			5	11
1969	Romuald	Cathérine			7	11
1970	David-Alexandre Winter	Je Suis Tombé Du Ciel			0	12
1971	Monique Melsen	Pomme, Pomme, Pomme			70	13
1972	Vicky Leandros	Après Toi			128	1
1973	Anne-Marie David	Tu Te Reconnaîtras			129	1
1974	Ireen Sheer	Bye, Bye, I Love You			14	4
1975	Géraldine	Toi			84	5
1976	Jürgen Marcus	Chansons Pour Ceux Qui S'aiment			17	4
1977	Anne Marie B	Frère Jacques			17	16
1978	Baccara	Parlez-vous Français?			73	7
1979	Jeane Manson	J'ai Déjà Vu ça Dans Tes Yeux			44	13
1980	Sophie & Magaly	Papa Pingouin			56	9
1981	Jean-Claude Pascal	C'est Peut-être Pas L'Amérique			41	11
1982	Svetlana	Cours Après le Temps			78	6
1983	Corinne Hermès	Si La Vie Est Cadeau			142	1
1984	Sophie Carle	100% D'amour			39	10
1985	Margo, Franck Olivier, Diane Solomon, Ireen Sheer, Malcolm Roberts & Chris Roberts	Children, Kinder, Enfants			37	13
1986	Sherisse Laurence	L'amour De Ma Vie			117	3
1987	Plastic Bertrand	Amour Amour			4	21
1988	Lara Fabian	Croire			90	4
1989	Park Café	Monsieur			8	20
1990	Céline Carzo	Quand Je Te Rêve			38	13
1991	Sarah Bray	Un Baiser Volé			29	14
1992	Marion Welter & Kontinent	Sou Fräi			10	21
1993	Modern Times	Donne-moi Une Chance			11	20

Malta

Year	Artist	Song	Semi-Final Points	Semi-Final Position	Final Points	Final Position
1971	Joe Grech	Marija L-maltija			52	18
1972	Helen & Joseph	L-imhabba			48	18
1973	-	-			-	-
1974	-	-			-	-
1975	Renato	Singing This Song			32	12
1976	-	-			-	-
1977	-	-			-	-
1978	-	-			-	-
1979	-	-			-	-
1980	-	-			-	-
1981	-	-			-	-
1982	-	-			-	-
1983	-	-			-	-
1984	-	-			-	-
1985	-	-			-	-
1986	-	-			-	-
1987	-	-			-	-
1988	-	-			-	-
1989	-	-			-	-
1990	-	-			-	-
1991	Paul Giordimaina & Georgina	Could It Be			106	6
1992	Mary Spiteri	Little Child			123	3
1993	William Mangion	This Time			69	8
1994	Moira Stafrace & Christopher Scicluna	More Than Love			97	5
1995	Mike Spiteri	Keep Me In Mind			76	10
1996	Miriam Christine	In A Woman's Heart			68	10
1997	Debbie Scerri	Let Me Fly			66	9
1998	Chiara	The One That I Love			165	3
1999	Times 3	Believe 'n Peace			32	15
2000	Claudette Pace	Desire			73	8
2001	Fabrizio Faniello	Another Summer Night			48	9
2002	Ira Losco	7th Wonder			164	2
2003	Lynn Chircop	To Dream Again			4	25
2004	Julie & Ludwig	On Again... Off Again	74	8	50	12
2005	Chiara	Angel	-	-	192	2
2006	Fabrizio Faniello	I Do	-	-	1	24
2007	Olivia Lewis	Vertigo	15	25	-	-
2008	Morena	Vodka	38	14	-	-
2009	Chiara	What If We	86	6	31	22
2010	Thea Garrett	My Dream	45	12	-	-
2011	Glen Vella	One Life	54	11	-	-
2012	Kurt Calleja	This Is The Night	70	7	41	21
2013	Gianluca	Tomorrow	118	4	120	8
2014	Firelight	Coming Home	63	9	32	23

Moldova

Year	Artist	Song	Semi-Final Points	Semi-Final Position	Final Points	Final Position
2005	Zdob si Zdub	Boonika Bate Toba	207	2	148	6
2006	Arsenium & Natalia Gordienko	Loca	-	-	22	20
2007	Natalia Barbu	Fight	91	10	109	10
2008	Geta Burlacu	A Century Of Love	36	12	-	-
2009	Nelly Ciobanu	Hora Din Moldova	106	5	69	14
2010	Sunstroke Project & Olia Tira	Run Away	52	10	27	22
2011	Zdob și Zdub	So Lucky	54	10	97	12
2012	Pasha Parfeny	Lăutar	100	5	81	11
2013	Aliona Moon	O Mie	95	4	71	11
2014	Cristina Scarlat	Wild Soul	13	16	-	-

Monaco

Year	Artist	Song	Semi-Final Points	Semi-Final Position	Final Points	Final Position
1959	Jacques Pills	Mon Ami Pierrot			1	11
1960	François Deguelt	Ce Soir-là			15	3
1961	Colette Deréal	Allons, Allons Les Enfants			6	10
1962	François Deguelt	Dis Rien			13	2
1963	Françoise Hardy	L'amour S'en Va			25	5
1964	Romuald	Où Sont-elles Passées?			15	3
1965	Marjorie Noël	Va Dire à L'amour			7	9
1966	Tereza	Bien Plus Fort			0	17
1967	Minouche Barelli	Boum-badaboum			10	5
1968	Line & Willy	A Chacun Sa Chanson			8	7
1969	Jean-Jacques	Maman, Maman			11	6
1970	Dominique Dussault	Marlène			5	8
1971	Séverine	Un Banc, Un Arbre, Une Rue			128	1
1972	Anne-Marie Godart & Peter MacLane	Comme On S'aime			65	16
1973	Marie	Un Train Qui Part			85	8
1974	Romuald	Celui Qui Reste Et Celui Qui S'en Va			14	4
1975	Sophie	Une Chanson C'est Une Lettre			22	13
1976	Mary Christy	Toi, La Musique Et Moi			93	3
1977	Michèle Torr	Une Petite Française			96	4
1978	Caline & Olivier Toussaint	Les Jardins De Monaco			107	4
1979	Laurent Vaguener	Notre Vie, C'est La Musique			12	16
1980	-	-			-	-
1981	-	-			-	-
1982	-	-			-	-
1983	-	-			-	-
1984	-	-			-	-
1985	-	-			-	-
1986	-	-			-	-
1987	-	-			-	-
1988	-	-			-	-
1989	-	-			-	-
1990	-	-			-	-
1991	-	-			-	-
1992	-	-			-	-
1993	-	-			-	-
1994	-	-			-	-
1995	-	-			-	-
1996	-	-			-	-
1997	-	-			-	-
1998	-	-			-	-
1999	-	-			-	-
2000	-	-			-	-
2001	-	-			-	-
2002	-	-			-	-
2003	-	-			-	-
2004	Maryon	Notre Planète	10	19	-	-
2005	Lise Darly	Tout De Moi	22	24	-	-
2006	Séverine Ferrer	La Coco-dance	14	21	-	-

Montenegro

Year	Artist	Song	Semi-Final Points	Semi-Final Position	Final Points	Final Position
2007	Stevan Faddy	Ajde Kroci	33	22	-	-
2008	Stefan Filipović	Zauvijek Volim Te	23	14	-	-
2009	Andrea Demirovic	Just Get Out of My Life	44	11	-	-
2010	-	-				-
2011	-	-				-
2012	Rambo Amadeus	Euro Neuro	20	15	-	-
2013	Who See	Igranka	41	12	-	-
2014	Sergej Ćetković	Moj Svijet	63	7	37	19

Morocco

Year	Artist	Song	Semi-Final Points	Semi-Final Position	Final Points	Final Position
1980	Samira Bensaïd	Bitakat Hob			7	18

Netherlands

Year	Artist	Song	Semi-Final Points	Semi-Final Position	Final Points	Final Position
1956	(1) Corry Brokken	Voorgoed Voorbij			-	2
1956	(2) Jetty Paerl	De Vogels Van Holland			-	2
1957	Corry Brokken	Net Als Toen			31	1
1958	Corry Brokken	Heel De Wereld			1	9
1959	Teddy Scholten	Een Beetje			21	1
1960	Rudi Carrell	Wat Een Geluk			2	12
1961	Greetje Kauffeld	Wat Een Dag			6	10
1962	De Spelbrekers	Katinka			0	13
1963	Annie Palmen	Een Speeldoos			0	13
1964	Anneke Grönloh	Jij Bent Mijn Leven			2	10
1965	Conny Van den Bos	Het Is Genoeg			5	11
1966	Milly Scott	Fernando En Philippo			2	15
1967	Thérèse Steinmetz	Ring-dinge			2	14
1968	Ronnie Tober	Morgen			1	16
1969	Lenny Kuhr	De Troubadour			18	1
1970	Patricia & Hearts of Soul	Waterman			7	7
1971	Saskia & Serge	De Tijd			85	6
1972	Sandra & Andres	Als Het Om De Liefde Gaat			106	4
1973	Ben Cramer	De Oude Muzikant			69	14
1974	Mouth & MacNeal	I See A Star			15	3
1975	Teach-In	Ding-A-Dong			152	1
1976	Sandra Reemer	The Party's Over Now			56	9
1977	Heddy Lester	De Mallemolen			35	12
1978	Harmony	't Is Ok			37	13
1979	Xandra	Colorado			51	12
1980	Maggie MacNeal	Amsterdam			93	5
1981	Linda Williams	Het Is Een Wonder			51	9
1982	Bill van Dijk	Jij En Ik			8	16
1983	Bernadette	Sing Me A Song			66	7
1984	Maribelle	Ik Hou Van Jou			34	13
1985	-	-			-	-
1986	Frizzle Sizzle	Alles Heeft Ritme			40	13
1987	Marcha	Rechtop In De Wind			83	5
1988	Gerard Joling	Shangri-la			70	9
1989	Justine Pelmelay	Blijf Zoals Je Bent			45	15
1990	Maywood	Ik Wil Alles Met Je Delen			25	15
1991	-	-			-	-
1992	Humphrey Campbell	Wijs Me De Weg			67	13
1993	Ruth Jacott	Vrede			92	6

Netherlands (continued)

Year	Artist	Song	Semi-Final Points	Semi-Final Position	Final Points	Final Position
1994	Willeke Alberti	Waar Is De Zon			4	23
1995	-	-			-	-
1996	Maxine & Franklin Brown	De Eerste Keer			78	7
1997	Mrs Einstein	Niemand Heeft Nog Tijd			5	22
1998	Edsilia Rombley	Hemel En Aarde			150	4
1999	Marlayne	One Good Reason			71	9
2000	Linda Wagenmakers	No Goodbyes			40	13
2001	Michelle	Out On My Own			16	18
2002	-	-			-	-
2003	Esther Hart	One More Night			45	13
2004	Re-union	Without You	146	6	11	20
2005	Glennis Grace	My Impossible Dream	53	14	-	-
2006	Treble	Amambanda	22	19	-	-
2007	Edsilia Rombley	On Top Of The World	38	21	-	-
2008	Hind	Your Heart Belongs To Me	27	13	-	-
2009	The Toppers	Shine	11	17	-	-
2010	Sieneke	Ik Ben Verliefd (Sha-la-lie)	29	14	-	-
2011	3JS	Never Alone	13	19	-	-
2012	Joan Franka	You And Me	35	15	-	-
2013	Anouk	Birds	75	6	114	9
2014	The Common Linnets	Calm After the Storm	150	1	238	2

Norway

Year	Artist	Song	Semi-Final Points	Semi-Final Position	Final Points	Final Position
1960	Nora Brockstedt	Voi-voi			11	4
1961	Nora Brockstedt	Sommer I Palma			10	7
1962	Inger Jacobsen	Kom Sol, Kom Regn			2	10
1963	Anita Thallaug	Solhverv			0	13
1964	Arne Bendiksen	Spiral			6	8
1965	Kirsti Sparboe	Karusell			1	13
1966	Åse Kleveland	Intet Er Nytt Under Solen			15	3
1967	Kirsti Sparboe	Dukkemann			2	14
1968	Odd Børre	Stress			2	13
1969	Kirsti Sparboe	Oj, Oj, Oj, Så Glad, Jeg Skal Bli			1	16
1970	-	-			-	-
1971	Hanne Krogh	Lykken Er...			65	17
1972	Grethe Kausland & Benny Borg	Småting			73	14
1973	Bendik Singers	It's Just A Game			89	7
1974	Anne-Karine Ström & the Bendik Singers	The First Day Of Love			3	14
1975	Ellen Nikolaysen	You Touched My Life With Summer			11	18
1976	Anne-Karine Ström	Mata Hari			7	17
1977	Anita Skorgan	Casanova			18	14
1978	Jahn Teigen	Mil Etter Mil			0	20
1979	Anita Skorgan	Oliver			57	11
1980	Sverre Kjellsberg & Mattis Hætta	Sámiid Ædnan			15	16
1981	Finn Kalvik	Aldri I Livet			0	20
1982	Jahn Teigen & Anita Skorgan	Adieu			40	12
1983	Jahn Teigen	Do Re Mi			53	9
1984	Dollie de Luxe	Lenge Leve Livet			29	17
1985	Bobbysocks	La Det Swinge			123	1
1986	Ketil Stokkan	Romeo			44	12
1987	Kate Gulbrandsen	Mitt Liv			65	9
1988	Karoline Krüger	For Vår Jord			88	5
1989	Britt Synnøve Johansen	Venners Nærhet			30	17
1990	Ketil Stokkan	Brandenburger Tor			8	21
1991	Just 4 Fun	Mrs Thompson			14	17

Norway (continued)

Year	Artist	Song	Semi-Final Points	Position	Final Points	Position
1992	Merethe Trøan	Visjoner			23	18
1993	Silje Vige	Alle Mine Tankar			120	4
1994	Elisabeth Andreasson & Jan Werner Danielsen	Duett			76	6
1995	Secret Garden	Nocturne			148	1
1996	Elisabeth Andreasson	I Evighet			114	2
1997	Tor Endresen	San Francisco			0	24
1998	Lars Fredriksen	Alltid Sommer			79	8
1999	Stig André Van Eijk	Living My Life Without You			35	13
2000	Charmed	My Heart Goes Boom			57	11
2001	Haldor Lægreid	On My Own			3	22
2002	-	-			-	-
2003	Jostein Hasselgård	I'm Not Afraid To Move On			123	4
2004	Knut Anders Sørum	High	-	-	3	24
2005	Wig Wam	In My Dreams	164	6	125	9
2006	Christine Guldbrandsen	Alvedansen	-	-	36	14
2007	Guri Schanke	Ven A Bailar Conmigo	48	18	-	-
2008	Maria	Hold On Be Strong	106	4	182	5
2009	Alexander Rybak	Fairytale	201	1	387	1
2010	Didrik Solli-Tangen	My Heart Is Yours	-	-	35	20
2011	Stella Mwangi	Haba Haba	30	17	-	-
2012	Tooji	Stay	45	10	7	26
2013	Margaret Berger	I Feed You My Love	120	3	191	4
2014	Carl Espen	Silent Storm	77	6	88	8

Poland

Year	Artist	Song	Semi-Final Points	Position	Final Points	Position
1994	Edyta Górniak	To Nie Ja!			166	2
1995	Justyna	Sama			15	18
1996	Kasia Kowalska	Chce Znac Swój Grzech			31	15
1997	Anna Maria Jopek	Ale Jestem			54	11
1998	Sixteen	To Takie Proste			19	17
1999	Mietek (Mieczyslaw) Szczesniak	Przytul Mnie Mocno			17	19
2000	-	-			-	-
2001	Piasek	2 Long			11	20
2002	-	-			-	-
2003	Ich Troje	Keine Grenzen - Zadnych Granic			90	7
2004	Blue Cafe	Love Song			27	17
2005	Ivan & Delfin	Czarna Dziewczyna	81	11	-	-
2006	Ich Troje	Follow My Heart	70	11	-	-
2007	The Jet Set	Time To Party	75	14	-	-
2008	Isis Gee	For Life	42	10	14	24
2009	Lidia Kopania	I Don't Wanna Leave	43	12	-	-
2010	Marcin Mroziński	Legenda	44	13	-	-
2011	Magdalena Tul	Jestem	18	19	-	-
2012	-	-	-	-	-	-
2013	-	-	-	-	-	-
2014	Donatan & Cleo	My Słowianie - We Are Slavic	70	8	62	14

Portugal

Year	Artist	Song	Semi-Final Points	Semi-Final Position	Final Points	Final Position
1964	António Calvário	Oração			0	13
1965	Simone de Oliviera	Sol De Inverno			1	13
1966	Madalena Iglesias	Ele E Ela			6	13
1967	Eduardo Nascimento	O Vento Mudou			3	12
1968	Carlos Mendes	Verão			5	11
1969	Simone de Oliviera	Desfolhada Portuguesa			4	15
1970	-	-			-	-
1971	Tonicha	Menina Do Alto Da Serra			83	9
1972	Carlos Mendes	A Festa Da Vida			90	7
1973	Fernando Tordo	Tourada			80	10
1974	Paulo de Carvalho	E Depois Do Adeus			3	14
1975	Duarte Mendes	Madrugada			16	16
1976	Carlos do Carmo	Uma Flor De Verde Pinho			24	12
1977	Os Amigos	Portugal No Coração			18	14
1978	Gemini	Dai-li-dou			5	17
1979	Manuela Bravo	Sobe, Sobe, Balão Sobe			64	9
1980	José Cid	Um Grande, Grande Amor			71	7
1981	Carlos Paião	Play-back			9	18
1982	Doce	Bem-bom			32	13
1983	Armando Gama	Esta Balada Que Te Dou			33	13
1984	Maria Guinot	Silêncio E Tanta Gente			38	11
1985	Adelaïde	Penso Em Ti, Eu Sei			9	18
1986	Dora	Não Sejas Mau Para Mim			28	14
1987	Nevada	Neste Barco à Vela			15	18
1988	Dora	Voltarei			5	18
1989	Da Vinci	Conquistador			39	16
1990	Nucha	Há Sempre Alguém			9	20
1991	Dulce	Lusitana Paixão			62	8
1992	Diná	Amor D'água Fresca			26	17
1993	Anabela	A Cidade Até Ser Dia			60	10
1994	Sara Tavares	Chamar A Música			73	8
1995	Tó Cruz	Baunilha E Chocolate			5	21
1996	Lúcia Moniz	O Meu Coração Não Tem Cor			92	6
1997	Célia Lawson	Antes Do Adeus			0	24
1998	Alma Lusa	Se Eu Te Pudesse Abraçar			36	12
1999	Rui Bandeira	Como Tudo Começou			12	21
2000	-	-			-	-
2001	MTM	Só Sei Ser Feliz Assim			18	17
2002	-	-			-	-
2003	Rita Guerra	Deixa-me Sonhar			13	22
2004	Sofia	Foi Magia	38	15	-	-
2005	2B	Amar	51	17	-	-
2006	Nonstop	Coisas De Nada	26	19	-	-
2007	Sabrina	Dança Comigo (vem Ser Feliz)	88	11	-	-
2008	Vânia Fernandes	Senhora Do Mar (Negras Águas)	120	2	69	13
2009	Flor-de-lis	Todas As Ruas Do Amor	70	8	57	15
2010	Filipa Azevedo	Há Dias Assim	89	4	43	18
2011	Homens Da Luta	Luta É Alegria	22	18	-	-
2012	Filipa Sousa	Vida Minha	39	13	-	-
2013	-	-	-	-	-	-
2014	Suzy	Quero Ser Tua	39	11	-	-

Romania

Year	Artist	Song	Semi-Final Points	Semi-Final Position	Final Points	Final Position
1994	Dan Bittman	Dincolo De Nori			14	21
1995	-	-			-	-
1996	-	-			-	-
1997	-	-			-	-
1998	Malina Olinescu	Eu Cred			6	22
1999	-	-			-	-
2000	Taxi	The Moon			25	17
2001	-	-			-	-
2002	Monica Anghel & Marcel Pavel	Tell Me Why			72	8
2003	Nicola	Don't Break My Heart			73	10
2004	Sanda Ladosi	I Admit	-	-	18	18
2005	Luminita Anghel & Sistem	Let Me Try	235	1	158	3
2006	Mihai Traistariu	Tornero	-	-	172	4
2007	Todomondo	Liubi, Liubi, I Love You	-	-	84	13
2008	Nico & Vlad	Pe-o Margine De Lume	94	7	45	20
2009	Elena	The Balkan Girls	67	9	40	19
2010	Paula Seling & Ovi	Playing With Fire	104	4	162	3
2011	Hotel FM	Change	111	4	77	17
2012	Mandinga	Zaleilah	120	3	71	12
2013	Cezar	It's My Life	83	5	65	13
2014	Paul Seling & Ovi	Miracle	125	2	72	12

Russia

Year	Artist	Song	Semi-Final Points	Semi-Final Position	Final Points	Final Position
1994	Youddiph	Vechni Stranik			70	9
1995	Philipp Kirkorov	Kolybelnaya Dlya Vulkana			18	17
1996	-	-			-	-
1997	Alla Pugachova	Primadonna			33	15
1998	-	-			-	-
1999	-	-			-	-
2000	Alsou	Solo			155	2
2001	Mumiy Troll	Lady Alpine Blue			37	12
2002	Prime Minister	Northern Girl			55	10
2003	t.A.T.u.	Ne Ver', Ne Boisia			164	3
2004	Julia Savicheva	Believe Me	-	-	67	11
2005	Natalia Podolskaya	Nobody Hurt No One	-	-	57	15
2006	Dima Bilan	Never Let You Go	217	3	248	2
2007	Serebro	Song # 1	-	-	207	3
2008	Dima Bilan	Believe	135	3	272	1
2009	Anastasia Prikhodko	Mamo	-	-	91	11
2010	Peter Nalitch & Friends	Lost And Forgotten	74	7	90	11
2011	Alexej Vorobjov	Get You	64	9	77	16
2012	Buranovskiye Babushki	Party for Everybody	152	1	259	2
2013	Dina Garipova	What If	156	2	174	5
2014	Tolmachevy Sisters	Shine	63	6	89	7

San Marino

Year	Artist	Song	Semi-Final Points	Position	Final Points	Position
2008	Miodio	Complice	5	19	-	-
2009	-	-	-	-	-	-
2010	-	-	-	-	-	-
2011	Senit	Stand By	34	16	-	-
2012	Valentina Monetta	The Social Network Song (Oh Oh - Uh - Oh Oh)	31	14	-	-
2013	Valentina Monetta	Crisalide (Vola)	47	11	-	-
2014	Valentina Monetta	Maybe (Forse)	40	10	14	24

Serbia

Year	Artist	Song	Semi-Final Points	Position	Final Points	Position
2007	Marija Šerifović	Molitva	298	1	268	1
2008	Jelena Tomašević feat Bora Dugic	Oro	-	-	160	6
2009	Marko Kon & Milaan	Cipela	60	10	-	-
2010	Milan Stanković	Ovo Je Balkan	79	5	72	13
2011	Nina	Čaroban	67	8	85	14
2012	Željko Joksimović	Nije Ljubav Stvar	159	2	214	3
2013	Moje 3	Ljubav Je Svuda	46	11	-	-

Serbia & Montenegro

Year	Artist	Song	Semi-Final Points	Position	Final Points	Position
2004	Željko Joksimović	Lane Moje	263	1	263	2
2005	No Name	Zauvijek Moja	-	-	137	7
2006	-	-	-	-	-	-

Slovakia

Year	Artist	Song	Semi-Final Points	Position	Final Points	Position
1994	Martin Durinda & Tublatanka	Nekovecná Piesen			15	19
1995	-	-			-	-
1996	Marcel Palonder	Kým Nás Máš			19	18
1997	-	-			-	-
1998	Katarína Hasprová	Modlitba			8	21
1999	-	-			-	-
2000	-	-			-	-
2001	-	-			-	-
2002	-	-			-	-
2003	-	-			-	-
2004	-	-	-	-	-	-
2005	-	-	-	-	-	-
2006	-	-	-	-	-	-
2007	-	-	-	-	-	-
2008	-	-	-	-	-	-
2009	Kamil Mikulčík & Nela Pocisková	Leť Tmou	8	18	-	-
2010	Kristina Pelakova	Horehronie	24	16	-	-
2011	TWiiNS	I'm Still Alive	48	13	-	-
2012	Max Jason Mai	Don't Close Your Eyes	22	18	-	-

Slovenia

Year	Artist	Song	Semi-Final Points	Semi-Final Position	Final Points	Final Position
1993	1X Band	Tih Dezeven Dan			9	22
1994	-	-			-	-
1995	Darja Svajger	Prisluhni Mi			83	7
1996	Regina	Dan Najlepših Sanj			16	21
1997	Tanja Ribic	Zbudi Se			60	10
1998	Vili Resnik	Naj Bogovi Slišijo			17	18
1999	Darja Svajger	For A Thousand Years			50	11
2000	-	-			-	-
2001	Nuša Derenda	Energy			70	7
2002	Sestre	Samo Ljubezen			32	15
2003	Karmen	Nanana			7	23
2004	Platin	Stay Forever	5	21	-	-
2005	Omar Naber	Stop	69	12	-	-
2006	Anžej Dežan	Mr Nobody	49	16	-	-
2007	Alenka Gotar	Cvet Z Juga	140	7	66	15
2008	Rebeka Dremelj	Vrag Naj Vzame	36	11	-	-
2009	Quartissimo featuring Martina	Love Symphony	14	16	-	-
2010	Ansambel Žlindra & Kalamari	Narodnozabavni Rock	6	16	-	-
2011	Maja Keuc	No One	112	3	96	13
2012	Eva Boto	Verjamem	31	17	-	-
2013	Hannah	Straight Into Love	8	16	-	-
2014	Tinkara Kovač	Round and Round	52	10		

Spain

Year	Artist	Song	Semi-Final Points	Semi-Final Position	Final Points	Final Position
1961	Conchita Bautista	Estando Contigo			8	9
1962	Victor Balaguer	Llámame			0	13
1963	José Guardiola	Algo Prodigioso			2	12
1964	Tim, Nelly & Tony	Caracola			1	12
1965	Conchita Bautista	Qué Bueno, Qué Bueno			0	15
1966	Raphael	Yo Soy Aquél			9	7
1967	Raphael	Hablemos Del Amor			9	6
1968	Massiel	La, La, La...			29	1
1969	Salomé	Vivo Cantando			18	1
1970	Julio Iglesias	Gwendolyne			8	4
1971	Karina	En Un Mundo Nuevo			115	2
1972	Jaime Morey	Amanece			83	10
1973	Mocedades	Eres Tú			125	2
1974	Peret	Canta Y Se Feliz			10	9
1975	Sergio & Estíbaliz	Tú Volverás			53	10
1976	Braulio	Sobran Las Palabras			11	16
1977	Micky	Enséñame A Cantar			52	9
1978	José Vélez	Bailemos Un Vals			65	9
1979	Betty Missiego	Su Canción			116	2
1980	Trigo Limpio	Qué Date Esta Noche			38	12
1981	Bacchelli	Y Solo Tú			38	14
1982	Lucía	Él			52	10
1983	Remedios Amaya	¿Quién Maneja Mi Barca?			0	9
1984	Bravo	Lady, Lady			106	3
1985	Paloma San Basilio	La Fiesta Terminó			36	14
1986	Cadillac	Valentino			51	10
1987	Patricia Kraus	No Estás Solo			10	19
1988	La Década	La Chica Que Yo Quiero (Made In Spain)			58	11
1989	Nina	Nacida Para Amar			88	6
1990	Azúcar Moreno	Bandido			96	5
1991	Sergio Dalma	Bailar Pegados			119	4

Spain (continued)

Year	Artist	Song	Semi-Final Points	Semi-Final Position	Final Points	Final Position
1992	Serafin	Todo Esto Es La Música			37	14
1993	Eva Santamaria	Hombres			58	11
1994	Alejandro Abad	Ella No Es Ella			17	18
1995	Anabel Conde	Vuelve Conmigo			119	2
1996	Antonio Carbonell	¡Ay, Qué Deseo!			17	20
1997	Marcos Llunas	Sin Rencor			96	6
1998	Mikel Herzog	¿Qué Voy A Hacer Sin Ti?			21	16
1999	Lydia	No Quiero Escuchar			1	23
2000	Serafín Zubiri	Colgado De Un Sueño			18	18
2001	David Civera	Dile Que La Quiero			76	6
2002	Rosa	Europe's Living A Celebration			81	7
2003	Beth	Dime			81	8
2004	Ramón	Para Llenarme De Ti	-	-	87	10
2005	Son de sol	Brujería	-	-	28	21
2006	Las Ketchup	Bloody Mary	-	-	18	21
2007	NASH	I Love You Mi Vida	-	-	43	20
2008	Rodolfo Chikilicuatre	Baila El Chiki Chiki	-	-	55	16
2009	Soraya	La Noche Es Para Mí	-	-	23	24
2010	Daniel Diges	Algo Pequeñito (Something Tiny)	-	-	68	15
2011	Lucía Pérez	Que Me Quiten Lo Bailao	-	-	50	23
2012	Pastora Soler	Quédate Conmigo (Stay With Me)	-	-	97	10
2013	ESDM	Contigo Hasta El Final (With You Until The End)	-	-	8	25
2014	Ruth Lorenzo	Dancing in the Rain	-	-	74	10

Sweden

Year	Artist	Song	Semi-Final Points	Semi-Final Position	Final Points	Final Position
1958	Alice Babs	Lilla Stjärna			10	4
1959	Brita Borg	Augustin			4	9
1960	Siw Malmkvist	Alla Andra Får Varann			4	10
1961	Lill-Babs	April, April			2	14
1962	Inger Berggren	Sol Och Vår			4	7
1963	Monica Zetterlund	En Gång I Stockholm			0	13
1964	-	-			-	-
1965	Ingvar Wixell	Absent Friend			6	10
1966	Lill Lindfors & Svante Thuresson	Nygammal Vals Eller Hip Man Svinaherde			16	2
1967	Östen Warnebring	Som En Dröm			7	8
1968	Claes-Göran Hederström	Det Börjar Verka Kärlek, Banne Mej			15	5
1969	Tommy Körberg	Judy, Min Vän			8	9
1970	-	-			-	-
1971	Family Four	Vita Vidder			85	6
1972	Family Four	Härliga Sommardag			75	13
1973	The Nova & The Dolls	You're Summer			94	5
1974	ABBA	Waterloo			24	1
1975	Lars Berghagen & The Dolls	Jennie, Jennie			72	8
1976	-	-			-	-
1977	Forbes	Beatles			2	18
1978	Björn Skifs	Det Blir Alltid Värre Framåt Natten			26	14
1979	Ted Gärdestad	Satellit			8	17
1980	Tomas Ledin	Just Nu!			47	10
1981	Björn Skifs	Fångad I En Dröm			50	10
1982	Chips	Dag Efter Dag			67	8
1983	Carola Häggkvist	Främling			126	3
1984	Herrey's	Diggi-loo Diggy-ley			145	1
1985	Kikki Danielsson	Bra Vibrationer			103	3
1986	Lasse Holm and Monica Törnell	E' De' Det Här Du Kallar Kärlek			78	5

Sweden (continued)

Year	Artist	Song	Semi-Final Points	Semi-Final Position	Final Points	Final Position
1987	Lotta Engberg	Boogaloo			50	12
1988	Tommy Körberg	Stad I Ljus			52	12
1989	Tommy Nilsson	En Dag			110	4
1990	Edin-Ådahl	Som En Vind			24	16
1991	Carola	Fångad Av En Stormvind			146	1
1992	Christer Björkmann	I Morgon är En Annan Dag			9	22
1993	Arvingarna	Eloïse			89	7
1994	Marie Bergman & Roger Pontare	Stjärnorna			48	13
1995	Jan Johansen	Se På Mej			100	3
1996	One More Time	Den Vilda			100	3
1997	Blond	Bara Hon älskar Mig			36	14
1998	Jill Johnson	Kärleken är			53	10
1999	Charlotte Nilsson	Take Me To Your Heaven			163	1
2000	Roger Pontare	When Spirits Are Calling My Name			88	7
2001	Friends	Listen To Your Heartbeat			100	5
2002	Afro-dite	Never Let It Go			72	8
2003	Fame	Give Me Your Love			107	5
2004	Lena Philipsson	It Hurts	-	-	170	5
2005	Martin Stenmarck	Las Vegas	-	-	30	19
2006	Carola	Invincible	214	4	170	5
2007	The Ark	The Worrying Kind	-	-	51	18
2008	Charlotte Perrelli	Hero	54	12	47	18
2009	Malena Ernman	La Voix	105	4	33	21
2010	Anna Bergendahl	This Is My Life	62	11	-	-
2011	Eric Saade	Popular	155	1	185	3
2012	Loreen	Euphoria	181	1	372	1
2013	Robin Stjernberg	You	-	-	62	14
2014	Sanna Nielsen	Undo	131	2	218	3

Switzerland

Year	Artist	Song	Semi-Final Points	Semi-Final Position	Final Points	Final Position
1956	(1) Lys Assia	Refrain			-	1
1956	(2) Lys Assia	Das Alte Karussell			-	2
1957	Lys Assia	L'enfant Que J'étais			5	8
1958	Lys Assia	Giorgio			24	2
1959	Christa Williams	Irgendwoher			14	4
1960	Anita Traversi	Cielo E Terra			5	8
1961	Franca di Rienzo	Nous Aurons Demain			16	13
1962	Jean Philippe	Le Retour			2	10
1963	Esther Ofarim	T'en Va Pas			40	2
1964	Anita Traversi	I Miei Pensieri			0	13
1965	Yovanna	Non à Jamais Sans Toi			8	8
1966	Madeleine Pascal	Ne Vois-tu Pas?			12	6
1967	Géraldine	Quel Coeur Vas-tu Briser?			0	17
1968	Gianni Mascolo	Guardando Il Sole			2	13
1969	Paola del Medico	Bonjour, Bonjour			13	5
1970	Henri Dès	Retour			8	4
1971	Peter, Sue & Marc	Les Illusions De Nos Vingt Ans			78	12
1972	Véronique Müller	C'est La Chanson De Mon Amour			88	8
1973	Patrick Juvet	Je Me Vais Marier, Marie			79	12
1974	Piera Martell	Mein Ruf Nach Dir			3	14
1975	Simone Drexel	Mikado			77	6
1976	Peter, Sue & Marc	Djambo, Djambo			91	4
1977	Pepe Lienhard Band	Swiss Lady			71	6
1978	Carole Vinci	Vivre			65	9
1979	Peter, Sue & Marc & Pfuri, Gorps & Kniri	Trödler Und Co			60	10

Switzerland (continued)

Year	Artist	Song	Semi-Final Points	Semi-Final Position	Final Points	Final Position
1980	Paola	Cinéma			104	4
1981	Peter, Sue & Marc	Io Senza Tei			121	4
1982	Arlette Zola	Amour On T'aime			97	3
1983	Mariella Farré	Io Così Non Ci Sto			28	15
1984	Rainy Day	Welche Farbe Hat Der Sonnenschein			30	16
1985	Mariella Farré & Pino Gasparini	Piano Piano			39	12
1986	Daniela Simons	Pas Pour Moi			140	2
1987	Carole Rich	Moitié Moitié			26	17
1988	Céline Dion	Ne Partez Pas Sans Moi			137	1
1989	Furbaz	Viver Senza Tei			47	13
1990	Egon Egemann	Musik Klingt In Die Welt Hinaus			51	11
1991	Sandra Simò	Canzone Per Te			118	5
1992	Daisy Auvray	Mister Music Man			32	15
1993	Annie Cotton	Moi, Tout Simplement			148	3
1994	Duilio	Sto Pregando			15	19
1995	-	-			-	-
1996	Cathy Leander	Mon Coeur L'aime			22	16
1997	Barbara Berta	Dentro Di Me			5	22
1998	Gunvor	Lass Ihn			0	25
1999	-	-			-	-
2000	Jane Bogaert	La Vita Cos'è?			14	20
2001	-	-			-	-
2002	Francine Jordi	Dans Le Jardin De Mon Âme			15	22
2003	-	-			-	-
2004	Piero Esteriore & the MusicStars	Celebrate	0	22	-	-
2005	Vanilla Ninja	Cool Vibes	114	8	128	8
2006	Six4One	If We All Give A Little	-	-	30	16
2007	DJ BoBo	Vampires Are Alive	40	20	-	-
2008	Paolo Meneguzzi	Era Stupendo	47	13	-	-
2009	Lovebugs	The Highest Heights	15	14	-	-
2010	Michael von der Heide	Il Pleut de L'Or	2	17	-	-
2011	Anna Rossinelli	In Love For A While	55	10	19	25
2012	Sinplus	Unbreakable	45	11	-	-
2013	Takasa	You And Me	41	13	-	-
2014	Sebalter	Hunter of Stars	92	4	64	13

Turkey

Year	Artist	Song	Semi-Final Points	Semi-Final Position	Final Points	Final Position
1975	Semiha Yanki	Seninle Bir Dakika			3	19
1976	-	-			-	-
1977	-	-			-	-
1978	Nazar	Sevinçe			2	18
1979	-	-			-	-
1980	Ajda Pekkan	Petr'oil			23	15
1981	Modern Folk Trio & Aysegül	Dönme Dolap			9	18
1982	Neço	Hani			20	15
1983	Çetin Alp & the Short Wave	Opera			0	19
1984	Bes Yil Önce, On Yil Sonra	Halay			37	12
1985	MFÖ	Di Dai Di Dai Dai (A'sik Oldum)			36	14
1986	Klips ve Onlar	Halley			53	9
1987	Seyyal Tanner & Lokomotif	Sarkim Sevgi üstüne			0	22
1988	MFÖ	Sufi (Hey Ya Hey)			37	15
1989	Pan	Bana Bana			5	21
1990	Kayahan	Gözlerinin Hapsindeyim			21	17
1991	Izel Çeliköz, Rayhan Soykarçi & Can Ugurluér	Iki Dakika			44	12

Turkey (continued)

Year	Artist	Song	Semi-Final Points	Semi-Final Position	Final Points	Final Position
1992	Aylin Vatankos	Yaz Bitti			17	19
1993	Burak Aydos, Öztürk Baybora & Serter	Esmer Yarim			10	21
1994	-	-			-	-
1995	Arzu Ece	Sev!			21	16
1996	Sebnem Paker	Besinçi Mevsim			57	12
1997	Sebnem Paker & Group Etnic	Dinle			121	3
1998	Tüzmen	Unutamazsin			25	14
1999	Tuba Önal & Grup Mystik	Dön Artik			21	16
2000	Pinar Ayhan & SOS Band	Yorgunum Anla			59	10
2001	Sedat Yüce	Sevgiliye Son			41	11
2002	Buket Bengisu & Saphire	Leylaklar Soldu Kalbinde			29	16
2003	Sertab Erener	Everyway That I Can			167	1
2004	Athena	For Real	-	-	195	4
2005	Gülseren	Rimi Rimi Ley	-	-	92	13
2006	Sibel Tüzün	Superstar	91	9	91	11
2007	Kenan Dogulu	Shake It Up Shekerim	197	3	163	4
2008	Mor ve Ötesi	Deli	85	7	138	7
2009	Hadise	Düm Tek Tek	172	2	177	4
2010	maNga	We Could Be The Same	118	1	170	2
2011	Yüksek Sadakat	Live It Up	47	13	-	-
2012	Can Bonomo	Love Me Back	80	5	112	7

Ukraine

Year	Artist	Song	Semi-Final Points	Semi-Final Position	Final Points	Final Position
2003	Olexandr	Hasta La Vista			30	14
2004	Ruslana	Wild Dances	256	2	280	1
2005	Greenjolly	Razom Nas Bahato	-	-	30	19
2006	Tina Karol	Show Me Your Love	146	6	145	7
2007	Verka Serduchka	Dancing Lasha Tumbai	-	-	235	2
2008	Ani Lorak	Shady Lady	152	1	230	2
2009	Svetlana Loboda	Be my Valentine! (Anti-crisis Girl)	80	6	76	12
2010	Alyosha	Sweet People	77	7	108	10
2011	Mika Newton	Angel	81	6	159	4
2012	Gaitana	Be My Guest	64	8	65	15
2013	Zlata Ognevich	Gravity	140	3	214	3
2014	Mariya Yaremchuk	Tick-Tock	118	5	113	6

United Kingdom

Year	Artist	Song	Semi-Final Points	Semi-Final Position	Final Points	Final Position
1957	Patricia Bredin	All			6	7
1958	-	-			-	-
1959	Pearl Carr & Teddy Johnson	Sing Little Birdie			16	2
1960	Bryan Johnson	Looking High, High, High			25	2
1961	The Allisons	Are You Sure?			24	2
1962	Ronnie Carroll	Ring-a-ding Girl			10	4
1963	Ronnie Carroll	Say Wonderful Things			28	4
1964	Matt Monro	I Love The Little Things			17	2
1965	Kathy Kirby	I Belong			26	2
1966	Kenneth McKellar	A Man Without Love			8	9
1967	Sandie Shaw	Puppet On A String			47	1
1968	Cliff Richard	Congratulations			28	2
1969	Lulu	Boom Bang-a-bang			18	1
1970	Mary Hopkin	Knock, Knock (Who's There?)			26	2
1971	Clodagh Rodgers	Jack In The Box			98	4

United Kingdom (continued)

Year	Artist	Song	Semi-Final Points	Semi-Final Position	Final Points	Final Position
1972	The New Seekers	Beg, Steal Or Borrow			114	2
1973	Cliff Richard	Power To All Our Friends			123	3
1974	Olivia Newton-John	Long Live Love			14	4
1975	The Shadows	Let Me Be The One			138	2
1976	Brotherhood of Man	Save Your Kisses For Me			164	1
1977	Lynsey de Paul & Mike Moran	Rock Bottom			121	2
1978	Co-Co	The Bad Old Days			61	11
1979	Black Lace	Mary Ann			73	7
1980	Prima Donna	Love Enough For Two			106	3
1981	Bucks Fizz	Making Your Mind Up			136	1
1982	Bardo	One Step Further			76	7
1983	Sweet Dreams	I'm Never Giving Up			79	6
1984	Belle & The Devotions	Love Games			63	7
1985	Vikki	Love Is...			100	4
1986	Ryder	Runner In The Night			72	7
1987	Rikki	Only The Light			47	13
1988	Scott Fitzgerald	Go			136	2
1989	Live Report	Why Do I Always Get It Wrong			130	2
1990	Emma	Give A Little Love Back To The World			87	6
1991	Samantha Janus	A Message To Your Heart			47	10
1992	Michael Ball	One Step Out Of Time			139	2
1993	Sonia	Better The Devil You Know			164	2
1994	Frances Ruffelle	We Will Be Free (Lonely Symphony)			63	10
1995	Love City Groove	Love City Groove			76	10
1996	Gina G	Just A Little Bit			77	8
1997	Katrina & The Waves	Love Shine A Light			227	1
1998	Imaani	Where Are You?			166	2
1999	Precious	Say It Again			38	14
2000	Nicki French	Don't Play That Song Again			28	16
2001	Lindsay D	No Dream Impossible			28	15
2002	Jessica Garlick	Come Back			111	3
2003	Jemini	Cry Baby			0	26
2004	James Fox	Hold On To Our Love	-	-	29	16
2005	Javine	Touch My Fire	-	-	18	22
2006	Daz Sampson	Teenage Life	-	-	25	19
2007	Scooch	Flying The Flag (For You)	-	-	19	22
2008	Andy Abraham	Even If	-	-	14	25
2009	Jade Ewen	It's My Time	-	-	173	5
2010	Josh Dubovie	That Sounds Good To Me	-	-	10	25
2011	Blue	I Can	-	-	100	11
2012	Engelbert Humperdinck	Love Will Set You Free	-	-	12	25
2013	Bonnie Tyler	Believe in Me	-	-	23	19
2014	Molly	Children of the Universe	-	-	40	17

Yugoslavia

Year	Artist	Song	Semi-Final Points	Semi-Final Position	Final Points	Final Position
1961	Ljiljana Petrovic	Neke Davne Zvezde			9	8
1962	Lola Novakovic	Ne Pali Svetlo U Sumrak			10	4
1963	Vice Vukov	Brodovi			3	11
1964	Sabahudin Kurt	Zivot Je Sklopio Krug			0	13
1965	Vice Vukov	Ceznja			2	12
1966	Berta Ambroz	Brez Besed			9	7
1967	Lado Leskovar	Vse Roze Sveta			7	8
1968	Luci Kapurso & Hamo Hajdarhodzic	Jedan Dan			8	7
1969	Ivan	Pozdrav Svijetu			5	13
1970	Eva Sršen	Pridi, Dala Ti Bom Cvet			4	11

Yugoslavia (continued)

Year	Artist	Song	Semi-Final Points	Semi-Final Position	Final Points	Final Position
1971	Krunoslav Slabinac	Tvoj Djecak Je Tuzan			68	14
1972	Tereza	Muzika I Ti			87	9
1973	Zdravko Colic	Gori Vatra			65	15
1974	Korni	Generacija 42			6	12
1975	Pepel In Kri	Dan Ljubezni			22	13
1976	Ambasadori	Ne Mogu Skriti Svoju Bol			10	18
1977	-	-			-	-
1978	-	-			-	-
1979	-	-			-	-
1980	-	-			-	-
1981	Seid-Memic Vajta	Leila			35	15
1982	Aska	Halo Halo			21	14
1983	Danijel	Dzuli			125	4
1984	Vlado & Isolda	Ciao Amore			26	18
1985	-	-			-	-
1986	Doris Dragovic	Zeljo Moja			49	11
1987	Novi Fosili	Ja Sam Za Ples			92	4
1988	Srebrna Krila	Mangup			87	6
1989	Riva	Rock Me			137	1
1990	Tajci	Hajde Da Ludujemo			81	7
1991	Baby Doll	Brazil			1	21
1992	Extra Nena	Ljubim Te Pesmama			44	12

SECTION 3

Statistics and Records

Who votes for who? Who are the best and worst in the history of Eurovision?

Do acts performing at the end score more highly?

All the facts & figures and full analysis of the results

Eurovision Winners - Average age and gender (solo performers & duos only)

Year	Winner	Performer	Date of Contest	Date of Birth	Age when won
1956	Switzerland	Lys Assia	24 May 1956	03 March 1924	32
1957	Netherlands	Corry Brokken	03 March 1957	03 December 1932	24
1958	France	André Claveau	12 March 1958	17 December 1911	46
1959	Netherlands	Teddy Scholten	11 March 1959	11 May 1926	32
1960	France	Jacqueline Boyer	29 March 1960	23 April 1941	18
1961	Luxembourg	Jean-Claude Pascal	18 March 1961	24 October 1927	33
1962	France	Isabelle Aubret	18 March 1962	28 July 1938	23
1963	Denmark	Grethe and Jørgen Ingmann - Grethe	23 March 1963	17 June 1938	24
		Grethe and Jørgen Ingmann - Jørgen	23 March 1963	26 April 1925	37
1964	Italy	Gigliola Cinquetti	21 March 1964	20 December 1947	16
1965	Luxembourg	France Gall	20 March 1965	09 October 1947	17
1966	Austria	Udo Jürgens	05 March 1966	30 September 1934	31
1967	United Kingdom	Sandie Shaw	08 April 1967	26 February 1947	20
1968	Spain	Massiel	06 April 1968	02 August 1947	20
1969	Spain	Salomé	29 March 1969	21 June 1943	25
	United Kingdom	Lulu	29 March 1969	03 November 1948	20
	Netherlands	Lenny Kuhr	29 March 1969	22 February 1950	19
	France	Frida Boccara	29 March 1969	29 October 1940	28
1970	Ireland	Dana	21 March 1970	30 August 1951	18
1971	Monaco	Séverine	03 April 1971	10 October 1948	22
1972	Luxembourg	Vicky Leandros	25 March 1972	23 August 1949	22
1973	Luxembourg	Anne-Marie David	07 April 1973	23 May 1952	20
1974	Sweden	ABBA	06 April 1974	-	-
1975	Netherlands	Teach-In	22 March 1975	-	-
1976	United Kingdom	Brotherhood of Man	03 April 1976	-	-
1977	France	Marie Myriam	07 May 1977	08 May 1957	19
1978	Israel	Izhar Cohen and the Alphabeta	22 April 1978	13 May 1951	26
1979	Israel	Gali Atari and Milk and Honey	31 March 1979	29 December 1953	25
1980	Ireland	Johnny Logan	19 April 1980	13 May 1954	25
1981	United Kingdom	Bucks Fizz	04 April 1981	-	-
1982	Germany	Nicole	24 April 1982	25 October 1964	17
1983	Luxembourg	Corinne Hermès	23 April 1983	16 November 1961	21
1984	Sweden	Herreys	05 May 1984	-	-
1985	Norway	Bobbysocks! - Hanne Krogh	04 May 1985	24 January 1956	29
		Bobbysocks! - Elisabeth Andreassen	04 May 1985	28 March 1958	27
1986	Belgium	Sandra Kim	03 May 1986	15 October 1972	13
1987	Ireland	Johnny Logan	09 May 1987	13 May 1954	32
1988	Switzerland	Celine Dion	30 April 1988	30 March 1968	20
1989	Yugoslavia	Riva	06 May 1989	-	-
1990	Italy	Toto Cutugno	05 May 1990	07 July 1943	46
1991	Sweden	Carola	04 May 1991	08 September 1966	24
1992	Ireland	Linda Martin	09 May 1992	17 April 1947	45
1993	Ireland	Niamh Kavanagh	15 May 1993	13 February 1968	25
1994	Ireland	Paul Harrington & Charlie McGettigan - Paul	30 April 1994	08 May 1960	33
		Paul Harrington & Charlie McGettigan - Charlie	30 April 1994	07 December 1950	43
1995	Norway	Secret Garden - Fionnuala Sherry	13 May 1995	20 September 1962	32
		Secret Garden - Rolf Løvland	13 May 1995	19 April 1955	40
1996	Ireland	Eimear Quinn	18 May 1996	01 January 1973	23
1997	United Kingdom	Katrina and the Waves	03 May 1997	-	-
1998	Israel	Dana International	09 May 1998	02 February 1969	29

Eurovision Winners - Average age and gender (solo performers & duos only)

Year	Winner	Performer	Date of Contest	Date of Birth	Age when won
1999	Sweden	Charlotte Nilsson	29 May 1999	07 October 1974	24
2000	Denmark	Olsen Brothers - Jørgen	13 May 2000	15 March 1950	50
		Olsen Brothers - Niels	13 May 2000	13 April 1954	46
2001	Estonia	Tanel Padar, Dave Benton and 2XL - Tanel	12 May 2001	27 October 1980	20
		Tanel Padar, Dave Benton and 2XL - Dave	12 May 2001	31 January 1951	50
2002	Latvia	Marie N	25 May 2002	23 June 1973	28
2003	Turkey	Sertab Erener	24 May 2003	04 December 1964	38
2004	Ukraine	Ruslana	15 May 2004	24 May 1973	30
2005	Greece	Helena Paparizou	21 May 2005	31 January 1982	23
2006	Finland	Lordi	20 May 2006	-	-
2007	Serbia	Marija Šerifović	12 May 2007	14 November 1984	22
2008	Russia	Dima Bilan	24 May 2008	24 December 1981	26
2009	Norway	Alexander Rybak	16 May 2009	13 May 1986	23
2010	Germany	Lena Meyer-Landrut	29 May 2010	23 May 1991	19
2011	Azerbaijan	Ell/Nikki - Eldar Gasimov	14 May 2011	04 June 1989	21
		Ell/Nikki - Nigar Jamal	14 May 2011	07 September 1980	30
2012	Sweden	Loreen	26 May 2012	16 October 1983	28
2013	Denmark	Emmelie de Forest	18 May 2013	28 February 1993	20
2014	Austria	Conchita Wurst (performs as female)	10 May 2014	06 November 1988	25

61 performers	Average:	27
45 solo acts	Average (solo acts):	25
18 male performers	Average (men):	34
43 female performers	Average (women):	24

Eurovision 2014 - What type of act?

Following last year's winning solo female artist, what did each country choose to send to this year's Contest?

Country	Presented by	Accompanied by
Albania	solo female	musician & female backing singers
Armenia	solo male	none
Austria	solo female	none
Azerbaijan	solo female	female performer
Belarus	male group	none
Belgium	solo male	female performer
Denmark	solo male	mixed backing singers
Estonia	solo female	male performer
Finland	male group	none
France	male group	male performers
FYR Macedonia	solo female	mixed backing singers & male performer
Georgia	mixed group	none
Germany	solo female	musicians
Greece	male group	male performer
Hungary	solo male	mixed performers
Iceland	male group	none
Ireland	solo female	musicians & male performers
Israel	solo female	female performers
Italy	solo female	musicians
Latvia	mixed group	none
Lithuania	solo female	female backing singers & male perfomer
Malta	mixed group	none
Moldova	solo female	male performers
Montenegro	solo male	female performer & mixed backing singers
Netherlands	male/female duo	musicians
Norway	solo male	musicians
Poland	female group	female performer
Portugal	solo female	female backing singers and musicians
Romania	male/female duo	none
Russia	female duo	none
San Marino	solo female	none
Slovenia	solo female	female backing singers
Spain	solo female	none
Sweden	solo female	none
Switzerland	solo male	musicians
Ukraine	solo female	male performer
United Kingdom	solo female	musicians & mixed backing singers
Totals:	solo female	18
	solo male	7
	others	12

Language selection over 7 year period (predominant language only)

Country	2008	2009	2010	2011	2012	2013	2014
Albania	Albanian	English	English	English	Albanian	Albanian	English
Andorra	English	English					
Armenia	English	English	English			English	English
Austria				English	German	English	English
Azerbaijan	English	English	English	English	English	English	English
Belarus	English	English	English	English	English	English	English
Belgium	Invented lang.	English	English	English	English	English	English
Bosnia & H	Bosnian	Bosnian	English	English	Bosnian		
Bulgaria	English	English	Bulgarian	Bulgarian	Bulgarian	Bulgarian	
Croatia	Croatian	Croatian	Croatian	English	Croatian	Croatian	
Cyprus	Greek	English	English	Greek	English	Greek	
Czech Republic	English	English					
Denmark	English	English	English	English	English	English	English
Estonia	Serbian	Estonian	English	English	Estonian	Estonian	English
Finland	Finnish	English	Finnish	English	Swedish	English	English
France	English	French	French	Corsican	French	French	French
FYR Macedonia	English	Macedonian	Macedonian	Macedonian	Macedonian	Macedonian	English
Georgia	English		English	English	English	English	English
Germany	English	English	English	English	English	English	English
Greece	English	English	Greek	English	English	Greek	English
Hungary	English	English		English	English	Hungarian	English
Iceland	English	English	English	English	English	Icelandic	English
Ireland	English	English	English	English	English	English	English
Israel	Hebrew	English	Hebrew	Hebrew	English	Hebrew	English
Italy				Italian	English	Italian	Italian
Latvia	English	Russian	English	English	English	English	English
Lithuania	English	English	English	English	English	English	English
Malta	English	English	English	English	English	English	English
Moldova	English	Romanian	English	English	English	Romanian	English
Montenegro	Montenegrin	English			English	Montenegrin	Montenegrin
Netherlands	English	English	Dutch	English	English	English	English
Norway	English	English	English	English	English	English	English
Poland	English	English	English	Polish			Polish
Portugal	Portuguese	Portuguese	Portuguese	Portuguese	Portuguese		Portuguese
Romania	Romanian	English	English	English	Spanish	English	English
Russia	English	Russian	English	English	Udmurt	English	English
San Marino	Italian			English	English	Italian	English
Serbia	Serbian	Serbian	Serbian	Serbian	Serbian	Serbian	
Slovakia		Slovak	Slovak	English	English		
Slovenia	Slovene	English	Slovene	English	Slovene	English	English
Spain	Spanish	Spanish	Spanish	Spanish	Spanish	Spanish	English
Sweden	English	French	English	English	English	English	English
Switzerland	Italian	English	French	English	English	English	English
Turkey	Turkish	English	English	English	English		
Ukraine	English	English	English	English	English	English	English
United Kingdom	English	English	English	English	English	English	English
Number of songs:	43	42	39	43	42	39	37
Sung in English:	26	27	25	33	27	22	32
Percentage:	60%	64%	64%	77%	64%	56%	86%

The Most Successful Countries in Eurovision history....

Rank 2014	Rank 2013	Change	Country	Winners	2nd	3rd	4th	5th
1	1		Ireland	7	3	2	3	3
2	2		United Kingdom	5	15	3	4	1
3	3		France	5	4	7	6	3
4	4		Sweden	5	1	6	2	6
5	5		Luxembourg	5	0	2	2	4
6	6		Netherlands	4	1	1	2	2
7	7		Israel	3	2	1	2	2
8	8		Denmark	3	1	3	2	3
9	9		Norway	3	1	1	4	3
10	10		Germany	2	4	5	2	3
11	11		Spain	2	4	1	2	1
12	12		Switzerland	2	3	3	4	2
13	13		Italy	2	2	4	2	3
14	25	+11	Austria	2	0	0	1	4
15	14	-1	Russia	1	3	2	0	1
16	15	-1	Ukraine	1	2	1	1	0
17	16	-1	Belgium	1	2	0	1	2
18	17	-1	Monaco	1	1	3	3	1
19	18	-1	Turkey	1	1	1	3	0
20	19	-1	Azerbaijan	1	1	1	1	1
21	20	-1	Greece	1	0	3	0	2
22	21	-1	Latvia	1	0	1	0	1
23	22	-1	Serbia	1	0	1	0	0
24	23	-1	Estonia	1	0	0	2	1
24	23	-1	Yugoslavia	1	0	0	2	1
26	26		Finland	1	0	0	0	0
27	27		Malta	0	2	2	0	1
28	28		Iceland	0	2	0	1	0
29	29		Poland	0	1	0	0	0
29	29		Serbia & Montenegro	0	1	0	0	0
31	31		Romania	0	0	2	1	0
32	32		Bosnia & Herzegovina	0	0	1	0	0
33	33		Croatia	0	0	0	2	1
34	34		Armenia	0	0	0	2	0
35	35		Hungary	0	0	0	1	1
36	36		Cyprus	0	0	0	0	3
37	37		Bulgaria	0	0	0	0	1
37	37		Albania	0	0	0	0	1
39	39		Andorra	0	0	0	0	0
39	39		Belarus	0	0	0	0	0
39	39		Czech Republic	0	0	0	0	0
39	39		FYR Macedonia	0	0	0	0	0
39	39		Georgia	0	0	0	0	0
39	39		Lithuania	0	0	0	0	0
39	39		Moldova	0	0	0	0	0
39	39		Montenegro	0	0	0	0	0
39	39		Morocco	0	0	0	0	0
39	39		Portugal	0	0	0	0	0
39	39		San Marino	0	0	0	0	0
39	39		Slovakia	0	0	0	0	0
39	39		Slovenia	0	0	0	0	0

…And The Least Successful Countries in Eurovision history

Rank 2014	Rank 2013	Change	Country	Last	2nd last	3rd Last	4th Last	5th Last
1	1		Norway	9	3	2	4	1
2	2		Belgium	6	2	7	4	2
3	3		Austria	6	2	5	3	1
4	4		Finland	5	3	5	2	7
5	5		Switzerland	4	1	1	3	3
6	6		Turkey	3	3	0	1	4
7	7		United Kingdom	3	2	1	1	0
8	8		Luxembourg	3	1	3	0	1
9	9		Malta	3	1	0	2	0
10	10		Spain	2	3	2	5	3
11	11		Sweden	2	2	2	1	2
12	12		Germany	2	1	4	5	1
13	13		Ireland	2	1	2	1	1
14	14		Yugoslavia	1	5	0	1	2
15	15		Netherlands	1	4	3	3	2
16	23	+7	France	1	3	4	2	3
17	16	-1	Denmark	1	1	3	3	3
18	17	-1	Cyprus	1	1	1	2	2
19	18	-1	Lithuania	1	1	1	2	1
20	19	-1	Monaco	1	1	1	1	1
21	20	-1	Iceland	1	1	0	0	1
22	21	-1	Italy	1	0	1	1	4
23	22	-1	Portugal	0	4	4	4	4
24	24		Israel	0	3	1	0	1
25	25		Estonia	0	2	0	0	0
26	26		Hungary	0	1	2	1	0
27	31	+4	Slovenia	0	1	1	2	0
28	27	-1	Poland	0	1	0	1	0
29	28	-1	Bosnia & Herzegovina	0	1	0	0	1
30	29	-1	Morocco	0	1	0	0	0
31	30	-1	Belarus	0	1	0	0	0
32	32		Latvia	0	0	1	0	0
32	38	+6	San Marino	0	0	1	0	0
34	33	-1	Greece	0	0	0	2	1
35	34	-1	Romania	0	0	0	1	1
36	35	-1	Moldova	0	0	0	0	2
37	36	-1	Slovakia	0	0	0	0	1
37	36	-1	Croatia	0	0	0	0	1
39	38	-1	Ukraine	0	0	0	0	0
39	38	-1	Albania	0	0	0	0	0
39	38	-1	Andorra	0	0	0	0	0
39	38	-1	Armenia	0	0	0	0	0
39	38	-1	Azerbaijan	0	0	0	0	1
39	38	-1	Bulgaria	0	0	0	0	0
39	38	-1	Czech Republic	0	0	0	0	0
39	38	-1	FYR Macedonia	0	0	0	0	0
39	38	-1	Georgia	0	0	0	0	0
39	38	-1	Montenegro	0	0	0	0	0
39	38	-1	Russia	0	0	0	0	0
39	38	-1	Serbia	0	0	0	0	0
39	38	-1	Serbia & Montenegro	0	0	0	0	0

The Most Finishes in the Top 3…

Country	Top 3	Winners	2nd	3rd
United Kingdom	23	5	15	3
France	16	5	4	7
Ireland	12	7	3	2
Sweden	12	5	1	6
Germany	11	2	4	5
Switzerland	8	2	3	3
Italy	8	2	2	4
Luxembourg	7	5	0	2
Denmark	7	3	1	3
Spain	7	2	4	1
Israel	6	3	2	1
Russia	6	1	3	2

… And the Most Finishes in the Bottom 3

Country	Bottom 3	Last	2nd last	3rd Last
Belgium	15	6	2	7
Norway	14	9	3	2
Austria	13	6	2	5
Finland	13	5	3	5
Netherlands	8	1	4	3
France	8	1	3	4
Portugal	8	0	4	4
Luxembourg	7	3	1	3
Spain	7	2	3	2
Germany	7	2	1	4
Switzerland	6	4	1	1
Turkey	6	3	3	0
United Kingdom	6	3	2	1
Sweden	6	2	2	2
Yugoslavia	6	1	5	0

Failing to Qualify for the Final

Who has been eliminated at the semi-final stage the most times?

Country	SF Failures	SF Appearances	Failure rate
Andorra	6	6	100%
Slovakia	4	4	100%
Czech Republic	3	3	100%
Monaco	3	3	100%
Bulgaria	8	9	89%
Montenegro	5	6	83%
Belgium	8	10	80%
San Marino	4	5	80%
Poland	6	8	75%
Netherlands	8	11	73%
Slovenia	8	11	73%
Switzerland	7	10	70%
Portugal	7	10	70%
Latvia	7	10	70%
Cyprus	6	9	67%
Belarus	7	11	64%
Estonia	7	11	64%
Israel	6	10	60%
Croatia	5	9	56%
FYR Macedonia	6	11	55%
Lithuania	5	10	50%
Albania	5	10	50%
Malta	4	9	44%
Ireland	4	9	44%
Finland	4	10	40%
Austria	4	11	36%
Hungary	2	6	33%
Serbia	2	6	33%
Iceland	3	10	30%
Norway	2	8	25%
Moldova	2	9	22%
Denmark	2	10	20%
Armenia	1	7	14%
Turkey	1	7	14%
Sweden	1	8	13%

..And the Most Successful Semi-Finalists

Country	SF Failures	SF Appearances	Success Rate
Ukraine	0	9	100%
Greece	0	8	100%
Romania	0	8	100%
Bosnia & Herzegovina	0	7	100%
Russia	0	7	100%
Azerbaijan	0	6	100%

The Best Semi-Final to Compete In

(analysis of semi-finalists from the introduction of the two semi-finals in 2008)

Top 3 in final   Bottom in final

Year	Winner	Second	Third	Last place
2008	Semi-final 1	Semi-final 2	Semi-final 1	n/a (United Kingdom)
2009	Semi-final 2	Semi-final 1	Semi-final 2	Semi-final 1
2010	n/a (Germany)	Semi-final 2	Semi-final 2	n/a (United Kingdom)
2011	Semi-final 1	n/a (Italy)	Semi-final 2	Semi-final 1
2012	Semi-final 2	Semi-final 1	Semi-final 2	Semi-final 2
2013	Semi-final 1	Semi-final 2	Semi-final 1	Semi-final 1
2014	Semi-final 2	Semi-final 1	Semi-final 1	n/a (France)

Average points received in the Final by semi-finalist   Average position in final

Year	Semi-final 1	Semi-final 2	Semi-final 1	Semi-final 2
2008	133	87	10	13
2009	83	118	14	11
2010	69	113	15	10
2011	87	110	15	11
2012	82	113	15	12
2013	101	100	13	12
2014	117	76	10	14

Winner's position in the Semi-finals

Year	Winner	Position in SF	Semi-final winners	Finished in Final
2008	Russia	3rd	Greece, Ukraine	3rd, 2nd
2009	Norway	1st	Iceland, Norway	2nd, 1st
2010	Germany	n/a	Belgium, Turkey	6th, 2nd
2011	Azerbaijan	2nd	Greece, Sweden	7th, 3rd
2012	Sweden	1st	Russia, Sweden	2nd, 1st
2013	Denmark	1st	Denmark, Azerbaijan	1st, 2nd
2014	Austria	1st	Netherlands, Austria	2nd, 1st

Most semi-final consecutive failures

Country	Number of Years	Last Final appearance
Albania	2	2012
Andorra	6	Never qualified
Armenia		
Austria		
Azerbaijan		
Belarus		
Belgium	1	2013
Bosnia & H		
Bulgaria	6	2007
Croatia	4	2009
Cyprus	1	2012
Czech Republic	3	Never qualified
Denmark		
Estonia	1	2013
Finland		
FYR Macedonia	2	2012
Georgia	1	2013
Greece		
Hungary		
Iceland		
Ireland	1	2013
Israel	4	2010
Latvia	6	2008
Lithuania	1	2013
Malta		
Moldova	1	2013
Montenegro		
Netherlands		
Norway		
Poland		
Portugal	3	2010
Romania		
Russia		
San Marino		
Serbia	1	2012
Slovakia	4	1998
Slovenia		
Sweden		
Switzerland	2	2011
Turkey		
Ukraine		

Congratulations to Montenegro and San Marino, who qualified for the Grand Final for the first time in 2014.
All the countries who currently participate have now reached the final at least once.

The Best & Worst Positions in the Order of Performance

(Since the introduction of the modern points scoring system in 1975)

Order of Performance	Points received and frequency (Finals only)															
	1	2	3	4	5	6	7	8	10	12	Total	Points	Rank	Av Vote	Rank	Change
1	56	41	52	56	47	44	43	45	48	46	478	2710	9	5.669	13	+1
2	44	32	31	36	43	37	37	37	20	23	340	1813	24	5.332	25	
3	51	42	46	41	30	36	42	39	38	37	402	2233	19	5.555	19	
4	38	36	45	48	43	48	38	33	39	30	398	2220	20	5.578	18	-3
5	46	48	40	44	44	43	40	40	29	41	415	2298	15	5.537	20	-3
6	38	49	48	35	41	46	32	47	35	29	400	2199	21	5.498	22	-1
7	45	60	50	49	45	50	46	35	52	33	465	2554	13	5.492	24	-1
8	39	57	43	47	56	37	48	40	40	32	439	2412	14	5.494	23	-1
9	48	54	50	36	42	32	47	56	47	51	463	2711	8	5.855	11	-1
10	35	49	35	56	61	44	50	54	46	57	487	2957	3	6.072	6	-1
11	49	48	50	48	65	53	53	43	38	45	492	2765	5	5.620	15	+9
12	52	48	44	44	34	52	43	44	63	44	468	2749	6	5.874	10	+1
13	44	37	34	49	39	34	41	45	57	50	430	2632	11	6.121	4	+2
14	53	42	50	58	42	52	47	39	58	40	481	2742	7	5.701	12	+1
15	52	39	46	31	50	37	44	38	34	40	411	2296	16	5.586	17	+1
16	45	42	41	39	47	45	47	40	31	33	410	2268	17	5.532	21	-1
17	44	44	38	46	50	63	63	54	55	79	536	3429	1	6.397	3	-1
18	45	52	70	50	53	68	61	59	51	57	566	3325	2	5.875	9	
19	48	44	43	47	35	52	36	60	47	47	459	2706	10	5.895	8	
20	32	47	43	37	31	29	47	41	60	67	434	2793	4	6.435	2	-1
21	44	36	39	46	41	51	43	38	30	36	404	2265	18	5.606	16	
22	39	39	48	35	46	30	34	45	52	55	423	2589	12	6.121	5	-1
23	36	27	30	46	32	40	34	36	42	33	356	2106	22	5.916	7	
24	25	28	27	27	30	27	27	40	41	46	318	2053	23	6.456	1	+2
25	14	21	20	12	16	16	20	16	14	15	164	928	25	5.659	14	-2
26	5	5	4	4	4	1	4	3	0	1	31	133	26	4.290	26	
First 3	151	115	129	133	120	117	122	121	106	106	1220	6756		5.538		
Top Half	506	537	509	516	517	492	497	497	469	446	4984	28198		5.658		
Bottom Half	561	531	559	552	551	575	570	570	598	621	5686	33688		5.925		
Last 3	140	137	153	144	162	146	157	169	176	196	1580	9698		6.138		
Last	38	49	41	49	45	38	50	52	56	63	481	2990		6.216		

Notes:

Countries performing first have received some votes 478 times but because these votes have most often been either 1 point, 3 points or 4 points, the average points scored is much lower in the league table.

On average the act performing last has received the 3rd highest points (no change on last year) and the 4th highest average vote (again, no change).

Performing in the second half of the contest is also a big advantage. Conchita Wurst was the first winner from the top half of the draw for 10 years.

Six of the top seven countries in this year's final performed at 18th or later in the running order.

Performing 24th in the running order becomes the best place in terms of the average value of votes received, thanks to Netherlands' second place this year. The biggest change was the average vote for the 11th performer, up 9 places thanks to Austria's win.

Until 2004, the total number of votes cast varied on how many countries took part each year. When the semi-finals were introduced, all countries could vote in the final even if they had not qualified. This has resulted in a big increase in the number of points awarded.

Winners & Losers by Order of Performance

(Since the introduction of the modern points scoring system in 1975)

Contest	Finalists	Position in Running Order				Running Order	Number of times:	
		Winner	Second	Third	Last		Winner	Last
1975	19	1	9	19	13	1	3	0
1976	18	1	17	16	18	2	0	2
1977	18	18	9	1	13	3	1	4
1978	20	18	10	6	2	4	1	2
1979	19	10	19	11	18	5	1	2
1980	19	17	12	13	10	6	0	3
1981	20	14	3	9	13	7	0	3
1982	18	18	15	7	6	8	2	1
1983	20	20	16	4	6 & 7	9	1	1
1984	19	1	9	4	13	10	2	3
1985	19	13	10	16	8	11	1	0
1986	20	13	10	1	5	12	0	4
1987	22	20	16	7	10	13	2	6
1988	21	9	4	13	12	14	3	1
1989	22	22	7	12	20	15	1	1
1990	22	19	14	17	9	16	0	1
1991	22	8	9	15	6	17	6	1
1992	23	17	16	10	12	18	4	3
1993	25	14	19	4	7	19	3	0
1994	25	3	24	14	16	20	4	1
1995	23	5	9	18	3	21	0	0
1996	23	17	12	23	18	22	2	0
1997	25	24	5	2	3	23	1	0
1998	25	8	16	10	5	24	2	1
1999	23	15	13	21	3	25	0	0
2000	24	14	9	21	10	26	0	1
2001	23	20	23	22	4			
2002	24	23	20	2	14			
2003	26	4	22	11	15			
2004	24	10	5	16	3			
2005	24	19	3	4	17			
2006	24	17	10	13	7			
2007	24	17	18	15	4			
2008	25	24	18	21	2			
2009	25	20	7	11	24			
2010	25	22	14	19	12			
2011	25	19	12	7	13			
2012	26	17	6	24	12			
2013	26	18	20	22	26			
2014	26	11	24	13	14			

12 Points: Recent Final History
(Spot the Trend - Who has received the maximum 12 points in Finals in the last 10 years?)

Voting country	Kiev 2005	Athens 2006	Helsinki 2007	Belgrade 2008	Moscow 2009	Oslo 2010	Düsseldorf 2011	Baku 2012	Malmö 2013	Copenhagen 2014
Albania	Greece	Bosnia & H	Spain	Greece	Greece	Greece	Italy	Greece	Italy	Spain
Andorra	Spain	Spain	Ukraine	Spain	Spain	-	-	-	-	-
Armenia	-	Russia	Russia	Russia	Russia	Georgia	Ukraine	-	Ukraine	Montenegro
Austria	Serbia & Mont	-	Serbia	-	-	-	Bosnia & H	Sweden	Azerbaijan	Armenia
Azerbaijan	-	-	-	Turkey	Turkey	Turkey	Ukraine	Turkey	Ukraine	Russia
Belarus	Russia	Russia	Russia	Russia	Norway	Russia	Georgia	Russia	Ukraine	Russia
Belgium	Greece	Armenia	Turkey	Armenia	Turkey	Greece	France	Sweden	Netherlands	Austria
Bosnia & H	Croatia	Croatia	Serbia	Serbia	Croatia	Serbia	Slovenia	FYR Macedonia	-	-
Bulgaria	Greece	Greece	Greece	Germany	Greece	Azerbaijan	United Kingdom	Serbia	Azerbaijan	-
Croatia	Serbia & Mont	Bosnia & H	Serbia	Bosnia & H	Bosnia & H	Turkey	Slovenia	Serbia	Ukraine	-
Cyprus	Greece	Greece	Greece	Greece	Greece	Greece	Greece	Greece	Greece	-
Czech Rep	-	-	Ukraine	Armenia	Armenia	-	-	-	-	-
Denmark	Norway	Finland	Sweden	Iceland	Norway	Germany	Ireland	Sweden	Norway	Sweden
Estonia	Switzerland	Finland	Russia	Russia	Norway	Germany	Sweden	Sweden	Russia	Netherlands
Finland	Norway	Russia	Serbia	Norway	Estonia	Germany	Hungary	Sweden	Norway	Austria
France	Turkey	Turkey	Turkey	Armenia	Turkey	Turkey	Spain	Sweden	Denmark	Armenia
FYR Macedonia	Albania	Bosnia & H	Serbia	Albania	Turkey	Albania	Bosnia & H	Albania	Denmark	Montenegro
Georgia	-	-	Armenia	Armenia	-	-	Lithuania	Lithuania	Azerbaijan	Armenia
Germany	Greece	Turkey	Turkey	Greece	Norway	Belgium	Austria	Sweden	Hungary	Netherlands
Greece	Cyprus	Finland	Bulgaria	Armenia	United Kingdom	Cyprus	France	Cyprus	Azerbaijan	Austria
Hungary	Greece	-	Serbia	Azerbaijan	Norway	-	Iceland	Sweden	Azerbaijan	Netherlands
Iceland	Norway	Finland	Finland	Denmark	Norway	Denmark	Denmark	Sweden	Denmark	Netherlands
Ireland	Latvia	Lithuania	Lithuania	Latvia	Iceland	Denmark	Denmark	Sweden	Denmark	Austria
Israel	Romania	Russia	Belarus	Russia	Norway	Armenia	Sweden	Sweden	Azerbaijan	Austria
Italy	-	-	-	-	-	-	Romania	Albania	Denmark	Austria
Latvia	Switzerland	Russia	Ukraine	Russia	Norway	Germany	Italy	Sweden	Russia	Netherlands
Lithuania	Latvia	Russia	Georgia	Russia	Norway	Georgia	Georgia	Azerbaijan	Azerbaijan	Netherlands
Malta	Cyprus	Switzerland	United Kingdom	Sweden	Iceland	Azerbaijan	Azerbaijan	Azerbaijan	Azerbaijan	Italy
Moldova	Latvia	Romania	Romania	Romania	Romania	Romania	Romania	Romania	Ukraine	Romania
Monaco	Israel	Bosnia & H	-	-	-	-	-	-	-	-
Montenegro	-	-	Serbia	Serbia	Bosnia & H	-	-	Serbia	Azerbaijan	Hungary
Netherlands	Turkey	Turkey	Turkey	Armenia	Norway	Armenia	Denmark	Sweden	Belgium	Austria
Norway	Finland	Sweden	Denmark	Iceland	Germany	Finland	Denmark	Sweden	Sweden	Netherlands

12 Points: Recent Final History

(Spot the Trend - Who has received the maximum 12 points in Finals in the last 10 years?)

Voting country	Kiev 2005	Athens 2006	Helsinki 2007	Belgrade 2008	Moscow 2009	Oslo 2010	Düsseldorf 2011	Baku 2012	Malmö 2013	Copenhagen 2014
Poland	Ukraine	Finland	Ukraine	Armenia	Norway	Denmark	Lithuania	-	-	Netherlands
Portugal	Romania	Ukraine	Ukraine	Ukraine	Moldova	Spain	Spain	Spain	-	Austria
Romania	Moldova	Moldova	Moldova	Greece	Moldova	Denmark	Moldova	Moldova	Moldova	Sweden
Russia	Malta	Armenia	Belarus	Armenia	Norway	Armenia	Azerbaijan	Sweden	Azerbaijan	Belarus
San Marino	-	-	-	Greece	-	-	Italy	Albania	Greece	Azerbaijan
Serbia	-	-	Hungary	Bosnia & H	Bosnia & H	Bosnia & H	Bosnia & H	FYR Macedonia	Denmark	-
Serbia & Mont	Greece	Bosnia & H	-	-	-	-	-	-	-	-
Slovakia	-	-	-	-	Estonia	Germany	Ukraine	Sweden	-	Austria
Slovenia	Croatia	Bosnia & H	Serbia	Serbia	Norway	Denmark	Bosnia & H	Serbia	Denmark	Austria
Spain	Romania	Romania	Romania	Romania	Norway	Germany	Italy	Sweden	Italy	Austria
Sweden	Greece	Finland	Finland	Norway	Norway	Germany	Ireland	Cyprus	Norway	Austria
Switzerland	Serbia & Mont	Bosnia & H	Serbia	Serbia	Turkey	Germany	Bosnia & H	Albania	Italy	-
Turkey	Greece	Bosnia & H	Armenia	Azerbaijan	Azerbaijan	Azerbaijan	Azerbaijan	Azerbaijan	-	-
Ukraine	Moldova	Russia	Belarus	Russia	Norway	Azerbaijan	Georgia	Azerbaijan	Belarus	Sweden
United Kingdom	Greece	Finland	Turkey	Greece	Turkey	Greece	Ireland	Sweden	Denmark	Austria

Highest number of 12 points scored by one entry

Since the introduction of the modern points scoring system in 1975, including semi-finals

Country	Contest	Performer	12 points	Out of	%	Position
Sweden	2012 Final	Loreen	18	41	44%	1
Norway	2009 Final	Alexander Rybak	16	41	39%	1
Austria	2014 Final	Conchita Wurst	13	36	36%	1
United Kingdom	1997	Katrina and The Waves	10	24	42%	1
Azerbaijan	2013 Final	Farid Mammadov	10	38	26%	2
Greece	2005 Final	Helena Paparizou	10	38	26%	1
Germany	1982	Nicole	9	17	53%	1
Estonia	2001	Tanel Padar, Dave Benton & 2XL	9	22	41%	1
Serbia & Montenegro	2004 Semi	Željko Joksimović	9	35	26%	1
Germany	2010 Final	Lena Meyer-Landrut	9	38	24%	1
Bosnia-Herzegovina	2006 Semi	Hari Mata Hari	9	37	24%	2
Serbia	2007 Semi	Marija Šerifović	9	41	22%	1
Serbia	2007 Final	Marija Šerifović	9	41	22%	1
Netherlands	2014 Semi	The Common Linnets	8	18	44%	1
Norway	1985	Bobbysocks	8	18	44%	1
Turkey	2009 Semi	Hadise	8	19	42%	2
Ireland	1987	Johnny Logan	8	21	38%	1
Denmark	2000	Olsen Brothers	8	23	35%	1
Ireland	1994	P Harrington & C McGettigan	8	24	33%	1
Ukraine	2004 Final	Ruslana	8	35	23%	1
Bosnia-H	2006 Final	Hari Mata Hari	8	37	22%	3
Finland	2006 Final	Lordi	8	37	22%	1
Russia	2006 Semi	Dima Bilan	8	37	22%	3
Netherlands	2014 Final	The Common Linnets	8	36	22%	2
Denmark	2013 Final	Emmelie de Forest	8	38	21%	1

Winners with the lowest number of 12 points

Country	Contest	Performer	12 points	Out of	%
United Kingdom	1981	Bucks Fizz	2	19	11%
Azerbaijan	2011	Ell/Nikki	3	42	7%
Israel	1998	Dana International	3	24	13%
Ireland	1992	Linda Martin	3	22	14%
Italy	1990	Toto Cutugno	3	21	14%
Switzerland	1988	Céline Dion	3	20	15%
France	1977	Marie Myriam	3	17	18%
Turkey	2003	Sertab Erener	4	25	16%
Yugoslavia	1989	Riva	4	21	19%
Sweden	1991	Carola	4	21	19%
Latvia	2002	Marie N	5	23	22%
Sweden	1999	Charlotte Nilsson	5	22	23%
Belgium	1986	Sandra Kim	5	19	26%
Sweden	1984	Herrey's	5	18	28%

... And Countries finishing with No Points

From 1975 onwards, including semi-finals

Country	No Points	Years
Norway	3	1978, 1997, 1981
Austria	2	1988, 1991
Turkey	2	1983, 1987
Switzerland	2	1998, 2004 Semi
Finland	1	1982
Spain	1	1983
Iceland	1	1989
Lithuania	1	1994
Portugal	1	1997
United Kingdom	1	2003
Czech Republic	1	2009 Semi

Performance of the "Big 5"

Since automatic qualification to the final was introduced in 2004.

Contest	Countries in Final		France		Germany		Spain		United Kingdom		Italy	
Final	Voting	Max pts	Points	% of max	Points	% of max	Points	% of max	Points	% of max	Points	% of max
2004	36	420	40	10%	93	22%	87	21%	29	7%	-	0%
2005	39	456	11	2%	4	1%	28	6%	18	4%	-	0%
2006	38	444	5	1%	36	8%	18	4%	25	6%	-	0%
2007	42	492	19	4%	49	10%	43	9%	19	4%	-	0%
2008	43	504	47	9%	14	3%	55	11%	14	3%	-	0%
2009	42	492	107	22%	35	7%	23	5%	173	35%	-	0%
2010	38	444	82	18%	246	55%	68	15%	10	2%	-	0%
2011	43	504	82	16%	107	21%	50	10%	100	20%	189	38%
2012	42	492	21	4%	110	22%	97	20%	12	2%	101	21%
2013	39	456	14	3%	18	4%	8	2%	23	5%	126	28%
2014	37	432	2	0%	39	9%	74	17%	40	9%	33	8%

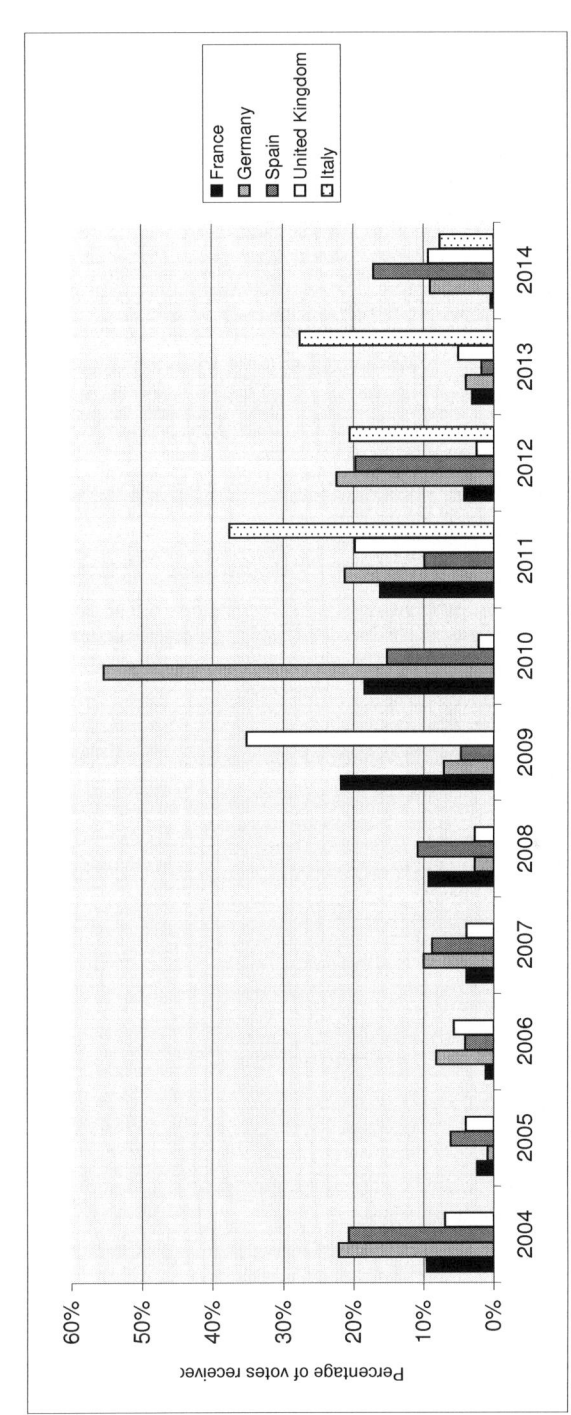

Hosts Performance
(Or are viewers influenced by an impressive show?)

Since the introduction of the modern points system in 1975.

Year	Host Country	Points	% of max	Finished	Out of	Countries voting
1975	Sweden	72	33%	8	19	19
1976	Netherlands	56	27%	9	18	18
1977	United Kingdom	121	59%	2	18	18
1978	France	119	52%	3	20	20
1979	Israel	125	58%	1	19	19
1980	Netherlands	93	43%	5	19	19
1981	Ireland	105	46%	5	20	20
1982	United Kingdom	76	37%	7	18	18
1983	Germany	94	41%	5	20	20
1984	Luxembourg	39	18%	10	19	19
1985	Sweden	103	48%	3	19	19
1986	Norway	44	19%	12	20	20
1987	Belgium	56	22%	11	22	22
1988	Ireland	79	33%	8	21	21
1989	Switzerland	47	19%	13	22	22
1990	Yugoslavia	81	32%	7	22	22
1991	Italy	89	35%	7	22	22
1992	Sweden	9	3%	22	23	23
1993	Ireland	187	65%	1	25	25
1994	Ireland	226	78%	1	25	25
1995	Ireland	44	17%	14	23	23
1996	Norway	114	43%	2	23	23
1997	Ireland	157	55%	2	25	25
1998	United Kingdom	166	58%	2	25	25
1999	Israel	93	35%	5	23	23
2000	Sweden	88	32%	7	24	24
2001	Denmark	177	67%	2	23	23
2002	Estonia	111	40%	4	24	24
2003	Latvia	5	2%	24	26	26
2004	Turkey	195	46%	4	24	36
2005	Ukraine	30	7%	19	24	39
2006	Greece	128	29%	9	24	38
2007	Finland	53	11%	17	24	42
2008	Serbia	160	32%	6	25	43
2009	Russia	91	18%	11	25	42
2010	Norway	35	8%	20	25	39
2011	Germany	107	21%	10	25	43
2012	Azerbaijan	150	30%	4	26	42
2013	Sweden	62	14%	14	26	39
2014	Denmark	74	17%	9	26	37

Eurovision Winners - Winning Margins

Year	Winner	Points	Runner-up	Points	Winning Margin	Margin as % of total pts
2009	Norway	387	Iceland	218	169	6.94%
2012	Sweden	372	Russia	259	113	4.64%
2010	Germany	246	Turkey	170	76	3.36%
1997	United Kingdom	227	Ireland	157	70	4.83%
1982	Germany	161	Israel	100	61	5.84%
1994	Ireland	226	Poland	166	60	4.14%
2014	Austria	290	Netherlands	238	52	2.42%
1996	Ireland	162	Norway	114	48	3.60%
2013	Denmark	281	Azerbaijan	234	47	2.08%
2006	Finland	292	Russia	248	44	2.00%
2008	Russia	272	Ukraine	230	42	1.68%
2000	Denmark	195	Russia	155	40	2.87%
2005	Greece	230	Malta	192	38	1.68%
1986	Belgium	176	Switzerland	140	36	3.10%
2007	Serbia	268	Ukraine	235	33	1.35%
1978	Israel	157	Belgium	125	32	2.76%
2011	Azerbaijan	221	Italy	189	32	1.28%
1987	Ireland	172	Germany	141	31	2.43%
1995	Norway	148	Spain	119	29	2.17%
1993	Ireland	187	United Kingdom	164	23	1.59%
2001	Estonia	198	Denmark	177	21	1.57%
1985	Norway	123	Germany	105	18	1.63%
1976	United Kingdom	164	France	147	17	1.63%
1990	Italy	149	France	132	17	1.33%
1999	Sweden	163	Iceland	146	17	1.27%
2004	Ukraine	280	Serbia & Mont	263	17	0.81%
1992	Ireland	155	United Kingdom	139	16	1.20%
1977	France	136	United Kingdom	121	15	1.44%
1980	Ireland	143	Germany	128	15	1.36%
1975	Netherlands	152	United Kingdom	138	14	1.27%
2002	Latvia	176	Malta	164	12	0.86%
1998	Israel	176	United Kingdom	166	10	0.69%
1979	Israel	125	Spain	116	9	0.82%
1984	Sweden	145	Ireland	137	8	0.73%
1989	Yugoslavia	137	United Kingdom	130	7	0.55%
1983	Luxembourg	142	Israel	136	6	0.52%
1981	United Kingdom	136	Germany	132	4	0.34%
2003	Turkey	167	Belgium	165	2	0.13%
1988	Switzerland	137	United Kingdom	136	1	0.08%
1991	Sweden	146	France	146	0	0.00%

Top 5 closest voting relationships

Since the introduction of the modern points scoring system in 1975, including semi-finals.

"% of max" is the percentage of the maximum one country could give to the other in all contests.

1) Most Points Awarded Between Two Countries

Pos		Gave to	Total	% of max		Gave to	Total	% of max	Average Total	% of max
1	Cyprus	Greece	328	94%	Greece	Cyprus	275	88%	302	91%
2	Denmark	Sweden	310	70%	Sweden	Denmark	241	53%	276	61%
3	Norway	Sweden	297	62%	Sweden	Norway	196	42%	247	52%
4	United Kingdom	Ireland	258	55%	Ireland	United Kingdom	191	41%	225	48%
5	Iceland	Denmark	229	55%	Denmark	Iceland	157	48%	193	51%

(IcelandDenmark replaces the previous 5th place relationship between Sweden/Ireland)

2) Highest Percentage of Possible Points Awarded Between Two Countries (min 2 contests)

Pos		Gave to	Total	% of max		Gave to	Total	% of max	Average Total	% of max
1	Turkey	Azerbaijan	72	100%	Azerbaijan	Turkey	84	100%	78	100%
2	Romania	Moldova	150	96%	Moldova	Romania	161	96%	156	96%
3	Italy	Albania	24	100%	Albania	Italy	41	85%	33	93%
4	Cyprus	Greece	328	94%	Greece	Cyprus	275	88%	302	91%
5	Montenegro	Serbia	58	97%	Serbia	Montenegro	20	83%	39	90%

(No change in positions compared to 2013)

3) Most Number of Times Any Points Awarded Between Two Countries

Pos		Voted for	Times	% of max		Voted for	Times	% of max	Average Times	% of max
1	Sweden	Denmark	33	87%	Denmark	Sweden	33	89%	33	88%
2	Ireland	United Kingdom	32	82%	United Kingdom	Ireland	32	82%	32	82%
3	Norway	Sweden	34	85%	Sweden	Norway	28	72%	31	78%
4	Greece	Cyprus	25	96%	Cyprus	Greece	29	100%	27	98%
5	Ireland	Norway	25	61%	Norway	Ireland	29	73%	27	67%

(No change in positions compared to 2013)

4) Highest Percentage of Possible Times Two Countries Have Voted for each Other

Pos		Voted for	Times	% of max		Voted for	Times	% of max	Average Times	% of max
1	Albania	Greece	17	100%	Greece	Albania	14	100%	16	100%
2	Russia	Ukraine	16	100%	Ukraine	Russia	15	100%	16	100%
3	Croatia	FYR Macedonia	14	100%	FYR Macedonia	Croatia	13	100%	14	100%
4	Moldova	Romania	14	100%	Romania	Moldova	13	100%	14	100%
5	Albania	FYR Macedonia	12	100%	FYR Macedonia	Albania	12	100%	12	100%

(Perhaps surprisingly, Russia/Ukraine move up one place this year)

.. And the Bottom 5 (or the Countries who receive points but don't reciprocate)

Since the introduction of the modern points scoring system in 1975, including semi-finals.

"% of max" is the percentage of the maximum one country could give to the other in all contests.

1) The Most One-Sided Points Totals

Pos	Gave to		Total	% of max	Gave to		Total	% of max	Difference Total	% of max
1	Turkey	France	38	10%	France	Turkey	190	44%	-152	-34%
2	Russia	Estonia	36	17%	Estonia	Russia	182	69%	-146	-52%
3	Russia	Latvia	24	14%	Latvia	Russia	157	69%	-133	-55%
4	Italy	Portugal	26	13%	Portugal	Italy	154	64%	-128	-51%
5	Turkey	Germany	86	22%	Germany	Turkey	208	48%	-122	-26%

(no change in positions compared to 2013)

2) The Most One-Sided Points as a percentage of the total points possible (min 2 contests)

Pos	Gave to		Total	% of max	Gave to		Total	% of max	Difference Total	% of max
1	Armenia	Czech Republic	0	0%	Czech Republic	Armenia	46	96%	-46	-96%
2	Bulgara	Italy	0	0%	Italy	Bulgaria	10	83%	-10	-83%
3	Ukraine	Czech Republic	0	0%	Czech Republic	Ukraine	37	77%	-37	-77%
4	Serbia	Switzerland	7	15%	Switzerland	Serbia	74	88%	-67	-73%
5	Serbia	Austria	2	6%	Austria	Serbia	47	78%	-45	-72%

(Armenia/Belgium dropped out of the top 5 following the 6 points awarded by Armenia to Belgium in the SF this year)

3) The biggest difference between the number of times countries vote for each other

Pos	Voted for		Times	% of max	Voted for		Times	% of max	Difference Times	% of max
1	Ireland	Portugal	4	12%	Portugal	Ireland	22	65%	-18	-53%
2	Sweden	Spain	7	18%	Spain	Sweden	24	60%	-17	-42%
3	United Kingdom	Portugal	9	24%	Portugal	United Kingdom	25	68%	-16	-44%
4	Russia	Estonia	7	39%	Estonia	Russia	22	100%	-15	-61%
5	Ireland	Turkey	7	20%	Turkey	Ireland	22	69%	-15	-49%

(Russia/Estonia make an appearance in the top 5 this year, France/Norway drop out)

4) Countries who keep voting for others but get nothing in return - based on percentage of maximum possible

Pos	Voted for		Times	% of max	Voted for		Times	% of max	Difference Times	% of max
1	Hungary	Andorra	0	0%	Andorra	Hungary	4	100%	-4	-100%
1	Armenia	Czech Republic	0	0%	Czech Republic	Armenia	4	100%	-4	-100%
1	Ukraine	Czech Republic	0	0%	Czech Republic	Ukraine	4	100%	-4	-100%
1	Netherlands	San Marino	0	0%	San Marino	Netherlands	4	100%	-4	-100%

(excludes statistics for Yugoslavia and Serbia & Montenegro - as those entities no longer exist, their figures will be permanent, and also excludes those for Morocco whose appearance in 1980 looks to be one-off.)

Which Countries Have Never Awarded Points To Another?

(In semi-finals and finals, where voting for the recipient would have been possible, due to being drawn in the same semi-final).

Voting Country	Number never voted for:	Net Change on 2013	The Unfortunates:	First time voted for in 2014
Albania	4		Czech Republic, Latvia, Lithuania, Georgia	
Andorra	8		Belarus, Bulgaria, Croatia, Czech Republic, Estonia, FYR Macedonia, Georgia, Serbia	
Armenia	4	-3	Andorra, Czech Republic, Latvia, Monaco	Estonia, Germany, Hungary
Austria	6	-2	Andorra, Czech Republic, Georgia, Lithuania, Montenegro, Morocco	Belarus, San Marino
Azerbaijan	8	-4	Andorra, Armenia, France, FYR Macedonia, Iceland, Slovakia, Spain, Switzerland	Austria, Belgium, Montenegro, Portugal
Belarus	3		Czech Republic, Monaco, San Marino	
Belgium	7		Andorra, Belarus, Czech Republic, FYR Macedonia, Montenegro, Morocco, San Marino	Austria
Bosnia-H	6		Andorra, Cyprus, Czech Republic, Luxembourg, Monaco, San Marino	
Bulgaria	9		Andorra, Czech Republic, France, Italy, Monaco, Montenegro, Poland, San Marino, Slovakia	
Croatia	3		Armenia, Luxembourg, Monaco	
Cyprus	5		Andorra, Czech Republic, Montenegro, San Marino, Slovakia	
Czech Republic	16		Austria, Belgium, Cyprus, Estonia, Finland, France, Germany, Ireland, Lithuania, Moldova, Montenegro, Netherlands, Poland, Romania, Spain, Switzerland	
Denmark	6	-1	Andorra, Czech Republic, Georgia, Morocco, San Marino, Slovakia	San Marino
Estonia	2	-1	FYR Macedonia, Montenegro	Montenegro
Finland	3		Czech Republic, Montenegro, Morocco	Finland, Slovenia
France	4	-1	Andorra, Czech Republic, FYR Macedonia, Morocco	Georgia
FYR Macedonia	1		Monaco	
Georgia	5	-2	Andorra, Czech Republic, Ireland, Montenegro, Slovakia	Montenegro
Germany	6	-1	Andorra, Belarus, Czech Republic, Morocco, San Marino	San Marino
Greece	3		Czech Republic, Montenegro, Morocco	
Hungary	5	-1	Andorra, Czech Republic, FYR Macedonia, Monaco, Slovakia	
Iceland	4	-1	Czech Republic, Monaco, Montenegro, Morocco	
Ireland	5		Czech Republic, FYR Macedonia, Montenegro, Morocco, San Marino	
Israel	2		Czech Republic, Slovakia	
Italy	7	+2	Armenia, Azerbaijan, Croatia, Georgia, Latvia, Montenegro, Slovakia	
Latvia	6		Andorra, Czech Republic, FYR Macedonia, Monaco, Montenegro, Slovakia	
Lithuania	7	-1	Albania, Czech Republic, FYR Macedonia, Monaco, Montenegro, San Marino, Slovakia	Austria
Luxembourg	4		Bosnia, Croatia, Morocco, Slovenia	
Moldova	2	-1	Czech Republic, Malta	Netherlands
Monaco	8		Andorra, Armenia, Bulgaria, Hungary, Moldova, Poland, Russia, Yugoslavia	

Which Countries Have Never Awarded Points To Another? (continued)

Voting Country	Number never voted for:	Net Change on 2013	The Unfortunates:	First time voted for in 2014
Montenegro	5	-4	Andorra, Czech Republic, Estonia, Germany, United Kingdom	Austria, Hungary, Portugal, Switzerland
Morocco	8		Belgium, Finland, Greece, Ireland, Italy, Luxembourg, Netherlands, Portugal	
Netherlands	4	-1	Czech Republic, Morocco, San Marino, Slovakia	Montenegro
Norway	6		Czech Republic, FYR Macedonia, Montenegro, Morocco, San Marino, Slovakia	
Poland	5		Bulgaria, Czech Republic, FYR Macedonia, Montenegro, San Marino	
Portugal	4	+1	Czech Republic, FYR Macedonia, Morocco, San Marino	
Romania	4		Andorra, Czech Republic, Monaco, Montenegro	
Russia	2	-2	Czech Republic, Monaco	Montenegro, San Marino
San Marino	8	-1	Andorra, Austria, Belarus, Bosnia, Cyprus, Estonia, Germany, Lithuania	Latvia, Ukraine
Serbia	4		Andorra, Czech Republic, San Marino, Spain	
Serbia & Mont	15		Andorra, Armenia, Austria, Belarus, Belgium, Denmark, France, Germany, Latvia, Malta, Monaco, Poland, Portugal, Spain, United Kingdom	
Slovakia	4		Bulgaria, France, Georgia, Latvia	
Slovenia	3		Czech Republic, Monaco, San Marino	
Spain	4	-1	Belarus, Czech Republic, FYR Macedonia, Morocco	Montenegro
Sweden	3	+1	Czech Republic, Morocco, San Marino	
Switzerland	8		Andorra, Belarus, Bulgaria, Czech Republic, Estonia, Morocco, San Marino, Slovakia	
Turkey	3		Morocco, Serbia, Slovakia	
Ukraine	3		Andorra, Czech Republic, Monaco	
United Kingdom	8		Andorra, Belarus, Czech Republic, FYR Macedonia, Montenegro, Morocco, San Marino, Slovakia	

(Net change takes into account the first time one country could vote for another, so the number of countries never voted for can increase, as for Italy, depending on the semi-final voting draw.)

The Least Friendly Pairs

Countries who have never given each other a single point no matter how many opportunities they've had.

Country	Have never awarded points to or received points from:	Total
Albania	Lithuania	1
Andorra	Bulgaria, Georgia, Serbia	3
Armenia	Monaco	1
Austria	Czech Republic	1
Azerbaijan	-	0
Belarus	-	0
Belgium	Czech Republic, Morocco	2
Bosnia & Herzegovina	Luxembourg, San Marino	2
Bulgaria	Andorra, Monaco, Poland, Slovakia	4
Croatia	Luxembourg	1
Cyprus	Czech Republic, San Marino	2
Czech Republic	Austria, Belgium, Cyprus, Finland, France, Germany, Ireland, Lithuania, Moldova, Montenegro, Netherlands, Poland, Romania, Spain, Switzerland	15
Denmark	-	0
Estonia	Montenegro	1
Finland	Czech Republic, Morocco	2
France	Czech Republic	1
FYR Macedonia	-	0
Georgia	Andorra, Slovakia	0
Germany	Czech Republic, San Marino	2
Greece	Morocco	1
Hungary	Monaco	1
Iceland	-	0
Ireland	Czech Republic, Morocco	2
Israel	-	0
Italy	-	0
Latvia	Slovakia	1
Lithuania	Albania, Czech Republic, San Marino	3
Luxembourg	Bosnia & H, Croatia, Morocco	3
Malta	-	0
Moldova	Czech Republic	1
Monaco	Armenia, Bulgaria, Hungary, Russia	4
Montenegro	Czech Republic, Estonia, United Kingdom	3
Morocco	Belgium, Finland, Greece, Ireland, Luxembourg, Netherlands, Portugal	7
Netherlands	Czech Republic, Morocco	2
Norway	-	0
Poland	Bulgaria, Czech Republic	2
Portugal	Morocco	1
Romania	Czech Republic	1
Russia	Monaco	1
San Marino	Bosnia & H, Cyprus, Germany, Lithuania	4
Serbia	Andorra	1
Slovakia	Bulgaria, Georgia, Latvia	3
Slovenia	-	0
Spain	Czech Republic	1
Sweden	-	0
Switzerland	Czech Republic	1
Turkey	-	0
Ukraine	-	0
United Kingdom	Montenegro	1

Eurovision 2014 - Who Votes for Who? (And Who Doesn't)

Since the introduction of the modern points scoring system in 1975, including semi-finals.
"% of max" is the percentage of the maximum one country could have given to the other in the semi-finals and final.
Since 2008, this figure is based on which semi-final each country was drawn to vote/perform in and which countries then made the final.
Previous voting arrangements are also taken into account, including the 2004 voting boycott by France, Poland & Russia.

Albania

	Albania awarded points to:				Frequency		Albania received points from:				Frequency	
	Total	% of max	12's	% of max	Times	% of max	Total	% of max	12's	% of max	Times	% of max
Albania	-	-	-	-	-	-	-	-	-	-	-	-
Andorra	6	13%	0	0%	1	25%	6	7%	0	0%	1	14%
Armenia	18	14%	0	0%	4	36%	1	1%	0	0%	1	13%
Austria	10	14%	0	0%	2	33%	38	53%	1	17%	6	100%
Azerbaijan	53	40%	0	0%	8	73%	22	20%	1	11%	5	56%
Belarus	6	5%	0	0%	2	20%	5	4%	0	0%	1	9%
Belgium	7	6%	0	0%	3	33%	39	27%	0	0%	7	58%
Bosnia & Herzegovina	70	49%	1	8%	8	67%	43	36%	0	0%	9	90%
Bulgaria	17	24%	0	0%	4	67%	6	6%	0	0%	2	22%
Croatia	26	20%	0	0%	6	55%	75	52%	0	0%	12	100%
Cyprus	33	28%	0	0%	6	60%	15	10%	0	0%	3	25%
Czech Republic	0	0%	0	0%	0	0%	1	2%	0	0%	1	25%
Denmark	12	7%	0	0%	4	27%	31	20%	0	0%	6	46%
Estonia	2	2%	0	0%	2	18%	2	1%	0	0%	2	17%
Finland	9	5%	0	0%	3	21%	24	15%	0	0%	5	38%
France	10	8%	0	0%	5	45%	14	9%	0	0%	5	38%
FYR Macedonia	103	72%	4	33%	12	100%	135	94%	9	75%	12	100%
Georgia	0	0%	0	0%	0	0%	3	4%	0	0%	1	14%
Germany	35	27%	0	0%	8	73%	29	22%	0	0%	7	64%
Greece	171	84%	8	47%	17	100%	132	79%	2	14%	14	100%
Hungary	48	29%	0	0%	7	50%	24	18%	0	0%	4	36%
Iceland	19	9%	0	0%	3	18%	29	16%	0	0%	6	40%
Ireland	13	10%	0	0%	3	27%	8	6%	0	0%	3	27%
Israel	26	22%	0	0%	6	60%	9	7%	0	0%	2	18%
Italy	41	85%	2	50%	4	100%	24	100%	2	100%	2	100%
Latvia	0	0%	0	0%	0	0%	11	6%	0	0%	4	27%
Lithuania	0	0%	0	0%	0	0%	0	0%	0	0%	0	0%
Luxembourg	0	-	0	-	0	-	0	-	0	-	0	-
Malta	43	28%	0	0%	10	77%	25	16%	0	0%	4	31%
Moldova	11	7%	0	0%	3	21%	6	5%	0	0%	2	18%
Monaco	2	6%	0	0%	1	33%	3	6%	0	0%	1	25%
Montenegro	37	77%	2	50%	4	100%	54	75%	2	33%	6	100%
Morocco	0	-	0	-	0	-	0	-	0	-	0	-
Netherlands	18	17%	0	0%	4	44%	8	6%	0	0%	4	36%
Norway	27	16%	0	0%	6	43%	19	13%	0	0%	4	33%
Poland	12	10%	0	0%	2	20%	12	10%	0	0%	3	30%
Portugal	16	13%	0	0%	4	40%	8	6%	0	0%	3	25%
Romania	27	16%	0	0%	6	43%	13	10%	0	0%	5	45%
Russia	20	10%	0	0%	5	31%	6	4%	0	0%	3	23%
San Marino	29	48%	0	0%	4	80%	44	61%	1	17%	6	100%
Serbia	18	17%	0	0%	8	89%	3	3%	0	0%	2	22%
Serbia & Montenegro	17	47%	0	0%	3	100%	22	46%	0	0%	3	75%
Slovakia	4	17%	0	0%	1	50%	4	7%	0	0%	1	20%
Slovenia	17	18%	0	0%	3	38%	26	22%	0	0%	7	70%
Spain	49	37%	2	18%	7	64%	10	6%	0	0%	3	20%
Sweden	42	27%	0	0%	9	69%	25	19%	0	0%	6	55%
Switzerland	15	11%	0	0%	3	27%	111	71%	2	15%	13	100%
Turkey	113	78%	3	25%	12	100%	60	45%	0	0%	11	100%
Ukraine	22	11%	0	0%	5	31%	7	5%	0	0%	3	25%
United Kingdom	15	11%	0	0%	3	27%	14	11%	0	0%	6	55%
Yugoslavia	0	-	0	-	0	-	0	-	0	-	0	-

Eurovision 2014 - Who Votes for Who? (And Who Doesn't)

Andorra

	Andorra awarded points to:				Frequency		Andorra received points from:				Frequency	
	Total	% of max	12's	% of max	Times	% of max	Total	% of max	12's	% of max	Times	% of max
Albania	6	7%	0	0%	1	14%	6	13%	0	0%	1	25%
Andorra	-	-	-	-	-	-	0	-	0	-	0	-
Armenia	3	4%	0	0%	1	14%	0	0%	0	0%	0	0%
Austria	8	22%	0	0%	2	67%	0	0%	0	0%	0	0%
Azerbaijan	15	42%	0	0%	2	67%	0	0%	0	0%	0	0%
Belarus	0	0%	0	0%	0	0%	4	7%	0	0%	1	20%
Belgium	8	11%	0	0%	2	33%	0	0%	0	0%	0	0%
Bosnia & Herzegovina	6	5%	0	0%	2	20%	0	0%	0	0%	0	0%
Bulgaria	0	0%	0	0%	0	0%	0	0%	0	0%	0	0%
Croatia	0	0%	0	0%	0	0%	2	4%	0	0%	1	25%
Cyprus	6	10%	0	0%	2	40%	0	0%	0	0%	0	0%
Czech Republic	0	0%	0	0%	0	0%	7	29%	0	0%	1	50%
Denmark	18	21%	0	0%	4	57%	0	0%	0	0%	0	0%
Estonia	0	0%	0	0%	0	0%	8	13%	0	0%	2	40%
Finland	49	45%	1	11%	7	78%	5	7%	0	0%	1	17%
France	26	36%	0	0%	5	83%	0	0%	0	0%	0	0%
FYR Macedonia	0	0%	0	0%	0	0%	1	2%	0	0%	1	20%
Georgia	0	0%	0	0%	0	0%	0	0%	0	0%	0	0%
Germany	5	7%	0	0%	1	17%	0	0%	0	0%	0	0%
Greece	34	35%	0	0%	6	75%	4	7%	0	0%	1	20%
Hungary	17	35%	0	0%	4	100%	0	0%	0	0%	0	0%
Iceland	24	29%	0	0%	3	43%	6	10%	0	0%	1	20%
Ireland	6	8%	0	0%	2	33%	5	8%	0	0%	2	40%
Israel	45	42%	1	11%	6	67%	6	8%	0	0%	2	33%
Italy	0	-	0	-	0	-	0	-	0	-	0	-
Latvia	12	14%	0	0%	2	29%	0	0%	0	0%	0	0%
Lithuania	13	18%	0	0%	3	50%	2	4%	0	0%	1	25%
Luxembourg	0	-	0	-	0	-	0	-	0	-	0	-
Malta	18	21%	0	0%	4	57%	3	5%	0	0%	1	20%
Moldova	5	6%	0	0%	2	29%	4	8%	0	0%	1	25%
Monaco	17	47%	0	0%	3	100%	0	0%	0	0%	0	0%
Montenegro	1	3%	0	0%	1	33%	0	0%	0	0%	0	0%
Morocco	0	-	0	-	0	-	0	-	0	-	0	-
Netherlands	19	26%	0	0%	4	67%	7	12%	0	0%	1	20%
Norway	26	27%	0	0%	5	63%	2	3%	0	0%	1	20%
Poland	10	14%	0	0%	1	17%	7	15%	0	0%	2	50%
Portugal	64	76%	4	57%	6	86%	10	17%	0	0%	2	40%
Romania	34	31%	0	0%	6	67%	0	0%	0	0%	0	0%
Russia	22	23%	0	0%	5	63%	4	8%	0	0%	1	25%
San Marino	2	17%	0	0%	1	100%	0	0%	0	0%	0	0%
Serbia	0	0%	0	0%	0	0%	0	0%	0	0%	0	0%
Serbia & Montenegro	3	8%	0	0%	2	67%	0	0%	0	0%	0	0%
Slovakia	0	-	0	-	0	-	0	-	0	-	0	-
Slovenia	8	11%	0	0%	1	17%	5	8%	0	0%	2	40%
Spain	60	83%	5	83%	5	83%	54	90%	3	60%	5	100%
Sweden	32	33%	0	0%	6	75%	2	3%	0	0%	1	20%
Switzerland	9	13%	0	0%	3	50%	0	0%	0	0%	0	0%
Turkey	15	14%	0	0%	3	33%	3	5%	0	0%	2	40%
Ukraine	49	51%	1	13%	6	75%	0	0%	0	0%	0	0%
United Kingdom	6	8%	0	0%	2	33%	0	0%	0	0%	0	0%
Yugoslavia	0	-	0	-	0	-	0	-	0	-	0	-

Eurovision 2014 - Who Votes for Who? (And Who Doesn't)

Armenia

	Armenia awarded points to:				Frequency		Armenia received points from:				Frequency	
	Total	% of max	12's	% of max	Times	% of max	Total	% of max	12's	% of max	Times	% of max
Albania	1	1%	0	0%	1	13%	18	14%	0	0%	4	36%
Andorra	0	0%	0	0%	0	0%	3	4%	0	0%	1	14%
Armenia	-	-	-	-	-	-	0	-	0	-	0	-
Austria	3	8%	0	0%	1	33%	17	47%	1	33%	2	67%
Azerbaijan	3	2%	0	0%	2	18%	0	0%	0	0%	0	0%
Belarus	39	46%	1	14%	5	71%	55	51%	0	0%	9	100%
Belgium	7	8%	0	0%	2	29%	85	64%	4	36%	9	82%
Bosnia & Herzegovina	17	16%	0	0%	4	44%	13	14%	0	0%	3	38%
Bulgaria	15	21%	0	0%	3	50%	70	58%	0	0%	9	90%
Croatia	9	13%	0	0%	2	33%	0	0%	0	0%	0	0%
Cyprus	17	35%	0	0%	3	75%	60	63%	2	25%	7	88%
Czech Republic	0	0%	0	0%	0	0%	46	96%	3	75%	4	100%
Denmark	15	14%	0	0%	4	44%	7	6%	0	0%	2	20%
Estonia	5	6%	0	0%	1	14%	12	10%	0	0%	3	30%
Finland	6	4%	0	0%	1	8%	10	7%	0	0%	4	33%
France	27	28%	0	0%	7	88%	99	83%	5	50%	10	100%
FYR Macedonia	15	21%	0	0%	2	33%	16	13%	0	0%	5	50%
Georgia	87	81%	3	33%	9	100%	84	88%	3	38%	8	100%
Germany	6	6%	0	0%	1	13%	57	43%	0	0%	9	82%
Greece	87	66%	0	0%	11	100%	79	60%	2	18%	9	82%
Hungary	1	1%	0	0%	1	13%	18	19%	0	0%	3	38%
Iceland	20	14%	1	8%	4	33%	17	12%	0	0%	6	50%
Ireland	4	4%	0	0%	2	25%	2	2%	0	0%	1	10%
Israel	34	31%	0	0%	5	56%	97	67%	2	17%	11	92%
Italy	7	19%	0	0%	2	67%	0	0%	0	0%	0	0%
Latvia	0	0%	0	0%	0	0%	18	15%	0	0%	4	40%
Lithuania	6	6%	0	0%	2	25%	3	3%	0	0%	2	20%
Luxembourg	0	-	0	-	0	-	0	-	0	-	0	-
Malta	23	24%	0	0%	4	50%	22	17%	0	0%	4	36%
Moldova	18	17%	0	0%	4	44%	28	23%	0	0%	8	80%
Monaco	0	0%	0	0%	0	0%	0	0%	0	0%	0	0%
Montenegro	25	42%	1	20%	3	60%	31	32%	0	0%	5	63%
Morocco	0	-	0	-	0	-	0	-	0	-	0	-
Netherlands	21	25%	0	0%	4	57%	102	77%	5	45%	10	91%
Norway	38	32%	0	0%	9	90%	7	5%	0	0%	2	17%
Poland	9	11%	0	0%	3	43%	52	48%	2	22%	9	100%
Portugal	13	15%	0	0%	3	43%	12	11%	0	0%	3	33%
Romania	19	13%	0	0%	6	50%	55	38%	0	0%	10	83%
Russia	126	88%	7	58%	12	100%	105	80%	6	55%	11	100%
San Marino	14	23%	0	0%	4	80%	40	48%	0	0%	6	86%
Serbia	21	29%	0	0%	4	67%	6	8%	0	0%	2	33%
Serbia & Montenegro	0	-	0	-	0	-	0	0%	0	0%	0	0%
Slovakia	0	-	0	-	0	-	7	29%	0	0%	2	100%
Slovenia	6	7%	0	0%	2	29%	10	8%	0	0%	2	20%
Spain	10	10%	0	0%	3	38%	73	51%	1	8%	10	83%
Sweden	31	23%	0	0%	6	55%	32	24%	0	0%	8	73%
Switzerland	10	10%	0	0%	3	38%	7	5%	0	0%	3	25%
Turkey	16	13%	0	0%	3	30%	75	69%	1	11%	9	100%
Ukraine	88	67%	3	27%	10	91%	71	59%	1	10%	10	100%
United Kingdom	9	9%	0	0%	2	25%	8	6%	0	0%	2	18%
Yugoslavia	0	-	0	-	0	-	0	-	0	-	0	-

Eurovision 2014 - Who Votes for Who? (And Who Doesn't)

Austria

	Austria awarded points to:				Frequency		Austria received points from:				Frequency	
	Total	% of max	12's	% of max	Times	% of max	Total	% of max	12's	% of max	Times	% of max
Albania	38	53%	1	17%	6	100%	10	14%	0	0%	2	33%
Andorra	0	0%	0	0%	0	0%	8	22%	0	0%	2	67%
Armenia	17	47%	1	33%	2	67%	3	8%	0	0%	1	33%
Austria	-	-	-	-	-	-	0	-	0	-	0	-
Azerbaijan	20	42%	1	25%	2	50%	1	3%	0	0%	1	33%
Belarus	10	9%	0	0%	1	11%	7	7%	0	0%	1	13%
Belgium	44	11%	0	0%	14	44%	83	21%	2	6%	17	52%
Bosnia & Herzegovina	96	50%	3	19%	11	69%	42	27%	1	8%	6	46%
Bulgaria	14	29%	0	0%	3	75%	15	31%	0	0%	2	50%
Croatia	68	35%	1	6%	10	63%	14	8%	0	0%	4	29%
Cyprus	22	7%	0	0%	6	21%	47	15%	0	0%	10	37%
Czech Republic	0	0%	0	0%	0	0%	0	0%	0	0%	0	0%
Denmark	101	26%	2	6%	16	48%	73	21%	0	0%	15	52%
Estonia	28	15%	0	0%	7	44%	28	17%	0	0%	6	43%
Finland	35	10%	0	0%	7	23%	48	13%	2	7%	10	33%
France	111	28%	4	12%	15	45%	51	14%	1	3%	10	32%
FYR Macedonia	12	9%	0	0%	4	36%	11	10%	0	0%	3	33%
Georgia	0	0%	0	0%	0	0%	23	48%	0	0%	3	75%
Germany	111	28%	1	3%	20	61%	77	20%	2	6%	14	44%
Greece	53	14%	0	0%	14	45%	88	25%	3	10%	16	55%
Hungary	38	26%	0	0%	7	58%	21	22%	0	0%	4	50%
Iceland	39	14%	0	0%	10	43%	46	12%	0	0%	7	23%
Ireland	158	39%	3	9%	21	62%	91	22%	3	9%	15	44%
Israel	79	23%	1	3%	16	55%	59	17%	1	3%	9	31%
Italy	57	24%	0	0%	11	55%	69	26%	4	18%	10	45%
Latvia	23	17%	0	0%	4	36%	15	13%	0	0%	3	30%
Lithuania	0	0%	0	0%	0	0%	20	17%	0	0%	2	20%
Luxembourg	47	22%	0	0%	9	50%	14	6%	0	0%	3	17%
Malta	41	17%	0	0%	9	45%	40	20%	1	6%	6	35%
Moldova	31	26%	0	0%	7	70%	10	12%	0	0%	2	29%
Monaco	14	19%	0	0%	3	50%	10	14%	0	0%	2	33%
Montenegro	0	0%	0	0%	0	0%	2	4%	0	0%	1	25%
Morocco	0	0%	0	0%	0	0%	3	25%	0	0%	1	100%
Netherlands	90	24%	2	6%	16	52%	44	13%	1	3%	10	34%
Norway	47	12%	1	3%	11	32%	47	13%	0	0%	9	29%
Poland	45	31%	1	8%	7	58%	24	17%	0	0%	5	42%
Portugal	19	6%	0	0%	4	14%	49	14%	1	3%	10	34%
Romania	61	34%	1	7%	10	67%	21	15%	1	8%	3	25%
Russia	51	27%	0	0%	7	44%	9	6%	0	0%	3	23%
San Marino	3	13%	0	0%	1	50%	0	0%	0	0%	0	0%
Serbia	47	78%	2	40%	5	100%	2	6%	0	0%	1	33%
Serbia & Montenegro	36	100%	3	100%	3	100%	0	0%	0	0%	0	0%
Slovakia	3	8%	0	0%	1	33%	9	19%	0	0%	3	75%
Slovenia	28	14%	0	0%	7	41%	59	33%	1	7%	9	60%
Spain	68	17%	0	0%	12	35%	64	17%	1	3%	10	31%
Sweden	134	33%	3	9%	18	53%	63	16%	1	3%	15	47%
Switzerland	103	28%	1	3%	19	61%	72	20%	2	7%	12	40%
Turkey	70	21%	1	4%	11	39%	71	23%	1	4%	13	50%
Ukraine	20	15%	0	0%	6	55%	9	9%	0	0%	2	25%
United Kingdom	167	41%	7	21%	23	68%	106	27%	2	6%	18	55%
Yugoslavia	24	17%	0	0%	5	42%	23	16%	0	0%	5	42%

Eurovision 2014 - Who Votes for Who? (And Who Doesn't)

Azerbaijan

	Azerbaijan awarded points to:				Frequency		Azerbaijan received points from:				Frequency	
	Total	% of max	12's	% of max	Times	% of max	Total	% of max	12's	% of max	Times	% of max
Albania	22	20%	1	11%	5	56%	53	40%	0	0%	8	73%
Andorra	0	0%	0	0%	0	0%	15	42%	0	0%	2	67%
Armenia	0	0%	0	0%	0	0%	3	2%	0	0%	2	18%
Austria	1	3%	0	0%	1	33%	20	42%	1	25%	2	50%
Azerbaijan	-	-	-	-	-	-	0	-	0	-	0	-
Belarus	14	39%	0	0%	2	67%	50	60%	0	0%	7	100%
Belgium	4	7%	0	0%	1	20%	28	26%	0	0%	6	67%
Bosnia & Herzegovina	9	13%	0	0%	3	50%	28	39%	0	0%	5	83%
Bulgaria	4	17%	0	0%	1	50%	64	67%	3	38%	7	88%
Croatia	5	8%	0	0%	2	40%	53	49%	0	0%	6	67%
Cyprus	6	10%	0	0%	3	60%	62	65%	0	0%	7	88%
Czech Republic	0	-	0	-	0	-	20	83%	0	0%	2	100%
Denmark	17	14%	0	0%	4	40%	23	19%	0	0%	4	40%
Estonia	12	14%	0	0%	3	43%	33	28%	0	0%	5	50%
Finland	6	6%	0	0%	2	22%	20	17%	0	0%	5	50%
France	0	0%	0	0%	0	0%	25	21%	0	0%	5	50%
FYR Macedonia	0	0%	0	0%	0	0%	24	25%	0	0%	5	63%
Georgia	60	71%	0	0%	7	100%	88	81%	4	44%	9	100%
Germany	1	1%	0	0%	1	14%	13	12%	0	0%	3	33%
Greece	70	49%	1	8%	10	83%	67	51%	2	18%	10	91%
Hungary	28	26%	0	0%	5	56%	73	61%	4	40%	8	80%
Iceland	0	0%	0	0%	0	0%	36	30%	0	0%	6	60%
Ireland	9	9%	0	0%	3	38%	27	23%	0	0%	6	60%
Israel	35	42%	0	0%	5	71%	62	52%	2	20%	9	90%
Italy	1	2%	0	0%	1	25%	0	0%	0	0%	0	0%
Latvia	10	17%	0	0%	2	40%	32	27%	0	0%	8	80%
Lithuania	14	17%	0	0%	4	57%	66	55%	2	20%	8	80%
Luxembourg	0	-	0	-	0	-	0	-	0	-	0	-
Malta	40	56%	1	17%	5	83%	71	66%	5	56%	7	78%
Moldova	39	36%	0	0%	7	78%	81	68%	1	10%	9	90%
Monaco	0	-	0	-	0	-	0	-	0	-	0	-
Montenegro	2	4%	0	0%	1	25%	33	39%	1	14%	5	71%
Morocco	0	-	0	-	0	-	0	-	0	-	0	-
Netherlands	5	7%	0	0%	2	33%	37	28%	0	0%	8	73%
Norway	40	33%	1	10%	7	70%	30	21%	0	0%	5	42%
Poland	6	8%	0	0%	3	50%	59	61%	1	13%	7	88%
Portugal	1	2%	0	0%	1	25%	17	20%	0	0%	3	43%
Romania	60	45%	0	0%	10	91%	53	44%	1	10%	7	70%
Russia	74	56%	1	9%	10	91%	111	84%	3	27%	11	100%
San Marino	18	25%	0	0%	4	67%	42	39%	1	11%	7	78%
Serbia	2	3%	0	0%	1	17%	18	19%	0	0%	4	50%
Serbia & Montenegro	0	-	0	-	0	-	0	-	0	-	0	-
Slovakia	0	0%	0	0%	0	0%	29	48%	1	20%	4	80%
Slovenia	1	2%	0	0%	1	20%	19	16%	0	0%	5	50%
Spain	0	0%	0	0%	0	0%	24	17%	0	0%	5	42%
Sweden	12	13%	0	0%	3	38%	14	13%	0	0%	3	33%
Switzerland	0	0%	0	0%	0	0%	19	16%	0	0%	6	60%
Turkey	72	100%	6	100%	6	100%	84	100%	7	100%	7	100%
Ukraine	97	81%	3	30%	10	100%	94	78%	4	40%	10	100%
United Kingdom	7	8%	0	0%	2	29%	9	8%	0	0%	3	33%
Yugoslavia	0	-	0	-	0	-	0	-	0	-	0	-

Eurovision 2014 - Who Votes for Who? (And Who Doesn't)

Belarus

	Belarus awarded points to:				Frequency		Belarus received points from:				Frequency	
	Total	% of max	12's	% of max	Times	% of max	Total	% of max	12's	% of max	Times	% of max
Albania	5	4%	0	0%	1	9%	6	5%	0	0%	2	20%
Andorra	4	7%	0	0%	1	20%	0	0%	0	0%	0	0%
Armenia	55	51%	0	0%	9	100%	39	46%	1	14%	5	71%
Austria	7	7%	0	0%	1	13%	10	9%	0	0%	1	11%
Azerbaijan	50	60%	0	0%	7	100%	14	39%	0	0%	2	67%
Belarus	-	-	-	-	-	-	0	-	0	-	0	-
Belgium	11	9%	0	0%	2	20%	0	0%	0	0%	0	0%
Bosnia & Herzegovina	21	12%	0	0%	5	33%	8	7%	0	0%	3	30%
Bulgaria	2	2%	0	0%	1	13%	21	18%	1	10%	5	50%
Croatia	21	16%	0	0%	5	45%	2	2%	0	0%	1	10%
Cyprus	15	13%	0	0%	3	30%	34	28%	0	0%	6	60%
Czech Republic	0	0%	0	0%	0	0%	8	17%	0	0%	3	75%
Denmark	18	10%	0	0%	5	33%	1	1%	0	0%	1	9%
Estonia	19	13%	0	0%	6	50%	24	17%	0	0%	5	42%
Finland	23	15%	0	0%	4	31%	11	8%	0	0%	2	18%
France	7	5%	0	0%	1	9%	1	1%	0	0%	1	9%
FYR Macedonia	12	7%	0	0%	4	27%	44	26%	0	0%	9	64%
Georgia	60	56%	1	11%	8	89%	53	55%	2	25%	7	88%
Germany	8	6%	0	0%	1	9%	0	0%	0	0%	0	0%
Greece	55	33%	1	7%	10	71%	35	29%	0	0%	6	60%
Hungary	12	11%	0	0%	4	44%	6	8%	0	0%	2	33%
Iceland	26	15%	1	7%	6	43%	10	8%	0	0%	4	36%
Ireland	5	3%	0	0%	2	17%	10	8%	0	0%	3	27%
Israel	47	36%	1	9%	8	73%	39	30%	2	18%	7	64%
Italy	3	6%	0	0%	1	25%	7	12%	0	0%	1	20%
Latvia	32	27%	0	0%	7	70%	37	28%	0	0%	6	55%
Lithuania	52	33%	0	0%	9	69%	59	41%	1	8%	10	83%
Luxembourg	0	-	0	-	0	-	0	-	0	-	0	-
Malta	35	21%	0	0%	8	57%	42	27%	0	0%	8	62%
Moldova	83	53%	1	8%	11	85%	65	54%	1	10%	9	90%
Monaco	0	0%	0	0%	0	0%	1	3%	0	0%	1	33%
Montenegro	5	10%	0	0%	2	50%	19	26%	0	0%	6	100%
Morocco	0	-	0	-	0	-	0	-	0	-	0	-
Netherlands	7	6%	0	0%	2	20%	3	2%	0	0%	2	18%
Norway	37	24%	1	8%	8	62%	4	3%	0	0%	2	20%
Poland	35	36%	0	0%	6	75%	22	23%	0	0%	5	63%
Portugal	15	11%	0	0%	2	18%	9	7%	0	0%	3	27%
Romania	18	10%	0	0%	7	47%	13	10%	0	0%	4	36%
Russia	151	90%	10	71%	14	100%	68	63%	4	44%	8	89%
San Marino	0	0%	0	0%	0	0%	0	0%	0	0%	0	0%
Serbia	27	25%	0	0%	5	56%	10	10%	0	0%	3	38%
Serbia & Montenegro	20	56%	0	0%	3	100%	0	0%	0	0%	0	0%
Slovakia	3	8%	0	0%	1	33%	4	8%	0	0%	2	50%
Slovenia	14	11%	0	0%	4	36%	10	7%	0	0%	2	17%
Spain	2	2%	0	0%	1	9%	0	0%	0	0%	0	0%
Sweden	46	26%	0	0%	8	53%	4	3%	0	0%	2	15%
Switzerland	23	19%	0	0%	4	40%	0	0%	0	0%	0	0%
Turkey	18	12%	0	0%	5	38%	8	7%	0	0%	2	22%
Ukraine	166	81%	6	35%	16	94%	96	67%	5	42%	11	92%
United Kingdom	6	5%	0	0%	3	27%	0	0%	0	0%	0	0%
Yugoslavia	0	-	0	-	0	-	0	-	0	-	0	-

Eurovision 2014 - Who Votes for Who? (And Who Doesn't)

Belgium

	Belgium awarded points to:				Frequency		Belgium received points from:				Frequency	
	Total	% of max	12's	% of max	Times	% of max	Total	% of max	12's	% of max	Times	% of max
Albania	39	27%	0	0%	7	58%	7	6%	0	0%	3	33%
Andorra	0	0%	0	0%	0	0%	8	11%	0	0%	2	33%
Armenia	85	64%	4	36%	9	82%	7	8%	0	0%	2	29%
Austria	83	21%	2	6%	17	52%	44	11%	0	0%	14	44%
Azerbaijan	28	26%	0	0%	6	67%	4	7%	0	0%	1	20%
Belarus	0	0%	0	0%	0	0%	11	9%	0	0%	2	20%
Belgium	-	-	-	-	-	-	0	-	0	-	0	-
Bosnia & Herzegovina	26	10%	0	0%	7	32%	22	11%	0	0%	3	19%
Bulgaria	7	10%	0	0%	3	50%	6	7%	0	0%	1	14%
Croatia	19	9%	0	0%	8	44%	9	5%	0	0%	3	19%
Cyprus	52	14%	0	0%	12	40%	41	12%	0	0%	9	31%
Czech Republic	0	0%	0	0%	0	0%	0	0%	0	0%	0	0%
Denmark	103	25%	1	3%	16	46%	57	16%	0	0%	9	30%
Estonia	19	8%	0	0%	6	30%	51	24%	0	0%	11	61%
Finland	41	9%	0	0%	9	24%	80	19%	2	6%	14	40%
France	107	24%	1	3%	17	46%	124	30%	4	11%	19	54%
FYR Macedonia	0	0%	0	0%	0	0%	12	8%	0	0%	3	25%
Georgia	11	15%	0	0%	3	50%	12	33%	1	33%	1	33%
Germany	134	30%	0	0%	21	57%	77	18%	2	6%	14	39%
Greece	134	31%	2	6%	22	61%	59	16%	1	3%	9	29%
Hungary	45	29%	1	8%	7	54%	7	7%	0	0%	2	25%
Iceland	65	19%	1	3%	10	34%	44	10%	1	3%	6	17%
Ireland	153	34%	4	11%	26	68%	97	22%	2	6%	14	39%
Israel	117	28%	1	3%	22	63%	48	12%	0	0%	11	33%
Italy	44	18%	0	0%	8	40%	28	12%	0	0%	6	30%
Latvia	33	20%	1	7%	4	29%	27	17%	0	0%	5	38%
Lithuania	17	11%	0	0%	3	23%	13	11%	0	0%	4	40%
Luxembourg	53	23%	0	0%	8	42%	48	21%	1	5%	8	42%
Malta	53	19%	0	0%	8	35%	32	13%	1	5%	4	20%
Moldova	20	10%	0	0%	7	44%	26	20%	0	0%	5	45%
Monaco	16	17%	0	0%	3	38%	26	27%	1	13%	3	38%
Montenegro	0	0%	0	0%	0	0%	3	4%	0	0%	2	29%
Morocco	0	0%	0	0%	0	0%	0	0%	0	0%	0	0%
Netherlands	179	44%	6	18%	25	74%	158	40%	2	6%	23	70%
Norway	115	25%	1	3%	22	58%	59	15%	0	0%	13	39%
Poland	17	9%	0	0%	4	27%	52	33%	3	23%	6	46%
Portugal	63	15%	0	0%	13	38%	107	27%	3	9%	15	45%
Romania	57	23%	0	0%	10	48%	21	12%	0	0%	4	27%
Russia	62	23%	1	5%	12	55%	45	23%	0	0%	7	44%
San Marino	0	0%	0	0%	0	0%	6	13%	0	0%	2	50%
Serbia	19	20%	0	0%	4	50%	15	25%	0	0%	3	60%
Serbia & Montenegro	10	28%	0	0%	2	67%	0	0%	0	0%	0	0%
Slovakia	4	7%	0	0%	2	40%	26	36%	0	0%	3	50%
Slovenia	10	5%	0	0%	3	18%	25	13%	0	0%	6	38%
Spain	121	27%	3	8%	23	61%	95	21%	2	5%	16	43%
Sweden	146	30%	2	5%	25	63%	58	13%	0	0%	13	36%
Switzerland	98	25%	3	9%	15	45%	43	11%	0	0%	7	22%
Turkey	140	34%	6	18%	18	53%	63	18%	1	3%	10	34%
Ukraine	42	21%	0	0%	8	47%	11	9%	0	0%	2	20%
United Kingdom	147	32%	7	18%	20	53%	90	21%	1	3%	17	49%
Yugoslavia	45	29%	1	8%	7	54%	32	21%	0	0%	5	38%

Eurovision 2014 - Who Votes for Who? (And Who Doesn't)

Bosnia & Herzegovina

	Bosnia awarded points to:				Frequency		Bosnia received points from:				Frequency	
	Total	% of max	12's	% of max	Times	% of max	Total	% of max	12's	% of max	Times	% of max
Albania	43	36%	0	0%	9	90%	70	49%	1	8%	8	67%
Andorra	0	0%	0	0%	0	0%	6	5%	0	0%	2	20%
Armenia	13	14%	0	0%	3	38%	17	16%	0	0%	4	44%
Austria	42	27%	1	8%	6	46%	96	50%	3	19%	11	69%
Azerbaijan	28	39%	0	0%	5	83%	9	13%	0	0%	3	50%
Belarus	8	7%	0	0%	3	30%	21	12%	0	0%	5	33%
Belgium	22	11%	0	0%	3	19%	26	10%	0	0%	7	32%
Bosnia & Herzegovina	-	-	-	-	-	-	0	-	0	-	0	-
Bulgaria	13	15%	0	0%	4	57%	31	22%	0	0%	6	50%
Croatia	145	67%	5	28%	16	89%	178	71%	5	24%	20	95%
Cyprus	0	0%	0	0%	0	0%	7	3%	0	0%	2	10%
Czech Republic	0	0%	0	0%	0	0%	13	27%	0	0%	3	75%
Denmark	12	6%	0	0%	4	24%	76	35%	1	6%	12	67%
Estonia	19	9%	0	0%	5	28%	2	1%	0	0%	2	9%
Finland	20	11%	0	0%	5	33%	53	23%	1	5%	8	42%
France	48	22%	1	6%	9	50%	65	25%	0	0%	12	55%
FYR Macedonia	114	68%	1	7%	13	93%	116	60%	3	19%	16	100%
Georgia	5	7%	0	0%	2	33%	2	3%	0	0%	1	17%
Germany	33	16%	0	0%	6	35%	79	27%	0	0%	13	54%
Greece	63	26%	0	0%	12	60%	20	8%	0	0%	4	19%
Hungary	8	7%	0	0%	4	44%	1	1%	0	0%	1	11%
Iceland	9	4%	0	0%	3	16%	18	7%	0	0%	5	24%
Ireland	54	25%	1	6%	9	50%	24	9%	0	0%	7	32%
Israel	34	17%	0	0%	7	41%	6	3%	0	0%	3	15%
Italy	12	25%	0	0%	2	50%	11	18%	0	0%	3	60%
Latvia	5	3%	0	0%	1	8%	4	2%	0	0%	2	13%
Lithuania	4	3%	0	0%	2	15%	7	4%	0	0%	2	13%
Luxembourg	0	0%	0	0%	0	0%	0	0%	0	0%	0	0%
Malta	61	27%	2	11%	11	58%	30	11%	0	0%	8	35%
Moldova	10	7%	0	0%	2	17%	20	14%	0	0%	4	33%
Monaco	0	0%	0	0%	0	0%	28	47%	2	40%	3	60%
Montenegro	27	75%	1	33%	3	100%	59	82%	3	50%	6	100%
Morocco	0	-	0	-	0	-	0	-	0	-	0	-
Netherlands	20	11%	0	0%	5	33%	83	33%	0	0%	13	62%
Norway	44	19%	0	0%	10	53%	92	37%	3	14%	11	52%
Poland	25	15%	0	0%	4	29%	20	9%	0	0%	4	22%
Portugal	12	6%	0	0%	5	28%	20	8%	0	0%	4	18%
Romania	24	13%	0	0%	6	38%	24	12%	1	6%	3	18%
Russia	31	14%	0	0%	8	44%	15	7%	0	0%	3	17%
San Marino	0	0%	0	0%	0	0%	0	0%	0	0%	0	0%
Serbia	90	94%	5	63%	8	100%	78	81%	5	63%	8	100%
Serbia & Montenegro	34	94%	2	67%	3	100%	41	68%	2	40%	5	100%
Slovakia	11	18%	0	0%	2	40%	41	38%	1	11%	6	67%
Slovenia	110	54%	2	12%	17	100%	151	57%	5	23%	17	77%
Spain	30	14%	0	0%	5	28%	12	5%	0	0%	4	18%
Sweden	74	29%	2	10%	14	67%	115	42%	0	0%	16	70%
Switzerland	8	6%	0	0%	3	25%	84	41%	3	18%	12	71%
Turkey	133	55%	4	20%	16	80%	175	69%	6	29%	19	90%
Ukraine	35	21%	0	0%	8	57%	22	13%	0	0%	3	21%
United Kingdom	33	15%	0	0%	7	39%	16	6%	0	0%	5	23%
Yugoslavia	0	-	0	-	0	-	0	-	0	-	0	-

Eurovision 2014 - Who Votes for Who? (And Who Doesn't)

Bulgaria

	Bulgaria awarded points to:				Frequency		Bulgaria received points from:				Frequency	
	Total	% of max	12's	% of max	Times	% of max	Total	% of max	12's	% of max	Times	% of max
Albania	6	6%	0	0%	2	22%	17	24%	0	0%	4	67%
Andorra	0	0%	0	0%	0	0%	0	0%	0	0%	0	0%
Armenia	70	58%	0	0%	9	90%	15	21%	0	0%	3	50%
Austria	15	31%	0	0%	2	50%	14	29%	0	0%	3	75%
Azerbaijan	64	67%	3	38%	7	88%	4	17%	0	0%	1	50%
Belarus	21	18%	1	10%	5	50%	2	2%	0	0%	1	13%
Belgium	6	7%	0	0%	1	14%	7	10%	0	0%	3	50%
Bosnia & Herzegovina	31	22%	0	0%	6	50%	13	15%	0	0%	4	57%
Bulgaria	-	-	-	-	-	-	0	-	0	-	0	-
Croatia	19	18%	0	0%	4	44%	13	15%	0	0%	3	43%
Cyprus	36	38%	0	0%	6	75%	63	75%	1	14%	7	100%
Czech Republic	0	0%	0	0%	0	0%	19	40%	0	0%	3	75%
Denmark	25	16%	1	8%	5	38%	4	5%	0	0%	1	14%
Estonia	7	6%	0	0%	2	22%	1	1%	0	0%	1	17%
Finland	15	13%	0	0%	3	30%	7	10%	0	0%	2	33%
France	0	0%	0	0%	0	0%	30	31%	0	0%	7	88%
FYR Macedonia	84	58%	1	8%	11	92%	51	47%	0	0%	9	100%
Georgia	27	23%	0	0%	6	60%	7	10%	0	0%	2	33%
Germany	15	14%	1	11%	2	22%	14	15%	0	0%	4	50%
Greece	91	76%	4	40%	10	100%	34	57%	1	20%	5	100%
Hungary	28	26%	0	0%	5	56%	22	37%	0	0%	4	80%
Iceland	11	8%	0	0%	2	17%	5	6%	0	0%	1	14%
Ireland	11	9%	0	0%	3	30%	1	1%	0	0%	1	17%
Israel	15	11%	0	0%	5	45%	6	6%	0	0%	1	13%
Italy	0	0%	0	0%	0	0%	10	83%	0	0%	1	100%
Latvia	1	1%	0	0%	1	11%	3	4%	0	0%	2	29%
Lithuania	17	13%	0	0%	5	45%	1	1%	0	0%	1	14%
Luxembourg	0	-	0	-	0	-	0	-	0	-	0	-
Malta	12	10%	0	0%	3	30%	14	15%	0	0%	4	50%
Moldova	22	17%	0	0%	6	55%	20	33%	0	0%	4	80%
Monaco	0	0%	0	0%	0	0%	0	0%	0	0%	0	0%
Montenegro	0	0%	0	0%	0	0%	10	28%	0	0%	2	67%
Morocco	0	-	0	-	0	-	0	-	0	-	0	-
Netherlands	5	6%	0	0%	1	14%	2	2%	0	0%	1	14%
Norway	16	12%	0	0%	7	64%	7	8%	0	0%	2	29%
Poland	0	0%	0	0%	0	0%	0	0%	0	0%	0	0%
Portugal	7	6%	0	0%	2	22%	19	23%	0	0%	5	71%
Romania	35	21%	0	0%	9	64%	7	7%	0	0%	3	38%
Russia	48	40%	1	10%	7	70%	4	8%	0	0%	1	25%
San Marino	0	0%	0	0%	0	0%	8	67%	0	0%	1	100%
Serbia	42	50%	2	29%	5	71%	18	38%	0	0%	4	100%
Serbia & Montenegro	4	33%	0	0%	1	100%	1	4%	0	0%	1	50%
Slovakia	0	0%	0	0%	0	0%	0	0%	0	0%	0	0%
Slovenia	13	14%	0	0%	2	25%	14	17%	0	0%	3	43%
Spain	5	5%	0	0%	2	22%	37	62%	0	0%	5	100%
Sweden	26	15%	0	0%	4	29%	1	1%	0	0%	1	11%
Switzerland	4	4%	0	0%	2	22%	0	0%	0	0%	0	0%
Turkey	96	62%	2	15%	13	100%	49	51%	1	13%	8	100%
Ukraine	67	40%	1	7%	11	79%	12	13%	0	0%	4	50%
United Kingdom	19	18%	1	11%	2	22%	22	23%	0	0%	4	50%
Yugoslavia	0	-	0	-	0	-	0	-	0	-	0	-

Eurovision 2014 - Who Votes for Who? (And Who Doesn't)

Croatia

	Croatia awarded points to:			Frequency		Croatia received points from:			Frequency	
	Total	% of max	12's	% of max	Times	% of max	Total	% of max	12's	% of max	Times	% of max
Albania	75	52%	0	0%	12	100%	26	20%	0	0%	6	55%
Andorra	2	4%	0	0%	1	25%	0	0%	0	0%	0	0%
Armenia	0	0%	0	0%	0	0%	9	13%	0	0%	2	33%
Austria	14	8%	0	0%	4	29%	68	35%	1	6%	10	63%
Azerbaijan	53	49%	0	0%	6	67%	5	8%	0	0%	2	40%
Belarus	2	2%	0	0%	1	10%	21	16%	0	0%	5	45%
Belgium	9	5%	0	0%	3	19%	19	9%	0	0%	8	44%
Bosnia & Herzegovina	178	71%	5	24%	20	95%	145	67%	5	28%	16	89%
Bulgaria	13	15%	0	0%	3	43%	19	18%	0	0%	4	44%
Croatia	-	-	-	-	-	-	0	-	0	-	0	-
Cyprus	52	21%	1	5%	10	48%	41	16%	0	0%	9	41%
Czech Republic	2	8%	0	0%	1	50%	3	6%	0	0%	1	25%
Denmark	51	19%	2	9%	8	36%	5	2%	0	0%	2	11%
Estonia	23	10%	0	0%	5	25%	17	7%	0	0%	5	25%
Finland	23	12%	0	0%	3	19%	14	7%	0	0%	6	38%
France	26	10%	0	0%	5	24%	25	10%	0	0%	4	19%
FYR Macedonia	109	65%	2	14%	14	100%	97	62%	2	15%	13	100%
Georgia	16	13%	0	0%	3	30%	9	13%	0	0%	2	33%
Germany	32	13%	0	0%	9	45%	58	25%	0	0%	14	74%
Greece	66	25%	0	0%	12	55%	31	14%	0	0%	8	42%
Hungary	42	25%	0	0%	8	57%	26	18%	0	0%	4	33%
Iceland	14	6%	0	0%	4	19%	30	13%	0	0%	8	42%
Ireland	52	20%	1	5%	13	59%	26	10%	0	0%	7	32%
Israel	14	7%	0	0%	3	18%	27	13%	0	0%	9	53%
Italy	20	33%	0	0%	3	60%	0	0%	0	0%	0	0%
Latvia	31	20%	0	0%	7	54%	24	14%	0	0%	5	36%
Lithuania	20	9%	0	0%	6	32%	25	12%	0	0%	6	33%
Luxembourg	0	0%	0	0%	0	0%	0	0%	0	0%	0	0%
Malta	96	36%	3	14%	15	68%	74	28%	2	9%	8	36%
Moldova	15	10%	0	0%	6	50%	11	11%	0	0%	3	38%
Monaco	0	0%	0	0%	0	0%	16	27%	0	0%	3	60%
Montenegro	11	46%	0	0%	2	100%	22	46%	0	0%	4	100%
Morocco	0	-	0	-	0	-	0	-	0	-	0	-
Netherlands	21	9%	0	0%	5	26%	23	9%	0	0%	7	33%
Norway	47	17%	1	4%	8	35%	30	11%	0	0%	9	41%
Poland	10	6%	0	0%	2	13%	23	11%	0	0%	6	35%
Portugal	24	11%	0	0%	4	21%	40	18%	0	0%	13	68%
Romania	14	7%	0	0%	4	24%	20	12%	0	0%	4	29%
Russia	75	31%	2	10%	12	60%	25	12%	0	0%	7	41%
San Marino	1	8%	0	0%	1	100%	4	17%	0	0%	1	50%
Serbia	106	88%	5	50%	10	100%	70	73%	3	38%	8	100%
Serbia & Montenegro	36	100%	3	100%	3	100%	42	70%	1	20%	5	100%
Slovakia	8	13%	0	0%	1	20%	32	44%	2	33%	4	67%
Slovenia	118	52%	2	11%	18	95%	164	65%	6	29%	19	90%
Spain	36	14%	0	0%	7	33%	33	13%	2	10%	6	29%
Sweden	33	11%	0	0%	9	38%	20	7%	0	0%	6	26%
Switzerland	16	8%	0	0%	6	38%	74	34%	0	0%	16	89%
Turkey	56	19%	1	4%	11	46%	55	21%	0	0%	9	41%
Ukraine	72	33%	1	6%	12	67%	46	27%	0	0%	9	64%
United Kingdom	69	27%	2	10%	11	52%	15	5%	0	0%	11	46%
Yugoslavia	0	-	0	-	0	-	0	-	0	-	0	-

Eurovision 2014 - Who Votes for Who? (And Who Doesn't)

Cyprus

	Cyprus awarded points to:				Frequency		Cyprus received points from:				Frequency	
	Total	% of max	12's	% of max	Times	% of max	Total	% of max	12's	% of max	Times	% of max
Albania	15	10%	0	0%	3	25%	33	28%	0	0%	6	60%
Andorra	0	0%	0	0%	0	0%	6	10%	0	0%	2	40%
Armenia	60	63%	2	25%	7	88%	17	35%	0	0%	3	75%
Austria	47	15%	0	0%	10	37%	22	7%	0	0%	6	21%
Azerbaijan	62	65%	0	0%	7	88%	6	10%	0	0%	3	60%
Belarus	34	28%	0	0%	6	60%	15	13%	0	0%	3	30%
Belgium	41	12%	0	0%	9	31%	52	14%	0	0%	12	40%
Bosnia & Herzegovina	7	3%	0	0%	2	10%	0	0%	0	0%	0	0%
Bulgaria	63	75%	1	14%	7	100%	36	38%	0	0%	6	75%
Croatia	41	16%	0	0%	9	41%	52	21%	1	5%	10	48%
Cyprus	-	-	-	-	-	-	0	-	0	-	0	-
Czech Republic	0	0%	0	0%	0	0%	0	0%	0	0%	0	0%
Denmark	81	20%	0	0%	17	50%	74	21%	0	0%	14	47%
Estonia	22	10%	0	0%	5	26%	26	12%	0	0%	6	33%
Finland	36	11%	0	0%	8	30%	63	20%	0	0%	10	38%
France	73	20%	0	0%	16	53%	39	11%	1	3%	9	31%
FYR Macedonia	5	3%	0	0%	2	14%	4	3%	0	0%	1	8%
Georgia	39	41%	1	13%	6	75%	2	3%	0	0%	1	20%
Germany	52	14%	2	7%	8	27%	42	13%	0	0%	11	39%
Greece	328	94%	24	83%	29	100%	275	88%	18	69%	25	96%
Hungary	22	13%	0	0%	4	29%	18	15%	1	10%	3	30%
Iceland	38	12%	1	4%	8	31%	76	23%	3	11%	10	36%
Ireland	100	25%	1	3%	15	45%	63	16%	0	0%	14	44%
Israel	59	18%	0	0%	14	50%	65	20%	0	0%	15	56%
Italy	55	35%	1	8%	10	77%	37	22%	0	0%	8	57%
Latvia	13	8%	0	0%	5	36%	19	11%	0	0%	5	36%
Lithuania	26	14%	0	0%	7	44%	19	11%	0	0%	6	43%
Luxembourg	32	22%	0	0%	5	42%	8	6%	0	0%	2	17%
Malta	50	20%	0	0%	11	52%	70	29%	3	15%	13	65%
Moldova	33	20%	0	0%	7	50%	9	8%	0	0%	2	22%
Monaco	4	11%	0	0%	1	33%	24	50%	1	25%	3	75%
Montenegro	0	0%	0	0%	0	0%	6	13%	0	0%	1	25%
Morocco	0	-	0	-	0	-	0	-	0	-	0	-
Netherlands	35	11%	0	0%	9	33%	58	17%	1	4%	7	25%
Norway	80	22%	0	0%	14	45%	54	16%	1	3%	11	38%
Poland	10	6%	0	0%	4	31%	10	6%	0	0%	3	23%
Portugal	25	8%	1	4%	6	22%	37	11%	0	0%	10	37%
Romania	86	38%	1	5%	14	74%	37	21%	0	0%	9	60%
Russia	100	44%	1	5%	16	84%	28	16%	0	0%	7	47%
San Marino	0	0%	0	0%	0	0%	0	0%	0	0%	0	0%
Serbia	32	33%	0	0%	7	88%	14	19%	0	0%	4	67%
Serbia & Montenegro	30	83%	0	0%	3	100%	6	13%	0	0%	3	75%
Slovakia	0	0%	0	0%	0	0%	3	4%	0	0%	3	43%
Slovenia	18	8%	0	0%	4	22%	31	14%	0	0%	7	37%
Spain	112	30%	1	3%	17	55%	56	16%	0	0%	10	33%
Sweden	97	24%	2	6%	17	50%	53	14%	1	3%	11	34%
Switzerland	66	20%	0	0%	15	56%	42	13%	0	0%	14	50%
Turkey	12	3%	0	0%	2	6%	10	3%	0	0%	3	10%
Ukraine	98	45%	1	6%	14	78%	24	15%	0	0%	5	38%
United Kingdom	75	20%	0	0%	20	65%	117	31%	2	6%	19	61%
Yugoslavia	59	49%	1	10%	9	90%	52	43%	1	10%	8	80%

Eurovision 2014 - Who Votes for Who? (And Who Doesn't)

Czech Republic

	Czech Rep awarded points to:				Frequency		Czech Rep received points from:				Frequency	
	Total	% of max	12's	% of max	Times	% of max	Total	% of max	12's	% of max	Times	% of max
Albania	1	2%	0	0%	1	25%	0	0%	0	0%	0	0%
Andorra	7	29%	0	0%	1	50%	0	0%	0	0%	0	0%
Armenia	46	96%	3	75%	4	100%	0	0%	0	0%	0	0%
Austria	0	0%	0	0%	0	0%	0	0%	0	0%	0	0%
Azerbaijan	20	83%	0	0%	2	100%	0	-	0	-	0	-
Belarus	8	17%	0	0%	3	75%	0	0%	0	0%	0	0%
Belgium	0	0%	0	0%	0	0%	0	0%	0	0%	0	0%
Bosnia & Herzegovina	13	27%	0	0%	3	75%	0	0%	0	0%	0	0%
Bulgaria	19	40%	0	0%	3	75%	0	0%	0	0%	0	0%
Croatia	3	6%	0	0%	1	25%	2	8%	0	0%	1	50%
Cyprus	0	0%	0	0%	0	0%	0	0%	0	0%	0	0%
Czech Republic	-	-	-	-	-	-	0	-	0	-	0	-
Denmark	12	25%	0	0%	2	50%	0	0%	0	0%	0	0%
Estonia	0	0%	0	0%	0	0%	1	8%	0	0%	1	100%
Finland	0	0%	0	0%	0	0%	0	0%	0	0%	0	0%
France	0	0%	0	0%	0	0%	0	0%	0	0%	0	0%
FYR Macedonia	18	38%	0	0%	4	100%	5	14%	0	0%	1	33%
Georgia	13	27%	0	0%	3	75%	0	0%	0	0%	0	0%
Germany	0	0%	0	0%	0	0%	0	0%	0	0%	0	0%
Greece	8	22%	0	0%	2	67%	0	0%	0	0%	0	0%
Hungary	8	22%	0	0%	1	33%	0	0%	0	0%	0	0%
Iceland	12	20%	0	0%	2	40%	0	0%	0	0%	0	0%
Ireland	0	0%	0	0%	0	0%	0	0%	0	0%	0	0%
Israel	10	21%	0	0%	3	75%	0	0%	0	0%	0	0%
Italy	0	-	0	-	0	-	0	-	0	-	0	-
Latvia	11	23%	0	0%	3	75%	0	0%	0	0%	0	0%
Lithuania	0	0%	0	0%	0	0%	0	0%	0	0%	0	0%
Luxembourg	0	-	0	-	0	-	0	-	0	-	0	-
Malta	13	27%	0	0%	2	50%	1	3%	0	0%	1	33%
Moldova	0	0%	0	0%	0	0%	0	0%	0	0%	0	0%
Monaco	0	-	0	-	0	-	0	-	0	-	0	-
Montenegro	0	0%	0	0%	0	0%	0	0%	0	0%	0	0%
Morocco	0	-	0	-	0	-	0	-	0	-	0	-
Netherlands	0	0%	0	0%	0	0%	0	0%	0	0%	0	0%
Norway	3	8%	0	0%	1	33%	0	0%	0	0%	0	0%
Poland	0	0%	0	0%	0	0%	0	0%	0	0%	0	0%
Portugal	16	27%	0	0%	3	60%	0	0%	0	0%	0	0%
Romania	0	0%	0	0%	0	0%	0	0%	0	0%	0	0%
Russia	21	58%	0	0%	3	100%	0	0%	0	0%	0	0%
San Marino	0	-	0	-	0	-	0	-	0	-	0	-
Serbia	26	72%	1	33%	3	100%	0	0%	0	0%	0	0%
Serbia & Montenegro	0	-	0	-	0	-	0	-	0	-	0	-
Slovakia	0	-	0	-	0	-	0	-	0	-	0	-
Slovenia	4	17%	0	0%	1	50%	0	0%	0	0%	0	0%
Spain	0	0%	0	0%	0	0%	0	0%	0	0%	0	0%
Sweden	6	10%	0	0%	1	20%	0	0%	0	0%	0	0%
Switzerland	0	0%	0	0%	0	0%	0	0%	0	0%	0	0%
Turkey	7	10%	0	0%	3	50%	1	3%	0	0%	1	33%
Ukraine	37	77%	2	50%	4	100%	0	0%	0	0%	0	0%
United Kingdom	6	17%	0	0%	1	33%	0	0%	0	0%	0	0%
Yugoslavia	0	-	0	-	0	-	0	-	0	-	0	-

Eurovision 2014 - Who Votes for Who? (And Who Doesn't)

Denmark

	Denmark awarded points to:				Frequency		Denmark received points from:				Frequency	
	Total	% of max	12's	% of max	Times	% of max	Total	% of max	12's	% of max	Times	% of max
Albania	31	20%	0	0%	6	46%	12	7%	0	0%	4	27%
Andorra	0	0%	0	0%	0	0%	18	21%	0	0%	4	57%
Armenia	7	6%	0	0%	2	20%	15	14%	0	0%	4	44%
Austria	73	21%	0	0%	15	52%	101	26%	2	6%	16	48%
Azerbaijan	23	19%	0	0%	4	40%	17	14%	0	0%	4	40%
Belarus	1	1%	0	0%	1	9%	18	10%	0	0%	5	33%
Belgium	57	16%	0	0%	9	30%	103	25%	1	3%	16	46%
Bosnia & Herzegovina	76	35%	1	6%	12	67%	12	6%	0	0%	4	24%
Bulgaria	4	5%	0	0%	1	14%	25	16%	1	8%	5	38%
Croatia	5	2%	0	0%	2	11%	51	19%	2	9%	8	36%
Cyprus	74	21%	0	0%	14	47%	81	20%	0	0%	17	50%
Czech Republic	0	0%	0	0%	0	0%	12	25%	0	0%	2	50%
Denmark	-	-	-	-	-	-	0	-	0	-	0	-
Estonia	52	25%	0	0%	12	71%	100	42%	2	10%	15	75%
Finland	62	18%	1	3%	10	34%	91	24%	1	3%	15	47%
France	66	17%	1	3%	14	44%	110	26%	2	6%	18	51%
FYR Macedonia	3	2%	0	0%	2	15%	17	9%	1	6%	3	19%
Georgia	0	0%	0	0%	0	0%	13	12%	0	0%	3	33%
Germany	159	40%	4	12%	25	76%	124	30%	2	6%	18	51%
Greece	42	11%	0	0%	13	42%	44	11%	1	3%	9	28%
Hungary	36	21%	1	7%	7	50%	47	28%	1	7%	9	64%
Iceland	157	48%	3	11%	22	81%	229	55%	9	26%	25	71%
Ireland	168	41%	4	12%	25	74%	184	40%	8	21%	25	66%
Israel	58	16%	0	0%	14	47%	129	32%	2	6%	20	59%
Italy	17	8%	0	0%	5	28%	47	19%	1	5%	9	43%
Latvia	46	26%	0	0%	9	60%	91	40%	2	11%	13	68%
Lithuania	20	10%	0	0%	6	38%	52	23%	0	0%	13	68%
Luxembourg	32	17%	0	0%	9	56%	26	14%	0	0%	6	38%
Malta	70	31%	1	5%	12	63%	68	26%	0	0%	15	68%
Moldova	19	11%	0	0%	3	20%	20	11%	1	7%	4	27%
Monaco	14	23%	0	0%	2	40%	33	46%	0	0%	4	67%
Montenegro	5	8%	0	0%	1	20%	18	19%	0	0%	2	25%
Morocco	0	0%	0	0%	0	0%	2	17%	0	0%	1	100%
Netherlands	98	27%	1	3%	15	50%	144	35%	5	15%	21	62%
Norway	152	38%	6	18%	22	67%	220	52%	7	20%	28	80%
Poland	11	8%	0	0%	4	33%	54	32%	1	7%	9	64%
Portugal	16	5%	0	0%	6	21%	74	19%	0	0%	19	59%
Romania	44	22%	0	0%	9	53%	54	26%	1	6%	11	65%
Russia	54	23%	2	10%	9	45%	44	19%	1	5%	7	37%
San Marino	0	0%	0	0%	0	0%	11	15%	0	0%	4	67%
Serbia	12	13%	0	0%	2	25%	24	20%	1	10%	4	40%
Serbia & Montenegro	17	47%	0	0%	2	67%	0	0%	0	0%	0	0%
Slovakia	0	0%	0	0%	0	0%	16	22%	0	0%	3	50%
Slovenia	15	7%	0	0%	2	12%	100	38%	2	9%	12	55%
Spain	30	8%	1	3%	8	24%	92	21%	0	0%	17	47%
Sweden	310	70%	12	32%	33	89%	241	53%	8	21%	33	87%
Switzerland	88	25%	1	3%	17	59%	60	15%	0	0%	15	44%
Turkey	90	23%	0	0%	14	42%	32	8%	0	0%	12	36%
Ukraine	51	22%	0	0%	11	58%	26	13%	0	0%	6	35%
United Kingdom	135	34%	2	6%	23	70%	144	32%	4	11%	22	59%
Yugoslavia	52	39%	2	18%	6	55%	7	5%	0	0%	2	18%

Eurovision 2014 - Who Votes for Who? (And Who Doesn't)

Estonia

	Estonia awarded points to:				Frequency		Estonia received points from:				Frequency	
	Total	% of max	12's	% of max	Times	% of max	Total	% of max	12's	% of max	Times	% of max
Albania	2	1%	0	0%	2	17%	2	2%	0	0%	2	18%
Andorra	8	13%	0	0%	2	40%	0	0%	0	0%	0	0%
Armenia	12	10%	0	0%	3	30%	5	6%	0	0%	1	14%
Austria	28	17%	0	0%	6	43%	28	15%	0	0%	7	44%
Azerbaijan	33	28%	0	0%	5	50%	12	14%	0	0%	3	43%
Belarus	24	17%	0	0%	5	42%	19	13%	0	0%	6	50%
Belgium	51	24%	0	0%	11	61%	19	8%	0	0%	6	30%
Bosnia & Herzegovina	2	1%	0	0%	2	9%	19	9%	0	0%	5	28%
Bulgaria	1	1%	0	0%	1	17%	7	6%	0	0%	2	22%
Croatia	17	7%	0	0%	5	25%	23	10%	0	0%	5	25%
Cyprus	26	12%	0	0%	6	33%	22	10%	0	0%	5	26%
Czech Republic	1	8%	0	0%	1	100%	0	0%	0	0%	0	0%
Denmark	100	42%	2	10%	15	75%	52	25%	0	0%	12	71%
Estonia	-	-	-	-	-	-	0	-	0	-	0	-
Finland	116	57%	3	18%	14	82%	125	69%	5	33%	14	93%
France	43	18%	1	5%	8	40%	57	23%	0	0%	9	43%
FYR Macedonia	0	0%	0	0%	0	0%	6	4%	0	0%	1	7%
Georgia	35	42%	0	0%	6	86%	9	15%	0	0%	2	40%
Germany	42	18%	1	5%	10	53%	44	18%	0	0%	8	40%
Greece	28	11%	0	0%	7	32%	24	11%	1	6%	5	28%
Hungary	47	30%	0	0%	9	69%	22	17%	0	0%	5	45%
Iceland	71	30%	1	5%	13	65%	66	32%	1	6%	11	65%
Ireland	71	28%	1	5%	13	62%	92	37%	0	0%	16	76%
Israel	20	10%	0	0%	5	31%	25	13%	0	0%	6	38%
Italy	13	22%	0	0%	2	40%	17	24%	1	17%	2	33%
Latvia	115	64%	2	13%	15	100%	151	79%	7	44%	15	94%
Lithuania	46	24%	0	0%	9	56%	89	49%	1	7%	13	87%
Luxembourg	0	-	0	-	0	-	0	-	0	-	0	-
Malta	54	23%	0	0%	12	60%	36	16%	1	5%	5	26%
Moldova	16	8%	0	0%	4	25%	33	21%	0	0%	8	62%
Monaco	2	6%	0	0%	1	33%	5	14%	0	0%	1	33%
Montenegro	0	0%	0	0%	0	0%	0	0%	0	0%	0	0%
Morocco	0	-	0	-	0	-	0	-	0	-	0	-
Netherlands	60	24%	2	10%	8	38%	53	20%	1	5%	9	41%
Norway	109	41%	2	9%	16	73%	53	23%	0	0%	9	47%
Poland	19	9%	1	6%	3	18%	50	28%	1	7%	7	47%
Portugal	8	4%	0	0%	3	19%	36	18%	1	6%	6	35%
Romania	12	5%	0	0%	4	21%	9	5%	0	0%	3	20%
Russia	182	69%	4	18%	22	100%	36	17%	0	0%	7	39%
San Marino	3	8%	0	0%	1	33%	0	0%	0	0%	0	0%
Serbia	2	2%	0	0%	2	20%	4	4%	0	0%	1	11%
Serbia & Montenegro	1	3%	0	0%	1	33%	4	11%	0	0%	1	33%
Slovakia	6	7%	0	0%	1	14%	50	42%	1	10%	6	60%
Slovenia	16	7%	0	0%	4	21%	41	17%	1	5%	8	40%
Spain	13	5%	0	0%	4	20%	29	12%	0	0%	8	38%
Sweden	161	58%	6	26%	20	87%	106	42%	3	14%	15	71%
Switzerland	26	17%	2	15%	3	23%	0	0%	0	0%	0	0%
Turkey	14	6%	0	0%	3	16%	22	11%	1	6%	3	19%
Ukraine	98	43%	2	11%	15	79%	29	17%	0	0%	8	57%
United Kingdom	44	18%	0	0%	9	45%	65	29%	1	5%	11	58%
Yugoslavia	0	-	0	-	0	-	0	-	0	-	0	-

Eurovision 2014 - Who Votes for Who? (And Who Doesn't)

Finland

	Finland awarded points to:				Frequency		Finland received points from:				Frequency	
	Total	% of max	12's	% of max	Times	% of max	Total	% of max	12's	% of max	Times	% of max
Albania	24	15%	0	0%	5	38%	9	5%	0	0%	3	21%
Andorra	5	7%	0	0%	1	17%	49	45%	1	11%	7	78%
Armenia	10	7%	0	0%	4	33%	6	4%	0	0%	1	8%
Austria	48	13%	2	7%	10	33%	35	10%	0	0%	7	23%
Azerbaijan	20	17%	0	0%	5	50%	6	6%	0	0%	2	22%
Belarus	11	8%	0	0%	2	18%	23	15%	0	0%	4	31%
Belgium	80	19%	2	6%	14	40%	41	9%	0	0%	9	24%
Bosnia & Herzegovina	53	23%	1	5%	8	42%	20	11%	0	0%	5	33%
Bulgaria	7	10%	0	0%	2	33%	15	13%	0	0%	3	30%
Croatia	14	7%	0	0%	6	38%	23	12%	0	0%	3	19%
Cyprus	63	20%	0	0%	10	38%	36	11%	0	0%	8	30%
Czech Republic	0	0%	0	0%	0	0%	0	0%	0	0%	0	0%
Denmark	91	24%	1	3%	15	47%	62	18%	1	3%	10	34%
Estonia	125	69%	5	33%	14	93%	116	57%	3	18%	14	82%
Finland	-	-	-	-	-	-	0	-	0	-	0	-
France	108	26%	3	9%	20	57%	50	12%	0	0%	11	32%
FYR Macedonia	2	1%	0	0%	2	13%	27	13%	0	0%	6	35%
Georgia	12	11%	0	0%	3	33%	1	1%	0	0%	1	13%
Germany	80	19%	2	6%	15	43%	82	18%	2	5%	18	47%
Greece	85	19%	0	0%	19	51%	82	19%	1	3%	13	36%
Hungary	88	52%	3	21%	10	71%	29	20%	1	8%	4	33%
Iceland	122	38%	3	11%	16	59%	137	31%	5	14%	18	49%
Ireland	117	29%	1	3%	23	68%	87	20%	1	3%	13	36%
Israel	152	37%	2	6%	24	71%	72	17%	0	0%	16	46%
Italy	118	49%	4	20%	16	80%	28	11%	0	0%	4	19%
Latvia	30	21%	1	8%	5	42%	40	22%	0	0%	7	47%
Lithuania	18	12%	0	0%	3	23%	38	23%	0	0%	6	43%
Luxembourg	55	24%	1	5%	9	47%	21	9%	0	0%	6	32%
Malta	41	14%	0	0%	10	42%	30	10%	0	0%	7	29%
Moldova	11	7%	0	0%	3	23%	19	13%	0	0%	3	25%
Monaco	17	18%	0	0%	4	50%	27	25%	0	0%	4	44%
Montenegro	0	0%	0	0%	0	0%	5	5%	0	0%	2	25%
Morocco	0	0%	0	0%	0	0%	0	0%	0	0%	0	0%
Netherlands	63	18%	0	0%	11	38%	46	12%	0	0%	11	34%
Norway	153	33%	6	15%	20	51%	147	33%	4	11%	22	59%
Poland	8	5%	0	0%	1	7%	58	32%	2	13%	9	60%
Portugal	37	9%	0	0%	13	39%	34	9%	0	0%	8	24%
Romania	21	8%	0	0%	5	24%	22	10%	0	0%	6	32%
Russia	84	35%	2	10%	14	70%	35	18%	1	6%	5	31%
San Marino	1	2%	0	0%	1	20%	17	18%	0	0%	4	50%
Serbia	31	32%	1	13%	5	63%	3	4%	0	0%	1	14%
Serbia & Montenegro	20	56%	0	0%	2	67%	15	31%	0	0%	2	50%
Slovakia	2	4%	0	0%	1	25%	2	3%	0	0%	1	17%
Slovenia	14	8%	0	0%	4	29%	23	12%	0	0%	4	25%
Spain	80	19%	0	0%	14	39%	68	15%	0	0%	14	36%
Sweden	189	44%	3	8%	26	72%	145	36%	3	9%	20	59%
Switzerland	138	32%	2	6%	22	61%	80	17%	1	3%	15	38%
Turkey	55	14%	0	0%	13	39%	40	11%	0	0%	9	30%
Ukraine	31	20%	0	0%	7	54%	13	11%	0	0%	2	20%
United Kingdom	104	24%	0	0%	17	47%	67	15%	2	5%	10	27%
Yugoslavia	35	22%	1	8%	7	54%	22	14%	0	0%	5	38%

Eurovision 2014 - Who Votes for Who? (And Who Doesn't)

France

	France awarded points to:				Frequency		France received points from:				Frequency	
	Total	% of max	12's	% of max	Times	% of max	Total	% of max	12's	% of max	Times	% of max
Albania	14	9%	0	0%	5	38%	10	8%	0	0%	5	45%
Andorra	0	0%	0	0%	0	0%	26	36%	0	0%	5	83%
Armenia	99	83%	5	50%	10	100%	27	28%	0	0%	7	88%
Austria	51	14%	1	3%	10	32%	111	28%	4	12%	15	45%
Azerbaijan	25	21%	0	0%	5	50%	0	0%	0	0%	0	0%
Belarus	1	1%	0	0%	1	9%	7	5%	0	0%	1	9%
Belgium	124	30%	4	11%	19	54%	107	24%	1	3%	17	46%
Bosnia & Herzegovina	65	25%	0	0%	12	55%	48	22%	1	6%	9	50%
Bulgaria	30	31%	0	0%	7	88%	0	0%	0	0%	0	0%
Croatia	25	10%	0	0%	4	19%	26	10%	0	0%	5	24%
Cyprus	39	11%	1	3%	9	31%	73	20%	0	0%	16	53%
Czech Republic	0	0%	0	0%	0	0%	0	0%	0	0%	0	0%
Denmark	110	26%	2	6%	18	51%	66	17%	1	3%	14	44%
Estonia	57	23%	0	0%	9	43%	43	18%	1	5%	8	40%
Finland	50	12%	0	0%	11	32%	108	26%	3	9%	20	57%
France	-	-	-	-	-	-	0	-	0	-	0	-
FYR Macedonia	0	0%	0	0%	0	0%	4	2%	0	0%	3	21%
Georgia	4	4%	0	0%	1	11%	2	2%	0	0%	1	14%
Germany	108	24%	1	3%	17	45%	115	25%	3	8%	17	45%
Greece	104	23%	0	0%	20	54%	126	31%	2	6%	20	59%
Hungary	30	16%	0	0%	9	56%	12	8%	0	0%	2	17%
Iceland	40	11%	0	0%	10	32%	86	19%	1	3%	13	35%
Ireland	100	23%	0	0%	20	54%	123	27%	1	3%	19	50%
Israel	177	46%	2	6%	27	84%	115	28%	2	6%	19	56%
Italy	96	38%	1	5%	16	76%	98	39%	1	5%	13	62%
Latvia	11	6%	0	0%	2	13%	21	12%	0	0%	6	40%
Lithuania	10	6%	0	0%	3	20%	39	22%	0	0%	7	47%
Luxembourg	56	26%	2	11%	9	50%	89	41%	3	17%	12	67%
Malta	42	13%	0	0%	10	38%	13	4%	0	0%	4	16%
Moldova	25	15%	0	0%	6	43%	2	2%	0	0%	1	10%
Monaco	27	32%	0	0%	5	71%	53	55%	2	25%	7	88%
Montenegro	7	19%	0	0%	1	33%	1	1%	0	0%	1	17%
Morocco	0	0%	0	0%	0	0%	1	8%	0	0%	1	100%
Netherlands	100	25%	2	6%	15	44%	119	28%	4	11%	19	54%
Norway	50	10%	0	0%	11	27%	134	29%	3	8%	25	66%
Poland	46	23%	1	6%	10	59%	39	19%	1	6%	6	35%
Portugal	198	47%	5	14%	25	71%	113	26%	3	8%	21	58%
Romania	55	24%	0	0%	11	58%	10	5%	0	0%	2	13%
Russia	28	11%	0	0%	8	38%	48	22%	1	6%	7	39%
San Marino	5	14%	0	0%	1	33%	11	18%	0	0%	2	40%
Serbia	76	70%	3	33%	8	89%	7	8%	0	0%	2	29%
Serbia & Montenegro	16	67%	0	0%	2	100%	0	0%	0	0%	0	0%
Slovakia	1	1%	0	0%	1	14%	0	0%	0	0%	0	0%
Slovenia	19	9%	0	0%	6	33%	33	14%	0	0%	7	35%
Spain	129	28%	2	5%	21	54%	93	20%	0	0%	16	41%
Sweden	122	24%	3	7%	26	62%	104	23%	0	0%	22	58%
Switzerland	85	22%	1	3%	13	41%	145	35%	4	11%	21	60%
Turkey	190	44%	8	22%	21	58%	38	10%	0	0%	12	36%
Ukraine	13	6%	0	0%	5	28%	8	6%	0	0%	2	17%
United Kingdom	146	31%	5	13%	21	54%	83	18%	0	0%	18	46%
Yugoslavia	21	15%	0	0%	7	58%	56	39%	3	25%	7	58%

Eurovision 2014 - Who Votes for Who? (And Who Doesn't)

FYR Macedonia

	Macedonia awarded points to:			Frequency			Macedonia received points from:			Frequency	
	Total	% of max	12's	% of max	Times	% of max	Total	% of max	12's	% of max	Times	% of max
Albania	135	94%	9	75%	12	100%	103	72%	4	33%	12	100%
Andorra	1	2%	0	0%	1	20%	0	0%	0	0%	0	0%
Armenia	16	13%	0	0%	5	50%	15	21%	0	0%	2	33%
Austria	11	10%	0	0%	3	33%	12	9%	0	0%	4	36%
Azerbaijan	24	25%	0	0%	5	63%	0	0%	0	0%	0	0%
Belarus	44	26%	0	0%	9	64%	12	7%	0	0%	4	27%
Belgium	12	8%	0	0%	3	25%	0	0%	0	0%	0	0%
Bosnia & Herzegovina	116	60%	3	19%	16	100%	114	68%	1	7%	13	93%
Bulgaria	51	47%	0	0%	9	100%	84	58%	1	8%	11	92%
Croatia	97	62%	2	15%	13	100%	109	65%	2	14%	14	100%
Cyprus	4	3%	0	0%	1	8%	5	3%	0	0%	2	14%
Czech Republic	5	14%	0	0%	1	33%	18	38%	0	0%	4	100%
Denmark	17	9%	1	6%	3	19%	3	2%	0	0%	2	15%
Estonia	6	4%	0	0%	1	7%	0	0%	0	0%	0	0%
Finland	27	13%	0	0%	6	35%	2	1%	0	0%	2	13%
France	4	2%	0	0%	3	21%	0	0%	0	0%	0	0%
FYR Macedonia	-	-	-	-	-	-	0	-	0	-	0	-
Georgia	11	9%	0	0%	3	30%	4	5%	0	0%	3	43%
Germany	8	5%	0	0%	1	7%	5	2%	0	0%	2	11%
Greece	50	25%	0	0%	10	59%	4	2%	0	0%	1	7%
Hungary	15	11%	0	0%	3	27%	0	0%	0	0%	0	0%
Iceland	7	4%	0	0%	3	19%	1	1%	0	0%	1	7%
Ireland	14	9%	0	0%	2	15%	0	0%	0	0%	0	0%
Israel	23	13%	0	0%	6	40%	5	3%	0	0%	2	13%
Italy	18	38%	0	0%	4	100%	3	8%	0	0%	2	67%
Latvia	16	10%	0	0%	4	31%	0	0%	0	0%	0	0%
Lithuania	7	4%	0	0%	2	15%	0	0%	0	0%	0	0%
Luxembourg	0	-	0	-	0	-	0	-	0	-	0	-
Malta	61	28%	2	11%	10	56%	16	7%	0	0%	6	33%
Moldova	35	24%	0	0%	6	50%	5	5%	0	0%	2	22%
Monaco	0	0%	0	0%	0	0%	4	6%	0	0%	2	33%
Montenegro	23	64%	1	33%	3	100%	38	79%	0	0%	4	100%
Morocco	0	-	0	-	0	-	0	-	0	-	0	-
Netherlands	15	11%	0	0%	4	36%	4	3%	0	0%	2	15%
Norway	29	15%	0	0%	5	31%	0	0%	0	0%	0	0%
Poland	10	9%	0	0%	3	33%	0	0%	0	0%	0	0%
Portugal	6	4%	0	0%	2	17%	0	0%	0	0%	0	0%
Romania	62	27%	2	11%	11	58%	38	20%	1	6%	8	50%
Russia	47	26%	0	0%	8	53%	8	6%	0	0%	2	18%
San Marino	5	21%	0	0%	1	50%	2	8%	0	0%	1	50%
Serbia	81	84%	3	38%	8	100%	60	83%	2	33%	6	100%
Serbia & Montenegro	30	83%	0	0%	3	100%	59	82%	2	33%	6	100%
Slovakia	3	6%	0	0%	1	25%	6	10%	0	0%	3	60%
Slovenia	49	34%	0	0%	10	83%	95	57%	1	7%	13	93%
Spain	5	3%	0	0%	2	14%	0	0%	0	0%	0	0%
Sweden	41	19%	0	0%	10	56%	10	5%	0	0%	4	25%
Switzerland	5	3%	0	0%	3	21%	66	34%	0	0%	12	75%
Turkey	125	65%	2	13%	16	100%	72	40%	0	0%	12	80%
Ukraine	54	28%	0	0%	11	69%	24	17%	0	0%	5	42%
United Kingdom	25	15%	0	0%	4	29%	0	0%	0	0%	0	0%
Yugoslavia	0	-	0	-	0	-	0	-	0	-	0	-

Eurovision 2014 - Who Votes for Who? (And Who Doesn't)

Georgia

	Georgia awarded points to:				Frequency		Georgia received points from:				Frequency	
	Total	% of max	12's	% of max	Times	% of max	Total	% of max	12's	% of max	Times	% of max
Albania	3	4%	0	0%	1	14%	0	0%	0	0%	0	0%
Andorra	0	0%	0	0%	0	0%	0	0%	0	0%	0	0%
Armenia	84	88%	3	38%	8	100%	87	81%	3	33%	9	100%
Austria	23	48%	0	0%	3	75%	0	0%	0	0%	0	0%
Azerbaijan	88	81%	4	44%	9	100%	60	71%	0	0%	7	100%
Belarus	53	55%	2	25%	7	88%	60	56%	1	11%	8	89%
Belgium	12	33%	1	33%	1	33%	11	15%	0	0%	3	50%
Bosnia & Herzegovina	2	3%	0	0%	1	17%	5	7%	0	0%	2	33%
Bulgaria	7	10%	0	0%	2	33%	27	23%	0	0%	6	60%
Croatia	9	13%	0	0%	2	33%	16	13%	0	0%	3	30%
Cyprus	2	3%	0	0%	1	20%	39	41%	1	13%	6	75%
Czech Republic	0	0%	0	0%	0	0%	13	27%	0	0%	3	75%
Denmark	13	12%	0	0%	3	33%	0	0%	0	0%	0	0%
Estonia	9	15%	0	0%	2	40%	35	42%	0	0%	6	86%
Finland	1	1%	0	0%	1	13%	12	11%	0	0%	3	33%
France	2	2%	0	0%	1	14%	4	4%	0	0%	1	11%
FYR Macedonia	4	5%	0	0%	3	43%	11	9%	0	0%	3	30%
Georgia	-	-	-	-	-	-	0	-	0	-	0	-
Germany	7	10%	0	0%	2	33%	1	1%	0	0%	1	13%
Greece	31	26%	0	0%	8	80%	48	44%	0	0%	9	100%
Hungary	19	18%	0	0%	4	44%	14	15%	0	0%	5	63%
Iceland	1	1%	0	0%	1	10%	8	7%	0	0%	3	33%
Ireland	0	0%	0	0%	0	0%	13	14%	0	0%	3	38%
Israel	17	24%	0	0%	4	67%	36	33%	0	0%	7	78%
Italy	13	27%	0	0%	3	75%	0	0%	0	0%	0	0%
Latvia	20	33%	0	0%	4	80%	35	36%	0	0%	5	63%
Lithuania	65	60%	2	22%	8	89%	109	83%	6	55%	11	100%
Luxembourg	0	-	0	-	0	-	0	-	0	-	0	-
Malta	27	25%	0	0%	5	56%	29	22%	0	0%	5	45%
Moldova	16	22%	0	0%	4	67%	30	42%	0	0%	6	100%
Monaco	0	-	0	-	0	-	0	-	0	-	0	-
Montenegro	0	0%	0	0%	0	0%	2	4%	0	0%	1	25%
Morocco	0	-	0	-	0	-	0	-	0	-	0	-
Netherlands	1	2%	0	0%	1	20%	12	13%	0	0%	3	38%
Norway	28	23%	0	0%	5	50%	1	1%	0	0%	1	9%
Poland	10	17%	0	0%	2	40%	24	29%	0	0%	5	71%
Portugal	9	13%	0	0%	2	33%	9	11%	0	0%	3	43%
Romania	10	8%	0	0%	2	20%	2	2%	0	0%	1	11%
Russia	43	45%	0	0%	7	88%	50	60%	0	0%	7	100%
San Marino	2	6%	0	0%	2	67%	10	17%	0	0%	3	60%
Serbia	24	25%	0	0%	3	38%	11	10%	0	0%	2	22%
Serbia & Montenegro	0	-	0	-	0	-	0	-	0	-	0	-
Slovakia	0	0%	0	0%	0	0%	0	0%	0	0%	0	0%
Slovenia	4	5%	0	0%	1	14%	10	9%	0	0%	3	33%
Spain	2	2%	0	0%	1	14%	8	8%	0	0%	3	38%
Sweden	23	21%	1	11%	4	44%	9	8%	0	0%	3	33%
Switzerland	3	3%	0	0%	2	25%	2	2%	0	0%	2	18%
Turkey	37	34%	0	0%	8	89%	65	60%	0	0%	9	100%
Ukraine	82	68%	1	10%	10	100%	81	75%	2	22%	9	100%
United Kingdom	6	7%	0	0%	2	29%	1	1%	0	0%	1	9%
Yugoslavia	0	-	0	-	0	-	0	-	0	-	0	-

Eurovision 2014 - Who Votes for Who? (And Who Doesn't)

Germany

	Germany awarded points to:				Frequency		Germany received points from:				Frequency	
	Total	% of max	12's	% of max	Times	% of max	Total	% of max	12's	% of max	Times	% of max
Albania	29	22%	0	0%	7	64%	35	27%	0	0%	8	73%
Andorra	0	0%	0	0%	0	0%	5	7%	0	0%	1	17%
Armenia	57	43%	0	0%	9	82%	6	6%	0	0%	1	13%
Austria	77	20%	2	6%	14	44%	111	28%	1	3%	20	61%
Azerbaijan	13	12%	0	0%	3	33%	1	1%	0	0%	1	14%
Belarus	0	0%	0	0%	0	0%	8	6%	0	0%	1	9%
Belgium	77	18%	2	6%	14	39%	134	30%	0	0%	21	57%
Bosnia & Herzegovina	79	27%	0	0%	13	54%	33	16%	0	0%	6	35%
Bulgaria	14	15%	0	0%	4	50%	15	14%	1	11%	2	22%
Croatia	58	25%	0	0%	14	74%	32	13%	0	0%	9	45%
Cyprus	42	13%	0	0%	11	39%	52	14%	2	7%	8	27%
Czech Republic	0	0%	0	0%	0	0%	0	0%	0	0%	0	0%
Denmark	124	30%	2	6%	18	51%	159	40%	4	12%	25	76%
Estonia	44	18%	0	0%	8	40%	42	18%	1	5%	10	53%
Finland	82	18%	2	5%	18	47%	80	19%	2	6%	15	43%
France	115	25%	3	8%	17	45%	108	24%	1	3%	17	45%
FYR Macedonia	5	2%	0	0%	2	11%	8	5%	0	0%	1	7%
Georgia	1	1%	0	0%	1	13%	7	10%	0	0%	2	33%
Germany	-	-	-	-	-	-	0	-	0	-	0	-
Greece	148	32%	3	8%	22	58%	34	8%	0	0%	9	26%
Hungary	42	27%	1	8%	5	38%	23	16%	1	8%	3	25%
Iceland	73	21%	1	3%	13	45%	61	14%	1	3%	11	30%
Ireland	138	30%	2	5%	24	63%	127	28%	1	3%	24	63%
Israel	125	28%	2	5%	23	62%	71	17%	2	6%	10	29%
Italy	59	23%	1	5%	13	62%	73	29%	1	5%	13	62%
Latvia	26	15%	1	7%	3	21%	41	23%	1	7%	7	47%
Lithuania	2	1%	0	0%	2	13%	20	11%	0	0%	5	33%
Luxembourg	42	18%	1	5%	7	37%	67	29%	2	11%	11	58%
Malta	72	22%	0	0%	16	59%	28	10%	0	0%	9	38%
Moldova	10	6%	0	0%	3	23%	2	2%	0	0%	1	10%
Monaco	23	21%	0	0%	4	44%	32	33%	1	13%	5	63%
Montenegro	2	4%	0	0%	1	25%	0	0%	0	0%	0	0%
Morocco	0	0%	0	0%	0	0%	10	83%	0	0%	1	100%
Netherlands	102	25%	1	3%	18	53%	125	30%	3	9%	23	66%
Norway	109	22%	2	5%	20	48%	84	18%	1	3%	17	45%
Poland	99	52%	2	13%	14	88%	53	28%	1	6%	8	50%
Portugal	82	19%	1	3%	15	42%	157	36%	4	11%	22	61%
Romania	42	16%	0	0%	9	41%	29	15%	1	6%	7	44%
Russia	68	27%	0	0%	13	62%	34	16%	0	0%	6	33%
San Marino	0	0%	0	0%	0	0%	0	0%	0	0%	0	0%
Serbia	55	57%	0	0%	7	88%	8	10%	0	0%	1	14%
Serbia & Montenegro	25	69%	1	33%	3	100%	0	0%	0	0%	0	0%
Slovakia	0	0%	0	0%	0	0%	27	38%	1	17%	3	50%
Slovenia	17	7%	0	0%	5	26%	30	13%	0	0%	6	32%
Spain	78	17%	2	5%	12	31%	190	41%	8	21%	27	69%
Sweden	151	31%	6	15%	24	59%	118	26%	2	5%	18	47%
Switzerland	106	26%	2	6%	17	50%	125	30%	4	11%	21	60%
Turkey	208	48%	8	22%	22	61%	86	22%	3	9%	13	39%
Ukraine	17	9%	0	0%	3	19%	10	7%	0	0%	2	17%
United Kingdom	146	31%	2	5%	23	59%	144	31%	1	3%	26	67%
Yugoslavia	16	10%	0	0%	6	46%	33	21%	1	8%	6	46%

Eurovision 2014 - Who Votes for Who? (And Who Doesn't)

Greece

	Greece awarded points to:				Frequency		Greece received points from:				Frequency	
	Total	% of max	12's	% of max	Times	% of max	Total	% of max	12's	% of max	Times	% of max
Albania	132	79%	2	14%	14	100%	171	84%	8	47%	17	100%
Andorra	4	7%	0	0%	1	20%	34	35%	0	0%	6	75%
Armenia	79	60%	2	18%	9	82%	87	66%	0	0%	11	100%
Austria	88	25%	3	10%	16	55%	53	14%	0	0%	14	45%
Azerbaijan	67	51%	2	18%	10	91%	70	49%	1	8%	10	83%
Belarus	35	29%	0	0%	6	60%	55	33%	1	7%	10	71%
Belgium	59	16%	1	3%	9	29%	134	31%	2	6%	22	61%
Bosnia & Herzegovina	20	8%	0	0%	4	19%	63	26%	0	0%	12	60%
Bulgaria	34	57%	1	20%	5	100%	91	76%	4	40%	10	100%
Croatia	31	14%	0	0%	8	42%	66	25%	0	0%	12	55%
Cyprus	275	88%	18	69%	25	96%	328	94%	24	83%	29	100%
Czech Republic	0	0%	0	0%	0	0%	8	22%	0	0%	2	67%
Denmark	44	11%	1	3%	9	28%	42	11%	0	0%	13	42%
Estonia	24	11%	1	6%	5	28%	28	11%	0	0%	7	32%
Finland	82	19%	1	3%	13	36%	85	19%	0	0%	19	51%
France	126	31%	2	6%	20	59%	104	23%	0	0%	20	54%
FYR Macedonia	4	2%	0	0%	1	7%	50	25%	0	0%	10	59%
Georgia	48	44%	0	0%	9	100%	31	26%	0	0%	8	80%
Germany	34	8%	0	0%	9	26%	148	32%	3	8%	22	58%
Greece	-	-	-	-	-	-	0	-	0	-	0	-
Hungary	20	10%	0	0%	5	31%	63	33%	1	6%	10	63%
Iceland	48	14%	0	0%	10	36%	57	16%	0	0%	12	41%
Ireland	104	25%	2	6%	13	37%	60	14%	0	0%	14	38%
Israel	52	14%	0	0%	13	41%	122	29%	1	3%	20	57%
Italy	63	28%	0	0%	12	63%	57	23%	1	5%	13	62%
Latvia	12	7%	0	0%	3	21%	25	11%	0	0%	6	32%
Lithuania	11	6%	0	0%	4	27%	35	16%	0	0%	7	39%
Luxembourg	24	13%	1	6%	5	31%	29	16%	0	0%	6	40%
Malta	72	25%	0	0%	15	63%	126	39%	2	7%	20	74%
Moldova	49	29%	0	0%	10	71%	49	29%	0	0%	11	79%
Monaco	16	19%	1	14%	2	29%	31	32%	0	0%	4	50%
Montenegro	0	0%	0	0%	0	0%	33	34%	0	0%	5	63%
Morocco	0	0%	0	0%	0	0%	0	0%	0	0%	0	0%
Netherlands	64	18%	1	3%	13	45%	113	29%	0	0%	21	64%
Norway	81	17%	2	5%	15	38%	87	19%	0	0%	20	51%
Poland	39	18%	0	0%	11	61%	52	21%	0	0%	13	62%
Portugal	45	12%	0	0%	14	44%	99	24%	1	3%	15	44%
Romania	101	42%	1	5%	14	70%	159	66%	5	25%	18	90%
Russia	89	34%	0	0%	16	73%	87	33%	0	0%	17	77%
San Marino	8	13%	0	0%	4	80%	69	64%	4	44%	7	78%
Serbia	34	31%	0	0%	6	67%	62	52%	0	0%	9	90%
Serbia & Montenegro	24	67%	0	0%	3	100%	35	73%	1	25%	4	100%
Slovakia	7	12%	0	0%	2	40%	23	21%	0	0%	4	44%
Slovenia	17	8%	0	0%	4	22%	55	20%	0	0%	11	48%
Spain	136	32%	0	0%	22	63%	170	35%	3	7%	25	61%
Sweden	46	11%	0	0%	9	26%	68	17%	2	6%	15	44%
Switzerland	73	19%	1	3%	15	47%	103	24%	1	3%	20	56%
Turkey	36	10%	0	0%	6	19%	81	23%	2	7%	14	47%
Ukraine	60	33%	0	0%	11	73%	35	21%	0	0%	6	43%
United Kingdom	84	20%	2	6%	14	40%	141	32%	5	14%	19	51%
Yugoslavia	30	25%	0	0%	7	70%	17	16%	0	0%	4	44%

Eurovision 2014 - Who Votes for Who? (And Who Doesn't)

Hungary

	Hungary awarded points to:				Frequency		Hungary received points from:				Frequency	
	Total	% of max	12's	% of max	Times	% of max	Total	% of max	12's	% of max	Times	% of max
Albania	24	18%	0	0%	4	36%	48	29%	0	0%	7	50%
Andorra	0	0%	0	0%	0	0%	17	35%	0	0%	4	100%
Armenia	18	19%	0	0%	3	38%	1	1%	0	0%	1	13%
Austria	21	22%	0	0%	4	50%	38	26%	0	0%	7	58%
Azerbaijan	73	61%	4	40%	8	80%	28	26%	0	0%	5	56%
Belarus	6	8%	0	0%	2	33%	12	11%	0	0%	4	44%
Belgium	7	7%	0	0%	2	25%	45	29%	1	8%	7	54%
Bosnia & Herzegovina	1	1%	0	0%	1	11%	8	7%	0	0%	4	44%
Bulgaria	22	37%	0	0%	4	80%	28	26%	0	0%	5	56%
Croatia	26	18%	0	0%	4	33%	42	25%	0	0%	8	57%
Cyprus	18	15%	1	10%	3	30%	22	13%	0	0%	4	29%
Czech Republic	0	0%	0	0%	0	0%	8	22%	0	0%	1	33%
Denmark	47	28%	1	7%	9	64%	36	21%	1	7%	7	50%
Estonia	22	17%	0	0%	5	45%	47	30%	0	0%	9	69%
Finland	29	20%	1	8%	4	33%	88	52%	3	21%	10	71%
France	12	8%	0	0%	2	17%	30	16%	0	0%	9	56%
FYR Macedonia	0	0%	0	0%	0	0%	15	11%	0	0%	3	27%
Georgia	14	15%	0	0%	5	63%	19	18%	0	0%	4	44%
Germany	23	16%	1	8%	3	25%	42	27%	1	8%	5	38%
Greece	63	33%	1	6%	10	63%	20	10%	0	0%	5	31%
Hungary	-	-	-	-	-	-	0	-	0	-	0	-
Iceland	85	44%	2	13%	11	69%	74	39%	1	6%	10	63%
Ireland	40	30%	0	0%	5	45%	29	17%	1	7%	5	36%
Israel	26	24%	0	0%	5	56%	26	18%	0	0%	4	33%
Italy	12	20%	0	0%	3	60%	3	4%	0	0%	1	17%
Latvia	7	6%	0	0%	3	30%	27	17%	0	0%	7	54%
Lithuania	5	4%	0	0%	1	10%	16	11%	0	0%	3	25%
Luxembourg	0	-	0	-	0	-	0	-	0	-	0	-
Malta	30	19%	0	0%	5	38%	10	6%	0	0%	5	33%
Moldova	24	18%	0	0%	6	55%	14	11%	0	0%	4	36%
Monaco	0	0%	0	0%	0	0%	0	0%	0	0%	0	0%
Montenegro	4	8%	0	0%	1	25%	12	14%	1	14%	1	14%
Morocco	0	-	0	-	0	-	0	-	0	-	0	-
Netherlands	46	43%	3	33%	5	56%	43	28%	0	0%	6	46%
Norway	52	29%	1	7%	9	60%	43	24%	0	0%	8	53%
Poland	32	24%	0	0%	8	73%	49	34%	2	17%	6	50%
Portugal	13	11%	0	0%	2	20%	38	24%	0	0%	7	54%
Romania	34	22%	1	8%	5	38%	77	53%	0	0%	11	92%
Russia	47	28%	0	0%	8	57%	32	18%	0	0%	7	47%
San Marino	13	22%	0	0%	3	60%	25	26%	0	0%	4	50%
Serbia	37	44%	2	29%	5	71%	50	52%	2	25%	7	88%
Serbia & Montenegro	2	17%	0	0%	1	100%	14	58%	0	0%	2	100%
Slovakia	0	0%	0	0%	0	0%	10	17%	0	0%	2	40%
Slovenia	23	21%	0	0%	4	44%	15	10%	0	0%	3	25%
Spain	13	9%	0	0%	3	25%	41	20%	0	0%	9	53%
Sweden	52	31%	1	7%	8	57%	56	33%	1	7%	8	57%
Switzerland	29	20%	0	0%	6	50%	41	23%	1	7%	8	53%
Turkey	30	23%	0	0%	7	64%	25	19%	0	0%	6	55%
Ukraine	45	34%	0	0%	8	73%	31	23%	0	0%	6	55%
United Kingdom	33	23%	1	8%	5	42%	27	16%	0	0%	6	43%
Yugoslavia	0	-	0	-	0	-	0	-	0	-	0	-

Eurovision 2014 - Who Votes for Who? (And Who Doesn't)

Iceland

	Iceland awarded points to:				Frequency		Iceland received points from:				Frequency	
	Total	% of max	12's	% of max	Times	% of max	Total	% of max	12's	% of max	Times	% of max
Albania	29	16%	0	0%	6	40%	19	9%	0	0%	3	18%
Andorra	6	10%	0	0%	1	20%	24	29%	0	0%	3	43%
Armenia	17	12%	0	0%	6	50%	20	14%	1	8%	4	33%
Austria	46	12%	0	0%	7	23%	39	14%	0	0%	10	43%
Azerbaijan	36	30%	0	0%	6	60%	0	0%	0	0%	0	0%
Belarus	10	8%	0	0%	4	36%	26	15%	1	7%	6	43%
Belgium	44	10%	1	3%	6	17%	65	19%	1	3%	10	34%
Bosnia & Herzegovina	18	7%	0	0%	5	24%	9	4%	0	0%	3	16%
Bulgaria	5	6%	0	0%	1	14%	11	8%	0	0%	2	17%
Croatia	30	13%	0	0%	8	42%	14	6%	0	0%	4	19%
Cyprus	76	23%	3	11%	10	36%	38	12%	1	4%	8	31%
Czech Republic	0	0%	0	0%	0	0%	12	20%	0	0%	2	40%
Denmark	229	55%	9	26%	25	71%	157	48%	3	11%	22	81%
Estonia	66	32%	1	6%	11	65%	71	30%	1	5%	13	65%
Finland	137	31%	5	14%	18	49%	122	38%	3	11%	16	59%
France	86	19%	1	3%	13	35%	40	11%	0	0%	10	32%
FYR Macedonia	1	1%	0	0%	1	7%	7	4%	0	0%	3	19%
Georgia	8	7%	0	0%	3	33%	1	1%	0	0%	1	10%
Germany	61	14%	1	3%	11	30%	73	21%	1	3%	13	45%
Greece	57	16%	0	0%	12	41%	48	14%	0	0%	10	36%
Hungary	74	39%	1	6%	10	63%	85	44%	2	13%	11	69%
Iceland	-	-	-	-	-	-	0	-	0	-	0	-
Ireland	66	21%	1	4%	13	50%	55	16%	1	4%	9	32%
Israel	35	9%	0	0%	8	24%	63	19%	1	4%	10	37%
Italy	20	8%	0	0%	5	24%	29	19%	0	0%	7	54%
Latvia	40	22%	0	0%	8	53%	51	22%	0	0%	11	58%
Lithuania	21	13%	0	0%	4	29%	41	21%	0	0%	7	44%
Luxembourg	9	4%	0	0%	3	16%	13	14%	0	0%	2	25%
Malta	40	13%	0	0%	9	35%	73	23%	3	11%	8	30%
Moldova	16	10%	0	0%	2	15%	25	16%	0	0%	4	31%
Monaco	0	0%	0	0%	0	0%	6	17%	0	0%	2	67%
Montenegro	0	0%	0	0%	0	0%	17	16%	0	0%	3	33%
Morocco	0	0%	0	0%	0	0%	0	-	0	-	0	-
Netherlands	56	15%	2	6%	10	31%	51	16%	0	0%	9	35%
Norway	164	34%	6	15%	22	55%	155	45%	3	10%	23	79%
Poland	26	14%	0	0%	7	44%	27	13%	0	0%	7	39%
Portugal	67	15%	0	0%	10	27%	95	27%	2	7%	15	52%
Romania	41	19%	0	0%	8	44%	20	10%	0	0%	2	12%
Russia	54	20%	0	0%	14	64%	22	9%	0	0%	8	38%
San Marino	4	7%	0	0%	1	20%	18	17%	0	0%	3	33%
Serbia	30	31%	0	0%	6	75%	11	9%	0	0%	2	20%
Serbia & Montenegro	7	19%	0	0%	1	33%	2	6%	0	0%	1	33%
Slovakia	5	14%	0	0%	1	33%	24	29%	0	0%	5	71%
Slovenia	11	7%	0	0%	4	29%	25	12%	0	0%	7	39%
Spain	26	6%	0	0%	9	24%	93	24%	1	3%	17	53%
Sweden	185	39%	3	8%	27	68%	166	46%	3	10%	23	77%
Switzerland	69	16%	1	3%	13	37%	70	21%	0	0%	12	43%
Turkey	31	7%	0	0%	8	22%	34	10%	0	0%	7	26%
Ukraine	60	31%	1	6%	9	56%	8	5%	0	0%	3	21%
United Kingdom	37	8%	1	3%	8	21%	99	28%	2	7%	16	53%
Yugoslavia	48	31%	1	8%	6	46%	4	5%	0	0%	1	14%

Eurovision 2014 - Who Votes for Who? (And Who Doesn't)

Ireland

	Ireland awarded points to:			Frequency		Ireland received points from:			Frequency	
	Total	% of max	12's	% of max	Times	% of max	Total	% of max	12's	% of max	Times	% of max
Albania	8	6%	0	0%	3	27%	13	10%	0	0%	3	27%
Andorra	5	8%	0	0%	2	40%	6	8%	0	0%	2	33%
Armenia	2	2%	0	0%	1	10%	4	4%	0	0%	2	25%
Austria	91	22%	3	9%	15	44%	158	39%	3	9%	21	62%
Azerbaijan	27	23%	0	0%	6	60%	9	9%	0	0%	3	38%
Belarus	10	8%	0	0%	3	27%	5	3%	0	0%	2	17%
Belgium	97	22%	2	6%	14	39%	153	34%	4	11%	26	68%
Bosnia & Herzegovina	24	9%	0	0%	7	32%	54	25%	1	6%	9	50%
Bulgaria	1	1%	0	0%	1	17%	11	9%	0	0%	3	30%
Croatia	26	10%	0	0%	7	32%	52	20%	1	5%	13	59%
Cyprus	63	16%	0	0%	14	44%	100	25%	1	3%	15	45%
Czech Republic	0	0%	0	0%	0	0%	0	0%	0	0%	0	0%
Denmark	184	40%	8	21%	25	66%	168	41%	4	12%	25	74%
Estonia	92	37%	0	0%	16	76%	71	28%	1	5%	13	62%
Finland	87	20%	1	3%	13	36%	117	29%	1	3%	23	68%
France	123	27%	1	3%	19	50%	100	23%	0	0%	20	54%
FYR Macedonia	0	0%	0	0%	0	0%	14	9%	0	0%	2	15%
Georgia	13	14%	0	0%	3	38%	0	0%	0	0%	0	0%
Germany	127	28%	1	3%	24	63%	138	30%	2	5%	24	63%
Greece	60	14%	0	0%	14	38%	104	25%	2	6%	13	37%
Hungary	29	17%	1	7%	5	36%	40	30%	0	0%	5	45%
Iceland	55	16%	1	4%	9	32%	66	21%	1	4%	13	50%
Ireland	-	-	-	-	-	-	0	-	0	-	0	-
Israel	87	20%	1	3%	14	39%	82	19%	1	3%	17	47%
Italy	80	33%	3	15%	11	55%	93	34%	5	22%	12	52%
Latvia	79	47%	3	21%	10	71%	50	28%	0	0%	9	60%
Lithuania	105	51%	5	29%	14	82%	51	27%	1	6%	7	44%
Luxembourg	65	30%	1	6%	10	56%	96	44%	0	0%	14	78%
Malta	91	32%	2	8%	15	63%	89	32%	2	9%	14	61%
Moldova	29	16%	0	0%	8	53%	4	3%	0	0%	3	23%
Monaco	17	18%	0	0%	3	38%	31	29%	0	0%	4	44%
Montenegro	0	0%	0	0%	0	0%	2	3%	0	0%	2	33%
Morocco	0	0%	0	0%	0	0%	0	0%	0	0%	0	0%
Netherlands	123	28%	2	6%	22	61%	144	32%	3	8%	23	61%
Norway	158	32%	2	5%	25	61%	171	36%	5	13%	29	73%
Poland	58	28%	1	6%	7	41%	44	20%	1	6%	10	56%
Portugal	19	5%	0	0%	4	12%	117	29%	0	0%	22	65%
Romania	77	29%	1	5%	15	68%	37	17%	0	0%	8	44%
Russia	72	27%	0	0%	11	50%	39	17%	1	5%	6	32%
San Marino	0	0%	0	0%	0	0%	12	20%	1	20%	1	20%
Serbia	12	13%	0	0%	2	25%	3	4%	0	0%	1	14%
Serbia & Montenegro	9	25%	0	0%	2	67%	1	2%	0	0%	1	25%
Slovakia	6	10%	0	0%	2	40%	29	30%	1	13%	5	63%
Slovenia	31	12%	1	5%	6	27%	41	15%	1	4%	12	52%
Spain	47	10%	0	0%	10	26%	131	28%	2	5%	21	54%
Sweden	159	33%	5	13%	23	58%	216	47%	6	16%	28	74%
Switzerland	92	23%	2	6%	17	50%	171	41%	7	20%	25	71%
Turkey	24	6%	0	0%	7	20%	124	32%	2	6%	22	69%
Ukraine	53	25%	0	0%	11	61%	8	5%	0	0%	4	29%
United Kingdom	191	41%	1	3%	32	82%	258	55%	8	21%	32	82%
Yugoslavia	34	24%	1	8%	8	67%	38	26%	0	0%	10	83%

Eurovision 2014 - Who Votes for Who? (And Who Doesn't)

Israel

	Israel awarded points to:				Frequency		Israel received points from:				Frequency	
	Total	% of max	12's	% of max	Times	% of max	Total	% of max	12's	% of max	Times	% of max
Albania	9	7%	0	0%	2	18%	26	22%	0	0%	6	60%
Andorra	6	8%	0	0%	2	33%	45	42%	1	11%	6	67%
Armenia	97	67%	2	17%	11	92%	34	31%	0	0%	5	56%
Austria	59	17%	1	3%	9	31%	79	23%	1	3%	16	55%
Azerbaijan	62	52%	2	20%	9	90%	35	42%	0	0%	5	71%
Belarus	39	30%	2	18%	7	64%	47	36%	1	9%	8	73%
Belgium	48	12%	0	0%	11	33%	117	28%	1	3%	22	63%
Bosnia & Herzegovina	6	3%	0	0%	3	15%	34	17%	0	0%	7	41%
Bulgaria	6	6%	0	0%	1	13%	15	11%	0	0%	5	45%
Croatia	27	13%	0	0%	9	53%	14	7%	0	0%	3	18%
Cyprus	65	20%	0	0%	15	56%	59	18%	0	0%	14	50%
Czech Republic	0	0%	0	0%	0	0%	10	21%	0	0%	3	75%
Denmark	129	32%	2	6%	20	59%	58	16%	0	0%	14	47%
Estonia	25	13%	0	0%	6	38%	20	10%	0	0%	5	31%
Finland	72	17%	0	0%	16	46%	152	37%	2	6%	24	71%
France	115	28%	2	6%	19	56%	177	46%	2	6%	27	84%
FYR Macedonia	5	3%	0	0%	2	13%	23	13%	0	0%	6	40%
Georgia	36	33%	0	0%	7	78%	17	24%	0	0%	4	67%
Germany	71	17%	2	6%	10	29%	125	28%	2	5%	23	62%
Greece	122	29%	1	3%	20	57%	52	14%	0	0%	13	41%
Hungary	26	18%	0	0%	4	33%	26	24%	0	0%	5	56%
Iceland	63	19%	1	4%	10	37%	35	9%	0	0%	8	24%
Ireland	82	19%	1	3%	17	47%	87	20%	1	3%	14	39%
Israel	-	-	-	-	-	-	0	-	0	-	0	-
Italy	28	13%	0	0%	8	44%	33	16%	0	0%	8	47%
Latvia	40	24%	1	7%	6	43%	6	3%	0	0%	3	20%
Lithuania	11	7%	0	0%	4	29%	12	8%	0	0%	4	31%
Luxembourg	35	17%	1	6%	6	35%	76	37%	1	6%	11	65%
Malta	51	18%	0	0%	10	43%	62	23%	1	5%	9	41%
Moldova	38	24%	0	0%	9	69%	18	15%	0	0%	4	40%
Monaco	19	20%	0	0%	4	50%	43	40%	2	22%	6	67%
Montenegro	1	2%	0	0%	1	20%	19	26%	0	0%	4	67%
Morocco	0	-	0	-	0	-	0	-	0	-	0	-
Netherlands	121	34%	2	7%	22	73%	138	37%	3	10%	23	74%
Norway	93	21%	2	5%	17	46%	109	26%	1	3%	20	57%
Poland	6	4%	0	0%	2	15%	33	20%	0	0%	5	36%
Portugal	20	6%	0	0%	5	17%	126	34%	2	6%	17	55%
Romania	157	57%	3	13%	20	87%	62	27%	0	0%	13	68%
Russia	140	61%	5	26%	17	89%	50	30%	0	0%	8	57%
San Marino	4	8%	0	0%	1	25%	12	25%	0	0%	2	50%
Serbia	10	14%	0	0%	2	33%	7	15%	0	0%	1	25%
Serbia & Montenegro	15	42%	0	0%	2	67%	6	13%	0	0%	2	50%
Slovakia	0	0%	0	0%	0	0%	20	42%	0	0%	3	75%
Slovenia	29	13%	0	0%	9	50%	29	13%	0	0%	6	32%
Spain	108	26%	3	9%	19	54%	113	27%	1	3%	19	54%
Sweden	150	34%	4	11%	21	57%	90	22%	1	3%	18	53%
Switzerland	71	18%	1	3%	16	50%	130	33%	1	3%	23	70%
Turkey	42	11%	0	0%	11	33%	63	17%	2	6%	11	35%
Ukraine	96	50%	1	6%	14	88%	27	20%	0	0%	6	55%
United Kingdom	138	33%	4	11%	22	63%	117	28%	2	6%	22	63%
Yugoslavia	52	36%	3	25%	6	50%	54	38%	2	17%	8	67%

Eurovision 2014 - Who Votes for Who? (And Who Doesn't)

Italy

	Italy awarded points to:			Frequency		Italy received points from:			Frequency	
	Total	% of max	12's	% of max	Times	% of max	Total	% of max	12's	% of max	Times	% of max
Albania	24	100%	2	100%	2	100%	41	85%	2	50%	4	100%
Andorra	0	-	0	-	0	-	0	-	0	-	0	-
Armenia	0	0%	0	0%	0	0%	7	19%	0	0%	2	67%
Austria	69	26%	4	18%	10	45%	57	24%	0	0%	11	55%
Azerbaijan	0	0%	0	0%	0	0%	1	2%	0	0%	1	25%
Belarus	7	12%	0	0%	1	20%	3	6%	0	0%	1	25%
Belgium	28	12%	0	0%	6	30%	44	18%	0	0%	8	40%
Bosnia & Herzegovina	11	18%	0	0%	3	60%	12	25%	0	0%	2	50%
Bulgaria	10	83%	0	0%	1	100%	0	0%	0	0%	0	0%
Croatia	0	0%	0	0%	0	0%	20	33%	0	0%	3	60%
Cyprus	37	22%	0	0%	8	57%	55	35%	1	8%	10	77%
Czech Republic	0	-	0	-	0	-	0	-	0	-	0	-
Denmark	47	19%	1	5%	9	43%	17	8%	0	0%	5	28%
Estonia	17	24%	1	17%	2	33%	13	22%	0	0%	2	40%
Finland	28	11%	0	0%	4	19%	118	49%	4	20%	16	80%
France	98	39%	1	5%	13	62%	96	38%	1	5%	16	76%
FYR Macedonia	3	8%	0	0%	2	67%	18	38%	0	0%	4	100%
Georgia	0	0%	0	0%	0	0%	13	27%	0	0%	3	75%
Germany	73	29%	1	5%	13	62%	59	23%	1	5%	13	62%
Greece	57	23%	1	5%	13	62%	63	28%	0	0%	12	63%
Hungary	3	4%	0	0%	1	17%	12	20%	0	0%	3	60%
Iceland	29	19%	0	0%	7	54%	20	8%	0	0%	5	24%
Ireland	93	34%	5	22%	12	52%	80	33%	3	15%	11	55%
Israel	33	16%	0	0%	8	47%	28	13%	0	0%	8	44%
Italy	-	-	-	-	-	-	0	-	0	-	0	-
Latvia	0	0%	0	0%	0	0%	12	25%	1	25%	1	25%
Lithuania	17	28%	0	0%	3	60%	14	29%	0	0%	2	50%
Luxembourg	41	21%	2	13%	7	44%	64	33%	1	6%	9	56%
Malta	42	39%	0	0%	7	78%	54	50%	1	11%	7	78%
Moldova	35	49%	0	0%	6	100%	5	10%	0	0%	1	25%
Monaco	33	55%	1	20%	5	100%	15	25%	0	0%	3	60%
Montenegro	0	0%	0	0%	0	0%	14	39%	0	0%	3	100%
Morocco	7	58%	0	0%	1	100%	0	0%	0	0%	0	0%
Netherlands	50	22%	0	0%	11	58%	30	13%	1	5%	5	26%
Norway	40	16%	0	0%	7	33%	50	20%	1	5%	10	48%
Poland	19	53%	0	0%	3	100%	18	50%	0	0%	2	67%
Portugal	26	13%	0	0%	7	41%	154	64%	5	25%	18	90%
Romania	51	61%	2	29%	7	100%	7	15%	0	0%	2	50%
Russia	16	19%	0	0%	3	43%	7	12%	0	0%	1	20%
San Marino	3	13%	0	0%	1	50%	23	48%	1	25%	3	75%
Serbia	12	33%	0	0%	3	100%	6	17%	0	0%	2	67%
Serbia & Montenegro	0	-	0	-	0	-	0	-	0	-	0	-
Slovakia	0	0%	0	0%	0	0%	5	21%	0	0%	1	50%
Slovenia	11	13%	0	0%	2	29%	26	36%	0	0%	4	67%
Spain	83	33%	1	5%	13	62%	147	58%	7	33%	18	86%
Sweden	39	15%	0	0%	7	33%	35	15%	0	0%	7	35%
Switzerland	81	32%	1	5%	15	71%	104	41%	1	5%	18	86%
Turkey	23	13%	0	0%	3	20%	76	40%	0	0%	12	75%
Ukraine	43	60%	1	17%	6	100%	4	8%	0	0%	1	25%
United Kingdom	94	37%	1	5%	15	71%	25	10%	0	0%	6	29%
Yugoslavia	17	14%	0	0%	3	30%	62	52%	1	10%	8	80%

Eurovision 2014 - Who Votes for Who? (And Who Doesn't)

Latvia

	Latvia awarded points to:				Frequency		Latvia received points from:				Frequency	
	Total	% of max	12's	% of max	Times	% of max	Total	% of max	12's	% of max	Times	% of max
Albania	11	6%	0	0%	4	27%	0	0%	0	0%	0	0%
Andorra	0	0%	0	0%	0	0%	12	14%	0	0%	2	29%
Armenia	18	15%	0	0%	4	40%	0	0%	0	0%	0	0%
Austria	15	13%	0	0%	3	30%	23	17%	0	0%	4	36%
Azerbaijan	32	27%	0	0%	8	80%	10	17%	0	0%	2	40%
Belarus	37	28%	0	0%	6	55%	32	27%	0	0%	7	70%
Belgium	27	17%	0	0%	5	38%	33	20%	1	7%	4	29%
Bosnia & Herzegovina	4	2%	0	0%	2	13%	5	3%	0	0%	1	8%
Bulgaria	3	4%	0	0%	2	29%	1	1%	0	0%	1	11%
Croatia	24	14%	0	0%	5	36%	31	20%	0	0%	7	54%
Cyprus	19	11%	0	0%	5	36%	13	8%	0	0%	5	36%
Czech Republic	0	0%	0	0%	0	0%	11	23%	0	0%	3	75%
Denmark	91	40%	2	11%	13	68%	46	26%	0	0%	9	60%
Estonia	151	79%	7	44%	15	94%	115	64%	2	13%	15	100%
Finland	40	22%	0	0%	7	47%	30	21%	1	8%	5	42%
France	21	12%	0	0%	6	40%	11	6%	0	0%	2	13%
FYR Macedonia	0	0%	0	0%	0	0%	16	10%	0	0%	4	31%
Georgia	35	36%	0	0%	5	63%	20	33%	0	0%	4	80%
Germany	41	23%	1	7%	7	47%	26	15%	1	7%	3	21%
Greece	25	11%	0	0%	6	32%	12	7%	0	0%	3	21%
Hungary	27	17%	0	0%	7	54%	7	6%	0	0%	3	30%
Iceland	51	22%	0	0%	11	58%	40	22%	0	0%	8	53%
Ireland	50	28%	0	0%	9	60%	79	47%	3	21%	10	71%
Israel	6	3%	0	0%	3	20%	40	24%	1	7%	6	43%
Italy	12	25%	1	25%	1	25%	0	0%	0	0%	0	0%
Latvia	-	-	-	-	-	-	0	-	0	-	0	-
Lithuania	94	60%	1	8%	12	92%	108	82%	5	45%	11	100%
Luxembourg	0	-	0	-	0	-	0	-	0	-	0	-
Malta	46	24%	0	0%	10	63%	58	35%	2	14%	7	50%
Moldova	23	13%	0	0%	5	33%	18	14%	1	9%	3	27%
Monaco	0	0%	0	0%	0	0%	10	21%	0	0%	2	50%
Montenegro	0	0%	0	0%	0	0%	5	8%	0	0%	2	40%
Morocco	0	-	0	-	0	-	0	-	0	-	0	-
Netherlands	26	17%	2	15%	3	23%	14	9%	0	0%	3	23%
Norway	84	44%	2	13%	11	69%	33	23%	1	8%	5	42%
Poland	17	13%	0	0%	5	45%	17	14%	1	10%	3	30%
Portugal	19	14%	0	0%	4	36%	39	27%	0	0%	6	50%
Romania	11	5%	0	0%	4	22%	7	4%	0	0%	2	15%
Russia	157	69%	6	32%	17	89%	24	14%	0	0%	7	50%
San Marino	4	8%	0	0%	2	50%	2	4%	0	0%	1	25%
Serbia	8	8%	0	0%	3	38%	2	3%	0	0%	1	17%
Serbia & Montenegro	10	28%	0	0%	3	100%	0	0%	0	0%	0	0%
Slovakia	0	0%	0	0%	0	0%	0	0%	0	0%	0	0%
Slovenia	16	11%	0	0%	4	33%	31	22%	0	0%	5	42%
Spain	13	7%	0	0%	3	20%	21	11%	1	6%	3	19%
Sweden	75	35%	1	6%	11	61%	33	20%	0	0%	8	57%
Switzerland	33	23%	1	8%	6	50%	18	13%	0	0%	4	33%
Turkey	2	1%	0	0%	1	7%	6	4%	0	0%	1	8%
Ukraine	106	49%	2	11%	14	78%	12	8%	0	0%	5	42%
United Kingdom	24	13%	0	0%	8	53%	50	35%	0	0%	8	67%
Yugoslavia	0	-	0	-	0	-	0	-	0	-	0	-

Eurovision 2014 - Who Votes for Who? (And Who Doesn't)

Lithuania

	Lithuania awarded points to:				Frequency		Lithuania received points from:				Frequency	
	Total	% of max	12's	% of max	Times	% of max	Total	% of max	12's	% of max	Times	% of max
Albania	0	0%	0	0%	0	0%	0	0%	0	0%	0	0%
Andorra	2	4%	0	0%	1	25%	13	18%	0	0%	3	50%
Armenia	3	3%	0	0%	2	20%	6	6%	0	0%	2	25%
Austria	20	17%	0	0%	2	20%	0	0%	0	0%	0	0%
Azerbaijan	66	55%	2	20%	8	80%	14	17%	0	0%	4	57%
Belarus	59	41%	1	8%	10	83%	52	33%	0	0%	9	69%
Belgium	13	11%	0	0%	4	40%	17	11%	0	0%	3	23%
Bosnia & Herzegovina	7	4%	0	0%	2	13%	4	3%	0	0%	2	15%
Bulgaria	1	1%	0	0%	1	14%	17	13%	0	0%	5	45%
Croatia	25	12%	0	0%	6	33%	20	9%	0	0%	6	32%
Cyprus	19	11%	0	0%	6	43%	26	14%	0	0%	7	44%
Czech Republic	0	0%	0	0%	0	0%	0	0%	0	0%	0	0%
Denmark	52	23%	0	0%	13	68%	20	10%	0	0%	6	38%
Estonia	89	49%	1	7%	13	87%	46	24%	0	0%	9	56%
Finland	38	23%	0	0%	6	43%	18	12%	0	0%	3	23%
France	39	22%	0	0%	7	47%	10	6%	0	0%	3	20%
FYR Macedonia	0	0%	0	0%	0	0%	7	4%	0	0%	2	15%
Georgia	109	83%	6	55%	11	100%	65	60%	2	22%	8	89%
Germany	20	11%	0	0%	5	33%	2	1%	0	0%	2	13%
Greece	35	16%	0	0%	7	39%	11	6%	0	0%	4	27%
Hungary	16	11%	0	0%	3	25%	5	4%	0	0%	1	10%
Iceland	41	21%	0	0%	7	44%	21	13%	0	0%	4	29%
Ireland	51	27%	1	6%	7	44%	105	51%	5	29%	14	82%
Israel	12	8%	0	0%	4	31%	11	7%	0	0%	4	29%
Italy	14	29%	0	0%	2	50%	17	28%	0	0%	3	60%
Latvia	108	82%	5	45%	11	100%	94	60%	1	8%	12	92%
Lithuania	-	-	-	-	-	-	0	-	0	-	0	-
Luxembourg	0	-	0	-	0	-	0	-	0	-	0	-
Malta	40	20%	0	0%	11	65%	19	9%	0	0%	5	29%
Moldova	29	20%	0	0%	5	42%	16	13%	0	0%	4	40%
Monaco	0	0%	0	0%	0	0%	11	23%	0	0%	2	50%
Montenegro	0	0%	0	0%	0	0%	1	2%	0	0%	1	20%
Morocco	0	-	0	-	0	-	0	-	0	-	0	-
Netherlands	36	21%	1	7%	7	50%	21	11%	0	0%	5	31%
Norway	66	31%	2	11%	10	56%	51	25%	0	0%	9	53%
Poland	47	33%	1	8%	9	75%	48	33%	2	17%	6	50%
Portugal	5	3%	0	0%	2	15%	22	14%	0	0%	4	31%
Romania	13	7%	0	0%	5	31%	4	3%	0	0%	2	15%
Russia	131	64%	3	18%	17	100%	43	26%	0	0%	9	64%
San Marino	0	0%	0	0%	0	0%	0	0%	0	0%	0	0%
Serbia	16	13%	0	0%	5	50%	14	12%	0	0%	3	30%
Serbia & Montenegro	3	8%	0	0%	2	67%	6	13%	0	0%	2	50%
Slovakia	0	0%	0	0%	0	0%	7	10%	0	0%	1	17%
Slovenia	18	10%	0	0%	4	27%	18	9%	0	0%	4	24%
Spain	12	7%	0	0%	2	13%	11	6%	0	0%	4	27%
Sweden	70	32%	0	0%	13	72%	14	7%	0	0%	5	29%
Switzerland	31	20%	0	0%	5	38%	3	2%	0	0%	1	7%
Turkey	16	8%	0	0%	4	24%	4	2%	0	0%	2	13%
Ukraine	114	53%	3	17%	16	89%	27	16%	0	0%	7	50%
United Kingdom	22	12%	0	0%	5	33%	102	45%	1	5%	14	74%
Yugoslavia	0	-	0	-	0	-	0	-	0	-	0	-

Eurovision 2014 - Who Votes for Who? (And Who Doesn't)

Luxembourg

	Luxembourg awarded points to				Frequency		Luxembourg received points from:				Frequency	
	Total	% of max	12's	% of max	Times	% of max	Total	% of max	12's	% of max	Times	% of max
Albania	0	-	0	-	0	-	0	-	0	-	0	-
Andorra	0	-	0	-	0	-	0	-	0	-	0	-
Armenia	0	-	0	-	0	-	0	-	0	-	0	-
Austria	14	6%	0	0%	3	17%	47	22%	0	0%	9	50%
Azerbaijan	0	-	0	-	0	-	0	-	0	-	0	-
Belarus	0	-	0	-	0	-	0	-	0	-	0	-
Belgium	48	21%	1	5%	8	42%	53	23%	0	0%	8	42%
Bosnia & Herzegovina	0	0%	0	0%	0	0%	0	0%	0	0%	0	0%
Bulgaria	0	-	0	-	0	-	0	-	0	-	0	-
Croatia	0	0%	0	0%	0	0%	0	0%	0	0%	0	0%
Cyprus	8	6%	0	0%	2	17%	32	22%	0	0%	5	42%
Czech Republic	0	-	0	-	0	-	0	-	0	-	0	-
Denmark	26	14%	0	0%	6	38%	32	17%	0	0%	9	56%
Estonia	0	-	0	-	0	-	0	-	0	-	0	-
Finland	21	9%	0	0%	6	32%	55	24%	1	5%	9	47%
France	89	41%	3	17%	12	67%	56	26%	2	11%	9	50%
FYR Macedonia	0	-	0	-	0	-	0	-	0	-	0	-
Georgia	0	-	0	-	0	-	0	-	0	-	0	-
Germany	67	29%	2	11%	11	58%	42	18%	1	5%	7	37%
Greece	29	16%	0	0%	6	40%	24	13%	1	6%	5	31%
Hungary	0	-	0	-	0	-	0	-	0	-	0	-
Iceland	13	14%	0	0%	2	25%	9	4%	0	0%	3	16%
Ireland	96	44%	0	0%	14	78%	65	30%	1	6%	10	56%
Israel	76	37%	1	6%	11	65%	35	17%	1	6%	6	35%
Italy	64	33%	1	6%	9	56%	41	21%	2	13%	7	44%
Latvia	0	-	0	-	0	-	0	-	0	-	0	-
Lithuania	0	-	0	-	0	-	0	-	0	-	0	-
Luxembourg	-	-	-	-	-	-	0	-	0	-	0	-
Malta	27	56%	1	25%	3	75%	25	52%	0	0%	3	75%
Moldova	0	-	0	-	0	-	0	-	0	-	0	-
Monaco	17	28%	1	20%	3	60%	10	17%	0	0%	2	40%
Montenegro	0	-	0	-	0	-	0	-	0	-	0	-
Morocco	0	0%	0	0%	0	0%	0	0%	0	0%	0	0%
Netherlands	61	30%	2	12%	11	65%	45	22%	1	6%	8	47%
Norway	33	14%	0	0%	9	47%	38	17%	1	5%	6	32%
Poland	0	-	0	-	0	-	0	-	0	-	0	-
Portugal	51	22%	0	0%	10	53%	76	33%	2	11%	12	63%
Romania	0	-	0	-	0	-	0	-	0	-	0	-
Russia	0	-	0	-	0	-	0	-	0	-	0	-
San Marino	0	-	0	-	0	-	0	-	0	-	0	-
Serbia	0	-	0	-	0	-	0	-	0	-	0	-
Serbia & Montenegro	0	-	0	-	0	-	0	-	0	-	0	-
Slovakia	0	-	0	-	0	-	0	-	0	-	0	-
Slovenia	0	0%	0	0%	0	0%	1	8%	0	0%	1	100%
Spain	67	29%	0	0%	12	63%	51	22%	1	5%	9	47%
Sweden	59	27%	0	0%	11	61%	52	24%	0	0%	8	44%
Switzerland	80	35%	3	16%	15	79%	26	11%	1	5%	5	26%
Turkey	19	10%	0	0%	4	25%	26	14%	0	0%	7	44%
Ukraine	0	-	0	-	0	-	0	-	0	-	0	-
United Kingdom	123	54%	4	21%	18	95%	57	25%	0	0%	10	53%
Yugoslavia	24	15%	0	0%	5	38%	37	24%	1	8%	6	46%

Eurovision 2014 - Who Votes for Who? (And Who Doesn't)

Malta

	Malta awarded points to:				Frequency		Malta received points from:				Frequency	
	Total	% of max	12's	% of max	Times	% of max	Total	% of max	12's	% of max	Times	% of max
Albania	25	16%	0	0%	4	31%	43	28%	0	0%	10	77%
Andorra	3	5%	0	0%	1	20%	18	21%	0	0%	4	57%
Armenia	22	17%	0	0%	4	36%	23	24%	0	0%	4	50%
Austria	40	20%	1	6%	6	35%	41	17%	0	0%	9	45%
Azerbaijan	71	66%	5	56%	7	78%	40	56%	1	17%	5	83%
Belarus	42	27%	0	0%	8	62%	35	21%	0	0%	8	57%
Belgium	32	13%	1	5%	4	20%	53	19%	0	0%	8	35%
Bosnia & Herzegovina	30	11%	0	0%	8	35%	61	27%	2	11%	11	58%
Bulgaria	14	15%	0	0%	4	50%	12	10%	0	0%	3	30%
Croatia	74	28%	2	9%	8	36%	96	36%	3	14%	15	68%
Cyprus	70	29%	3	15%	13	65%	50	20%	0	0%	11	52%
Czech Republic	1	3%	0	0%	1	33%	13	27%	0	0%	2	50%
Denmark	68	26%	0	0%	15	68%	70	31%	1	5%	12	63%
Estonia	36	16%	1	5%	5	26%	54	23%	0	0%	12	60%
Finland	30	10%	0	0%	7	29%	41	14%	0	0%	10	42%
France	13	4%	0	0%	4	16%	42	13%	0	0%	10	38%
FYR Macedonia	16	7%	0	0%	6	33%	61	28%	2	11%	10	56%
Georgia	29	22%	0	0%	5	45%	27	25%	0	0%	5	56%
Germany	28	10%	0	0%	9	38%	72	22%	0	0%	16	59%
Greece	126	39%	2	7%	20	74%	72	25%	0	0%	15	63%
Hungary	10	6%	0	0%	5	33%	30	19%	0	0%	5	38%
Iceland	73	23%	3	11%	8	30%	40	13%	0	0%	9	35%
Ireland	89	32%	2	9%	14	61%	91	32%	2	8%	15	63%
Israel	62	23%	1	5%	9	41%	51	18%	0	0%	10	43%
Italy	54	50%	1	11%	7	78%	42	39%	0	0%	7	78%
Latvia	58	35%	2	14%	7	50%	46	24%	0	0%	10	63%
Lithuania	19	9%	0	0%	5	29%	40	20%	0	0%	11	65%
Luxembourg	25	52%	0	0%	3	75%	27	56%	1	25%	3	75%
Malta	-	-	-	-	-	-	0	-	0	-	0	-
Moldova	9	7%	0	0%	2	18%	0	0%	0	0%	0	0%
Monaco	1	2%	0	0%	1	25%	5	8%	0	0%	1	20%
Montenegro	6	17%	0	0%	1	33%	1	1%	0	0%	1	17%
Morocco	0	-	0	-	0	-	0	-	0	-	0	-
Netherlands	65	29%	1	5%	11	58%	39	15%	0	0%	10	48%
Norway	66	20%	0	0%	16	57%	74	24%	2	8%	12	46%
Poland	14	7%	0	0%	4	24%	24	12%	0	0%	5	29%
Portugal	11	4%	0	0%	5	21%	50	17%	1	4%	12	50%
Romania	83	35%	1	5%	11	55%	43	21%	0	0%	8	47%
Russia	59	23%	1	5%	11	52%	32	16%	1	6%	4	24%
San Marino	12	33%	0	0%	2	67%	38	63%	1	20%	5	100%
Serbia	23	21%	0	0%	6	67%	21	22%	0	0%	4	50%
Serbia & Montenegro	10	28%	0	0%	2	67%	0	0%	0	0%	0	0%
Slovakia	27	45%	1	20%	3	60%	31	37%	1	14%	5	71%
Slovenia	26	12%	0	0%	7	39%	40	17%	2	10%	6	30%
Spain	46	15%	1	4%	8	32%	72	23%	1	4%	13	50%
Sweden	125	37%	3	11%	19	68%	68	22%	2	8%	13	50%
Switzerland	65	25%	2	9%	11	50%	58	20%	0	0%	11	46%
Turkey	87	27%	1	4%	12	44%	93	32%	1	4%	15	63%
Ukraine	73	38%	0	0%	12	75%	28	19%	0	0%	6	50%
United Kingdom	109	36%	1	4%	17	68%	132	39%	3	11%	21	75%
Yugoslavia	4	11%	0	0%	2	67%	13	36%	0	0%	3	100%

Eurovision 2014 - Who Votes for Who? (And Who Doesn't)

Moldova

	Moldova awarded points to:				Frequency		Moldova received points from:				Frequency	
	Total	% of max	12's	% of max	Times	% of max	Total	% of max	12's	% of max	Times	% of max
Albania	6	5%	0	0%	2	18%	11	7%	0	0%	3	21%
Andorra	4	8%	0	0%	1	25%	5	6%	0	0%	2	29%
Armenia	28	23%	0	0%	8	80%	18	17%	0	0%	4	44%
Austria	10	12%	0	0%	2	29%	31	26%	0	0%	7	70%
Azerbaijan	81	68%	1	10%	9	90%	39	36%	0	0%	7	78%
Belarus	65	54%	1	10%	9	90%	83	53%	1	8%	11	85%
Belgium	26	20%	0	0%	5	45%	20	10%	0	0%	7	44%
Bosnia & Herzegovina	20	14%	0	0%	4	33%	10	7%	0	0%	2	17%
Bulgaria	20	33%	0	0%	4	80%	22	17%	0	0%	6	55%
Croatia	11	11%	0	0%	3	38%	15	10%	0	0%	6	50%
Cyprus	9	8%	0	0%	2	22%	33	20%	0	0%	7	50%
Czech Republic	0	0%	0	0%	0	0%	0	0%	0	0%	0	0%
Denmark	20	11%	1	7%	4	27%	19	11%	0	0%	3	20%
Estonia	33	21%	0	0%	8	62%	16	8%	0	0%	4	25%
Finland	19	13%	0	0%	3	25%	11	7%	0	0%	3	23%
France	2	2%	0	0%	1	10%	25	15%	0	0%	6	43%
FYR Macedonia	5	5%	0	0%	2	22%	35	24%	0	0%	6	50%
Georgia	30	42%	0	0%	6	100%	16	22%	0	0%	4	67%
Germany	2	2%	0	0%	1	10%	10	6%	0	0%	3	23%
Greece	49	29%	0	0%	11	79%	49	29%	0	0%	10	71%
Hungary	14	11%	0	0%	4	36%	24	18%	0	0%	6	55%
Iceland	25	16%	0	0%	4	31%	16	10%	0	0%	2	15%
Ireland	4	3%	0	0%	3	23%	29	16%	0	0%	8	53%
Israel	18	15%	0	0%	4	40%	38	24%	0	0%	9	69%
Italy	5	10%	0	0%	1	25%	35	49%	0	0%	6	100%
Latvia	18	14%	1	9%	3	27%	23	13%	0	0%	5	33%
Lithuania	16	13%	0	0%	4	40%	29	20%	0	0%	5	42%
Luxembourg	0	-	0	-	0	-	0	-	0	-	0	-
Malta	0	0%	0	0%	0	0%	9	7%	0	0%	2	18%
Moldova	-	-	-	-	-	-	0	-	0	-	0	-
Monaco	2	8%	0	0%	1	50%	0	0%	0	0%	0	0%
Montenegro	11	15%	0	0%	2	33%	21	19%	0	0%	5	56%
Morocco	0	-	0	-	0	-	0	-	0	-	0	-
Netherlands	2	2%	0	0%	1	10%	10	6%	0	0%	2	13%
Norway	43	30%	0	0%	9	75%	15	10%	0	0%	4	33%
Poland	9	8%	0	0%	4	44%	25	19%	0	0%	5	45%
Portugal	15	18%	0	0%	3	43%	80	61%	2	18%	10	91%
Romania	161	96%	12	86%	14	100%	150	96%	10	77%	13	100%
Russia	137	71%	3	19%	16	100%	101	53%	3	19%	15	94%
San Marino	9	19%	0	0%	3	75%	18	25%	0	0%	3	50%
Serbia	18	17%	0	0%	5	56%	22	18%	0	0%	5	50%
Serbia & Montenegro	1	8%	0	0%	1	100%	11	31%	0	0%	2	67%
Slovakia	7	19%	0	0%	1	33%	16	19%	0	0%	3	43%
Slovenia	9	8%	0	0%	3	30%	22	13%	0	0%	6	43%
Spain	4	3%	0	0%	1	10%	56	31%	0	0%	11	73%
Sweden	48	33%	0	0%	9	75%	7	4%	0	0%	2	15%
Switzerland	8	10%	0	0%	1	14%	9	7%	0	0%	2	18%
Turkey	11	10%	0	0%	2	22%	42	39%	1	11%	6	67%
Ukraine	126	70%	2	13%	15	100%	87	52%	2	14%	11	79%
United Kingdom	5	4%	0	0%	2	20%	15	11%	0	0%	3	27%
Yugoslavia	0	-	0	-	0	-	0	-	0	-	0	-

Eurovision 2014 - Who Votes for Who? (And Who Doesn't)

Monaco

	Monaco awarded points to:				Frequency		Monaco received points from:				Frequency	
	Total	% of max	12's	% of max	Times	% of max	Total	% of max	12's	% of max	Times	% of max
Albania	3	6%	0	0%	1	25%	2	6%	0	0%	1	33%
Andorra	0	0%	0	0%	0	0%	17	47%	0	0%	3	100%
Armenia	0	0%	0	0%	0	0%	0	0%	0	0%	0	0%
Austria	10	14%	0	0%	2	33%	14	19%	0	0%	3	50%
Azerbaijan	0	-	0	-	0	-	0	-	0	-	0	-
Belarus	1	3%	0	0%	1	33%	0	0%	0	0%	0	0%
Belgium	26	27%	1	13%	3	38%	16	17%	0	0%	3	38%
Bosnia & Herzegovina	28	47%	2	40%	3	60%	0	0%	0	0%	0	0%
Bulgaria	0	0%	0	0%	0	0%	0	0%	0	0%	0	0%
Croatia	16	27%	0	0%	3	60%	0	0%	0	0%	0	0%
Cyprus	24	50%	1	25%	3	75%	4	11%	0	0%	1	33%
Czech Republic	0	-	0	-	0	-	0	-	0	-	0	-
Denmark	33	46%	0	0%	4	67%	14	23%	0	0%	2	40%
Estonia	5	14%	0	0%	1	33%	2	6%	0	0%	1	33%
Finland	27	25%	0	0%	4	44%	17	18%	0	0%	4	50%
France	53	55%	2	25%	7	88%	27	32%	0	0%	5	71%
FYR Macedonia	4	6%	0	0%	2	33%	0	0%	0	0%	0	0%
Georgia	0	-	0	-	0	-	0	-	0	-	0	-
Germany	32	33%	1	13%	5	63%	23	21%	0	0%	4	44%
Greece	31	32%	0	0%	4	50%	16	19%	1	14%	2	29%
Hungary	0	0%	0	0%	0	0%	0	0%	0	0%	0	0%
Iceland	6	17%	0	0%	2	67%	0	0%	0	0%	0	0%
Ireland	31	29%	0	0%	4	44%	17	18%	0	0%	3	38%
Israel	43	40%	2	22%	6	67%	19	20%	0	0%	4	50%
Italy	15	25%	0	0%	3	60%	33	55%	1	20%	5	100%
Latvia	10	21%	0	0%	2	50%	0	0%	0	0%	0	0%
Lithuania	11	23%	0	0%	2	50%	0	0%	0	0%	0	0%
Luxembourg	10	17%	0	0%	2	40%	17	28%	1	20%	3	60%
Malta	5	8%	0	0%	1	20%	1	2%	0	0%	1	25%
Moldova	0	0%	0	0%	0	0%	2	8%	0	0%	1	50%
Monaco	-	-	-	-	-	-	0	-	0	-	0	-
Montenegro	0	-	0	-	0	-	0	-	0	-	0	-
Morocco	0	-	0	-	0	-	0	-	0	-	0	-
Netherlands	32	30%	0	0%	6	67%	18	19%	0	0%	2	25%
Norway	9	8%	0	0%	3	33%	10	10%	0	0%	3	38%
Poland	0	0%	0	0%	0	0%	1	4%	0	0%	1	50%
Portugal	8	8%	0	0%	3	38%	18	19%	0	0%	5	63%
Romania	11	23%	0	0%	2	50%	0	0%	0	0%	0	0%
Russia	0	0%	0	0%	0	0%	0	0%	0	0%	0	0%
San Marino	0	-	0	-	0	-	0	-	0	-	0	-
Serbia	0	-	0	-	0	-	0	-	0	-	0	-
Serbia & Montenegro	14	39%	0	0%	3	100%	0	0%	0	0%	0	0%
Slovakia	0	-	0	-	0	-	0	-	0	-	0	-
Slovenia	7	19%	0	0%	2	67%	0	0%	0	0%	0	0%
Spain	14	15%	0	0%	4	50%	17	18%	0	0%	3	38%
Sweden	22	23%	0	0%	4	50%	22	26%	1	14%	2	29%
Switzerland	29	27%	0	0%	7	78%	16	17%	0	0%	3	38%
Turkey	11	15%	0	0%	2	33%	5	8%	0	0%	1	20%
Ukraine	15	25%	0	0%	4	80%	0	0%	0	0%	0	0%
United Kingdom	42	44%	2	25%	5	63%	24	25%	0	0%	4	50%
Yugoslavia	0	0%	0	0%	0	0%	4	17%	0	0%	1	50%

Eurovision 2014 - Who Votes for Who? (And Who Doesn't)

Montenegro

	Montenegro awarded points to:				Frequency		Montenegro received points from:				Frequency	
	Total	% of max	12's	% of max	Times	% of max	Total	% of max	12's	% of max	Times	% of max
Albania	54	75%	2	33%	6	100%	37	77%	2	50%	4	100%
Andorra	0	0%	0	0%	0	0%	1	3%	0	0%	1	33%
Armenia	31	32%	0	0%	5	63%	25	42%	1	20%	3	60%
Austria	2	4%	0	0%	1	25%	0	0%	0	0%	0	0%
Azerbaijan	33	39%	1	14%	5	71%	2	4%	0	0%	1	25%
Belarus	19	26%	0	0%	6	100%	5	10%	0	0%	2	50%
Belgium	3	4%	0	0%	2	29%	0	0%	0	0%	0	0%
Bosnia & Herzegovina	59	82%	3	50%	6	100%	27	75%	1	33%	3	100%
Bulgaria	10	28%	0	0%	2	67%	0	0%	0	0%	0	0%
Croatia	22	46%	0	0%	4	100%	11	46%	0	0%	2	100%
Cyprus	6	13%	0	0%	1	25%	0	0%	0	0%	0	0%
Czech Republic	0	0%	0	0%	0	0%	0	0%	0	0%	0	0%
Denmark	18	19%	0	0%	2	25%	5	8%	0	0%	1	20%
Estonia	0	0%	0	0%	0	0%	0	0%	0	0%	0	0%
Finland	5	5%	0	0%	2	25%	0	0%	0	0%	0	0%
France	1	1%	0	0%	1	17%	7	19%	0	0%	1	33%
FYR Macedonia	38	79%	0	0%	4	100%	23	64%	1	33%	3	100%
Georgia	2	4%	0	0%	1	25%	0	0%	0	0%	0	0%
Germany	0	0%	0	0%	0	0%	2	4%	0	0%	1	25%
Greece	33	34%	0	0%	5	63%	0	0%	0	0%	0	0%
Hungary	12	14%	1	14%	1	14%	4	8%	0	0%	1	25%
Iceland	17	16%	0	0%	3	33%	0	0%	0	0%	0	0%
Ireland	2	3%	0	0%	2	33%	0	0%	0	0%	0	0%
Israel	19	26%	0	0%	4	67%	1	2%	0	0%	1	20%
Italy	14	39%	0	0%	3	100%	0	0%	0	0%	0	0%
Latvia	5	8%	0	0%	2	40%	0	0%	0	0%	0	0%
Lithuania	1	2%	0	0%	1	20%	0	0%	0	0%	0	0%
Luxembourg	0	-	0	-	0	-	0	-	0	-	0	-
Malta	1	1%	0	0%	1	17%	6	17%	0	0%	1	33%
Moldova	21	19%	0	0%	5	56%	11	15%	0	0%	2	33%
Monaco	0	-	0	-	0	-	0	-	0	-	0	-
Montenegro	-	-	-	-	-	-	0	-	0	-	0	-
Morocco	0	-	0	-	0	-	0	-	0	-	0	-
Netherlands	3	4%	0	0%	2	33%	6	10%	0	0%	1	20%
Norway	20	24%	0	0%	4	57%	0	0%	0	0%	0	0%
Poland	5	8%	0	0%	2	40%	0	0%	0	0%	0	0%
Portugal	3	6%	0	0%	1	25%	7	15%	0	0%	2	50%
Romania	14	13%	0	0%	3	33%	0	0%	0	0%	0	0%
Russia	52	43%	0	0%	8	80%	5	7%	0	0%	1	17%
San Marino	4	8%	0	0%	1	25%	9	19%	0	0%	2	50%
Serbia	58	97%	4	80%	5	100%	20	83%	1	50%	2	100%
Serbia & Montenegro	-	-	-	-	-	-	0	-	0	-	0	-
Slovakia	0	-	0	-	0	-	0	-	0	-	0	-
Slovenia	37	62%	0	0%	5	100%	22	46%	0	0%	3	75%
Spain	4	6%	0	0%	1	17%	4	7%	0	0%	1	20%
Sweden	15	16%	0	0%	3	38%	5	8%	0	0%	2	40%
Switzerland	5	10%	0	0%	1	25%	2	4%	0	0%	1	25%
Turkey	15	21%	0	0%	4	67%	5	21%	0	0%	1	50%
Ukraine	33	34%	1	13%	5	63%	9	19%	0	0%	2	50%
United Kingdom	0	0%	0	0%	0	0%	0	0%	0	0%	0	0%
Yugoslavia	0	-	0	-	0	-	0	-	0	-	0	-

Eurovision 2014 - Who Votes for Who? (And Who Doesn't)

Morocco

	Morocco awarded points to:				Frequency		Morocco received points from :				Frequency	
	Total	% of max	12's	% of max	Times	% of max	Total	% of max	12's	% of max	Times	% of max
Albania	0	-	0	-	0	-	0	-	0	-	0	-
Andorra	0	-	0	-	0	-	0	-	0	-	0	-
Armenia	0	-	0	-	0	-	0	-	0	-	0	-
Austria	3	25%	0	0%	1	100%	0	0%	0	0%	0	0%
Azerbaijan	0	-	0	-	0	-	0	-	0	-	0	-
Belarus	0	-	0	-	0	-	0	-	0	-	0	-
Belgium	0	0%	0	0%	0	0%	0	0%	0	0%	0	0%
Bosnia & Herzegovina	0	-	0	-	0	-	0	-	0	-	0	-
Bulgaria	0	-	0	-	0	-	0	-	0	-	0	-
Croatia	0	-	0	-	0	-	0	-	0	-	0	-
Cyprus	0	-	0	-	0	-	0	-	0	-	0	-
Czech Republic	0	-	0	-	0	-	0	-	0	-	0	-
Denmark	2	17%	0	0%	1	100%	0	0%	0	0%	0	0%
Estonia	0	-	0	-	0	-	0	-	0	-	0	-
Finland	0	0%	0	0%	0	0%	0	0%	0	0%	0	0%
France	1	8%	0	0%	1	100%	0	0%	0	0%	0	0%
FYR Macedonia	0	-	0	-	0	-	0	-	0	-	0	-
Georgia	0	-	0	-	0	-	0	-	0	-	0	-
Germany	10	83%	0	0%	1	100%	0	0%	0	0%	0	0%
Greece	0	0%	0	0%	0	0%	0	0%	0	0%	0	0%
Hungary	0	-	0	-	0	-	0	-	0	-	0	-
Iceland	0	-	0	-	0	-	0	0%	0	0%	0	0%
Ireland	0	0%	0	0%	0	0%	0	0%	0	0%	0	0%
Israel	0	-	0	-	0	-	0	-	0	-	0	-
Italy	0	0%	0	0%	0	0%	7	58%	0	0%	1	100%
Latvia	0	-	0	-	0	-	0	-	0	-	0	-
Lithuania	0	-	0	-	0	-	0	-	0	-	0	-
Luxembourg	0	0%	0	0%	0	0%	0	0%	0	0%	0	0%
Malta	0	-	0	-	0	-	0	-	0	-	0	-
Moldova	0	-	0	-	0	-	0	-	0	-	0	-
Monaco	0	-	0	-	0	-	0	-	0	-	0	-
Montenegro	0	-	0	-	0	-	0	-	0	-	0	-
Morocco	-	-	-	-	-	-	0	-	0	-	0	-
Netherlands	0	0%	0	0%	0	0%	0	0%	0	0%	0	0%
Norway	4	33%	0	0%	1	100%	0	0%	0	0%	0	0%
Poland	0	-	0	-	0	-	0	-	0	-	0	-
Portugal	0	0%	0	0%	0	0%	0	0%	0	0%	0	0%
Romania	0	-	0	-	0	-	0	-	0	-	0	-
Russia	0	-	0	-	0	-	0	-	0	-	0	-
San Marino	0	-	0	-	0	-	0	-	0	-	0	-
Serbia	0	-	0	-	0	-	0	-	0	-	0	-
Serbia & Montenegro	0	-	0	-	0	-	0	-	0	-	0	-
Slovakia	0	-	0	-	0	-	0	-	0	-	0	-
Slovenia	0	-	0	-	0	-	0	-	0	-	0	-
Spain	5	42%	0	0%	1	100%	0	0%	0	0%	0	0%
Sweden	6	50%	0	0%	1	100%	0	0%	0	0%	0	0%
Switzerland	7	58%	0	0%	1	100%	0	0%	0	0%	0	0%
Turkey	12	100%	1	100%	1	100%	0	0%	0	0%	0	0%
Ukraine	0	-	0	-	0	-	0	-	0	-	0	-
United Kingdom	8	67%	0	0%	1	100%	0	0%	0	0%	0	0%
Yugoslavia	0	-	0	-	0	-	0	-	0	-	0	-

Eurovision 2014 - Who Votes for Who? (And Who Doesn't)

Netherlands

	Netherlands awarded points to:				Frequency		Netherlands received points from:				Frequency	
	Total	% of max	12's	% of max	Times	% of max	Total	% of max	12's	% of max	Times	% of max
Albania	8	6%	0	0%	4	36%	18	17%	0	0%	4	44%
Andorra	7	12%	0	0%	1	20%	19	26%	0	0%	4	67%
Armenia	102	77%	5	45%	10	91%	21	25%	0	0%	4	57%
Austria	44	13%	1	3%	10	34%	90	24%	2	6%	16	52%
Azerbaijan	37	28%	0	0%	8	73%	5	7%	0	0%	2	33%
Belarus	3	2%	0	0%	2	18%	7	6%	0	0%	2	20%
Belgium	158	40%	2	6%	23	70%	179	44%	6	18%	25	74%
Bosnia & Herzegovina	83	33%	0	0%	13	62%	20	11%	0	0%	5	33%
Bulgaria	2	2%	0	0%	1	14%	5	6%	0	0%	1	14%
Croatia	23	9%	0	0%	7	33%	21	9%	0	0%	5	26%
Cyprus	58	17%	1	4%	7	25%	35	11%	0	0%	9	33%
Czech Republic	0	0%	0	0%	0	0%	0	0%	0	0%	0	0%
Denmark	144	35%	5	15%	21	62%	98	27%	1	3%	15	50%
Estonia	53	20%	1	5%	9	41%	60	24%	2	10%	8	38%
Finland	46	12%	0	0%	11	34%	63	18%	0	0%	11	38%
France	119	28%	4	11%	19	54%	100	25%	2	6%	15	44%
FYR Macedonia	4	3%	0	0%	2	15%	15	11%	0	0%	4	36%
Georgia	12	13%	0	0%	3	38%	1	2%	0	0%	1	20%
Germany	125	30%	3	9%	23	66%	102	25%	1	3%	18	53%
Greece	113	29%	0	0%	21	64%	64	18%	1	3%	13	45%
Hungary	43	28%	0	0%	6	46%	46	43%	3	33%	5	56%
Iceland	51	16%	0	0%	9	35%	56	15%	2	6%	10	31%
Ireland	144	32%	3	8%	23	61%	123	28%	2	6%	22	61%
Israel	138	37%	3	10%	23	74%	121	34%	2	7%	22	73%
Italy	30	13%	1	5%	5	26%	50	22%	0	0%	11	58%
Latvia	14	9%	0	0%	3	23%	26	17%	2	15%	3	23%
Lithuania	21	11%	0	0%	5	31%	36	21%	1	7%	7	50%
Luxembourg	45	22%	1	6%	8	47%	61	30%	2	12%	11	65%
Malta	39	15%	0	0%	10	48%	65	29%	1	5%	11	58%
Moldova	10	6%	0	0%	2	13%	2	2%	0	0%	1	10%
Monaco	18	19%	0	0%	2	25%	32	30%	0	0%	6	67%
Montenegro	6	10%	0	0%	1	20%	3	4%	0	0%	2	33%
Morocco	0	0%	0	0%	0	0%	0	0%	0	0%	0	0%
Netherlands	-	-	-	-	-	-	0	-	0	-	0	-
Norway	130	28%	2	5%	25	64%	87	20%	2	6%	15	42%
Poland	22	11%	0	0%	6	38%	24	14%	1	7%	3	21%
Portugal	64	17%	1	3%	13	41%	85	22%	1	3%	14	44%
Romania	30	13%	0	0%	7	37%	12	7%	0	0%	5	36%
Russia	35	15%	0	0%	10	50%	19	11%	0	0%	5	33%
San Marino	0	0%	0	0%	0	0%	20	42%	1	25%	4	100%
Serbia	57	53%	0	0%	9	100%	1	2%	0	0%	1	20%
Serbia & Montenegro	26	72%	1	33%	3	100%	1	2%	0	0%	1	25%
Slovakia	0	0%	0	0%	0	0%	5	7%	0	0%	1	17%
Slovenia	26	11%	0	0%	5	25%	50	21%	0	0%	10	50%
Spain	57	13%	0	0%	12	33%	98	23%	1	3%	18	51%
Sweden	140	30%	3	8%	20	51%	99	23%	2	6%	17	47%
Switzerland	102	28%	1	3%	14	47%	91	25%	1	3%	18	60%
Turkey	168	42%	7	21%	23	70%	95	28%	1	4%	19	68%
Ukraine	43	18%	0	0%	9	45%	11	7%	0	0%	2	14%
United Kingdom	107	25%	2	6%	19	53%	94	22%	1	3%	21	60%
Yugoslavia	25	17%	0	0%	4	33%	40	28%	0	0%	7	58%

Eurovision 2014 - Who Votes for Who? (And Who Doesn't)

Norway

	Norway awarded points to:				Frequency		Norway received points from:				Frequency	
	Total	% of max	12's	% of max	Times	% of max	Total	% of max	12's	% of max	Times	% of max
Albania	19	13%	0	0%	4	33%	27	16%	0	0%	6	43%
Andorra	2	3%	0	0%	1	20%	26	27%	0	0%	5	63%
Armenia	7	5%	0	0%	2	17%	38	32%	0	0%	9	90%
Austria	47	13%	0	0%	9	29%	47	12%	1	3%	11	32%
Azerbaijan	30	21%	0	0%	5	42%	40	33%	1	10%	7	70%
Belarus	4	3%	0	0%	2	20%	37	24%	1	8%	8	62%
Belgium	59	15%	0	0%	13	39%	115	25%	1	3%	22	58%
Bosnia & Herzegovina	92	37%	3	14%	11	52%	44	19%	0	0%	10	53%
Bulgaria	7	8%	0	0%	2	29%	16	12%	0	0%	7	64%
Croatia	30	11%	0	0%	9	41%	47	17%	1	4%	8	35%
Cyprus	54	16%	1	3%	11	38%	80	22%	0	0%	14	45%
Czech Republic	0	0%	0	0%	0	0%	3	8%	0	0%	1	33%
Denmark	220	52%	7	20%	28	80%	152	38%	6	18%	22	67%
Estonia	53	23%	0	0%	9	47%	109	41%	2	9%	16	73%
Finland	147	33%	4	11%	22	59%	153	33%	6	15%	20	51%
France	134	29%	3	8%	25	66%	50	10%	0	0%	11	27%
FYR Macedonia	0	0%	0	0%	0	0%	29	15%	0	0%	5	31%
Georgia	1	1%	0	0%	1	9%	28	23%	0	0%	5	50%
Germany	84	18%	1	3%	17	45%	109	22%	2	5%	20	48%
Greece	87	19%	0	0%	20	51%	81	17%	2	5%	15	38%
Hungary	43	24%	0	0%	8	53%	52	29%	1	7%	9	60%
Iceland	155	45%	3	10%	23	79%	164	34%	6	15%	22	55%
Ireland	171	36%	5	13%	29	73%	158	32%	2	5%	25	61%
Israel	109	26%	1	3%	20	57%	93	21%	2	5%	17	46%
Italy	50	20%	1	5%	10	48%	40	16%	0	0%	7	33%
Latvia	33	23%	1	8%	5	42%	84	44%	2	13%	11	69%
Lithuania	51	25%	0	0%	9	53%	66	31%	2	11%	10	56%
Luxembourg	38	17%	1	5%	6	32%	33	14%	0	0%	9	47%
Malta	74	24%	2	8%	12	46%	66	20%	0	0%	16	57%
Moldova	15	10%	0	0%	4	33%	43	30%	0	0%	9	75%
Monaco	10	10%	0	0%	3	38%	9	8%	0	0%	3	33%
Montenegro	0	0%	0	0%	0	0%	20	24%	0	0%	4	57%
Morocco	0	0%	0	0%	0	0%	4	33%	0	0%	1	100%
Netherlands	87	20%	2	6%	15	42%	130	28%	2	5%	25	64%
Norway	-	-	-	-	-	-	0	-	0	-	0	-
Poland	42	19%	0	0%	11	61%	94	37%	2	10%	14	67%
Portugal	43	10%	1	3%	8	22%	76	17%	1	3%	19	50%
Romania	69	29%	0	0%	11	55%	49	23%	0	0%	10	56%
Russia	61	25%	0	0%	12	60%	72	30%	2	10%	9	45%
San Marino	0	0%	0	0%	0	0%	26	31%	0	0%	4	57%
Serbia	59	55%	0	0%	8	89%	29	27%	0	0%	4	44%
Serbia & Montenegro	16	44%	0	0%	2	67%	6	13%	0	0%	2	50%
Slovakia	0	0%	0	0%	0	0%	47	49%	0	0%	6	75%
Slovenia	15	6%	0	0%	3	15%	58	21%	1	4%	11	48%
Spain	50	11%	0	0%	12	31%	80	16%	3	7%	15	35%
Sweden	297	62%	10	25%	34	85%	196	42%	6	15%	28	72%
Switzerland	99	24%	1	3%	18	51%	77	17%	0	0%	16	42%
Turkey	59	13%	0	0%	16	43%	57	14%	1	3%	11	31%
Ukraine	29	14%	0	0%	8	47%	53	32%	1	7%	8	57%
United Kingdom	119	25%	2	5%	21	54%	101	20%	2	5%	16	38%
Yugoslavia	31	20%	1	8%	5	38%	11	7%	0	0%	2	15%

Eurovision 2014 - Who Votes for Who? (And Who Doesn't)

Poland

	Poland awarded points to:				Frequency		Poland received points from:				Frequency	
	Total	% of max	12's	% of max	Times	% of max	Total	% of max	12's	% of max	Times	% of max
Albania	12	10%	0	0%	3	30%	12	10%	0	0%	2	20%
Andorra	7	15%	0	0%	2	50%	10	14%	0	0%	1	17%
Armenia	52	48%	2	22%	9	100%	9	11%	0	0%	3	43%
Austria	24	17%	0	0%	5	42%	45	31%	1	8%	7	58%
Azerbaijan	59	61%	1	13%	7	88%	6	8%	0	0%	3	50%
Belarus	22	23%	0	0%	5	63%	35	36%	0	0%	6	75%
Belgium	52	33%	3	23%	6	46%	17	9%	0	0%	4	27%
Bosnia & Herzegovina	20	9%	0	0%	4	22%	25	15%	0	0%	4	29%
Bulgaria	0	0%	0	0%	0	0%	0	0%	0	0%	0	0%
Croatia	23	11%	0	0%	6	35%	10	6%	0	0%	2	13%
Cyprus	10	6%	0	0%	3	23%	10	6%	0	0%	4	31%
Czech Republic	0	0%	0	0%	0	0%	0	0%	0	0%	0	0%
Denmark	54	32%	1	7%	9	64%	11	8%	0	0%	4	33%
Estonia	50	28%	1	7%	7	47%	19	9%	1	6%	3	18%
Finland	58	32%	2	13%	9	60%	8	5%	0	0%	1	7%
France	39	19%	1	6%	6	35%	46	23%	1	6%	10	59%
FYR Macedonia	0	0%	0	0%	0	0%	10	9%	0	0%	3	33%
Georgia	24	29%	0	0%	5	71%	10	17%	0	0%	2	40%
Germany	53	28%	1	6%	8	50%	99	52%	2	13%	14	88%
Greece	52	21%	0	0%	13	62%	39	18%	0	0%	11	61%
Hungary	49	34%	2	17%	6	50%	32	24%	0	0%	8	73%
Iceland	27	13%	0	0%	7	39%	26	14%	0	0%	7	44%
Ireland	44	20%	1	6%	10	56%	58	28%	1	6%	7	41%
Israel	33	20%	0	0%	5	36%	6	4%	0	0%	2	15%
Italy	18	50%	0	0%	2	67%	19	53%	0	0%	3	100%
Latvia	17	14%	1	10%	3	30%	17	13%	0	0%	5	45%
Lithuania	48	33%	2	17%	6	50%	47	33%	1	8%	9	75%
Luxembourg	0	-	0	-	0	-	0	-	0	-	0	-
Malta	24	12%	0	0%	5	29%	14	7%	0	0%	4	24%
Moldova	25	19%	0	0%	5	45%	9	8%	0	0%	4	44%
Monaco	1	4%	0	0%	1	50%	0	0%	0	0%	0	0%
Montenegro	0	0%	0	0%	0	0%	5	8%	0	0%	2	40%
Morocco	0	-	0	-	0	-	0	-	0	-	0	-
Netherlands	24	14%	1	7%	3	21%	22	11%	0	0%	6	38%
Norway	94	37%	2	10%	14	67%	42	19%	0	0%	11	61%
Poland	-	-	-	-	-	-	0	-	0	-	0	-
Portugal	13	7%	0	0%	3	19%	10	6%	0	0%	3	20%
Romania	35	19%	0	0%	6	40%	23	17%	0	0%	4	36%
Russia	60	28%	0	0%	9	50%	25	13%	0	0%	5	31%
San Marino	0	0%	0	0%	0	0%	10	17%	0	0%	1	20%
Serbia	29	30%	0	0%	5	63%	2	3%	0	0%	1	20%
Serbia & Montenegro	5	21%	0	0%	1	50%	0	0%	0	0%	0	0%
Slovakia	5	8%	0	0%	1	20%	7	12%	0	0%	2	40%
Slovenia	28	15%	0	0%	7	44%	18	9%	0	0%	5	31%
Spain	16	8%	0	0%	5	29%	25	11%	0	0%	7	37%
Sweden	59	29%	0	0%	9	53%	10	6%	0	0%	5	33%
Switzerland	36	25%	1	8%	5	42%	13	9%	0	0%	2	17%
Turkey	11	5%	0	0%	3	18%	8	5%	0	0%	2	15%
Ukraine	95	66%	3	25%	12	100%	49	45%	0	0%	7	78%
United Kingdom	32	16%	0	0%	7	41%	31	16%	1	6%	7	44%
Yugoslavia	0	-	0	-	0	-	0	-	0	-	0	-

Eurovision 2014 - Who Votes for Who? (And Who Doesn't)

Portugal

	Portugal awarded points to:				Frequency		Portugal received points from:				Frequency	
	Total	% of max	12's	% of max	Times	% of max	Total	% of max	12's	% of max	Times	% of max
Albania	8	6%	0	0%	3	25%	16	13%	0	0%	4	40%
Andorra	10	17%	0	0%	2	40%	64	76%	4	57%	6	86%
Armenia	12	11%	0	0%	3	33%	13	15%	0	0%	3	43%
Austria	49	14%	1	3%	10	34%	19	6%	0	0%	4	14%
Azerbaijan	17	20%	0	0%	3	43%	1	2%	0	0%	1	25%
Belarus	9	7%	0	0%	3	27%	15	11%	0	0%	2	18%
Belgium	107	27%	3	9%	15	45%	63	15%	0	0%	13	38%
Bosnia & Herzegovina	20	8%	0	0%	4	18%	12	6%	0	0%	5	28%
Bulgaria	19	23%	0	0%	5	71%	7	6%	0	0%	2	22%
Croatia	40	18%	0	0%	13	68%	24	11%	0	0%	4	21%
Cyprus	37	11%	0	0%	10	37%	25	8%	1	4%	6	22%
Czech Republic	0	0%	0	0%	0	0%	16	27%	0	0%	3	60%
Denmark	74	19%	0	0%	19	59%	16	5%	0	0%	6	21%
Estonia	36	18%	1	6%	6	35%	8	4%	0	0%	3	19%
Finland	34	9%	0	0%	8	24%	37	9%	0	0%	13	39%
France	113	26%	3	8%	21	58%	198	47%	5	14%	25	71%
FYR Macedonia	0	0%	0	0%	0	0%	6	4%	0	0%	2	17%
Georgia	9	11%	0	0%	3	43%	9	13%	0	0%	2	33%
Germany	157	36%	4	11%	22	61%	82	19%	1	3%	15	42%
Greece	99	24%	1	3%	15	44%	45	12%	0	0%	14	44%
Hungary	38	24%	0	0%	7	54%	13	11%	0	0%	2	20%
Iceland	95	27%	2	7%	15	52%	67	15%	0	0%	10	27%
Ireland	117	29%	0	0%	22	65%	19	5%	0	0%	4	12%
Israel	126	34%	2	6%	17	55%	20	6%	0	0%	5	17%
Italy	154	64%	5	25%	18	90%	26	13%	0	0%	7	41%
Latvia	39	27%	0	0%	6	50%	19	14%	0	0%	4	36%
Lithuania	22	14%	0	0%	4	31%	5	3%	0	0%	2	15%
Luxembourg	76	33%	2	11%	12	63%	51	22%	0	0%	10	53%
Malta	50	17%	1	4%	12	50%	11	4%	0	0%	5	21%
Moldova	80	61%	2	18%	10	91%	15	18%	0	0%	3	43%
Monaco	18	19%	0	0%	5	63%	8	8%	0	0%	3	38%
Montenegro	7	15%	0	0%	2	50%	3	6%	0	0%	1	25%
Morocco	0	0%	0	0%	0	0%	0	0%	0	0%	0	0%
Netherlands	85	22%	1	3%	14	44%	64	17%	1	3%	13	41%
Norway	76	17%	1	3%	19	50%	43	10%	1	3%	8	22%
Poland	10	6%	0	0%	3	20%	13	7%	0	0%	3	19%
Portugal	-	-	-	-	-	-	0	-	0	-	0	-
Romania	74	41%	1	7%	11	73%	15	11%	0	0%	2	18%
Russia	51	24%	0	0%	12	67%	4	3%	0	0%	1	8%
San Marino	0	0%	0	0%	0	0%	5	21%	0	0%	1	50%
Serbia	25	26%	0	0%	6	75%	15	16%	0	0%	5	63%
Serbia & Montenegro	17	47%	0	0%	2	67%	0	0%	0	0%	0	0%
Slovakia	9	15%	0	0%	2	40%	11	13%	0	0%	3	43%
Slovenia	20	10%	0	0%	5	31%	6	3%	0	0%	3	19%
Spain	150	34%	6	16%	19	51%	164	38%	3	8%	24	67%
Sweden	145	30%	1	3%	22	55%	51	12%	0	0%	12	33%
Switzerland	94	24%	1	3%	19	59%	126	32%	2	6%	19	58%
Turkey	21	5%	0	0%	4	11%	48	12%	1	3%	10	29%
Ukraine	110	57%	5	31%	13	81%	14	12%	0	0%	3	30%
United Kingdom	156	35%	4	11%	25	68%	37	8%	0	0%	9	24%
Yugoslavia	11	7%	0	0%	3	23%	14	9%	0	0%	3	23%

Eurovision 2014 - Who Votes for Who? (And Who Doesn't)

Romania

	Romania awarded points to:				Frequency		Romania received points from:				Frequency	
	Total	% of max	12's	% of max	Times	% of max	Total	% of max	12's	% of max	Times	% of max
Albania	13	10%	0	0%	5	45%	27	16%	0	0%	6	43%
Andorra	0	0%	0	0%	0	0%	34	31%	0	0%	6	67%
Armenia	55	38%	0	0%	10	83%	19	13%	0	0%	6	50%
Austria	21	15%	1	8%	3	25%	61	34%	1	7%	10	67%
Azerbaijan	53	44%	1	10%	7	70%	60	45%	0	0%	10	91%
Belarus	13	10%	0	0%	4	36%	18	10%	0	0%	7	47%
Belgium	21	12%	0	0%	4	27%	57	23%	0	0%	10	48%
Bosnia & Herzegovina	24	12%	1	6%	3	18%	24	13%	0	0%	6	38%
Bulgaria	7	7%	0	0%	3	38%	35	21%	0	0%	9	64%
Croatia	20	12%	0	0%	4	29%	14	7%	0	0%	4	24%
Cyprus	37	21%	0	0%	9	60%	86	38%	1	5%	14	74%
Czech Republic	0	0%	0	0%	0	0%	0	0%	0	0%	0	0%
Denmark	54	26%	1	6%	11	65%	44	22%	0	0%	9	53%
Estonia	9	5%	0	0%	3	20%	12	5%	0	0%	4	21%
Finland	22	10%	0	0%	6	32%	21	8%	0	0%	5	24%
France	10	5%	0	0%	2	13%	55	24%	0	0%	11	58%
FYR Macedonia	38	20%	1	6%	8	50%	62	27%	2	11%	11	58%
Georgia	2	2%	0	0%	1	11%	10	8%	0	0%	2	20%
Germany	29	15%	1	6%	7	44%	42	16%	0	0%	9	41%
Greece	159	66%	5	25%	18	90%	101	42%	1	5%	14	70%
Hungary	77	53%	0	0%	11	92%	34	22%	1	8%	5	38%
Iceland	20	10%	0	0%	2	12%	41	19%	0	0%	8	44%
Ireland	37	17%	0	0%	8	44%	77	29%	1	5%	15	68%
Israel	62	27%	0	0%	13	68%	157	57%	3	13%	20	87%
Italy	7	15%	0	0%	2	50%	51	61%	2	29%	7	100%
Latvia	7	4%	0	0%	2	15%	11	5%	0	0%	4	22%
Lithuania	4	3%	0	0%	2	15%	13	7%	0	0%	5	31%
Luxembourg	0	-	0	-	0	-	0	-	0	-	0	-
Malta	43	21%	0	0%	8	47%	83	35%	1	5%	11	55%
Moldova	150	96%	10	77%	13	100%	161	96%	12	86%	14	100%
Monaco	0	0%	0	0%	0	0%	11	23%	0	0%	2	50%
Montenegro	0	0%	0	0%	0	0%	14	13%	0	0%	3	33%
Morocco	0	-	0	-	0	-	0	-	0	-	0	-
Netherlands	12	7%	0	0%	5	36%	30	13%	0	0%	7	37%
Norway	49	23%	0	0%	10	56%	69	29%	0	0%	11	55%
Poland	23	17%	0	0%	4	36%	35	19%	0	0%	6	40%
Portugal	15	11%	0	0%	2	18%	74	41%	1	7%	11	73%
Romania	-	-	-	-	-	-	0	-	0	-	0	-
Russia	78	36%	1	6%	11	61%	51	24%	2	11%	10	56%
San Marino	4	8%	0	0%	1	25%	13	14%	0	0%	3	38%
Serbia	24	33%	0	0%	4	67%	8	10%	0	0%	2	29%
Serbia & Montenegro	24	67%	0	0%	3	100%	12	25%	0	0%	3	75%
Slovakia	3	8%	0	0%	1	33%	7	8%	0	0%	2	29%
Slovenia	30	18%	0	0%	6	43%	30	13%	0	0%	6	32%
Spain	38	20%	0	0%	8	50%	149	62%	6	30%	16	80%
Sweden	67	29%	2	11%	10	53%	42	18%	0	0%	8	40%
Switzerland	23	12%	0	0%	5	31%	22	9%	0	0%	6	29%
Turkey	107	56%	1	6%	15	94%	55	29%	0	0%	12	75%
Ukraine	49	26%	0	0%	11	69%	15	8%	0	0%	6	40%
United Kingdom	20	10%	1	6%	4	25%	46	19%	1	5%	7	35%
Yugoslavia	0	-	0	-	0	-	0	-	0	-	0	-

Eurovision 2014 - Who Votes for Who? (And Who Doesn't)

Russia

	Russia awarded points to:			Frequency		Russia received points from:			Frequency	
	Total	% of max	12's	% of max	Times	% of max	Total	% of max	12's	% of max	Times	% of max
Albania	6	4%	0	0%	3	23%	20	10%	0	0%	5	31%
Andorra	4	8%	0	0%	1	25%	22	23%	0	0%	5	63%
Armenia	105	80%	6	55%	11	100%	126	88%	7	58%	12	100%
Austria	9	6%	0	0%	3	23%	51	27%	0	0%	7	44%
Azerbaijan	111	84%	3	27%	11	100%	74	56%	1	9%	10	91%
Belarus	68	63%	4	44%	8	89%	151	90%	10	71%	14	100%
Belgium	45	23%	0	0%	7	44%	62	23%	1	5%	12	55%
Bosnia & Herzegovina	15	7%	0	0%	3	17%	31	14%	0	0%	8	44%
Bulgaria	4	8%	0	0%	1	25%	48	40%	1	10%	7	70%
Croatia	25	12%	0	0%	7	41%	75	31%	2	10%	12	60%
Cyprus	28	16%	0	0%	7	47%	100	44%	1	5%	16	84%
Czech Republic	0	0%	0	0%	0	0%	21	58%	0	0%	3	100%
Denmark	44	19%	1	5%	7	37%	54	23%	2	10%	9	45%
Estonia	36	17%	0	0%	7	39%	182	69%	4	18%	22	100%
Finland	35	18%	1	6%	5	31%	84	35%	2	10%	14	70%
France	48	22%	1	6%	7	39%	28	11%	0	0%	8	38%
FYR Macedonia	8	6%	0	0%	2	18%	47	26%	0	0%	8	53%
Georgia	50	60%	0	0%	7	100%	43	45%	0	0%	7	88%
Germany	34	16%	0	0%	6	33%	68	27%	0	0%	13	62%
Greece	87	33%	0	0%	17	77%	89	34%	0	0%	16	73%
Hungary	32	18%	0	0%	7	47%	47	28%	0	0%	8	57%
Iceland	22	9%	0	0%	8	38%	54	20%	0	0%	14	64%
Ireland	39	17%	1	5%	6	32%	72	27%	0	0%	11	50%
Israel	50	30%	0	0%	8	57%	140	61%	5	26%	17	89%
Italy	7	12%	0	0%	1	20%	16	19%	0	0%	3	43%
Latvia	24	14%	0	0%	7	50%	157	69%	6	32%	17	89%
Lithuania	43	26%	0	0%	9	64%	131	64%	3	18%	17	100%
Luxembourg	0	-	0	-	0	-	0	-	0	-	0	-
Malta	32	16%	1	6%	4	24%	59	23%	1	5%	11	52%
Moldova	101	53%	3	19%	15	94%	137	71%	3	19%	16	100%
Monaco	0	0%	0	0%	0	0%	0	0%	0	0%	0	0%
Montenegro	5	7%	0	0%	1	17%	52	43%	0	0%	8	80%
Morocco	0	-	0	-	0	-	0	-	0	-	0	-
Netherlands	19	11%	0	0%	5	33%	35	15%	0	0%	10	50%
Norway	72	30%	2	10%	9	45%	61	25%	0	0%	12	60%
Poland	25	13%	0	0%	5	31%	60	28%	0	0%	9	50%
Portugal	4	3%	0	0%	1	8%	51	24%	0	0%	12	67%
Romania	51	24%	2	11%	10	56%	78	36%	1	6%	11	61%
Russia	-	-	-	-	-	-	0	-	0	-	0	-
San Marino	3	5%	0	0%	1	20%	13	12%	0	0%	3	33%
Serbia	29	24%	0	0%	6	60%	52	43%	0	0%	8	80%
Serbia & Montenegro	16	67%	0	0%	2	100%	12	25%	0	0%	3	75%
Slovakia	1	3%	0	0%	1	33%	9	13%	0	0%	2	33%
Slovenia	42	25%	0	0%	8	57%	77	34%	2	11%	10	53%
Spain	20	9%	0	0%	4	22%	53	18%	0	0%	9	38%
Sweden	37	16%	1	5%	9	47%	50	20%	0	0%	9	43%
Switzerland	14	10%	0	0%	3	25%	10	5%	0	0%	2	11%
Turkey	25	12%	0	0%	6	35%	50	25%	0	0%	9	53%
Ukraine	114	59%	1	6%	16	100%	129	72%	4	27%	15	100%
United Kingdom	32	15%	1	6%	7	39%	43	17%	0	0%	7	33%
Yugoslavia	0	-	0	-	0	-	0	-	0	-	0	-

Eurovision 2014 - Who Votes for Who? (And Who Doesn't)

San Marino

	San Marino awarded points to:				Frequency		San Marino received points from:				Frequency	
	Total	% of max	12's	% of max	Times	% of max	Total	% of max	12's	% of max	Times	% of max
Albania	44	61%	1	17%	6	100%	29	48%	0	0%	4	80%
Andorra	0	0%	0	0%	0	0%	2	17%	0	0%	1	100%
Armenia	40	48%	0	0%	6	86%	14	23%	0	0%	4	80%
Austria	0	0%	0	0%	0	0%	3	13%	0	0%	1	50%
Azerbaijan	42	39%	1	11%	7	78%	18	25%	0	0%	4	67%
Belarus	0	0%	0	0%	0	0%	0	0%	0	0%	0	0%
Belgium	6	13%	0	0%	2	50%	0	0%	0	0%	0	0%
Bosnia & Herzegovina	0	0%	0	0%	0	0%	0	0%	0	0%	0	0%
Bulgaria	8	67%	0	0%	1	100%	0	0%	0	0%	0	0%
Croatia	4	17%	0	0%	1	50%	1	8%	0	0%	1	100%
Cyprus	0	0%	0	0%	0	0%	0	0%	0	0%	0	0%
Czech Republic	0	-	0	-	0	-	0	-	0	-	0	-
Denmark	11	15%	0	0%	4	67%	0	0%	0	0%	0	0%
Estonia	0	0%	0	0%	0	0%	3	8%	0	0%	1	33%
Finland	17	18%	0	0%	4	50%	1	2%	0	0%	1	20%
France	11	18%	0	0%	2	40%	5	14%	0	0%	1	33%
FYR Macedonia	2	8%	0	0%	1	50%	5	21%	0	0%	1	50%
Georgia	10	17%	0	0%	3	60%	2	6%	0	0%	2	67%
Germany	0	0%	0	0%	0	0%	0	0%	0	0%	0	0%
Greece	69	64%	4	44%	7	78%	8	13%	0	0%	4	80%
Hungary	25	26%	0	0%	4	50%	13	22%	0	0%	3	60%
Iceland	18	17%	0	0%	3	33%	4	7%	0	0%	1	20%
Ireland	12	20%	1	20%	1	20%	0	0%	0	0%	0	0%
Israel	12	25%	0	0%	2	50%	4	8%	0	0%	1	25%
Italy	23	48%	1	25%	3	75%	3	13%	0	0%	1	50%
Latvia	2	4%	0	0%	1	25%	4	8%	0	0%	2	50%
Lithuania	0	0%	0	0%	0	0%	0	0%	0	0%	0	0%
Luxembourg	0	-	0	-	0	-	0	-	0	-	0	-
Malta	38	63%	1	20%	5	100%	12	33%	0	0%	2	67%
Moldova	18	25%	0	0%	3	50%	9	19%	0	0%	3	75%
Monaco	0	-	0	-	0	-	0	-	0	-	0	-
Montenegro	9	19%	0	0%	2	50%	4	8%	0	0%	1	25%
Morocco	0	-	0	-	0	-	0	-	0	-	0	-
Netherlands	20	42%	1	25%	4	100%	0	0%	0	0%	0	0%
Norway	26	31%	0	0%	4	57%	0	0%	0	0%	0	0%
Poland	10	17%	0	0%	1	20%	0	0%	0	0%	0	0%
Portugal	5	21%	0	0%	1	50%	0	0%	0	0%	0	0%
Romania	13	14%	0	0%	3	38%	4	8%	0	0%	1	25%
Russia	13	12%	0	0%	3	33%	3	5%	0	0%	1	20%
San Marino	-	-	-	-	-	-	0	-	0	-	0	-
Serbia	14	29%	0	0%	3	75%	0	0%	0	0%	0	0%
Serbia & Montenegro	0	-	0	-	0	-	0	-	0	-	0	-
Slovakia	0	-	0	-	0	-	0	-	0	-	0	-
Slovenia	1	3%	0	0%	1	33%	0	0%	0	0%	0	0%
Spain	1	2%	0	0%	1	20%	11	15%	0	0%	2	33%
Sweden	22	31%	0	0%	4	67%	0	0%	0	0%	0	0%
Switzerland	1	2%	0	0%	1	20%	0	0%	0	0%	0	0%
Turkey	19	53%	0	0%	3	100%	5	42%	0	0%	1	100%
Ukraine	4	6%	0	0%	1	17%	4	17%	0	0%	1	50%
United Kingdom	13	22%	0	0%	3	60%	0	0%	0	0%	0	0%
Yugoslavia	0	-	0	-	0	-	0	-	0	-	0	-

Eurovision 2014 - Who Votes for Who? (And Who Doesn't)

Serbia

	Serbia awarded points to:			Frequency		Serbia received points from:			Frequency	
	Total	% of max	12's	% of max	Times	% of max	Total	% of max	12's	% of max	Times	% of max
Albania	3	3%	0	0%	2	22%	18	17%	0	0%	8	89%
Andorra	0	0%	0	0%	0	0%	0	0%	0	0%	0	0%
Armenia	6	8%	0	0%	2	33%	21	29%	0	0%	4	67%
Austria	2	6%	0	0%	1	33%	47	78%	2	40%	5	100%
Azerbaijan	18	19%	0	0%	4	50%	2	3%	0	0%	1	17%
Belarus	10	10%	0	0%	3	38%	27	25%	0	0%	5	56%
Belgium	15	25%	0	0%	3	60%	19	20%	0	0%	4	50%
Bosnia & Herzegovina	78	81%	5	63%	8	100%	90	94%	5	63%	8	100%
Bulgaria	18	38%	0	0%	4	100%	42	50%	2	29%	5	71%
Croatia	70	73%	3	38%	8	100%	106	88%	5	50%	10	100%
Cyprus	14	19%	0	0%	4	67%	32	33%	0	0%	7	88%
Czech Republic	0	0%	0	0%	0	0%	26	72%	1	33%	3	100%
Denmark	24	20%	1	10%	4	40%	12	13%	0	0%	2	25%
Estonia	4	4%	0	0%	1	11%	2	2%	0	0%	2	20%
Finland	3	4%	0	0%	1	14%	31	32%	1	13%	5	63%
France	7	8%	0	0%	2	29%	76	70%	3	33%	8	89%
FYR Macedonia	60	83%	2	33%	6	100%	81	84%	3	38%	8	100%
Georgia	11	10%	0	0%	2	22%	24	25%	0	0%	3	38%
Germany	8	10%	0	0%	1	14%	55	57%	0	0%	7	88%
Greece	62	52%	0	0%	9	90%	34	31%	0	0%	6	67%
Hungary	50	52%	2	25%	7	88%	37	44%	2	29%	5	71%
Iceland	11	9%	0	0%	2	20%	30	31%	0	0%	6	75%
Ireland	3	4%	0	0%	1	14%	12	13%	0	0%	2	25%
Israel	7	15%	0	0%	1	25%	10	14%	0	0%	2	33%
Italy	6	17%	0	0%	2	67%	12	33%	0	0%	3	100%
Latvia	2	3%	0	0%	1	17%	8	8%	0	0%	3	38%
Lithuania	14	12%	0	0%	3	30%	16	13%	0	0%	5	50%
Luxembourg	0	-	0	-	0	-	0	-	0	-	0	-
Malta	21	22%	0	0%	4	50%	23	21%	0	0%	6	67%
Moldova	22	18%	0	0%	5	50%	18	17%	0	0%	5	56%
Monaco	0	-	0	-	0	-	0	-	0	-	0	-
Montenegro	20	83%	1	50%	2	100%	58	97%	4	80%	5	100%
Morocco	0	-	0	-	0	-	0	-	0	-	0	-
Netherlands	1	2%	0	0%	1	20%	57	53%	0	0%	9	100%
Norway	29	27%	0	0%	4	44%	59	55%	0	0%	8	89%
Poland	2	3%	0	0%	1	20%	29	30%	0	0%	5	63%
Portugal	15	16%	0	0%	5	63%	25	26%	0	0%	6	75%
Romania	8	10%	0	0%	2	29%	24	33%	0	0%	4	67%
Russia	52	43%	0	0%	8	80%	29	24%	0	0%	6	60%
San Marino	0	0%	0	0%	0	0%	14	29%	0	0%	3	75%
Serbia	-	-	-	-	-	-	0	-	0	-	0	-
Serbia & Montenegro	0	-	0	-	0	-	0	-	0	-	0	-
Slovakia	7	19%	0	0%	2	67%	21	29%	0	0%	3	50%
Slovenia	37	51%	0	0%	5	83%	95	88%	6	67%	9	100%
Spain	0	0%	0	0%	0	0%	23	21%	0	0%	6	67%
Sweden	24	25%	0	0%	6	75%	55	57%	0	0%	7	88%
Switzerland	7	15%	0	0%	2	50%	74	88%	4	57%	7	100%
Turkey	3	3%	0	0%	1	11%	0	0%	0	0%	0	0%
Ukraine	50	38%	0	0%	9	82%	26	24%	0	0%	5	56%
United Kingdom	8	10%	0	0%	1	14%	8	7%	0	0%	2	22%
Yugoslavia	0	-	0	-	0	-	0	-	0	-	0	-

Eurovision 2014 - Who Votes for Who? (And Who Doesn't)

Serbia & Montenegro

	Serbia & Montenegro awarded points				Frequency		Serbia & Montenegro received points fr				Frequency	
	Total	% of max	12's	% of max	Times	% of max	Total	% of max	12's	% of max	Times	% of max
Albania	22	46%	0	0%	3	75%	17	47%	0	0%	3	100%
Andorra	0	0%	0	0%	0	0%	3	8%	0	0%	2	67%
Armenia	0	0%	0	0%	0	0%	0	-	0	-	0	-
Austria	0	0%	0	0%	0	0%	36	100%	3	100%	3	100%
Azerbaijan	0	-	0	-	0	-	0	-	0	-	0	-
Belarus	0	0%	0	0%	0	0%	20	56%	0	0%	3	100%
Belgium	0	0%	0	0%	0	0%	10	28%	0	0%	2	67%
Bosnia & Herzegovina	41	68%	2	40%	5	100%	34	94%	2	67%	3	100%
Bulgaria	1	4%	0	0%	1	50%	4	33%	0	0%	1	100%
Croatia	42	70%	1	20%	5	100%	36	100%	3	100%	3	100%
Cyprus	6	13%	0	0%	3	75%	30	83%	0	0%	3	100%
Czech Republic	0	-	0	-	0	-	0	-	0	-	0	-
Denmark	0	0%	0	0%	0	0%	17	47%	0	0%	2	67%
Estonia	4	11%	0	0%	1	33%	1	3%	0	0%	1	33%
Finland	15	31%	0	0%	2	50%	20	56%	0	0%	2	67%
France	0	0%	0	0%	0	0%	16	67%	0	0%	2	100%
FYR Macedonia	59	82%	2	33%	6	100%	30	83%	0	0%	3	100%
Georgia	0	-	0	-	0	-	0	-	0	-	0	-
Germany	0	0%	0	0%	0	0%	25	69%	1	33%	3	100%
Greece	35	73%	1	25%	4	100%	24	67%	0	0%	3	100%
Hungary	14	58%	0	0%	2	100%	2	17%	0	0%	1	100%
Iceland	2	6%	0	0%	1	33%	7	19%	0	0%	1	33%
Ireland	1	2%	0	0%	1	25%	9	25%	0	0%	2	67%
Israel	6	13%	0	0%	2	50%	15	42%	0	0%	2	67%
Italy	0	-	0	-	0	-	0	-	0	-	0	-
Latvia	0	0%	0	0%	0	0%	10	28%	0	0%	3	100%
Lithuania	6	13%	0	0%	2	50%	3	8%	0	0%	2	67%
Luxembourg	0	-	0	-	0	-	0	-	0	-	0	-
Malta	0	0%	0	0%	0	0%	10	28%	0	0%	2	67%
Moldova	11	31%	0	0%	2	67%	1	8%	0	0%	1	100%
Monaco	0	0%	0	0%	0	0%	14	39%	0	0%	3	100%
Montenegro	-	-	-	-	-	-	0	-	0	-	0	-
Morocco	0	-	0	-	0	-	0	-	0	-	0	-
Netherlands	1	2%	0	0%	1	25%	26	72%	1	33%	3	100%
Norway	6	13%	0	0%	2	50%	16	44%	0	0%	2	67%
Poland	0	0%	0	0%	0	0%	5	21%	0	0%	1	50%
Portugal	0	0%	0	0%	0	0%	17	47%	0	0%	2	67%
Romania	12	25%	0	0%	3	75%	24	67%	0	0%	3	100%
Russia	12	25%	0	0%	3	75%	16	67%	0	0%	2	100%
San Marino	0	-	0	-	0	-	0	-	0	-	0	-
Serbia	0	-	0	-	0	-	0	-	0	-	0	-
Serbia & Montenegro	-	-	-	-	-	-	0	-	0	-	0	-
Slovakia	0	-	0	-	0	-	0	-	0	-	0	-
Slovenia	14	39%	0	0%	2	67%	34	94%	2	67%	3	100%
Spain	0	0%	0	0%	0	0%	14	39%	0	0%	2	67%
Sweden	9	19%	0	0%	3	75%	28	78%	2	67%	3	100%
Switzerland	2	4%	0	0%	1	25%	36	100%	3	100%	3	100%
Turkey	2	4%	0	0%	1	25%	15	42%	0	0%	2	67%
Ukraine	25	42%	0	0%	4	80%	27	75%	2	67%	3	100%
United Kingdom	0	0%	0	0%	0	0%	11	31%	0	0%	2	67%
Yugoslavia	0	-	0	-	0	-	0	-	0	-	0	-

Eurovision 2014 - Who Votes for Who? (And Who Doesn't)

Slovakia

	Slovakia awarded points to:				Frequency		Slovakia received points from:				Frequency	
	Total	% of max	12's	% of max	Times	% of max	Total	% of max	12's	% of max	Times	% of max
Albania	4	7%	0	0%	1	20%	4	17%	0	0%	1	50%
Andorra	0	-	0	-	0	-	0	-	0	-	0	-
Armenia	7	29%	0	0%	2	100%	0	-	0	-	0	-
Austria	9	19%	0	0%	3	75%	3	8%	0	0%	1	33%
Azerbaijan	29	48%	1	20%	4	80%	0	0%	0	0%	0	0%
Belarus	4	8%	0	0%	2	50%	3	8%	0	0%	1	33%
Belgium	26	36%	0	0%	3	50%	4	7%	0	0%	2	40%
Bosnia & Herzegovina	41	38%	1	11%	6	67%	11	18%	0	0%	2	40%
Bulgaria	0	0%	0	0%	0	0%	0	0%	0	0%	0	0%
Croatia	32	44%	2	33%	4	67%	8	13%	0	0%	1	20%
Cyprus	3	4%	0	0%	3	43%	0	0%	0	0%	0	0%
Czech Republic	0	-	0	-	0	-	0	-	0	-	0	-
Denmark	16	22%	0	0%	3	50%	0	0%	0	0%	0	0%
Estonia	50	42%	1	10%	6	60%	6	7%	0	0%	1	14%
Finland	2	3%	0	0%	1	17%	2	4%	0	0%	1	25%
France	0	0%	0	0%	0	0%	1	1%	0	0%	1	14%
FYR Macedonia	6	10%	0	0%	3	60%	3	6%	0	0%	1	25%
Georgia	0	0%	0	0%	0	0%	0	0%	0	0%	0	0%
Germany	27	38%	1	17%	3	50%	0	0%	0	0%	0	0%
Greece	23	21%	0	0%	4	44%	7	12%	0	0%	2	40%
Hungary	10	17%	0	0%	2	40%	0	0%	0	0%	0	0%
Iceland	24	29%	0	0%	5	71%	5	14%	0	0%	1	33%
Ireland	29	30%	1	13%	5	63%	6	10%	0	0%	2	40%
Israel	20	42%	0	0%	3	75%	0	0%	0	0%	0	0%
Italy	5	21%	0	0%	1	50%	0	0%	0	0%	0	0%
Latvia	0	0%	0	0%	0	0%	0	0%	0	0%	0	0%
Lithuania	7	10%	0	0%	1	17%	0	0%	0	0%	0	0%
Luxembourg	0	-	0	-	0	-	0	-	0	-	0	-
Malta	31	37%	1	14%	5	71%	27	45%	1	20%	3	60%
Moldova	16	19%	0	0%	3	43%	7	19%	0	0%	1	33%
Monaco	0	-	0	-	0	-	0	-	0	-	0	-
Montenegro	0	-	0	-	0	-	0	-	0	-	0	-
Morocco	0	-	0	-	0	-	0	-	0	-	0	-
Netherlands	5	7%	0	0%	1	17%	0	0%	0	0%	0	0%
Norway	47	49%	0	0%	6	75%	0	0%	0	0%	0	0%
Poland	7	12%	0	0%	2	40%	5	8%	0	0%	1	20%
Portugal	11	13%	0	0%	3	43%	9	15%	0	0%	2	40%
Romania	7	8%	0	0%	2	29%	3	8%	0	0%	1	33%
Russia	9	13%	0	0%	2	33%	1	3%	0	0%	1	33%
San Marino	0	-	0	-	0	-	0	-	0	-	0	-
Serbia	21	29%	0	0%	3	50%	7	19%	0	0%	2	67%
Serbia & Montenegro	0	-	0	-	0	-	0	-	0	-	0	-
Slovakia	-	-	-	-	-	-	0	-	0	-	0	-
Slovenia	9	13%	0	0%	2	33%	3	5%	0	0%	1	20%
Spain	4	5%	0	0%	2	29%	2	3%	0	0%	1	20%
Sweden	48	50%	2	25%	5	63%	3	5%	0	0%	1	20%
Switzerland	6	13%	0	0%	2	50%	0	0%	0	0%	0	0%
Turkey	3	4%	0	0%	1	17%	0	0%	0	0%	0	0%
Ukraine	30	36%	1	14%	5	71%	14	39%	1	33%	2	67%
United Kingdom	15	18%	0	0%	3	43%	0	0%	0	0%	0	0%
Yugoslavia	0	-	0	-	0	-	0	-	0	-	0	-

Eurovision 2014 - Who Votes for Who? (And Who Doesn't)

Slovenia

	Slovenia awarded points to:				Frequency		Slovenia received points from:				Frequency	
	Total	% of max	12's	% of max	Times	% of max	Total	% of max	12's	% of max	Times	% of max
Albania	26	22%	0	0%	7	70%	17	18%	0	0%	3	38%
Andorra	5	8%	0	0%	2	40%	8	11%	0	0%	1	17%
Armenia	10	8%	0	0%	2	20%	6	7%	0	0%	2	29%
Austria	59	33%	1	7%	9	60%	28	14%	0	0%	7	41%
Azerbaijan	19	16%	0	0%	5	50%	1	2%	0	0%	1	20%
Belarus	10	7%	0	0%	2	17%	14	11%	0	0%	4	36%
Belgium	25	13%	0	0%	6	38%	10	5%	0	0%	3	18%
Bosnia & Herzegovina	151	57%	5	23%	17	77%	110	54%	2	12%	17	100%
Bulgaria	14	17%	0	0%	3	43%	13	14%	0	0%	2	25%
Croatia	164	65%	6	29%	19	90%	118	52%	2	11%	18	95%
Cyprus	31	14%	0	0%	7	37%	18	8%	0	0%	4	22%
Czech Republic	0	0%	0	0%	0	0%	4	17%	0	0%	1	50%
Denmark	100	38%	2	9%	12	55%	15	7%	0	0%	2	12%
Estonia	41	17%	1	5%	8	40%	16	7%	0	0%	4	21%
Finland	23	12%	0	0%	4	25%	14	8%	0	0%	4	29%
France	33	14%	0	0%	7	35%	19	9%	0	0%	6	33%
FYR Macedonia	95	57%	1	7%	13	93%	49	34%	0	0%	10	83%
Georgia	10	9%	0	0%	3	33%	4	5%	0	0%	1	14%
Germany	30	13%	0	0%	6	32%	17	7%	0	0%	5	26%
Greece	55	20%	0	0%	11	48%	17	8%	0	0%	4	22%
Hungary	15	10%	0	0%	3	25%	23	21%	0	0%	4	44%
Iceland	25	12%	0	0%	7	39%	11	7%	0	0%	4	29%
Ireland	41	15%	1	4%	12	52%	31	12%	1	5%	6	27%
Israel	29	13%	0	0%	6	32%	29	13%	0	0%	9	50%
Italy	26	36%	0	0%	4	67%	11	13%	0	0%	2	29%
Latvia	31	22%	0	0%	5	42%	16	11%	0	0%	4	33%
Lithuania	18	9%	0	0%	4	24%	18	10%	0	0%	4	27%
Luxembourg	1	8%	0	0%	1	100%	0	0%	0	0%	0	0%
Malta	40	17%	2	10%	6	30%	26	12%	0	0%	7	39%
Moldova	22	13%	0	0%	6	43%	9	8%	0	0%	3	30%
Monaco	0	0%	0	0%	0	0%	7	19%	0	0%	2	67%
Montenegro	22	46%	0	0%	3	75%	37	62%	0	0%	5	100%
Morocco	0	-	0	-	0	-	0	-	0	-	0	-
Netherlands	50	21%	0	0%	10	50%	26	11%	0	0%	5	25%
Norway	58	21%	1	4%	11	48%	15	6%	0	0%	3	15%
Poland	18	9%	0	0%	5	31%	28	15%	0	0%	7	44%
Portugal	6	3%	0	0%	3	19%	20	10%	0	0%	5	31%
Romania	30	13%	0	0%	6	32%	30	18%	0	0%	6	43%
Russia	77	34%	2	11%	10	53%	42	25%	0	0%	8	57%
San Marino	0	0%	0	0%	0	0%	1	3%	0	0%	1	33%
Serbia	95	88%	6	67%	9	100%	37	51%	0	0%	5	83%
Serbia & Montenegro	34	94%	2	67%	3	100%	14	39%	0	0%	2	67%
Slovakia	3	5%	0	0%	1	20%	9	13%	0	0%	2	33%
Slovenia	-	-	-	-	-	-	0	-	0	-	0	-
Spain	20	8%	0	0%	7	35%	22	10%	0	0%	6	33%
Sweden	96	35%	0	0%	16	70%	17	7%	0	0%	3	15%
Switzerland	33	20%	0	0%	7	50%	8	5%	0	0%	2	14%
Turkey	18	7%	0	0%	4	19%	18	9%	0	0%	4	24%
Ukraine	51	22%	1	5%	10	53%	16	10%	0	0%	4	31%
United Kingdom	40	17%	0	0%	9	45%	18	8%	0	0%	3	15%
Yugoslavia	0	-	0	-	0	-	0	-	0	-	0	-

Eurovision 2014 - Who Votes for Who? (And Who Doesn't)

Spain

	Spain awarded points to:				Frequency		Spain received points from:				Frequency	
	Total	% of max	12's	% of max	Times	% of max	Total	% of max	12's	% of max	Times	% of max
Albania	10	6%	0	0%	3	20%	49	37%	2	18%	7	64%
Andorra	54	90%	3	60%	5	100%	60	83%	5	83%	5	83%
Armenia	73	51%	1	8%	10	83%	10	10%	0	0%	3	38%
Austria	64	17%	1	3%	10	31%	68	17%	0	0%	12	35%
Azerbaijan	24	17%	0	0%	5	42%	0	0%	0	0%	0	0%
Belarus	0	0%	0	0%	0	0%	2	2%	0	0%	1	9%
Belgium	95	21%	2	5%	16	43%	121	27%	3	8%	23	61%
Bosnia & Herzegovina	12	5%	0	0%	4	18%	30	14%	0	0%	5	28%
Bulgaria	37	62%	0	0%	5	100%	5	5%	0	0%	2	22%
Croatia	33	13%	2	10%	6	29%	36	14%	0	0%	7	33%
Cyprus	56	16%	0	0%	10	33%	112	30%	1	3%	17	55%
Czech Republic	0	0%	0	0%	0	0%	0	0%	0	0%	0	0%
Denmark	92	21%	0	0%	17	47%	30	8%	1	3%	8	24%
Estonia	29	12%	0	0%	8	38%	13	5%	0	0%	4	20%
Finland	68	15%	0	0%	14	36%	80	19%	0	0%	14	39%
France	93	20%	0	0%	16	41%	129	28%	2	5%	21	54%
FYR Macedonia	0	0%	0	0%	0	0%	5	3%	0	0%	2	14%
Georgia	8	8%	0	0%	3	38%	2	2%	0	0%	1	14%
Germany	190	41%	8	21%	27	69%	78	17%	2	5%	12	31%
Greece	170	35%	3	7%	25	61%	136	32%	0	0%	22	63%
Hungary	41	20%	0	0%	9	53%	13	9%	0	0%	3	25%
Iceland	93	24%	1	3%	17	53%	26	6%	0	0%	9	24%
Ireland	131	28%	2	5%	21	54%	47	10%	0	0%	10	26%
Israel	113	27%	1	3%	19	54%	108	26%	3	9%	19	54%
Italy	147	58%	7	33%	18	86%	83	33%	1	5%	13	62%
Latvia	21	11%	1	6%	3	19%	13	7%	0	0%	3	20%
Lithuania	11	6%	0	0%	4	27%	12	7%	0	0%	2	13%
Luxembourg	51	22%	1	5%	9	47%	67	29%	0	0%	12	63%
Malta	72	23%	1	4%	13	50%	46	15%	1	4%	8	32%
Moldova	56	31%	0	0%	11	73%	4	3%	0	0%	1	10%
Monaco	17	18%	0	0%	3	38%	14	15%	0	0%	4	50%
Montenegro	4	7%	0	0%	1	20%	4	6%	0	0%	1	17%
Morocco	0	0%	0	0%	0	0%	5	42%	0	0%	1	100%
Netherlands	98	23%	1	3%	18	51%	57	13%	0	0%	12	33%
Norway	80	16%	3	7%	15	35%	50	11%	0	0%	12	31%
Poland	25	11%	0	0%	7	37%	16	8%	0	0%	5	29%
Portugal	164	38%	3	8%	24	67%	150	34%	6	16%	19	51%
Romania	149	62%	6	30%	16	80%	38	20%	0	0%	8	50%
Russia	53	18%	0	0%	9	38%	20	9%	0	0%	4	22%
San Marino	11	15%	0	0%	2	33%	1	2%	0	0%	1	20%
Serbia	23	21%	0	0%	6	67%	0	0%	0	0%	0	0%
Serbia & Montenegro	14	39%	0	0%	2	67%	0	0%	0	0%	0	0%
Slovakia	2	3%	0	0%	1	20%	4	5%	0	0%	2	29%
Slovenia	22	10%	0	0%	6	33%	20	8%	0	0%	7	35%
Spain	-	-	-	-	-	-	0	-	0	-	0	-
Sweden	121	25%	2	5%	24	60%	41	9%	0	0%	7	18%
Switzerland	42	10%	0	0%	12	34%	149	34%	3	8%	25	69%
Turkey	55	13%	1	3%	14	39%	118	29%	2	6%	19	56%
Ukraine	78	41%	0	0%	13	81%	6	4%	0	0%	2	17%
United Kingdom	132	28%	1	3%	24	60%	58	12%	0	0%	17	43%
Yugoslavia	22	14%	0	0%	4	31%	26	17%	0	0%	7	54%

Eurovision 2014 - Who Votes for Who? (And Who Doesn't)

Sweden

	Sweden awarded points to:				Frequency		Sweden received points from:				Frequency	
	Total	% of max	12's	% of max	Times	% of max	Total	% of max	12's	% of max	Times	% of max
Albania	25	19%	0	0%	6	55%	42	27%	0	0%	9	69%
Andorra	2	3%	0	0%	1	20%	32	33%	0	0%	6	75%
Armenia	32	24%	0	0%	8	73%	31	23%	0	0%	6	55%
Austria	63	16%	1	3%	15	47%	134	33%	3	9%	18	53%
Azerbaijan	14	13%	0	0%	3	33%	12	13%	0	0%	3	38%
Belarus	4	3%	0	0%	2	15%	46	26%	0	0%	8	53%
Belgium	58	13%	0	0%	13	36%	146	30%	2	5%	25	63%
Bosnia & Herzegovina	115	42%	0	0%	16	70%	74	29%	2	10%	14	67%
Bulgaria	1	1%	0	0%	1	11%	26	15%	0	0%	4	29%
Croatia	20	7%	0	0%	6	26%	33	11%	0	0%	9	38%
Cyprus	53	14%	1	3%	11	34%	97	24%	2	6%	17	50%
Czech Republic	0	0%	0	0%	0	0%	6	10%	0	0%	1	20%
Denmark	241	53%	8	21%	33	87%	310	70%	12	32%	33	89%
Estonia	106	42%	3	14%	15	71%	161	58%	6	26%	20	87%
Finland	145	36%	3	9%	20	59%	189	44%	3	8%	26	72%
France	104	23%	0	0%	22	58%	122	24%	3	7%	26	62%
FYR Macedonia	10	5%	0	0%	4	25%	41	19%	0	0%	10	56%
Georgia	9	8%	0	0%	3	33%	23	21%	1	11%	4	44%
Germany	118	26%	2	5%	18	47%	151	31%	6	15%	24	59%
Greece	68	17%	2	6%	15	44%	46	11%	0	0%	9	26%
Hungary	56	33%	1	7%	8	57%	52	31%	1	7%	8	57%
Iceland	166	46%	3	10%	23	77%	185	39%	3	8%	27	68%
Ireland	216	47%	6	16%	28	74%	159	33%	5	13%	23	58%
Israel	90	22%	1	3%	18	53%	150	34%	4	11%	21	57%
Italy	35	15%	0	0%	7	35%	39	15%	0	0%	7	33%
Latvia	33	20%	0	0%	8	57%	75	35%	1	6%	11	61%
Lithuania	14	7%	0	0%	5	29%	70	32%	0	0%	13	72%
Luxembourg	52	24%	0	0%	8	44%	59	27%	0	0%	11	61%
Malta	68	22%	2	8%	13	50%	125	37%	3	11%	19	68%
Moldova	7	4%	0	0%	2	15%	48	33%	0	0%	9	75%
Monaco	22	26%	1	14%	2	29%	22	23%	0	0%	4	50%
Montenegro	5	8%	0	0%	2	40%	15	16%	0	0%	3	38%
Morocco	0	0%	0	0%	0	0%	6	50%	0	0%	1	100%
Netherlands	99	23%	2	6%	17	47%	140	30%	3	8%	20	51%
Norway	196	42%	6	15%	28	72%	297	62%	10	25%	34	85%
Poland	10	6%	0	0%	5	33%	59	29%	0	0%	9	53%
Portugal	51	12%	0	0%	12	33%	145	30%	1	3%	22	55%
Romania	42	18%	0	0%	8	40%	67	29%	2	11%	10	53%
Russia	50	20%	0	0%	9	43%	37	16%	1	5%	9	47%
San Marino	0	0%	0	0%	0	0%	22	31%	0	0%	4	67%
Serbia	55	57%	0	0%	7	88%	24	25%	0	0%	6	75%
Serbia & Montenegro	28	78%	2	67%	3	100%	9	19%	0	0%	3	75%
Slovakia	3	5%	0	0%	1	20%	48	50%	2	25%	5	63%
Slovenia	17	7%	0	0%	3	15%	96	35%	0	0%	16	70%
Spain	41	9%	0	0%	7	18%	121	25%	2	5%	24	60%
Sweden	-	-	-	-	-	-	0		0	-	0	-
Switzerland	56	14%	2	6%	12	35%	120	26%	1	3%	20	53%
Turkey	91	19%	0	0%	15	38%	97	21%	1	3%	20	53%
Ukraine	41	17%	0	0%	10	50%	58	28%	1	6%	10	59%
United Kingdom	133	28%	3	8%	21	54%	195	38%	3	7%	32	74%
Yugoslavia	35	24%	1	8%	6	50%	49	34%	1	8%	9	75%

Eurovision 2014 - Who Votes for Who? (And Who Doesn't)

Switzerland

	Switzerland awarded points to:			Frequency		Switzerland received points from:			Frequency	
	Total	% of max	12's	% of max	Times	% of max	Total	% of max	12's	% of max	Times	% of max
Albania	111	71%	2	15%	13	100%	15	11%	0	0%	3	27%
Andorra	0	0%	0	0%	0	0%	9	13%	0	0%	3	50%
Armenia	7	5%	0	0%	3	25%	10	10%	0	0%	3	38%
Austria	72	20%	2	7%	12	40%	103	28%	1	3%	19	61%
Azerbaijan	19	16%	0	0%	6	60%	0	0%	0	0%	0	0%
Belarus	0	0%	0	0%	0	0%	23	19%	0	0%	4	40%
Belgium	43	11%	0	0%	7	22%	98	25%	3	9%	15	45%
Bosnia & Herzegovina	84	41%	3	18%	12	71%	8	6%	0	0%	3	25%
Bulgaria	0	0%	0	0%	0	0%	4	4%	0	0%	2	22%
Croatia	74	34%	0	0%	16	89%	16	8%	0	0%	6	38%
Cyprus	42	13%	0	0%	14	50%	66	20%	0	0%	15	56%
Czech Republic	0	0%	0	0%	0	0%	0	0%	0	0%	0	0%
Denmark	60	15%	0	0%	15	44%	88	25%	1	3%	17	59%
Estonia	0	0%	0	0%	0	0%	26	17%	2	15%	3	23%
Finland	80	17%	1	3%	15	38%	138	32%	2	6%	22	61%
France	145	35%	4	11%	21	60%	85	22%	1	3%	13	41%
FYR Macedonia	66	34%	0	0%	12	75%	5	3%	0	0%	3	21%
Georgia	2	2%	0	0%	2	18%	3	3%	0	0%	2	25%
Germany	125	30%	4	11%	21	60%	106	26%	2	6%	17	50%
Greece	103	24%	1	3%	20	56%	73	19%	1	3%	15	47%
Hungary	41	23%	1	7%	8	53%	29	20%	0	0%	6	50%
Iceland	70	21%	0	0%	12	43%	69	16%	1	3%	13	37%
Ireland	171	41%	7	20%	25	71%	92	23%	2	6%	17	50%
Israel	130	33%	1	3%	23	70%	71	18%	1	3%	16	50%
Italy	104	41%	1	5%	18	86%	81	32%	1	5%	15	71%
Latvia	18	13%	0	0%	4	33%	33	23%	1	8%	6	50%
Lithuania	3	2%	0	0%	1	7%	31	20%	0	0%	5	38%
Luxembourg	26	11%	1	5%	5	26%	80	35%	3	16%	15	79%
Malta	58	20%	0	0%	11	46%	65	25%	2	9%	11	50%
Moldova	9	7%	0	0%	2	18%	8	10%	0	0%	1	14%
Monaco	16	17%	0	0%	3	38%	29	27%	0	0%	7	78%
Montenegro	2	4%	0	0%	1	25%	5	10%	0	0%	1	25%
Morocco	0	0%	0	0%	0	0%	7	58%	0	0%	1	100%
Netherlands	91	25%	1	3%	18	60%	102	28%	1	3%	14	47%
Norway	77	17%	0	0%	16	42%	99	24%	1	3%	18	51%
Poland	13	9%	0	0%	2	17%	36	25%	1	8%	5	42%
Portugal	126	32%	2	6%	19	58%	94	24%	1	3%	19	59%
Romania	22	9%	0	0%	6	29%	23	12%	0	0%	5	31%
Russia	10	5%	0	0%	2	11%	14	10%	0	0%	3	25%
San Marino	0	0%	0	0%	0	0%	1	2%	0	0%	1	20%
Serbia	74	88%	4	57%	7	100%	7	15%	0	0%	2	50%
Serbia & Montenegro	36	100%	3	100%	3	100%	2	4%	0	0%	1	25%
Slovakia	0	0%	0	0%	0	0%	6	13%	0	0%	2	50%
Slovenia	8	5%	0	0%	2	14%	33	20%	0	0%	7	50%
Spain	149	34%	3	8%	25	69%	42	10%	0	0%	12	34%
Sweden	120	26%	1	3%	20	53%	56	14%	2	6%	12	35%
Switzerland	-	-	-	-	-	-	0	-	0	-	0	-
Turkey	154	37%	3	9%	21	60%	60	16%	0	0%	11	35%
Ukraine	5	3%	0	0%	3	20%	5	5%	0	0%	1	11%
United Kingdom	142	33%	2	6%	22	61%	128	29%	3	8%	19	51%
Yugoslavia	18	12%	0	0%	4	31%	61	39%	1	8%	9	69%

Eurovision 2014 - Who Votes for Who? (And Who Doesn't)

Turkey

	Turkey awarded points to:				Frequency		Turkey received points from:				Frequency	
	Total	% of max	12's	% of max	Times	% of max	Total	% of max	12's	% of max	Times	% of max
Albania	60	45%	0	0%	11	100%	113	78%	3	25%	12	100%
Andorra	3	5%	0	0%	2	40%	15	14%	0	0%	3	33%
Armenia	75	69%	1	11%	9	100%	16	13%	0	0%	3	30%
Austria	71	23%	1	4%	13	50%	70	21%	1	4%	11	39%
Azerbaijan	84	100%	7	100%	7	100%	72	100%	6	100%	6	100%
Belarus	8	7%	0	0%	2	22%	18	12%	0	0%	5	38%
Belgium	63	18%	1	3%	10	34%	140	34%	6	18%	18	53%
Bosnia & Herzegovina	175	69%	6	29%	19	90%	133	55%	4	20%	16	80%
Bulgaria	49	51%	1	13%	8	100%	96	62%	2	15%	13	100%
Croatia	55	21%	0	0%	9	41%	56	19%	1	4%	11	46%
Cyprus	10	3%	0	0%	3	10%	12	3%	0	0%	2	6%
Czech Republic	1	3%	0	0%	1	33%	7	10%	0	0%	3	50%
Denmark	32	8%	0	0%	12	36%	90	23%	0	0%	14	42%
Estonia	22	11%	1	6%	3	19%	14	6%	0	0%	3	16%
Finland	40	11%	0	0%	9	30%	55	14%	0	0%	13	39%
France	38	10%	0	0%	12	36%	190	44%	8	22%	21	58%
FYR Macedonia	72	40%	0	0%	12	80%	125	65%	2	13%	16	100%
Georgia	65	60%	0	0%	9	100%	37	34%	0	0%	8	89%
Germany	86	22%	3	9%	13	39%	208	48%	8	22%	22	61%
Greece	81	23%	2	7%	14	47%	36	10%	0	0%	6	19%
Hungary	25	19%	0	0%	6	55%	30	23%	0	0%	7	64%
Iceland	34	10%	0	0%	7	26%	31	7%	0	0%	8	22%
Ireland	124	32%	2	6%	22	69%	24	6%	0	0%	7	20%
Israel	63	17%	2	6%	11	35%	42	11%	0	0%	11	33%
Italy	76	40%	0	0%	12	75%	23	13%	0	0%	3	20%
Latvia	6	4%	0	0%	1	8%	2	1%	0	0%	1	7%
Lithuania	4	2%	0	0%	2	13%	16	8%	0	0%	4	24%
Luxembourg	26	14%	0	0%	7	44%	19	10%	0	0%	4	25%
Malta	93	32%	1	4%	15	63%	87	27%	1	4%	12	44%
Moldova	42	39%	1	11%	6	67%	11	10%	0	0%	2	22%
Monaco	5	8%	0	0%	1	20%	11	15%	0	0%	2	33%
Montenegro	5	21%	0	0%	1	50%	15	21%	0	0%	4	67%
Morocco	0	0%	0	0%	0	0%	12	100%	1	100%	1	100%
Netherlands	95	28%	1	4%	19	68%	168	42%	7	21%	23	70%
Norway	57	14%	1	3%	11	31%	59	13%	0	0%	16	43%
Poland	8	5%	0	0%	2	15%	11	5%	0	0%	3	18%
Portugal	48	12%	1	3%	10	29%	21	5%	0	0%	4	11%
Romania	55	29%	0	0%	12	75%	107	56%	1	6%	15	94%
Russia	50	25%	0	0%	9	53%	25	12%	0	0%	6	35%
San Marino	5	42%	0	0%	1	100%	19	53%	0	0%	3	100%
Serbia	0	0%	0	0%	0	0%	3	3%	0	0%	1	11%
Serbia & Montenegro	15	42%	0	0%	2	67%	2	4%	0	0%	1	25%
Slovakia	0	0%	0	0%	0	0%	3	4%	0	0%	1	17%
Slovenia	18	9%	0	0%	4	24%	18	7%	0	0%	4	19%
Spain	118	29%	2	6%	19	56%	55	13%	1	3%	14	39%
Sweden	97	21%	1	3%	20	53%	91	19%	0	0%	15	38%
Switzerland	60	16%	0	0%	11	35%	154	37%	3	9%	21	60%
Turkey	-	-	-	-	-	-	0		0	-	0	-
Ukraine	69	38%	2	13%	10	67%	39	23%	0	0%	9	64%
United Kingdom	126	31%	2	6%	21	62%	143	30%	4	10%	24	60%
Yugoslavia	80	56%	4	33%	10	83%	42	29%	1	8%	6	50%

Eurovision 2014 - Who Votes for Who? (And Who Doesn't)

Ukraine

	Ukraine awarded points to:				Frequency		Ukraine received points from:				Frequency	
	Total	% of max	12's	% of max	Times	% of max	Total	% of max	12's	% of max	Times	% of max
Albania	7	5%	0	0%	3	25%	22	11%	0	0%	5	31%
Andorra	0	0%	0	0%	0	0%	49	51%	1	13%	6	75%
Armenia	71	59%	1	10%	10	100%	88	67%	3	27%	10	91%
Austria	9	9%	0	0%	2	25%	20	15%	0	0%	6	55%
Azerbaijan	94	78%	4	40%	10	100%	97	81%	3	30%	10	100%
Belarus	96	67%	5	42%	11	92%	166	81%	6	35%	16	94%
Belgium	11	9%	0	0%	2	20%	42	21%	0	0%	8	47%
Bosnia & Herzegovina	22	13%	0	0%	3	21%	35	21%	0	0%	8	57%
Bulgaria	12	13%	0	0%	4	50%	67	40%	1	7%	11	79%
Croatia	46	27%	0	0%	9	64%	72	33%	1	6%	12	67%
Cyprus	24	15%	0	0%	5	38%	98	45%	1	6%	14	78%
Czech Republic	0	0%	0	0%	0	0%	37	77%	2	50%	4	100%
Denmark	26	13%	0	0%	6	35%	51	22%	0	0%	11	58%
Estonia	29	17%	0	0%	8	57%	98	43%	2	11%	15	79%
Finland	13	11%	0	0%	2	20%	31	20%	0	0%	7	54%
France	8	6%	0	0%	2	17%	13	6%	0	0%	5	28%
FYR Macedonia	24	17%	0	0%	5	42%	54	28%	0	0%	11	69%
Georgia	81	75%	2	22%	9	100%	82	68%	1	10%	10	100%
Germany	10	7%	0	0%	2	17%	17	9%	0	0%	3	19%
Greece	35	21%	0	0%	6	43%	60	33%	0	0%	11	73%
Hungary	31	23%	0	0%	6	55%	45	34%	0	0%	8	73%
Iceland	8	5%	0	0%	3	21%	60	31%	1	6%	9	56%
Ireland	8	5%	0	0%	4	29%	53	25%	0	0%	11	61%
Israel	27	20%	0	0%	6	55%	96	50%	1	6%	14	88%
Italy	4	8%	0	0%	1	25%	43	60%	1	17%	6	100%
Latvia	12	8%	0	0%	5	42%	106	49%	2	11%	14	78%
Lithuania	27	16%	0	0%	7	50%	114	53%	3	17%	16	89%
Luxembourg	0	-	0	-	0	-	0	-	0	-	0	-
Malta	28	19%	0	0%	6	50%	73	38%	0	0%	12	75%
Moldova	87	52%	2	14%	11	79%	126	70%	2	13%	15	100%
Monaco	0	0%	0	0%	0	0%	15	25%	0	0%	4	80%
Montenegro	9	19%	0	0%	2	50%	33	34%	1	13%	5	63%
Morocco	0	0%	0	-	0	-	0	-	0	-	0	-
Netherlands	11	7%	0	0%	2	14%	43	18%	0	0%	9	45%
Norway	53	32%	1	7%	8	57%	29	14%	0	0%	8	47%
Poland	49	45%	0	0%	7	78%	95	66%	3	25%	12	100%
Portugal	14	12%	0	0%	3	30%	110	57%	5	31%	13	81%
Romania	15	8%	0	0%	6	40%	49	26%	0	0%	11	69%
Russia	129	72%	4	27%	15	100%	114	59%	1	6%	16	100%
San Marino	4	17%	0	0%	1	50%	4	6%	0	0%	1	17%
Serbia	26	24%	0	0%	5	56%	50	38%	0	0%	9	82%
Serbia & Montenegro	27	75%	2	67%	3	100%	25	42%	0	0%	4	80%
Slovakia	14	39%	1	33%	2	67%	30	36%	1	14%	5	71%
Slovenia	16	10%	0	0%	4	31%	51	22%	1	5%	10	53%
Spain	6	4%	0	0%	2	17%	78	41%	0	0%	13	81%
Sweden	58	28%	1	6%	10	59%	41	17%	0	0%	10	50%
Switzerland	5	5%	0	0%	1	11%	5	3%	0	0%	3	20%
Turkey	39	23%	0	0%	9	64%	69	38%	2	13%	10	67%
Ukraine	-	-	-	-	-	-	0	-	0	-	0	-
United Kingdom	9	6%	0	0%	2	17%	43	20%	0	0%	10	56%
Yugoslavia	0	-	0	-	0	-	0	-	0	-	0	-

Eurovision 2014 - Who Votes for Who? (And Who Doesn't)

United Kingdom

	UK awarded points to:				Frequency		UK received points from:				Frequency	
	Total	% of max	12's	% of max	Times	% of max	Total	% of max	12's	% of max	Times	% of max
Albania	14	11%	0	0%	6	55%	15	11%	0	0%	3	27%
Andorra	0	0%	0	0%	0	0%	6	8%	0	0%	2	33%
Armenia	8	6%	0	0%	2	18%	9	9%	0	0%	2	25%
Austria	106	27%	2	6%	18	55%	167	41%	7	21%	23	68%
Azerbaijan	0	0%	0	0%	3	33%	7	8%	0	0%	2	29%
Belarus	0	0%	0	0%	0	0%	6	5%	0	0%	3	27%
Belgium	90	21%	1	3%	17	49%	147	32%	7	18%	20	53%
Bosnia & Herzegovina	16	6%	0	0%	5	23%	33	15%	0	0%	7	39%
Bulgaria	22	23%	0	0%	4	50%	19	18%	1	11%	2	22%
Croatia	15	5%	0	0%	11	46%	69	27%	2	10%	11	52%
Cyprus	117	31%	2	6%	19	61%	75	20%	0	0%	20	65%
Czech Republic	0	0%	0	0%	0	0%	6	17%	0	0%	1	33%
Denmark	144	32%	4	11%	22	59%	135	34%	2	6%	23	70%
Estonia	65	29%	1	5%	11	58%	44	18%	0	0%	9	45%
Finland	67	15%	2	5%	10	27%	104	24%	0	0%	17	47%
France	83	18%	0	0%	18	46%	146	31%	5	13%	21	54%
FYR Macedonia	0	0%	0	0%	0	0%	25	15%	0	0%	4	29%
Georgia	1	1%	0	0%	1	9%	6	7%	0	0%	2	29%
Germany	144	31%	1	3%	26	67%	146	31%	2	5%	23	59%
Greece	141	32%	5	14%	19	51%	84	20%	2	6%	14	40%
Hungary	27	16%	0	0%	6	43%	33	23%	1	8%	5	42%
Iceland	99	28%	2	7%	16	53%	37	8%	1	3%	8	21%
Ireland	258	55%	8	21%	32	82%	191	41%	1	3%	32	82%
Israel	117	28%	2	6%	22	63%	138	33%	4	11%	22	63%
Italy	25	10%	0	0%	6	29%	94	37%	1	5%	15	71%
Latvia	50	35%	0	0%	8	67%	24	13%	0	0%	8	53%
Lithuania	102	45%	1	5%	14	74%	22	12%	0	0%	5	33%
Luxembourg	57	25%	0	0%	10	53%	123	54%	4	21%	18	95%
Malta	132	39%	3	11%	21	75%	109	36%	1	4%	17	68%
Moldova	15	11%	0	0%	3	27%	5	4%	0	0%	2	20%
Monaco	24	25%	0	0%	4	50%	42	44%	2	25%	5	63%
Montenegro	0	0%	0	0%	0	0%	0	0%	0	0%	0	0%
Morocco	0	0%	0	0%	0	0%	8	67%	0	0%	1	100%
Netherlands	94	22%	1	3%	21	60%	107	25%	2	6%	19	53%
Norway	101	20%	2	5%	16	38%	119	25%	2	5%	21	54%
Poland	31	16%	1	6%	7	44%	32	16%	0	0%	7	41%
Portugal	37	8%	0	0%	9	24%	156	35%	4	11%	25	68%
Romania	46	19%	1	5%	7	35%	20	10%	1	6%	4	25%
Russia	43	17%	0	0%	7	33%	32	15%	1	6%	7	39%
San Marino	0	0%	0	0%	0	0%	13	22%	0	0%	3	60%
Serbia	8	7%	0	0%	2	22%	8	10%	0	0%	1	14%
Serbia & Montenegro	11	31%	0	0%	2	67%	0	0%	0	0%	0	0%
Slovakia	0	0%	0	0%	0	0%	15	18%	0	0%	3	43%
Slovenia	18	8%	0	0%	3	15%	40	17%	0	0%	9	45%
Spain	58	12%	0	0%	17	43%	132	28%	1	3%	24	60%
Sweden	195	38%	3	7%	32	74%	133	28%	3	8%	21	54%
Switzerland	128	29%	3	8%	19	51%	142	33%	2	6%	22	61%
Turkey	143	30%	4	10%	24	60%	126	31%	2	6%	21	62%
Ukraine	43	20%	0	0%	10	56%	9	6%	0	0%	2	17%
United Kingdom	-	-	-	-	-	-	0	-	0	-	0	-
Yugoslavia	47	30%	2	15%	6	46%	57	37%	1	8%	8	62%

Eurovision 2014 - Who Votes for Who? (And Who Doesn't)

Yugoslavia

	Yugoslavia awarded points to:				Frequency		Yugoslavia received points from:				Frequency	
	Total	% of max	12's	% of max	Times	% of max	Total	% of max	12's	% of max	Times	% of max
Albania	0	-	0	-	0	-	0	-	0	-	0	-
Andorra	0	-	0	-	0	-	0	-	0	-	0	-
Armenia	0	-	0	-	0	-	0	-	0	-	0	-
Austria	23	16%	0	0%	5	42%	24	17%	0	0%	5	42%
Azerbaijan	0	-	0	-	0	-	0	-	0	-	0	-
Belarus	0	-	0	-	0	-	0	-	0	-	0	-
Belgium	32	21%	0	0%	5	38%	45	29%	1	8%	7	54%
Bosnia & Herzegovina	0	-	0	-	0	-	0	-	0	-	0	-
Bulgaria	0	-	0	-	0	-	0	-	0	-	0	-
Croatia	0	-	0	-	0	-	0	-	0	-	0	-
Cyprus	52	43%	1	10%	8	80%	59	49%	1	10%	9	90%
Czech Republic	0	-	0	-	0	-	0	-	0	-	0	-
Denmark	7	5%	0	0%	2	18%	52	39%	2	18%	6	55%
Estonia	0	-	0	-	0	-	0	-	0	-	0	-
Finland	22	14%	0	0%	5	38%	35	22%	1	8%	7	54%
France	56	39%	3	25%	7	58%	21	15%	0	0%	7	58%
FYR Macedonia	0	-	0	-	0	-	0	-	0	-	0	-
Georgia	0	-	0	-	0	-	0	-	0	-	0	-
Germany	33	21%	1	8%	6	46%	16	10%	0	0%	6	46%
Greece	17	16%	0	0%	4	44%	30	25%	0	0%	7	70%
Hungary	0	-	0	-	0	-	0	-	0	-	0	-
Iceland	4	5%	0	0%	1	14%	48	31%	1	8%	6	46%
Ireland	38	26%	0	0%	10	83%	34	24%	1	8%	8	67%
Israel	54	38%	2	17%	8	67%	52	36%	3	25%	6	50%
Italy	62	52%	1	10%	8	80%	17	14%	0	0%	3	30%
Latvia	0	-	0	-	0	-	0	-	0	-	0	-
Lithuania	0	-	0	-	0	-	0	-	0	-	0	-
Luxembourg	37	24%	1	8%	6	46%	24	15%	0	0%	5	38%
Malta	13	36%	0	0%	3	100%	4	11%	0	0%	2	67%
Moldova	0	-	0	-	0	-	0	-	0	-	0	-
Monaco	4	17%	0	0%	1	50%	0	0%	0	0%	0	0%
Montenegro	0	-	0	-	0	-	0	-	0	-	0	-
Morocco	0	-	0	-	0	-	0	-	0	-	0	-
Netherlands	40	28%	0	0%	7	58%	25	17%	0	0%	4	33%
Norway	11	7%	0	0%	2	15%	31	20%	1	8%	5	38%
Poland	0	-	0	-	0	-	0	-	0	-	0	-
Portugal	14	9%	0	0%	3	23%	11	7%	0	0%	3	23%
Romania	0	-	0	-	0	-	0	-	0	-	0	-
Russia	0	-	0	-	0	-	0	-	0	-	0	-
San Marino	0	-	0	-	0	-	0	-	0	-	0	-
Serbia	0	-	0	-	0	-	0	-	0	-	0	-
Serbia & Montenegro	0	-	0	-	0	-	0	-	0	-	0	-
Slovakia	0	-	0	-	0	-	0	-	0	-	0	-
Slovenia	0	-	0	-	0	-	0	-	0	-	0	-
Spain	26	17%	0	0%	7	54%	22	14%	0	0%	4	31%
Sweden	49	34%	1	8%	9	75%	35	24%	1	8%	6	50%
Switzerland	61	39%	1	8%	9	69%	18	12%	0	0%	4	31%
Turkey	42	29%	1	8%	6	50%	80	56%	4	33%	10	83%
Ukraine	0	-	0	-	0	-	0	-	0	-	0	-
United Kingdom	57	37%	1	8%	8	62%	47	30%	2	15%	6	46%
Yugoslavia	-	-	-	-	-	-	0	-	0	-	0	-